Humanity and Self-Cultivation:

Essays in Confucian Thought

Tu Wei-ming

Humanity
 and
Self-Cultivation:
*Essays in
Confucian Thought*

Asian Humanities Press

Berkeley · 1979

ISBN 0–89581–600–8

This book is dedicated to
Hsiao I-yü

PREFACE

The late Professor Benjamin Nelson of the New School for Social Research suggested in the spring of 1977 that I gather together several of my published essays on Confucian thought. I was delighted and honored to have been invited by him to put the materials into a volume for a projected series in comparative civilizational studies under his editorship. He also agreed to write a foreword, indicating his sense of my work for the project. Ben's tragic death, which occurred on September 17, 1977, while he was traveling in Germany, was a major loss to all of us who had been inspired by his dynamic personality and his creative scholarship. I was particularly saddened by the unexpected departure of this beloved "teacher and friend"; we had planned to write jointly at least three pieces on China and the West in a comparative civilizational perspective. One of them was to have been an intensive study of the Neo-Confucian concept of mind (*hsin*) in the light of the medieval Christian notion of conscience.

It was owing to the encouragement of my colleague, Professor Lewis Lancaster of the Department of Oriental Languages, that I again took courage to put these essays into book form. The decision of the Asian Humanities Press to reset the entire work provided me an opportunity to make a few typographic corrections and editorial improvements. I am indebted to Joseph Adler, Betsy Scheiner and Tracy Thompson for their kind assistance in this regard.

I am grateful to my teachers and friends in history and philosophy for their continuous intellectual support of my work. I would particularly like to note the inspiring conversations I have had over the years with Chang Hao, Wing-tsit Chan, Ch'en Ch'i-yün, W. T. de Bary, Hung Ming-shui, Lin Yü-sheng, James T. C. Liu, Liu Shu-hsien, Mei Kuang, Thomas A. Metzger, Fritz W. Mote, David N. Keightley, Irwin Scheiner, B. I. Schwartz, Frederic E. Wakeman Jr., L. S. Yang, and Yü Ying-shih. Thanks are also due to members of the Berkeley Regional Seminar in Confucian Studies under the sponsorship of the American Council of Learned Societies; their critiques of my work turned out to be truly liberating. I wish to express my special appreciation to John Ewell, the rapporteur of the seminar. He has given his time and energies to reading and criticizing several of the papers in draft form.

And I must also mention that, although they do not participate directly in my *academic* reflections on Confucian thought, the long-term informal association, the Fellowship of Oriental Humanism (Tung-fang Jen-wen Yu-hui), under the leadership of the late Professor T'ang Chün-i and Professors Mou Tsung-san and Hsü Fu-kuan, has created a genuine world of meaningful communication within which my work has been constantly nourished.

Berkeley, California   Tu Wei-ming
June 1978

ACKNOWLEDGMENTS

"The Creative Tension between *Jen* and *Li*," *Philosophy East and West*, 18:1–2 (January–April 1968), 29–39. Reprinted by permission of the University Press of Hawaii and Copyright © 1968 by the University Press of Hawaii.

"Li as Process of Humanization," *Philosophy East and West*, 22:2 (April 1972), 187–201. Reprinted by permission of the University Press of Hawaii and Copyright © 1972 by the University Press of Hawaii.

"The Confucian Perception of Adulthood," *Daedalus*, 105:2 (April 1976), 109–123. Reprinted by permission of *Daedalus, Journal of the American Academy of Arts and Sciences*, Boston, Mass. *Adulthood*, Spring 1976, pp. 113–127.

"On the Mencian Perception of Moral Self-Development," *The Monist*, 61:1 (January 1978), 72–81. Reprinted by permission of the Edward C. Hegeler Foundation and Copyright © 1978 by the Edward C. Hegeler Foundation, La Salle, Illinois.

"The Neo-Confucian Concept of Man," *Philosophy East and West*, 21:1 (January 1971), 72–81. Reprinted by permission of the University Press of Hawaii and Copyright © 1971 by the University Press of Hawaii.

"The Unity of Knowing and Acting: From a Neo-Confucian Perspective," in *Philosophy: Theory and Practice*, ed. T. M. P. Mahadevan (Madras: Proceedings of the International Seminar on World Philosophy, December 7–17, 1970), pp. 190–205. Reprinted by permission.

" 'Inner Experience': The Basis of Creativity in Neo-Confucian Thinking," in *Artists and Traditions: Uses of the Past in Chinese Culture*, ed. Christian F. Murck (Princeton: The Art Museum, Princeton University, 1976), pp. 9–15. Reprinted by permission of the Art Museum, Princeton University and Copyright © 1976 by the Trustees of Princeton University.

"Mind and Human Nature," *Journal of Asian Studies*, 30:3 (May 1971), 642–647. Reprinted by permission of the Association for Asian Studies and Copyright © 1971 by the Association for Asian Studies.

"Reconstituting the Confucian Tradition," *Journal of Asian Studies*, 33:3 (May 1974), 441–454. Reprinted by permission of the Association for Asian Studies and Copyright © 1974 by the Association for Asian Studies.

"Subjectivity and Ontological Reality: An Interpretation of Wang Yang-ming's Mode of Thinking," *Philosophy East and West*, 23:1–2 (January–April 1973), 187–205. Reprinted by permission of the University Press of Hawaii and Copyright © 1973 by the University Press of Hawaii.

"An Inquiry into Wang Yang-ming's Four-Sentence Teaching," *Eastern Buddhist*, n. s., 7:2 (October 1974), 32–48. Reprinted by permission.

"Transformational Thinking as Philosophy," *Philosophy East and West*, 24 (January–April 1976), 75–80. Reprinted by permission of the University Press of Hawaii and Copyright © 1976 by the University Press of Hawaii.

"Yen Yüan: From Inner Experience to Lived Concreteness," in *The Unfolding of Neo-Confucianism*, ed. Wm. T. de Bary (New York: Columbia University Press, 1975), pp. 511–541. Reprinted by permission of Columbia University Press and Copyright © 1975 by Columbia University Press.

"Hsiung Shih-li's Quest for Authentic Existence," in *The Limits of Change: Essays on Conservative Alternatives in Republican China*, ed. Charlotte Furth (Cambridge: Harvard University Press, 1976), pp. 242–275, 396–400. Reprinted by permission of Harvard University Press and Copyright © 1976 by the President and Fellows of Harvard College.

"Confucianism: Symbol and Substance in Recent Times," *Asian Thought and Society: An International Review*, 1:1 (April 1976), 42–66. Reprinted by permission of East-West Publishing Co. and Copyright © 1976 by East-West Publishing Co.

CONTENTS

INTRODUCTION

The twelve papers and three review articles included here constitute a series of attempts to come to an understanding of Confucian thought, one of the richest and longest spiritual traditions in human history. I use the word *spiritual* advisedly, after much reflection on what I have been doing in these preliminary explorations. I must note at the outset that my intention has been to examine some of the salient features of the Confucian mode of thinking in an analytical and descriptive manner. The fact that I have addressed myself to issues whose discussion may tend to put the Confucian tradition in a very positive light is a matter of methodological choice rather than a deliberate effort to defend a maligned system of ideas.

To be sure, the Confucian knowledge that lures me on is, I suppose, shared by only a small coterie of like-minded students of Chinese thought. The majority of Chinese intellectuals as well as China scholars in the West have, for more than half a century, focused their attention on what may be called the "dark side" of Confucian culture. As an intellectual historian, I am acutely aware of the Confucian contribution to despotic, gerontocratic, and male-oriented practices and tendencies in traditional and contemporary China. The upsurge of anti-Confucian campaigns in recent decades, with the possible exception of the most recent turn of events during the Cultural Revolution, is, in my view, an integral part of a serious intellectual critique of an outmoded way of life by some of the best minds in twentieth-century China.

However, it is one thing to evaluate Confucian ideas in a modern perspective and quite another to attack Confucian symbolism from the alleged vantage point of a modern ideology, be it scientism, nationalism, or socialism. The former is an interpretive art that seeks to understand and bring understanding to a cultural phenomenon in the spirit of discovery; the latter arises from a polemicist suasion with the explicit purpose of reducing a tradition to a set of formulaic utterances. The active participation of some of the most brilliant minds in contemporary China in wave after wave of critical reappraisals of the Confucian heritage certainly indicates that the tradition has not fared well in the eyes of China's modernizers. But as we inquire into the meaning of modernization in China, we are easily struck by the repeated failures of even the best champions of "new world," "new thought," "new tide," and "new life" to come to terms with the *Problematik* of cultural identity.

Indeed, the various strategies to modernize China on the ideological front have turned out to be visionary shortcuts intending to appropriate the "golden needle" of wealth and power from the West without being weighed down by the deep roots of the indigenous culture. Chinese intellectuals, I believe, have paid a heavy price for this kind of wishful thinking. Not the least of it is the superficiality of commitment the scholarly community has been willing to accept for the purpose of effecting any seemingly workable design that might give promise of saving the nation from foreign invasion, domestic dissension, and perpetual backwardness. As a result, the potency of idea is lost. In its place, brute power, with or without ideological justification, reigns over a country that for centuries has been characterized as the land of "ritual and music." The politicization of culture is, to borrow from Joseph Levenson, the tragic fate of Confucian China.

I do not think, however, that the fate of Confucianism has been sealed. On the contrary, there are authentic possibilities for the reemergence of Confucian thought as a predominant intellectual force in China. I am by no means prophesying the rise of a Confucian Phoenix, as it were, from the ashes of Marxism-Leninism-Maoism. But I believe that as the depoliticization of culture becomes a national creed rather than merely functioning as a strategy of modernization, Confucian spiritual values in art, literature, history, and philosophy will again assert a shaping influence on creative minds throughout China. That China's quest for cultural identity in the future can realistically bypass the challenge of the most profound and pervasive articulation of "Chineseness" in the past is inconceivable.

It is vitally important to note, nevertheless, that my work on Confucian thought has not been motivated by a single-minded determination to make it relevant to the ideological transformation of contemporary China. Even though I may have been influenced by such a desire, my central concern has been to learn as impartially as I could the distinctive characteristics of the Confucian tradition. For the sake of focus, my priority has been to probe its "inner dimension" as a step toward a more comprehensive appreciation of its cultural, social, and political manifestations. My methodological preference has therefore been to study first that aspect of Confucian thought which has, in the judgment of its leading proponents, inspired many generations of sophisticated thinkers in traditional China.

Needless to say, in so doing I have become committed to certain values that I have learned from my Confucian studies. Actually I am perfectly willing to define my own quest for cultural identity as being "Confucian" in nature. Of course, I am aware that personal choice of an existential sort may significantly limit one's ability to analyze and describe a spiritual tradition in a disinterested manner. It is commonly believed that the closer one moves toward the role of participant, the more difficult it becomes for one to perform the function of observer. The standard of objectivity that in practice necessitates the spirit of disinterestedness seems incompatible with the psychology of commitment.

Yet the difficulty of immersing oneself in a tradition without losing one's critical acumen is not insurmountable. In fact, the discipline of the humanities demands continuous interaction between fiduciary commitment on the one hand and judicious distancing on the other. It may not be farfetched to suggest that the keen edge of creative scholarship is often the result of a confrontation between these two modes of learning. The art of interpretation lies in part in our ability to negotiate a path between insensitivity and overwhelming enthusiasm.

It is in this sense that my essays in Confucian thought are explorations, with varying degrees of success or failure. By explorations, however, I do not mean to imply that I have really attempted to venture to unknown shores in order to open new frontiers of research. The metaphor of a voyage braving uncharted oceans is not what I have in mind. On the contrary, I have been working in areas too familiar to students of Chinese thought to engender that kind of excitement. Indeed, I have avoided problem areas that are peripheral to traditional Confucian concerns. Of course, I am aware that topics seemingly marginal to well-established interpretive positions on Confucian thought may turn out to be extremely fruitful for further exploration. But my own choice has been to examine, or, more appropriately, reexamine, issues that have long been thought to be settled. My method then is neither surveying nor constructing but, in Gabriel Marcel's sense, "digging" with a view to interpreting.

My exploration—a kind of intellectual archaeology, one might say—began more than a decade ago. The present volume is in a sense simply a collection of papers that I happened to write on different occasions for a variety of purposes over a period of twelve years. But the essays, while internally self-sufficient, are not really isolated adventures but rather part and parcel of a unified effort to explore the rich symbolic resources of the Confucian tradition. I did not, it is true, have an overall design when I set out; I did not have a blueprint to guide my activities. But having been trained in Confucian classics by traditional Chinese scholars in college tutorials and having been exposed to interpretations of Confucian culture by modern American professors in graduate seminars, I decided in 1966 to summon up the strength for a prolonged inquiry into Confucian spiritual values as a professional commitment. In a sense, these papers are emanations rather than realized goals of that commitment. But there is, I hope, an underlying unity that will direct the reader's attention to an appreciation of the "inner dimension" of Confucian thought.

Admittedly I do not yet have a definite notion of the intellectual map that is to emerge in the end. Nor can I, at this juncture, offer clear indications of how it should be put together. But I think that these intensive studies will show that Confucian spiritual values are not reducible to political, social, or psychological phenomena and that they can be fruitfully studied as independent realms of human endeavor by bringing disciplines such as ethics, aesthetics, comparative religion, and systematic philosophy to bear on them. It is not my intention to exaggerate the worth of these modes of investigation; I only wish to note that my aim has been to analyze and describe Confucian thought in the context of studies of the spiritual lives of its exemplary teachers and of the spiritual contents of its classical texts.

This is partly to redress a gross imbalance prevalent in sinological literature East and West. More importantly, it is an attempt to see if layers of opaque descriptions cannot be penetrated so that authentic possibilities for new interpretations will again present themselves. Indeed, I believe that by employing fresh perspectives on perennial issues, we can dig down through the strata of partial and distorted writings on the matter. Only then can we say that we have arrived at an understanding. In retrospect, nevertheless, I cannot claim that these papers are more than footprints on the intended way.

Part One, which consists of four essays on classical Confucian ideas, is a tentative solution to a confrontation between two radically different and yet, in a deeper sense, complementary perceptions of self-cultivation philosophy: the traditional ideals of harmony, integration, and unity and the modern emphases on alienation, tension, and contradiction. In these papers, I argue that if we take seriously the process of learning to be human, the Confucian persuasion, far from being a static adherence to a predetermined pattern, signifies an unceasing spiritual self-transformation.

The centrality of personal growth takes on an all-embracing significance in the Neo-Confucian modes of thinking. Part Two may thus be viewed as a series of concerted efforts to "apply" this particular insight to human situations of a divergent nature. Although owing to the circumstances under which they were composed they do not exhibit a formally unified pattern, they are by no means casual responses to contingent requests. In fact, the reader may find Part Two an extended, if still incomplete, exploration of the "inner landscape" of the Neo-Confucian way of life.

The reader may or may not see the connection between the application of this one insight to historically unrelated human situations and the so-called exploration of the inner landscape of a tradition. My central aim, however, has been to identify the "narrow ridge" that in a profound spiritual sense links the past to the present. The two relatively lengthy essays in Part Three are experiments of this kind. Despite their contemporary focus, they are, I hope, more than speculative accounts of what should have happened in the recent past and what could or might happen in the near future. To be sure, my research on modern Confucian symbolism is still tentative. And, undeniably, my interpretive position on the transformation of Confucian thought in contemporary China has been affected by a deep concern for the continuous well-being of this great tradition. My observations are, however, not purely "personal." I maintain that my sentiment against the modernist claim that it is neither desirable nor practicable to cherish the old in order to discover the new is being shared by an increasing number of academicians. In the spirit of my colleagues, notably Robert Bellah and Herbert Fingarette, I believe that it is because we can reanimate the old that we are hopeful of attaining the new.

Humanity
and
Self-Cultivation:

Essays in
Confucian Thought

Part One

Classical Confucian Ideas

1. The Creative Tension
Between Jen and Li

I

The purpose of this paper is neither to study two
Confucian concepts in an evolutionary perspective nor to present an
analysis of their linguistic meanings. It is rather an attempt to look
into the dynamism of the Confucian tradition by contrasting what is
probably its most important concept, *jen* (goodness, humanity)
with what is probably its most well-known concept, *li* (propriety).
This is, of course, just one of the many possible approaches. Similar
attempts can be made by relating *jen* to *i* (righteousness), *chih* (wisdom), *hsiao* (filial piety), *chung* (loyalty), *yung* (courage), or many
other particular virtues in Confucianism. Indeed, even in discussing
jen and *li* we are attracted to various lines of speculation. For example, we can follow Mencius and treat *jen* as the first among the
four cardinal virtues. We can also follow Hsün Tzu and treat *li* as
the most important system of social control. We may even show the
uniqueness of *jen* in Confucianism as against *Tao* in Taoism, universal
love (*chien-ai*) in Moism, and even God in Christianity, by placing
it in the context of *li*.

In a sense, all these possibilities will be touched on in the following discussion, but the main emphasis is on the "creative tension"
itself. It is hoped that by examining this specific problem, we may
attempt to rediscover the resourcefulness of some of the most original
and persistent Confucian concepts. However, it will become clear
later that the focus of the discussion is on *jen* rather than *li*. This is
not merely because the concept of *li* is more familiar and easier to
grasp, but also because *li* had been in existence long before the time
of Confucius.[1] It was, after all, the introduction of the new concept
of *jen* by Confucius himself that marked a qualitative break in the
field of Chinese intellectual history. Therefore, we shall first proceed

to the discussion of a passage in the *Analects* which has been regarded as the best attempt to characterize the concept of *jen*.

II

In response to a question asked by his best disciple about *jen*, Confucius answered, "To conquer yourself (*k'e-chi*) and return to property (*fu-li*) is *jen*."[2] It seems justifiable to begin the discussion with this quotation, for the three key concepts or issues involved here are most relevant to our purpose. However, difficulties also arise from the very beginning. The concept of *k'e-chi* may be rendered as "to conquer oneself," but the special connotation in English is quite misleading. The Confucian idea does not mean that one should engage in a bitter struggle with one's own corporeal desires. It suggests instead that one should fulfill them in an ethical context. The concept of *k'e-chi* is in fact closely linked to the concept of self-cultivation (*hsiu-shen*). Indeed, they are practically identical.

The Chinese phrase *fu-li* also conveys wider and more profound implications than its translation, "return to propriety," would suggest. First of all, *li* refers generally to norms and standards of proper behavior in a social, ethical, or even religious context. And the word *fu* does not mean passively responding to a given situation. Arthur Waley renders the whole idea as "to submit to rituals," which seems completely indefensible.[3] Actually, *fu-li* means to bring oneself in line with *li*. Instead of passive submission, it implies active participation. The concepts of *k'e-chi* and *fu-li* may seem elusive, but among the three, *jen* is probably still the most difficult to grasp. Although it has been freely translated as benevolence, charity, humanity, love, human-heartedness, and goodness, none is really satisfactory.[4] It seems that the best way to approach the concept of *jen* is to regard it first of all as the virtue of the highest order in the value system of Confucianism. In other words, *jen* gives "meaning" to all the other ethical norms that perform integrative functions in a Confucian society.

Therefore, it seems necessary to take different levels of meaning into consideration as we tackle these issues. Roughly, we can consider *jen* as a concept of personal morality in classical Confucianism and of metaphysical justification in Neo-Confucianism, and *li* as basically a concept of social relations. It should be pointed out, however, that such a generalization is only useful for analytical purposes. First, the great minds that brought forth these concepts were not necessarily aware of these categories themselves. Secondly, even if unconsciously or implicitly they did follow such distinctions, their main concern was the "harmony" and not the "tension" among them. Accordingly, by stressing "tension," we do not intend to contradict the main concern of the ancient philosophers. Rather, we wish to show that the "harmony" with which they were concerned had a very complicated symphonic structure. Indeed, ordinary ears were not accustomed to it. Of course, we face the danger of injecting too much meaning into the age-old text, but our primary emphasis is not textual criticism—although it is crucial to a study like this—but the possible range of flexibility that the text may endure. However, we must be careful not to jump into the other extreme of pure speculation. With these considerations, we proceed to the discussion of *jen*.

III

As a concept of personal morality, *jen* is used to describe the highest human achievement ever reached through moral self-cultivation.[5] It is not too difficult to become a *chün-tzu* (gentleman) but hardly anyone is qualified to be called a *jen-jen* (a man who embodies *jen*). Confucius almost never gave anyone such praise.[6] However, the Master also said, "Is *jen* indeed so far away? If we really wanted *jen*, we should find that it was at our very side."[7] Furthermore, he remarked, "A man who does not have *jen*, what can he have to do with ritual (*li*)? A man who does not have *jen*, what can he have to do with music?"[8] These two seemingly contradictory positions can be easily reconciled if we do not treat *jen* as an objective entity. The problem is not "either-or," for Confucius upholds a varied degree of actualization of *jen*. Every human being embodies *jen* to a certain extent, but in the process of becoming a man who more fully embodies *jen* no one can reach the perfect stage.

The central problem in this connection is the internal decision-making process. It is not just a moment or a stage. The internal decision-making process is in fact a permanent problem repeatedly confronting the individual in all situations. It is in this association that Confucius said, "The gentleman who ever parts company with *jen* does not fulfill that name. Never for a moment does a gentleman quit the way of *jen*. He is never so harried but that he cleaves to this; never so tottering but that he cleaves to this."[9] Furthermore, in the Neo-Confucian tradition the "becoming process" is not just "functional," or merely a means to an end; it is also "substantial" in the sense that the "becoming" is an end, or even an ultimate end in itself.[10]

From the functional point of view, the becoming process is characterized, again to use a Neo-Confucian expression, by constant "moral efforts" (*kung-fu*). The classical Confucian concept of *hsin* (new, renewal or renewing) and the Neo-Confucian concept of *chüeh* (awake or awaking) all refer to this everlasting and conscious effort within. In fact, a Christian may also accept *hsin* in terms of rebirth and *chüeh* in terms of responding to God's calling. However, unlike the Christian approach, the Confucian line of thinking rejects the idea that the ultimate source of such an effort derives from God's grace. It argues that in the process of self-realization, the very foundation of such an act relies on the moral mind, or in Confucian terminology, the mind of *jen*, which is intrinsic to every human being.

The contrast, nevertheless, does not lie between faith in a transcendental Him and loyalty to an immanent "Me." Confucianism also has a transcendental anchorage (a point to be discussed later) although it is in quite a different nature. In this connection, from the substantial point of view, *jen* is not only a personal virtue but also a metaphysical reality.[11] In other words, not only psychologically has every human being the potentiality to embody *jen*, but also metaphysically the moral mind, or the mind of *jen,* is in essence identical with the cosmic mind. *Jen* is thus both the moral and ontological basis of self-cultivation. It is, on the one hand, conceived as a driving force behind, and on the other hand, a meaning-structure above moral conduct. Actually, *jen* is morality, but in Confucianism, expecially in the Mencian version, morality is not merely confined to the ethical stage; it also conveys religious significance. Indeed, Confucian ethics necessarily extends to the religious realm.[12] Professor Mou Tsung-san actually argues that in the last analysis, as a metaphysical reality, *jen* means "creativity itself."[13] It is probably also in this sense that Professor Wing-tsit Chan uses activity and life (or production) to describe two of the three most important characteristics of *jen*.[14]

Consistent with this line of thinking, Mencius was able to say, "He who has exhausted all of his mind knows his nature. Knowing his nature, he knows Heaven. To preserve one's mind and nourish one's nature is the way to serve Heaven. When neither a premature death nor long life causes a man any doublemindedness, but he waits in the cultivation of his personal character for whatever may happen—this is the way in which he establishes his Heavenly ordained being."[15] The Confucianists, expecially in the Neo-Confucian tradition, therefore, refuse to accept the relevance of a personal God in the transcendental sense but add a transcendental and religious dimension to the "subjectivity" of *jen* that is both functional and substantial in the self-decision-making process. It is understandable that Confucianism by its very nature does not assume the role of a formal religion, but performs the comparable functions of an ethico-religious system in Chinese society. Therefore, although it is acceptable not to call Confucianism a religion, it is completely unjustified to deny its religiousness.[16]

Accordingly, *jen* is not primarily a concept of human relations, although they are extremely crucial to it. It is a rather a principle of inwardness. By "inwardness," it is meant that *jen* is not a quality acquired from outside; it is not a product of biological, social, or political forces. Confucius actually said that when it comes to *jen*, one need not yield even to one's teacher. Commenting on this passage, Chu Hsi remarked that *jen* is possessed by oneself and it can be realized only by oneself.[17] Hence, *jen* as an inner morality is not caused by the mechanism of *li* from outside. It is higher-order concept which gives meaning to *li*. *Jen* in this sense is basically linked with the self-reviving, self-perfecting, and self-fulfilling process of an individual. *Jen* is also a unifying concept. It not only gives meanings to other important Confucian concepts, but it also shapes their characteristics and unifies them in a comprehensive whole. It is in this association that Confucius refused to be called informative and argued, "I have one thread upon which I string them all (various kinds of information)."[18]

Confucius' refusal to be called informative, however, does not exclude his sincere concern for education and other social problems. Furthermore, if Confucius did want a "thread" to string his knowledge on, the information concerning the manifold world was valuable to him. After all, Confucius never preached asceticism.[19] Nor did Confucius ever discuss his philosophy outside of a specific social context. Therefore, the Neo-Confucian philosophers' concept of *jen*, while it can be treated as a metaphysical concept, must in practice be closely related to a given situation. Chan's third characterization of *jen* as sociality is most relevant in this connection.[20] This leads us to the concept of *li*.

IV

Li can be conceived as an externalization of *jen* in a specific social context. No matter how abstract it appears, *jen* almost by definition requires concrete manifestation. A Confucian personality does not speculate on the metaphysical connotations of *jen* for their own sake. He does not try to comprehend it purely intellectually. Nor does he accept it as a living faith. Unlike the Christian's relationship to his personal God and the Pure Land Buddhist's relationship to Amida Buddha, but like the Taoist's attitude toward *Tao*, in this particular case the Confucianist tries to embody *jen* (*t'i-jen*).

The psychological mechanism is compatible with the Taoist idea that a "true man" should be able to embody the *Tao* (*t'i-tao*). However, the concept of *Tao* is not only undifferentiated by itself; it also prevents any differentiation from taking place. Hence, terms such as *p'u* (uncarved block) and *su* (colorless, plain) become very prominent in Taoism. *Jen*, on the other hand, is required by ontological necessity to differentiate itself in the manifold world.[21] A Confucianist may practice meditation, as so many Neo-Confucianists, probably under the influence of Taoism and Ch'an Buddhism, actually did, but in addition he has to actualize his inner strength, so to speak, in a given social condition. The best expression in this connection is the phrase, "to actualize *jen*" (*chien-jen*). It is inconceivable to a Taoist that Tao should be actualized in this world by human efforts because the core of the Taoist doctrine is to teach its followers to transcend merely human affairs and psychologically dwell in "nothingness" (*wu*) so as to be in line with the "nonaction" (*wu-wei*) of the great *Tao*. It is quite possible that Taoism generates positive social consequences, but at any rate these are not its primary concerns. The Confucian concept of *jen*, on the other hand, is oriented toward the opposite direction. Social impact is inherent in the principle of inwardness because the main point is not to achieve perfect equilibrium in order to eliminate all worldly entanglements but to be of great "use," although this is quite different from both positivistic utilitarianism and Dewey-type instrumentalism. Nevertheless, it is in this concern for workability and practicability that the true "meaning" of *li* should be found.

Tseng Tzu once said, "When proper respect toward the dead is shown at the end and continued after they are far away, the moral force of a people has reached its highest point."[22] The *li* of ancestral worship, according to this argument, definitely exerts sound influence in social ethics. This is in line with Mencius when he severely attacked the Moist concept of universal love. Mencius even concluded that the Moist doctrine would eventually lead to universal indifference.[23] In the light of Christian theology, this accusation seems quite shocking. Yet since "universal love" in Moism is not based on a general concern for a transcendental God, it is very probable that parents will be treated like strangers simply because the intensity of intimate emotion decreases in a broadly diffused area. Therefore, Confucianists argue that if a person fails to understand the importance of the roots he definitely cannot be aware of the branches; how can a person who does not even love his parents and wife talk about loving his neighbors?[24] This approach obviously reflects some tendency toward particularism. From the Christian point of view, only by pledging loyalty to a transcendental God can one escape the dilemma of particularism—which is a kind of selfishness. Therefore, if one cannot forsake one's biological ties and obey a universalistic principle, one is not qualified to become a Christian. However, the Confucian particularism mentioned above is not considered by Confucian philosophers to be diametrically opposed to universalism. It is, rather, a concern for practicability. *Jen*, as a Confucian ideal, is universalistic rather than particularistic, but in the real process through which *jen* is concretely actualized, particular

11

considerations in the realm of *li* do exist.

Li, accordingly, can be considered as a principle of particularism that signifies how the process of *jen's* self-actualization is to take place. In other words, a Confucianist always carries out his moral self-cultivation in the social context. He does not refrain from involvement in the world. Nor does he conceive himself only in the world but not of the world. His orientation is this-worldly, and he regards this-worldly activities as both intrinsically valuable and necessary to self-fulfillment. However, this does not lead to the conclusion that *li* is *always* linked with active participation in society. On some special occasions, *li* may also cause contrary results. For example, the three-year mourning rites for the death of one's parent in the ideal case always force a Confucianist to practice celibacy after marriage, usually in the most productive years of his intellectual life. It is beyond doubt that some of the masterpieces in Chinese literature as well as philosophy are the products of such a period. Indeed, this kind of puritanic self-discipline is so important that to the Confucianists the idea of "withdraw and return" seems basically desirable and to a certain extent functionally necessary. The cases of Ssu-ma Ch'ien (who was not necessarily a typical Confucian historian), Wang Yang-ming, and Tseng Kuo-fan are frequently quoted by Confucian scholars to prove their point. The idea that a kind of puritanic self-discipline precedes successful activism thus becomes an accepted Confucian view of life. Mencius' remark that when a man receives a great mission from heaven he has to suffer severely first has been taken to be a necessary frustration or "forced withdrawal" in order to prepare oneself for a greater task.[25] Weber's thesis that "Confucian rationalism meant rational adjustment to the world"[26] is correct only if one bears in mind that "adjustment" does not mean compliance to the status quo. Comparable to the Christian idea that "It is written but I say unto you . . . ," a Confucianist may very well refute an established *li* by exposing its incompatibility with *jen*.

Consequently, with some qualification, the tension between *li* and *jen* in Confucianism can very well be illustrated by that between Law and Gospel in Christianity. To use Harvey Cox's analogy, *li* means the standards of this world, whereas *jen* means the summons to choice and answerability. *Li* signifies the fact that a man lives in society; *jen* points to the equally important fact that he is more than the intersection of social forces. He feels himself summoned to choose, to actualize a potential *selfhood* which is more than the sum of genes, plus glands, plus class. Man cannot live without *li*, but when *li* becomes wholly determinative, he is no longer really man.[27] In a deeper sense, therefore, the creative tension between *jen* and *li* suggests a kind of interdependence. As a result the Confucian philosophers acknowledge the coercive nature of society not only passively as a given condition, but also positively as a creative instrumentality. To use again a remark made by Mou Tsung-san, *jen* needs "windows" to expose itself to the outside world, otherwise it will become suffocated. It should be mentioned in passing that by contrast the undifferentiated Taoist image, *Hun-t'un* (the great saturation), simply dies as soon as seven holes are opened in it.[28] Similarly, *li* becomes empty formalism if *jen* is absent. Furthermore, *li* without *jen* easily degenerates into social coercion incapable of conscious improvement and liable to destroy any true human feelings. The so-called "doctrine of *li*" (*li-chiao*), which was under such violent criticism during the May 4th period, especially by literary writers like Lu Hsün, is a good example. A single case is sufficient to illustrate this point. During the Ming-Ch'ing period, quite a number of widows committed suicide hoping to show that their acts were in conformity with the *li* of chastity. In view of such stupidity, Lu Hsün was quite justified in calling this type of *li* "eating man" (*ch'ih-jen*).

Therefore, it is extremely important to keep the balance between *jen* and *li*, and the balance between *jen* and *li* must be sought in a dynamic process. Hence, a kind-hearted man who acts in perfect harmony with the existing rituals does not necessarily represent such a balance. Ironically, the ideal Confucian gentleman has frequently been delineated as exactly the type that Confucius and Mencius both strongly condemned, namely, the "good villager" (*hsiang-yüan*) who, though he acted as if he were following the Confucian norms, was actually only following convention without consciously engaging in moral practice at all. Confucius called this type of person "the thief of virtue,"[29] because the magic touch, self-cultivation, the conscious effort to bring oneself in line with *li*, was absent.[30]

V

To sum up the discussion so far, the passage quoted in the

13

very beginning—"To conquer yourself and return to *li* is *jen*"—thus suggests that the Confucian answer to the elimination of the conflict between *jen* and *li* is to maintain a creative tension between the two and to engage in moral self-cultivation. The best witness of this teaching is the testimony of Confucius himself.

In a quick review of the development of his own life history, the Master said, "At seventy, I could follow the dictates of my own heart; for what I desired no longer overstepped the boundaries of right."[31] The "boundaries of right" surely means the realm governed by *li*. In other words, Confucius claimed that at seventy he could follow his heart's desires, and yet every act performed by him was in line with *li*. This does not mean that he had become a virtuoso of *li*. It suggests, instead, that he was able to bridge the seemingly un-bridgeable gap between "what is" and "what ought to be." He was so versed in self-cultivation that he could operate in a specific social situation with an artistic maturity. In fact, Confucius used the image of music to describe this type of perfect harmony between one's inwardness and outer manifestation.

NOTES

[1]Although in the *Tso's Commentary on the Spring and Autumm Annals*, Duke Hsiang, 7th year, Sec. 6, we find a passage that says, "The three (goodness, correctness, and uprightness) in harmony constitute *jen*," the most important concept in the book is *li*. See James Legge, trans., "The *Ch'uen Ts'ew*, with the *Tso Chuen*," in *The Chinese Classics*, vol. 5 (London: Henry Frowede, 1871), p. 432.

[2]*The Analects* (*Lun-yü*), 12.1. See Arthur Waley, trans., *The Analects of Confucius* (London: George Allen & Unwin Ltd., 1938), p. 162.

[3]Under the translation, Waley has this to say: "In the *Tso Chuan* (Chao Kung, 12th year), Confucius is made to quote this as a saying from 'an old record.' The commentators, not understanding the archaic use of *k'e* (able to) turned *k'e-chi* into 'self-conquest,' an error fruitful in edification; see above, p. 74." I have checked his page 74 and all the original sources he has cited. I am convinced that the commentators are basically correct and Waley's remarks themselves are far-fetched. Waley failed to recognize that in the very first chapter of *Tso Chuan* the term *k'e* is used to mean "conquer" rather than "able to." See Legge, (*op. cit.*, p. 3.): "In summer, in the fifth month, the earl of Ch'ing overcame (*k'e*) Twan in Yen."

[4]See Wing-tsit Chan, "The Evolution of the Confucian Concept *Jen*," *Philosophy East and West* 4, no. 4 (January, 1955): 295.

[5]It seems difficult to accept Juan Yüan's statement that "Confucius considered the sage as the highest type of human being, the man of *jen* the next, followed by the man of wisdom." Although Confucius did make the distinction between the man of *jen* and the man of wisdom, he did not on any occasion suggest that the man of *jen* should be clearly differentiated from the man who had attained sagehood. See Juan Yüan, "Lun-yü lun-jen lun" (A treatise on *jen* in the *Analects*), in his *Yenching-shih chi*, Part 1, chüan 8, pp. 3a-5a. See also Chan, *op. cit.*, p. 298.

[6]The case of Kuan Chung should be considered as exceptional. It should be noted that Confucius praised Kuan Chung for his great achievement in suppressing the encroachment of the barbarians. Despite Kuan Chung's pretentiousness, which was quite contrary to *li*, his merits in the cultural sphere warranted such praise. See *Analects*, 14.17; 3.22.

[7]*Ibid.*, 7. 29.

[8]*Ibid.*, 3.3.

[9]*Ibid.*, 4.11.

[10]"Function" in Neo-Confucian terminology is the translation of *yung* and "substance" that of *t'i*. To be sure, the *t'i-yung* dichotomy is a monographical topic by itself. Suffice it to say that in the present study, it is used as one of the many possible approaches to the concept of *jen*.

[11]Chan, *op. cit.*, p. 306.

[12]For a penetrating discussion of this issue, see T'ang Chün-i, "The T'ien Ming (Heavenly Ordinance) in Pre-Ch'in China," *Philosophy East and West* 11, no. 4 (January, 1962): 195–218 and 12, no. 1 (April, 1962): 29–49.

[13]Mou Tsung-san, *Chung-kuo che-hsüeh te t'e-chih* (The characteristics of Chinese philosophy; Hong Kong: Young Sun, 1963), pp. 37–38.

[14]Chan, *op. cit.*, pp. 310-314.

[15]*Book of Mencius*, 7A.1; See James Legge, trans., *The Works of Mencius*, in *The Chinese Classics*, vol. 2 (Oxford: Clarendon Press, 1895).

[16]Terms like *religion, religions,* and *religiousness* are based on the usage in recent studies by Wilfred Cantwell Smith, Clifford Geertz, and Robert Bellah.

[17]*Analects*, 15.35.

[18]*Ibid.*, 15.2.

[19]See Étienne Balazs, "Political Philosophy and Social Crisis," in *Chinese Civilization and Bureaucracy* (New Haven: Yale University Press, 1964), p. 195.

[20]Chan, *op. cit.*, p. 311.

[21]This is related to the whole problem of "differentiation" (*ch'a-teng hsing*). Among modern Chinese philosophers on Confucianism, notably T'ang Chün-i, Mou Tsung-san, and Hsü Fu-kuan, the consensus is to regard "differentiation" as an intrinsic quality of *jen*.

[22]*Analects*, 1.9.

[23]*Mencius*, 3B.9.

[24]For a completely different position see Homer H. Dubs, "The Development of Altruism in Confucianism," *Philosophy East and West* 1, no. 1 (April, 1951): 48–55.

[25]*Mencius*, 6B.15.

[26]Max Weber, *The Religion of China: Confucianism and Taoism*, Hans H. Gerth, trans.

(Glencoe: Free Press, 1951), pp. 226–249.

[27]Throughout the whole paragraph, I have simply substituted *jen* for Gospel and *li* for Law. The whole argument made by Harvey Cox in his *Secular City* (New York: Macmillan Co., 1965) seems quite compatible with its Confucian counterpart; see p. 47.

[28]Chuang Tzu's symbol for the Taoistic state of pure consciousness, which sees without listening, knows without thinking, is the god *Hun-tun*: "Fuss, the god of the Southern Ocean, and Fret, the god of the Northern Ocean, happened once to meet in the realm of *Hun-tun*, the god of the center. *Hun-tun* treated them very handsomely and they discussed together what they could do to repay his kindness. They had noticed that, whereas everyone else has seven apertures, for sight, hearing, eating, breathing and so on, *Hun-tun* had none. So they decided to make the experiment of boring holes in him. Every day they bored a hole, and on the seventh day *Hun-tun* died." See Arthur Waley, *Three Ways of Thought in Ancient China* (London: George Allen & Unwin Ltd., 1953), p. 97. For the original text, see *Chuang Tzu*, 1.7.

[29]"The thief of virtue" is a widely used but loose translation of *te chih ts'e*, which literally means to inflict damage on virtue.

[30]*Analects*, 17.13; *Mencius* 7B.37.

[31]*Analects*, 2.4.

2. Li *as Process*
of Humanization

I

An inquiry into the concept of *li* necessarily involves broad issues of Confucian intentionality. In an earlier article, I made some preliminary attempts to investigate the "creative tension between *jen* and *li*." Although the study addressed itself to the two cardinal virtues in Confucianism, the real basis of such questioning lies in the assumption that the central concern of Confucian teaching is the process of becoming a sage, of becoming fully realized as an authentic human being. And it is in self-realization that the basis of *li* as an externalization of *jen* really lies.[1]

In this article I contend that the issue of the self versus society, especially as manifested in the conflict between an inner sense of personal morality and an outer expression of social responsibility, only scratches the surface of Confucian teaching. A much more prominent and, in my opinion, more profound issue is the distinction between authentic self and inauthentic self and that between partial self-realization and complete self-realization. To come to grips with this, I will first present an analysis of what may be called the ground of *li* in Confucian intentionality and then I will try to deal with the inevitable question: How can *li*, which is commonly translated as "ritual," be adequately understood as a process of humanization?

It should be noted that although this article is not intended to analyze the concept of *li* in terms of either its historical evolution or its linguistic ramifications, both the historical and linguistic dimensions are important as points of departure. But the primary concern of this paper is the ethicoreligious implication of *li* as viewed from the perspective of the philosophy of Mencius. I hope that such an approach, despite its obvious limitation of being one-sided, will raise relevant questions for those who are engaged in the study of Confucianism not only as a form of intellectual exercise but also as a quest for a deeper understanding of some perennial human problems.

II

In my study of the creative tension between *jen* and *li*, I attempted to refute the notion that *jen* is primarily a concept of human relations, for I believe that *jen* is "basically linked with the self-reviving, self-perfecting, and self-fulfilling process of an individual."[2] Further, I contended that *li* in this connection can be conceived of as an externalization of *jen* in a concrete social situation. And it is in *jen*'s inner demand for self-actualization that the meaning of *li* as a principle of particularism really lies. It is of paramount importance that we recognize the primacy of *jen* over *li* and the inseparability of *li* from *jen*. However, this article is an attempt to go beyond the dichotomy of "inner" and "outer" to arrive at a more sophisticated appreciation of the concept of *li*, which in turn may also help us to probe the inner resources of the concept of *jen*.

Nevertheless, to deny the validity of categorizing *jen* as primarily a concept of human relations is not to deemphasize the centrality of human-relatedness in the actualization of the ideal of *jen*. Indeed, it may very well be argued that just as *jen*, especially when used as a comprehensive virtue, gives meaning to *li*, *jen* without the manifestation of *li* is also inconceivable. Concrete application in the sociopolitical arena is such a salient feature of *jen* that to "embody" *jen* necessarily implies a profound care for the practical affairs of the world, which historically has been expressed in terms of the "five human relations," (*wu-lun*), sometimes referred to as the "five constancies," (*wu-ch'ang*). Therefore the five basic human relations become concrete manifestations of a deeper reality, namely cohumanity, to borrow Peter Boodberg's suggestive translation of *jen*.[3] Actually, the etymological meaning of *jen* is "man in society." According to one school of interpretation, the Chinese character for *jen* consists of the sign for man and the sign for two, designating the primordial form of human-relatedness.[4] Therefore, underlying the five human relations is the principle of reciprocity. Strictly speaking, man cannot become truly human if he does not feel the need to reciprocate the

18

affections of other people. For one's ability to relate to others in a meaningful way, such as in the spirit of filiality, brotherhood, or friendship, reflects one's level of self-cultivation.

From the Confucian point of view, therefore, although one can never become truly human if one fails to be sincere to one's inner self, one can never delve deeply into one's genuine selfhood if one refuses to manifest sincerity in the context of human-relatedness. On the surface this is an innocuous, some would say commonsensical, notion. But to probe its ethicoreligious implication necessitates a careful reflection on a few basic problems in Confucian humanism. One question readily comes to mind: Why must human-relatedness be an integral part of one's quest for self-realization? One wonders if Confucianism has not failed to recognize the agonizing reality that man's search for inner truth frequently, if not always, takes the form of a lonely struggle. When a truth seeker submits his burning desire for self-transcendence to the mores of the multitude, his spirit of detachment is damaged and the motivational force necessary for a high attainment in the religious realm may be lost also.

In many great spiritual traditions, human-relatedness as shown in one's attachment to the world is considered detrimental to man's religiosity and therefore must be forsaken before one can fully experience ultimate reality either in the form of a union with the "wholly other" or in the form of a unity with true selfhood.[5] In some standard expressions of this orientation, the argument runs as follows: human-relatedness must be totally eliminated because it gives rise to a false perception of the self. Unless that perception of the self that mainly results from the contaminating contacts with a variety of human situations is fundamentally transformed, real spiritual progress cannot be made. Accordingly spiritual self-purification becomes synonymous with a process of dehumanization, that is, to neutralize the distinctive properties of human-relatedness in man. The notion of "intercepting the multitudinous streams (of relations)"[6] in the teaching of Ch'an and the idea of the "leap of faith" from the ethical to the religious stage in the Kierkegaardian sense, notwithstanding the fundamental difference and conflict between them, both point to the necessity of transcending human relations to arrive at a level of self-awareness qualitatively different from social consciousness. To be religious in this connection is not to be social, but rather vehemently antisocial.

Indeed, it has been widely held that one of the most salient characteristics of spiritual self-transcendence is to say "no" to society at large. In the writings of many influential thinkers nowadays, to free oneself from human bondage and from the duress of moral authority has become such an accepted value that the glorification of personal liberation and the inculpation of social coerciveness become virtually two sides of the same coin. In light of this, it is natural to assume that the realization of the authentic self requires the courage to dwell spiritually as well as physically in ultimate isolation.

The Confucian approach, however, is fundamentally different. It contends that sociality is not only a desirable trait but also a defining characteristic of the highest human attainment. The position is based on two interrelated assumptions. One is that, although man has always been conditioned by a given structure beyond his control, the ultimate ground of his self-realization lies within his own nature. Man has the inner strength to actualize the full potential of his being, and his creativity is inherent in his humanness. Man, therefore, is not a creature but a creative agent who gives meaning to "Heaven, Earth, and the myriad things." The second reason is that, despite his ontological self-sufficiency, for man to become a fully actualized human being he must constantly engage in the process of learning to be a sage (the highest form of authentic humanity). It should be remarked that the process of learning to be a sage does not take the form of linear progression but that of gradual integration. Specifically man authenticates his being not by detaching himself from the world of human relations but by making sincere attempts to harmonize his relationships with others.

This article, however, does not purport to defend the Confucian position by rigorous analytical argument. It intends to understand the general direction of the "Confucian persuasion" by a preliminary inquiry into the concept of *li*.

III

Li is a concept pregnant with ethicoreligious connotations. The mere fact that it has been rendered as "ceremony," "ritual," "rites," "propriety," "rules of propriety," "good custom," "decorum," "good form," and a host of other ideas including that of natural law suggests the scope of its implications.[7] Etymologically, the ideograph *li* symbolizes a sacrificial act. As Wing-tsit Chan has pointed out, it originally meant "a religious sacrifice."[8] However, the earliest available dictionary meaning of *li* is "treading" or "following." Specifically it points to the step or act whereby spiritual beings are properly served and human happiness obtained.[9]

Whether we focus on its original meaning of sacrifice or its derivative meaning of propriety, *li* implies the existence of an "other." To dwell in *li*, therefore, is not to remain isolated. On the contrary, it necessarily involves a relationship or a process by which a relationship comes into being. Thus, to relate oneself to an other is the underlying structure of *li*. The problem of *li* does not even occur when one has absolutely nothing to relate to. The primacy of an other in the actualization of *li* is best shown in the saying, "The feeling of respect and reverence is what we call *li*."[10] Since, with the exception of an extreme form of narcissism, a feeling of respect and reverence presupposes something or someone which is respected and revered, it is very unlikely that one can have such a feeling without ever coming to terms with an other. It is also said, "In carrying out *li*, harmony (*ho*) is to be cherished."[11] It is conceivable that here the *ho* means harmony with oneself so that one can perform *li* with a peaceful state of mind. But it is undeniable that *li* involves the act of relating to an other, if only as a manifestation of an inward feeling.

Is our insistence on the point that otherness, which is thought to be outside the self, is inherent in the structure of *li*, necessarily in conflict with the Mencian idea that *li* is rooted in the mind (*hsin*) and not infused into us from without?[12] On the surface this seems reminiscent of the famous debate between Mencius and Kao Tzu on the internality and externality of righteousness (*i*).[13] By concentrating on the otherness of *li*, are we not committing the fallacy of subsuming *li* under a set of external principles? If this were the case, we would be arguing for an interpretation of *li* analogous to Kao Tzu's position on *i*. However, it scarcely need be said that our present line of thinking has been Mencian in character. How are we to account for this apparent incongruity?

The two assumptions mentioned earlier may provide an answer.

21

According to the Confucian contention, the ultimate ground of man's self-realization lies in his own nature, and yet for man to attain his personal authenticity, he must undergo a process of self-transformation. Such a process involves more than the sublimation of instinctual demands. Far from being a kind of asceticism, self-transformation in the Confucian sense must be manifested in the context of human relations. However, it does not take the form of internalizing social values. Man's authenticity, as seen from the Confucian perspective, is not predicated on the prescriptions of society. Indeed, man can never become authentic by uncritically submitting himself to the restrictions of society. It should be mentioned in passing that in the *Analects, hsiang-yüan,* a type of man who follows the convention and assumes the appearance of virtue, is in sharp conflict with the ideal personality of *chün-tzu.*[14]

In a deeper sense, Confucian self-transformation is based on neither isolated self-control nor collective social sanction. It is in what may be called the "between" that its basis really lies. If we follow this line of thinking, the road to sagehood is a "narrow ridge" between spiritual individualism and ethical socialism.[15] Nevertheless, nothing could be further from my intention than to suggest that the Confucian approach undermines either social collectivity or the individual self. Actually with reference to this particular point, the main issue in Confucianism is never conceived of in terms of an "either-or" proposition. Rather, to be an authentic man is to be truthful to *both* one's selfhood and one's sociality. The personality of Confucius bears witness to this. His single-minded effort to realize his inner self is manifested in his ability to purify its inauthentic expressions: "Confucius was completely free from four things: He had no arbitrariness of opinion, no dogmatism, no obstinacy, and no egotism."[16] On the other hand, his concern for self-cultivation never hindered his commitment to society at large: "It is impossible to associate with birds and beasts, as if they were the same with us. If I associate not with these people—with mankind—with whom shall I associate? If right principles prevailed through the empire, there would be no use for me to change its state."[17]

It is certainly misleading to leave the impression that Confucius as a moral optimist happily sails between the Scylla of self-isolation and the Charybdis of social coercion. It is true that Confucius has

22

clearly remarked, "Is humanity (*jen*) far away? I wish to be human, and lo! humanity is at hand."[18] But only after he had attained the adavanced age of seventy was he able to state with confidence that he could follow his heart's desire without transgressing moral principles.[19] The ability to harmonize childlike spontaneity with ethical responsibility, which entails a long and continuous process of self-cultivation, presupposes an awareness of the other. Yet the other, seen in human relationship, symbolizes a concrete path by which the true self becomes manifested. Ideally the dangers of self-isolation and social coercion can be conquered if a fundamental change has been made in the dichotomous way of perceiving the relationship between the self and society. In a practical sense, the source of such a change is located neither in the self nor in society exclusively. It has to be sought in both, and indeed in the "between."

Mencius' insistence on the internality of *i*, and for that matter of *li*, is actually an attempt to maintain that man's moral inwardness as a necessary requirement for self-realization is not reducible to a set of externalizable forces. If an inner decision is not made, no matter how ingeniously social values are imposed on the individual, the best consequence one can expect is a kind of passive submission reminiscent of the *hsiang-yüan*. Therefore, the Mencian position does not preclude the awareness that the existence of the other, specifically in the form of human-relatedness, is an integral part of man's struggle to attain his personal authenticity. In this connection, *Jen che jen yeh*, which is sometimes rendered as "Humanity is man," or "Man is *jen*,"[20] really points to the inseparability of man and his cohumanity.

It may be said that by stressing the otherness in the structure of *li*, we are not at all in conflict with Mencius' insistence on the internality of *li*. Mencius says, "the feeling of modesty and complaisance is the germ (*tuan*) of *li*."[21] The character *tuan* is interpreted by James Legge to mean *tuan-hsü* (the end of a clue), "that point outside, which may be laid hold of, and will guide us to all within."[22] Mencius does not say that *li* is inherent in the mind, in the sense that the actualization of *li* involves nothing other than introspective self-discipline. The issue of *li* is "like that of fire which has begun to burn, or that of a spring which has begun to find vent."[23] Its source is grounded in the natural feeling of the mind. But if the feeling in which the rationale of *li* rests is denied development, it may eventually die. Like a fire or a spring, *li* is a movement, a continuous process of extension. To paraphrase Mencius again, if *li* is fully extended it will be sufficient for a man to serve all within the four seas. If it is not at all extended, it will not even suffice for a man to serve his own parents.[24] Implicit in this proverbial statement is what may be called the inner dynamics of *li*.

IV

Viewed dynamically *li* points to a concrete way whereby one enters into communion with others. Reminiscent of its dictionary meaning of "following" or "treading," here *li* is understood as a movement leading toward an authentic relationship. Genetically the relationship was perceived as that between man and a supernatural being. The basic concern of *li* was then how to take the proper step so that one could either follow the given commands of a transcendent other or evoke the desired responses from it. Yet long before the birth of Confucius in 551 B.C., the concept of *li* had acquired a strong ethical meaning. The relationship between man and man gradually became its dominant trait. The sacrificial aspect of *li*, however, continued to play an important role in the Confucian tradition throughout Chinese history.

In the thought of Mencius, *li* together with humanity (*jen*), righteousness (*i*), and wisdom (*chih*) acquires an inner dimension.[25] The quest for an authentic relationship becomes essentially a problem of self-transformation. Mencius actually remarked, "All the ten thousand things are there in me. There is no greater joy for me than to find, on self-examination, that I am true to myself, Try your best to treat others as you would wish to be treated yourself, and you will find that this is the shortest way to benevolence (*jen*)."[26] He also stated that if a man can give full realization to his mind he will understand his own nature, and by understanding his own nature he will know Heaven.[27] But if we investigate the actual process of self-transformation in this connection, we will notice that it necessitates not only the awareness of an other but also the experience of mutual dependence. The Mencian emphasis on the internality of establishing authentic relationship with an other, far from being a

24

kind of subjectivism, points to both social and transcendent dimensions.

Hence the meaning of *li* evolved from a proper act of offering sacrifice to an authentic way of establishing human-relatedness, which in the Mencian version actually involves the act of self-transformation. *Li* in this connection is understood as movement instead of form. The emphasis is on its dynamic process rather than its static structure. Such a position can be supported on etymological as well as historical grounds. Our purpose for singling out this particular area for consideration is not to refute the commonly accepted interpretations of *li*. Rather, it is intended to be a preliminary step toward the formulation of a more comprehensive view of *li*.

If we seriously take the notion of *li* as movement, the dichotomy of self and society has to be understood in a new perspective. The self must be extended beyond its physical existence to attain its authenticity, for sociality is a constituent aspect of the authentic self. However, society is not conceived of as something out there that is being imposed on the individual. It is in essence an extended self. The internalization of social values, which is frequently criticized as the submission of the individual to a well-established authority, can therefore be interpreted as a creative step taken by the self to enter into human-relatedness for the sake of none other than its own realization.

When Mencius said, "All the ten thousand things are there in us," he was presenting an ontological understanding of the self: Heaven, Earth, and the myriad things are all inherent in the being of the self. Yet Mencius further suggested that in the concrete process of an individual's actualizing the authenticity of his self—the realization of *jen* in his human nature—the law of reciprocity (*shu*), which entails the existence of an other, has to be vigorously applied.[28] The apparent contradiction between the ontological assertion and the practical consideration can be resolved by perceiving the self as a continuum, an extension of its physical existence to the embodiment of the universe as a whole. Self and society therefore are not static concepts denoting two irreconcilable entities but are two mutually dependent aspects of the same dynamic process.

What is the movement of *li* then? Indeed, what is the direction toward which *li* actually moves? In the light of the earlier discussion,

25

I propose to answer this question by first returning to an earlier point. The basic concern in Confucianism is *how to become a sage*. Such a concern seems to involve a method (how), a process (becoming), and an end (sagehood). Since the attainment of Confucian sagehood is predicated on the belief that man is perfectible by self-effort, the method in question is not an acquired technique but self-cultivation. Similarly the process is not an external procedure but self-transformation, and the end is not an objectifiable goal but self-realization.

However, the means-and-end dichotomy is inadequate to express its basic spiritual orientation because strictly speaking the attainment of sagehood should not be conceived of as achieving something external to the structure of man. Rather, it is a manifestation of what constitutes true humanity. But as we have pointed out repeatedly, it is misleading to argue that since sagehood is inherent in the nature of man, the attainment of sagehood requires nothing more than a process of inner transformation, independent of society at large. This being so, self-transformation must be regarded as both a means and an end in the process of self-extension. In fact it points to a dialectical interplay between the means of self-cultivation as internal examination and the end of complete self-realization as communion with others and with the universe at large.

For example, one controls and sometimes even denies one's instinctual demands, and by so doing one is able to enter into a better communion with others. This may be interpreted as a form of self-mortification for the sake of social solidarity. Yet such an interpretation only scratches the surface of Confucian intentionality. For sociality as a spiritual value is justified neither on grounds of transcendent reference nor on grounds of collective goal. It is in the perfectibility of man as an ethicoreligious being that the justification for sociality really lies. Indeed, a Confucian tries to be social for the sake of self-realization. His personal authenticity is inseparable from his sociality. If he fails to relate himself to others in a meaningful way, he does violence not only to his social relations but also to his authentic self. Unless he cultivates himself in the context of human-relatedness, no matter how high a spiritual level he is able to attain, from the Confucian point of view, his claim to self-realization is inauthentic.

T'ang Chün-i has pointed out that "to live in definite ethical relations with others in the actual world, practicing the morality of doing one's duty to others but not asking them to do their duties, reciprocally," is the Confucian way.[29] We may add that the golden rule in Confucianism, which states, "Do not do to others what you would not want others to do to you," is basically "duty consciousness."[30] It does not lead to the demand of "rights-consciousness" that the other reciprocate what my sense of duty has dictated me to perform.[31] Underlying this kind of passivity is the awareness of the other as an irreducible entity in man's "searching in himself."[32] Since I can never be sure of the situations of the others to the same degree and in the same way that I can be of my own, it is presumptuous for me to impose my sense of duty on others. However, in the performance of my own duty I cannot afford to ignore the reality of otherness because it actually constitutes an integral part of the process in which my sense of duty is to be actualized.

Accordingly the principle of reciprocity as it is used in the present context involves the awareness of sociality as an integral part of man's self-realization. It is true that the Confucian concept of *shu*, which is frequently rendered as reciprocity, takes "inward examination" (*nei-hsing*) as its point of departure. But inward examination in this connection has a great deal to do with one's human-relatedness. Tseng Tzu's daily practice is a case in point. In the *Analects* he is recorded to have said, "Every day I examine myself on three points: whether in counseling others I have not been loyal; whether in intercourse with my friends I have not been faithful; and whether I have not repeated again and again and practiced the instructions of my teacher."[33] Therefore the ability to relate oneself to society at large becomes an important indicator of one's self-cultivation.

Seen from this particular standpoint, man's authentic being can be fully manifested if and only if the individual enters into human-relatedness in the spirit of reciprocity. *Li* thus may be understood as the movement of self-transformation, the dialectical path through which man becomes more human.

V

Concretely, *li* as a process of humanization is manifested in four developmental stages: (1) cultivating personal life (*hsiu-shen*), (2) regulating familial relations (*ch'i-chia*), (3) ordering the affairs of the state (*chih-kuo*), and (4) bringing peace to the world (*p'ing t'ien-hsia*).[34] It should be emphasized that the four developmental stages must not be regarded as merely a linear progression. It is true that to regulate one's familial relations one must first cultivate one's personal life, and to bring peace to the world one must first order the affairs of the state, and so forth. But it may be argued also that cultivating one's personal life necessarily leads to the regulation of familial relations, because in the Confucian context it is inconceivable that self-cultivation can be isolated from human-relatedness. Familial relationship, being the primordial dimension of human-relatedness, becomes an essential part of self-cultivation, which in an ultimate sense must also entail peace in the world. Indeed, unless self-cultivation eventually brings about peace in the world it cannot be said to have been fully manifested. Therefore, in a practical sense, self-cultivation is an unceasing process of gradual inclusion.

By analogy, regulating familial relations is, on the one hand, a more inclusive expression of self-cultivation, and on the other, an essential aspect of the affairs of the state. For the regulation of familial relations to complete its task, so to speak, ultimately it must bring peace to the world. Thus in Confucianism ideally self-cultivation results in universal peace, which in turn has its practical root in each man's cultivation of his personal life. But, as a concrete process of gradual inclusion, self-cultivation cannot bypass the regulation of familial relations or the ordering of the affairs of the state. The idea that one can somehow transcend both the family and the state to bring about universal peace is alien to the Confucian way of thinking.

Mencius' attack on the "universalism" of Mo Tzu is a case in point.[35] From the Mencian perspective, the central issue is not so much the desirability of universalizing one's basic value commitment as much as *how*, by a concrete path, it can be universally manifested. By advocating "love without discrimination" (*chien-ai*),[36] Mo Tzu failed to take into account the human reality: the affective intensity of the father-son relationship is a commonly experienced fact. Setting up an abstract standard of indiscriminate love without coming to terms with concrete human situations is to ignore the very context in which the ideal is to be actualized. Hence, the Confucianists believe that the realization of universal love must begin with a

28

concrete process of gradual inclusion.

This process of inclusion is characterized by an awareness of a given structure and a way to go beyond any finite form of restriction. The process must take the individual as its starting point, but complete self-realization implies the inclusion of the universe as a whole. In practice the given structure of an individual is necessarily an integral part of his self-realization, and yet for him to be fully developed he must transcend any limited version of the given structure, such as egocentrism, nepotism, ethnocentrism, and anthropocentrism. Ideally man's given structure is as inclusive as the universe. To use a common expression, "nothing is not included" (*wu-so-pu-pao*) in man's true being. However, at a specific juncture of development, it is important for the individual to be aware of his physical as well as his spiritual "locality."[37] *Li* in this sense involves not only a given structure but also a way by which any finite form of restriction is transcended (the dynamic process).

Descriptively *li* assumes the forms of integrating personality, family, state, and the world. It is thus understandable that as a comprehensible concept *li* denotes a variety of rituals concerning personal conduct, social relations, political organizations, and religious behavior. It includes virtually all aspects of human culture: psychological, social, and religious. In the Confucian context it is inconceivable that one can become truly human without going through the process of "ritualization," which in this particular connection means humanization. A brief survey of the available historical literature on *li* will be sufficient to show the tautological relationship between ritualization and humanization in the Confucian tradition. Works such as *Chou-li, Li-chi* and the more recently compiled *Wu-li t'ung-k'ao*[38] contain "rituals" of such a diverse nature that the only way to comprehend their scope is to consider them compendia of human culture as seen from the Confucian perspective. Terms such as Hsia-*li*, Yin-*li*, or Chou-*li* used in the time of Confucius should also be understood as generic concepts referring to the cultural traditions of Hsia, Yin, and Chou.[39] The famous "Li-yün" chapter of the *Book of Rites*, in the light of the present discussion, symbolizes the highest attainment of human culture in the ideal of *ta-t'ung* (great harmony or great unity).[40]

The humanization of *li* is best shown in an important dialogue in the *Analects*. The first part of the exchange between Yen Hui and Confucius was used in my earlier paper as a key to understanding the relationship between *jen* and *li*. Having given his reply to Yen Hui concerning the question of humanity (*jen*): "To conquer yourself and return to *li*," Confucius further commented on the specific items involved: "Do not look at what is contrary to *li*, do not listen to what is contrary to *li*, do not speak what is contrary to *li*, and do not make any movement which is contrary to *li*."[41] If *li* is perceived as fixed rituals that are being imposed on the individual without his moral consent, Confucius' instruction that one must see, listen, speak, and move in accordance with *li* does seem unreasonably demanding. However, *li* as a process of ritualization, which in this particular context refers to the process of humanization in general, varies according to the principle of "timeliness" (*shih*).[42] The situational dimension is so crucial to the structure of *li* that a fundamentalistic adherence to its forms is at best a demonstration of what was called "the small fidelity of common men and common women."[43]

The personality of Confucius as manifested in the "*Hsiang-tang*" chapter of the *Analects* is certainly "ritualized" in a form extremely difficult for us to comprehend.[44] But in his own time and place, his ritualism was a remarkable fruition of his humanness. After all, sagehood, which is the personality ideal beyond the reach of even Confucius himself, is none other than the authentic manifestation of humanity.

VI

In conclusion, we may indulge in a comparative note. The Confucian concept of *li* is actually much more inclusive than either the Christian concept of Law or the Indian concept of *dharma*. Abraham's attempt to sacrifice his own son in Genesis seems to symbolize that faith transcends not only Law but also human rationality. In Confucianism, the postulation of a realm of meaning, which sometimes takes the paradoxical form of "absurdity," completely beyond the humanization of *li*, is incomprehensible. Similarly the Indian concept of *mokṣa*, which symbolizes release from *saṃsāra* and liberation from *karman*, wherein the status of *dharma* becomes problematical if not completely irrelevant, is also unthinkable to the Confucian mind. For sagehood, as the full embodiment of *jen*, must also manifest *li*. Despite tension between *jen* and *li*, the actualization of *jen* cannot but travel the path of *li*.

NOTES

[1]Tu Wei-ming, "The Creative Tension between *Jen* and *Li*," *Philosophy East and West* 18, no.1–2 (January-April, 1968): 29–39.

[2]*Ibid.*, p. 34. See above, p. 9.

[3]"The Semasiology of Some Primary Confucian Concepts," *Philosophy East and West* 2, no. 4 (1953): 317–332.

[4]See Hsü Shen, *Shuo-wen chieh-tzu* (reprint, Taipei: I-wen Book Co., 1958), 8:1.4.

[5]Rudolf Otto, *Mysticism East and West*, trans. Bertha L. Bracey and Richenda C. Payne (New York: Macmillan Company, 1960), pp. 157–179.

[6]See Hsüeh-tou and Yüan-wu, *Pi-yen chi* (*Pi-yen lu*), 1:1. For some general information on this important collection of the spiritual tradition of Ch'an, see Suzuki Daisetz, "On the Hekigan Roku," *The Eastern Buddhist*, n.s., 1, no. 1 (Sept. 1965): 5–21.

[7]See Chu Hsi, *Reflections on Things at Hand*, trans. Wing-tsit Chan (New York: Columbia University Press, 1967), p. 367.

[8]*Ibid.*

[9]Hsü Shen, *Shuo-wen chieh-tzu*, 1a:4.3. See also *K'ang-hsi tzu-tien* (reprint, Taipei: I-wen Book Co., 1957), p. 1920.

[10]*Mencius*, 6A.6. See Wing-tsit Chan, trans, and comp., *A Source Book in Chinese Philosophy* (Princeton: Princeton University Press, 1963), p. 54 (hereafter cited as "Chan, *Source Book*"). Cf. D.C. Lau, trans., *Mencius* (Baltimore, Md.: Penguin Classics, 1970), p. 163.

[11]*Analects*, 1.12. In a slightly different context, *li* may also be understood as "harmonizing" the directions of some other important virtues in Confucianism: "Respectfulness without *li* becomes tiresome; carefulness without *li* becomes timidity; daring without *li* becomes turbulence; and straightforwardness without *li* becomes rudeness." For this quotation, see *Analects*, 8.2. Cf. *Confucian Analects*, in James Legge, trans., *The Chinese Analects*, 5 vols. (Oxford: Clarendon Press, 1893–95), 1:208; hereafter cited as "Legge, *Classics*."

[12]*Mencius*, 6A.6.

[13]*Ibid.*, 6A.4, 5.

[14]For the case of *hsiang-yüan*, see *Analects*, 17.13. A more detailed exposition on this issue can be found in *Mencius*, 7B.37. Also see D.C. Lau, *Mencius*, p. 203. For the personality ideal of *chün-tzu*, see *Analects*, 1.2, 8, 14; 2.12, 13; 4.5, 24; 6.16; 9.13; 13.3; 14.30; 15.17, 20, 31; 16.8, 10.

[15]For example Étienne Balazs has characterized Chinese philosophy as predom-

inantly a social philosophy. On the other hand, to emphasize the transcendent reference in Confucianism, D. Howard Smith has this to say about Confucius: "He was concerned to enunciate the basis of that integration and harmony of personality which results in good life and conduct. But that basis he found in obedience and conformity to the Way of Heaven. To suggest, as many scholars do, that Confucius found a satisfying solution in pure humanism, and that his ethics did not finally rest on deep religious insight and personal faith in *T'ien* is to discount many of the most pregnant sayings attributed to Confucius in the *Analects.*" (*Chinese Religions* [New York: Holt, Reinhart and Winston, 1968], p. 35.) It should be acknowledged in this connection that my struggle to go beyond the dichotomy of spiritual individualism and ethical socialism in formulating a more balanced interpretation of the Confucian spiritual orientation is made less painful by the original contributions of two eminent scholars in the philosophy of religion: Huston Smith, "Transcendence in Traditional China," *Religious Studies* 2:185–196; and Herbert Fingarette, "Human Community as Holy Rite: An Interpretation of Confucian *Analects,*" *Harvard Theological Review* 59, no. 1. (1966): 53–67.

[16]*Analects*, 9.4.

[17]*Ibid.*, 18.6.

[18]*Ibid.*, 7.29.

[19]*Ibid.*, 2.4.

[20]For a brief discussion on this issue, see Donald J. Munro, *The Concept of Man in Early China* (Stanford: Stanford University Press, 1969), p. 15. Also see *Mencius*, 7B.16. D.C. Lau gives the following translation: "Benevolence means 'man.' " In a footnote he adds, "This is not a simple phonetic gloss based on identical prounciations, as the two words are in fact cognate." See *Mencius*, p. 197.

[21]*Mencius*, 2A.6. See D.C. Lau, *Mencius*, p. 83. The word *germ* here is the translation of the Chinese character *tuan*, which is rendered in Legge as "principle." Cf. *The Works of Mencius* in James Legge, trans., *The Chinese Classics* (reprint, Taipei: Wen-hsing Book Co., 1966), 2:203.

[22]Legge, *ibid.*

[23]*Mencius*, 2A.6.

[24]*Ibid.*

[25]*Ibid.*

[26]*Ibid.*, 7.4. See D.C. Lau, *Mencius*, p. 182. Cf. Legge, *Classics*, 2:450–451.

[27]*Mencius*, 7A.1.

[28]Legge, *Classics*, 2:451.

[29]"The Development of Ideas of Spiritual Value in Chinese Philosophy," in Charles A. Moore, ed., *The Chinese Mind* (Honolulu: East-West Center Press, 1967), p. 192.

[30]*Analects*, 15.23. Cf. Legge's translation: "Tsze-kung asked, saying, 'Is there one word which may serve as a rule of practice for all one's life?' The Master said, 'Is not Reciprocity such a word? What you do not want done to yourself, do not do to others.'" It may be interesting to point out that "Reciprocity" is used here to translate the ideograph *shu*. See Legge, *Classics*, 1:301.

[31]The terms *duty-consciousness* and *rights-consciousness* are borrowed from T'ang Chün-i, "The Development of Ideas of Spiritual Value in Chinese Philosophy," p. 193.

[32]For the expression "searching in oneself," see *ibid.*

[33]*Analects*, 1.4. See Chan, *Source Book*, p. 20.

[34]*Ta-hsüeh* in Chu Hsi, comp., *Ssu-shu chi-chu* (reprint, Taipei: Shih-chieh Book Co., 1952), 1a-b.

[35]*Mencius*, 3B.9, 7A.26.

[36]See a brief note on Mo Tzu in D.C. Lau, *Mencius*, p. 274.

[37]In using the word *locality* I have the concept of *fen* in mind. Although *fen* as a key concept in Confucianism is best developed in the philosophy of Hsün Tzu, its prominence in the Mencian way of thinking is also quite evident. For instance, Mencius actually used the concept of *fen-ting* to characterize human nature. See *Mencius*, 7A.21. A very suggestive account on this issue can be found in Hsü Fu-kuan, *Chung-kuo jen-hsing-lun shih* (Taichung: Tunghai University Press, 1963), p. 167.

[38]For a succinct textual account of *Chou-li* and *Li-chi*, see Ch'ü Wan-li, *Ku-chi tao-tu* (Taipei: K'ai-ming Book Co., 1964), pp. 159–183. The anthology of *Wu-li t'ung-k'ao* in the Ch'ing dynasty (1880 ed.) was indeed voluminous. It was put together by a group of scholars under the editorship of Ch'in Hui-tien.

[39]For reference to Hsia-*li* and Yin-*li*, see *Analects*, 2.23; 3.9. For reference to Chou-*li* as well, see *Chung-yung*, 28.5. It should be noted that the term Chou-*li* used in this context is different from the name of the Confucian work *Chou-li*.

[40]It is certainly beyond our present concern to present a comprehensive analysis of the "Li-yün" chapter in *Li-chi*. Issues such as authentic authorship and intellectual origins are too complicated to come to grips with at this particular juncture of research. For example, some scholars have argued, "There are strong evidences in this piece of the syncretic tendencies of the Han, which suggest that the primitive ideal of Grand Harmony is actually a Taoist conception, while the age of Lesser Prosperity following it is the original sage-king ideal of Confucius and Mencius downgraded one step." However, the authors also state, "This passage from the *Book of Rites* (*Li-chi*) is one of the most celebrated in Confucian literature. It has been traditionally takes as representing Confucius' highest ideal in the social order, the age of Grand Unity (*ta-t'ung*) in which the world was shared by all the people." (Wm. Theodore de Bary, et al., comps., *Sources of Chinese Tradition* [New York Columbia University Press, 1960], p. 191.) *Li-yün*, which has been rendered as "Evolution of Rites," points to a dynamic process by which human culture gradually evolves into a state of universal peace. In the light of our discussion so far, this is by no means incompatible with Confucian intentionality. It seems to me that a close examination of the claim that the concept of *ta-t'ung* is basically Taoist in origin will show that such a claim, far from being a textual or a historical argument, is itself based on a rather restricted philosophical presupposition, namely that Confucianism is in essence a kind of pragmatic social philosophy.

[41]*Analects*, 12.1.

[42]For a vivid description of the Confucian concept of "timeliness" as manifested in the personality of Confucius, see *Mencius*, 6B.1. Also see *Analects*, 18.8 for Confucius' characterization of his own spiritual orientation.

[43]*Analects*, 14.18. See Legge, *Classics*, 1:282–293.

[44]See especially *Analects*, 10.8, 16.

3. The Confucian Perception of Adulthood

According to the Confucian *Book of Rites,* the "capping ceremony" (*kuan-li*) is performed on a man's twentieth birthday and declares that he has come of age. But only after he has married and become a father in his thirties is he considered a fully participating member of society. His career as a scholar-official normally begins at forty. He is then considered mature and responsible. If all goes well, he reaches the apex of his public service at fifty, and he does not retire from it until he is well over seventy. The "capping ceremony" is also preceded by an equally elaborate process of maturation: education at home begins at six, sex differentiation in education at seven, etiquette at eight, arithmetic at nine, formal schooling at ten, and by thirteen the student will have studied music, poetry, dance, ritual, archery, and horsemanship.[1] Thus from childhood to old age the learning to be human never ceases.

Adulthood conceived in this way is not so much a state of attainment as a process of becoming. The initiation rite as a gateway to manhood does not feature prominently in Confucian symbolism. And the idea that one's life on earth can and should be differentiated into discrete modes of existence and is, in essence, a preparation for an afterlife does not seem to have occurred in the Confucian tradition either. The emphasis instead is on the process of living itself. The maturation of a human being is viewed as an unfolding of humanity in the world. For without self-cultivation as a continuous effort to realize one's humanity, biological growth becomes meaningless. Adulthood, then, is "to become a person." The present paper is intended as an exploration of the underlying structure of this claim.

Metaphor

Tseng Tzu, one of Confucius' most respected disciples, envisioned the task of becoming a man as one of embarking on an endless journey with a heavy burden on one's shoulders:

> The true Knight of the Way [*shih*] must perforce be both broad-shouldered and stout of heart; his burden is heavy and he has far to go. For Humanity [*jen*] is the burden he has taken upon himself; and must we not grant that it is a heavy one to bear? Only with death does this journey end; then must we not grant that he has far to go?[2]

The image of being "on the way" is also present in Confucius' comment on his best disciple, Yen Hui, whose premature death deeply agonized him: "Alas, I saw his constant advance. I never saw him stop in his progress."[3] Similarly, as the *Analects* records, once standing by a stream the Master was moved to remark, "Could one but go on and on like this, never ceasing day or night!"[4] As many commentators have pointed out, the continuous flow of the water here symbolizes a ceaseless process of self-realization and is therefore an apt description of the Confucian understanding of the authentic way of being human.

Yet the Way, which is inseparable from the person who pursues it, is never perceived as an external path. Instead, it is assumed to be inherent in human nature and thus, as the *Doctrine of the Mean* clearly notes, cannot even for a moment be detached from it.[5] To follow the Way, so conceived, is neither a rejection of, nor a departure from, one's humanity. It is rather a fulfillment of it. Therefore, in a strict sense, a man does not follow the Way as a means to an end. Nor does he imitate the Way so that he can realize a specifiable destiny. The idea of achievement is not at all applicable to this mode of thinking. In fact, Confucius himself insisted that "the Way cannot make man great" and that "it is man who can make the Way great."[6] Understandably, in Confucian literature the imagery of *seeing* the Way is hardly used. The Way can be heard (presumably as an inner voice), obtained, and embodied, but it can never be found by casting our gaze outward.

The internality of the Way as an experienced presence is what accounts for much of the moral striving in Confucian self-cultivation. Since the Way is not shown as a norm that establishes a fixed pattern of behavior, a person cannot measure the success or failure of his conduct in terms of the degree of approximation to an external ideal. The Way is always near at hand, and the journey must be constantly renewed here and now. An often-quoted dictum in the *Great Learning* simply reads: "If you can renovate yourself one day, then you can do so every day, and keep doing so day after day." The instruction is not only to do what one ought to do but to "try at all times to do the utmost one can."[7] And furthermore, if one encounters difficulties, "do not complain against Heaven above or blame men below."[8] It is like the art of archery: "When the archer misses the center of the target, he turns around and seeks for the cause of failure within himself."[9] The Way, then, does not provide an ideal norm or a set of directives to be complied with. It functions as a governing perpective and a point of orientation.

The Confucians believe that ideally only those who steer the middle course can completely realize themselves and hence manifest the Way in its all-embracing fullness. But they are also aware that, although the course of the Mean is perfect, few people have been able to follow it consistently, "if just for a round month." The seemingly common and direct path of self-cultivation is in practice extremely difficult to maintain. It was probably not merely for dramatic effect that Confucius is alleged to have said, "The empire, the states, and the families can be put to order. Ranks and emolument can be declined. A bare, naked weapon can be tramped upon. But the Mean cannot [easily] be attained."[10] Thus the pursuit of the middle course is much more demanding and significant than even the most outstanding demonstration of power, honor, or valor. This may give one the impression that only those who can always pursue the due medium are the "true Knights of the Way." But, having come to the realization that the quality of the Mean rarely exists, Confucius was particularly concerned about finding the "ardent" (*k'uang*) and the "aloof" (*chüan*). For "the ardent will advance and lay hold of the Way; the aloof will keep themselves from pursuing the wrong ways."[11]

The Way is, then, particularly open to those who have the inner strength to "get hold of it, grasp it firmly as if wearing it on the breast and never lose it,"[12] and to those who are able to wait for the right moment to follow it. But it is more or less manifested in the lives and conduct of ordinary people as well. Even men and women of simple intelligence are in a sense witnesses of the Way.[13] Only the so-called hyperhonest villager (*hsiang-yüan*) has little chance of manifesting it. Confucius' distaste for this sort of person is shown in his characterization of him as "the enemy (or thief) of virtue."[14] The reason why Confucius was particularly disapproving of the hyperhonest villager is elaborated by Mencius as follows:

> If you want to censure him, you cannot find anything; if you want to find fault with him, you cannot find anything either. He shares with others the practices of the day and is in harmony with the sordid world. He pursues such a policy and appears to be conscientious and faithful, and to show integrity in his conduct. He is liked by the multitude and is self-righteous. It is impossible to embark on the way of Yao and Shun [the Confucian Way] with such a man. Hence the name "enemy of virtue."[15]

At first glance Confucius does seem unusually stringent toward the hyperhonest villager. One wonders what harm he has done merely because he believes that "being in this world, one must behave in a manner pleasing to this world."[16] After all, one of the primary Confucian concerns, also, is to bring peace and harmony to this world. Again, Mencius elaborates on how Confucius might have responded to our puzzlement:

> I dislike what is specious. I dislike weeds for fear they might be confused with rice plant; I dislike flattery for fear it might be confused with what is right; I dislike glibness for fear it might be confused with the truthful; . . . I dislike the hyperhonest villager for fear he might be confused with the virtuous.[17]

The real problem with the hyperhonest villager is his total lack of a commitment to the Way. Despite his apparent compatibility with the established social norms, he is absolutely devoid of any "ambition" for self-improvement. His complacency, as a result, is no more than a reflection of a hollow and unreal personality.

The Knight of the Way, however, never ceases to "set his heart on the Way." Nor does he relax his "firm grasp on virtue." Indeed, he always endeavors to "rely on humanity and find recreation in the arts"[18] so that he can broaden himself with "culture" (*wen*) and refine himself with "ritual" (*li*).[19] His "ambition" is to become a "man of humanity" who, "wishing to establish his own character, also establishes the character of others, and wishing to be prominent himself, also helps others to be prominent."[20] His learning is "for the sake of himself" (*wei-chi*),[21] and he does not regard himself as an "instrument" (*chi*), for his mode of existence is to be an end rather than a tool for any external purpose.[22] To be sure, this by no means implies that he somehow exemplifies the amateur ideal of "doing his own thing" for love alone. As we shall see, he is as much motivated by a duty consciousness[23] as by an aesthetic need for self-perfection.

In fact, no matter how hard he works and how much distance he covers, a true man is, as it were, all the time "on the Way." The aforementioned Tseng Tzu was gravely serious when he said that "only with death does this journey end." Even the sigh of relief he uttered with his dying words—"I feel now that whatever may betide I have got through safely"—was preceded by a verse from the *Book of Odes*:

> In fear and tembling,
> With caution and care,
> As though on the brink of a chasm,
> As though treading thin ice.[24]

Approach

The Way as a root metaphor or basic analogy is vitally important for understanding the Confucian concept of man, an understanding necessary for an appreciation of the Confucian idea of adulthood. Since the process of maturation is conceived as a continous effort toward self-realization, the creative development of a person depends as much on a sense of inner direction as on a prior knowledge of the established social norms. For a person to manifest his humanity, it is not enough simply to model himself on the proper ways of life and conduct approved by society. He must learn to control his own course through experience and furnish it with contents shaped by his concrete action. And as the Way cannot be fully mapped out in advance, he must, with a sense of discovery,

39

undergo a dynamic process of self-transformation in order to comport with it.[25] The Way, then, is always a way of "becoming" (*ch'eng*).

Understandably, the Confucian term for adulthood is *ch'eng-jen*, which literally means one who has *become* a person. Since the word *ch'eng*, like many other Chinese characters, is both a noun and a verb, the former signifying a state of completion and the latter a process of development, it is not far-fetched to understand the *ch'eng-jen* basically as one who has *gone far* toward a fully developed humanity. The notion of *ch'eng-jen* thus denotes not merely a stage of life but a many-sided manifestation of man's creative adaptation to the inevitable process of aging, a proven ability to mature further, as well as an obvious sign of maturity itself. The assumption is that the person who "has the Way" (*yu-tao*) has not only experiential knowledge of the Way but the wisdom and strength to lead the Way.

Strictly speaking, if adulthood means the process of becoming a person and an adult means not only a mature person but also a person capable of further maturing, it is difficult to imagine in such a context how "adulthood" could merely signify a culminating point of "adolescence." The idea of adolescence as a state of growing up, presumably from puberty to maturity, is alien to the Confucian view of life. For one thing, maturity can never be achieved in the sense of suddenly enveloping a hitherto incomprehensible mode of existence. Since the process of aging begins with birth, it does not make much sense to characterize a particular stage of human life as "growing up." It is one thing to underscore a distinctive pattern of physical maturation in youth and quite another to define the process of becoming human in terms of a period of nine to eleven years of alleged transition.

However, this should by no means suggest that the distinction between youth and manhood is absent in Confucian thought. It is only that attention is not so sharply focused on a "between" period, alleged to be characterized by mental and emotional instability as well as by other ingratiating attributes associated with this early stage of life. Since, in Confucianism, maturation is perceived mainly in terms of self-cultivation, human growth as a holistic process of realizing that which is thought to be the authentic human nature begins in early childhood and does not end even with old age.

Despite the critical quality of adolescence in both the "nature" and "art" of maturing, it is by and large equal in importance to other vital periods of life history. By implication, although old age must be recognized as a delicate situation and at times even confronted as a difficult problem, it is intrinsically valuable as a concluding chapter in man's self-realization.

Against this background, the tripartite division of "youth" (*shao*), "manhood" (*chuang*), and "old age" (*lao*) in the *Analects* must be taken as denoting three equally significant periods of human life and thus three integral aspects of adulthood (which, to reiterate an early point, means the state of being well on the way to becoming a fully realized person). The three things against which a Knight of the Way must, as Confucius recommended, be on his guard can therefore be seen as an integrated teaching on adulthood:

> In his youth, before his blood and vital humors have settled down, he is on his guard against lust. Having reached his prime, when the blood and vital humors have finally hardened, he is on his guard against strife. Having reached old age, when the blood and vital humors are already decaying, he is on his guard against avarice.[26]

The young adult should be on his guard against excessive indulgence in sex not so much because of an aversion toward sexual activity itself as because of the detrimental effect it is thought to have on one's mental as well as physical health. The physiological theories underlying this consideration, which are still prevalent in China, hold that a careful preservation of one's "blood and vital humors" at this juncture of maturation is a prerequisite for wholesome growth. The development of a personality, like the planting of crops, must not be hurried. The story of the farmer of Sung in *Mencius* whose over-zealousness led him to help his crops grow by artificially pulling up seedlings is a vivid description of how harmful imposition can frustrate the natural process of aging.[27] Just as unnecessary assistance withers the crops, "lust's effect," far from comforting to the body and mind, "is tempest after sun."

Similarly, strife is threatening to true manhood because the energy available for personal development and public service is misdirected. To be sure, Confucius encouraged moral striving. And

41

the reason why he was particularly pleased to teach the "ardent" is precisely that the latter have a strong will to forge ahead.[28] But competitiveness, which is what "strife" means in this connection, is a clear demonstration that the way of being human is here pursued not for the sake of self-realization but "for the sake of the others" (*wei-jen*).[29] As long as one's self-image is mainly dependent on the external responses of others, one's inner direction will be lost. As a result, the ability to "endure adversity" or "enjoy prosperity" for long will also be weakened.[30] Despite the fact that physically one's "blood and vital humors have finally hardened," one is not necessarily strong in the sense of being truly "steadfast" (*kang*). In fact, steadfastness in the Confucian sense means the ability to remain unaffected by external influences in determining how one is to pursue and manifest the Way.[31]

If strife, reflecting a profound inner uncertainty, becomes a kind of impulsive aggressiveness, "avarice" in old age seems to indicate a defensive attachment to what one has already gained. The Chinese character *te* in this particular context also suggests "possessiveness." The remark in the *Analects* may have been the source of a widely circulated proverb, which characterizes the small-minded person as one who is "distressed in mind trying to get more, and then troubled lest he lose it." A possessive old man may not present any serious threat to society. But from the viewpoint of self-realization, if one is overpowered by possessiveness in old age, the possibility for a safe and sound passage in the last phase of one's lifelong journey will be slim. Otherwise, old age may truly be the fruition of one's earnest endeavor to learn to be human through self-effort. Thus, like lust in youth and strife in manhood, the real danger of avarice lies in its detrimental effect on what ought to be a ceaseless process of realizing full humanity. In a deeper sense, since one of the most persistent attachments is to life itself, the art of dying is undoubtedly the principal challenge in old age. Unless one can peacefully accept the termination of one's life as a matter of fact, one somehow still falls short of a successful completion. This may have been the reason why a great many biographies of Confucian scholar-officials contain detailed descriptions of the last moments of their lives.

The common belief that, under the influence of Confucian thought, Chinese culture has developed a special respect for old age needs some explanation. Notwithstanding gerontocratic tendencies in Chinese history, old age in itself commands little admiration. Respect for the old is actually based on the assumption that, in the long and unavoidable journey of self-improvement, an old man ought to have forged way ahead in furnishing his life with inspiring contents. Ideally, therefore, being advanced in age is a sign of wisdom and resourcefulness as well as of experience and perseverance. But this hardly implies that in practice seniority of age automatically becomes an indisputable value. Simply "being old and not dying" does not get one very far. The manner in which Confucius approached an old man in the *Analects* may appear shockingly un-Confucian on the surface, but it is consistent with his overarching concerns:

> Yüan Jang [an unmannerly old man of Confucius' acquaintance] sat waiting for the Master in a sprawling position. The Master said to him, "In youth, not humble as befits a junior; in manhood, doing nothing worthy of being handed down. And merely to live on, getting older and older, is to be a useless pest." With this he hit him on the shank with his staff.[32]

Confucius' candid attitude toward Yüan Jang, by which many a commentator including Arthur Waley has been deeply perplexed.[33] is not at all inconceivable in light of the Confucian belief that old age, as a more matured manifestation of adulthood, is itself still "on the way." It is perhaps also in this sense that the Master instructed his followers to respect the young: "How do you know that they will not one day be all that you are now?" And since the emphasis is on actual performance as well as on promise of moral growth, Confucius continued, "[Only] if a man has reached forty or fifty and nothing has been heard of him, then I grant there is no need to respect him."[34] It would be misleading to suppose, however, that one's moral growth can significantly surpass one's physical maturation. An attempt to get on quickly without proper cultivation merely assumes the form rather than the content of maturity. A youth whom Confucius employed to carry messages is a case in point. When a friend commented that he seemed to have made great progress, the Master said, "I observe that he is fond of occupying the seat of a *full-grown man*; I observe that he walks shoulder to shoulder with his elders. He is not

43

one who is seeking to make progress *in learning*. He wishes quickly to become a man."[35]

It should be noted in this connection that learning (*hsüeh*) in the tradition of Confucian education is broadly defined to include not only intellectual and ethical growth but the development of the body as well. Actually the involvement of the body is such an integral part of the Confucian ideal of learning that the Confucian Way itself has been characterized by the Neo-Confucians as "the learning of the body and mind" (*shen-hsin chih chiao*). Indeed, each of the "six arts" (*liu-i*) that constitute the core of Confucian teaching involves the total participation of the body. Although only archery and charioteering are intended to be physical exercises, ritual and music both require the harmonization of bodily movements. Even in calligraphy and arithmetic, the importance of practice in the sense of acquiring an experiential understanding of the basic skills is always emphasized. One might even say that it is precisely in this sense that the Neo-Confucian masters often instruct their students to "embody" the Way. Therefore, the one who seeks to make progress in learning must have the courage and patience to wait for the "ripening of humanity" (*jen-shu*). After all, "only when the year grows cold do we see that the pine and cypress are the last to fade;"[36] likewise, human self-realization depends much on what may be called one's staying power.

The idea that youth, manhood, and old age are three inseparable dimensions of adulthood is compatible with the Confucian belief that a fully developed person should first be incited by "poetry," then established by "ritual," and finally perfected by "music."[37] It may not be far-fetched to suggest that adulthood, as a process of becoming, can be understood as a continuous "ritualization" from "poetry" to "music."

The poetic state, so to speak, symbolizes the eagerness and excitement of the young adult who has already developed an inner sense of direction. The technical term used to designate this kind of commitment is *li-chih*, which literally means "to establish one's will." The absolute necessity of an existential decision, not only as a commencement but also as an affirmation to be continuously reenacted, is taken for granted in Confucian literature. Thus, the Master insisted, "Only one who bursts with eagerness do I instruct; only one

44

who bubbles with excitement, do I enlighten."[38] In a strict sense, unless the young adult is personally motivated to embark on the Way, no teacher can force him to pursue it. Having been fully aware that, especially for the young, "the desire to build up [one's] moral power is never as strong as sexual desire,"[39] Confucius recommended the study of poetry as a guide for harmonizing basic emotions. He felt that the odes of the classical tradition can, among other things, "serve to stimulate the mind," "be used for purposes of self-contemplation," "teach the art of sociality," and "show how to regulate feelings of resentment." Through a careful reading of them, he further maintained, not only "the more immediate duty of serving one's father and the remoter one of serving one's prince" can be learned, but even knowledge about natural phenomena can be acquired.[40] On the other hand, he who does not have any acquaintance with the odes is "as though he stood with his face pressed against a wall!"[41] In such a situation, he can hardly advance a step toward self-realization. Poetry then marks an initial but critical step on the Way.

Similarly, ritual, symbolizing the state of manhood, is both a structure and a movement whereby one's character as a mature person is established. Like the tradition of the *Odes*, it involves a set of highly integrated rules of propriety, which the young adult must learn in order to become a full participating member of society. Also, like poetry, it harmonizes as well as directs human emotions toward a socially recognizable mode of expression. Since a person in the Confucian sense is always a center of relationships rather than an *individual* complete in himself and separable from others, the structure and movement by which he expresses himself in the context of human-relatedness becomes a defining characteristic of his humanity. Ritualization so conceived, far from being depersonalizing, is a necessary way of learning to be human. However, the order of priority as specified by Confucius clearly indicates that ritual itself must also be based on human feelings: "If a man is not humane [*jen*], what can he have to do with ritual?"[42] Ideally ritualization should be in perfect accord with humanization. And ritual is not thought to be a social imposition on nature but a refinement of nature according to well-articulated cultural values. It is perhaps in this sense that Confucius maintained that only through ritual can

45

those human feelings that exhibit basic virtues be properly manifested:

> Respectfulness without ritual becomes laborious bustle; carefulness without ritual becomes timidity; boldness without ritual becomes turbulence; straightforwardness without ritual becomes rudeness.[43]

It is also in this sense that the Master felt he could finally talk about the real meanings of the odes with Tzu-hsia, because this disciple had come to the realization that just as the art of laying on the colors follows the preparation of the plain ground, so is ritual subsequent to poetry.[44]

Example

The perception of adulthood as a continuous development from poetry to music is an idealized way of conceptualizing the process of growing up in accordance with the middle path. A close approximation to this pattern of maturation is certainly the case of Confucius himself. Yet, although the *Analects* does provide a good example of this, it has never been taken as a norm in the Confucian tradition. For the process of self-realization is so dependent on one's particular circumstances that it is pointless to set up one concrete experience as the single most important archetype. The Confucian Way, in a strict sense, is not one and the same as the way of Confucius. Strictly speaking, even the word *Confucianist* is a misnomer because the follower of the Confucian Way does not accept the Master's life and conduct as revealed truth; nor does he believe that Confucius actually attained the highest possible level of human perfection. His ultimate concern, then, is not to become a Confucianist but to become a genuine human being, a sage. To be sure, Confucius the symbol has been honored as the complete sage for more than two thousand years. But this by no means suggests that Confucius the person has ever been celebrated as the only true interpreter of the human Way (*jen-tao*). In fact, Confucius never claimed that he had himself attained sagehood. The way of Confucius therefore should be taken mainly as a standard of inspiration:

At fifteen I set my heart upon learning.
At thirty I established myself [in accordance with ritual].
At forty I no longer had perplexities.
At fifty I knew the Mandate of Heaven.
At sixty I was at ease with whatever I heard.
At seventy I could follow my heart's desire without
   transgressing the boundaries of right.[45]

"Learning" (*hsüeh*) was to Confucius much more than the acquisition of empirical knowledge; nor was it simply a method of internalizing the proper manner of behavior in society. It was the thing he did as a conscious human being. Through learning, which means through an ever deepening personal knowledge about how to be human, he transformed his life into a meaningful existence. Learning in this particular association was so much a cherished idea that Confucius almost refused to grant anyone else the characterization of being "given to learning"; "In a hamlet of ten houses you may be sure of finding someone quite as loyal and true to his word as I. But I doubt if you would find anyone with such a love of learning."[46] And he admitted that, after the death of his best disciple, no students of his were really "given to learning."[47] Confucius was absolutely serious about his self-image as a devoted learner; once after a disciple reported that he had been at a loss to describe his Master to a questioner, Confucius said, "Why didn't you say that I am a person who forgets his food when engaged in vigorous pursuit [of learning], is so happy as to forget his worries, and is not aware that old age is coming on?"[48]

If the setting of his heart on learning at fifteen signifies the opening of a new and continuous process of intellectual and moral growth, the establishment of his character in accordance with ritual at thirty further suggests a more refined expression of maturity. As ritual involves a network of human relations, self-establishment in this connection specifically points to the responsibility one assumes in reference to a variety of primordial ties. Concerning the major dyadic relationships, Confucius is alleged to have said that he had not been able to accomplish any of them:

To serve my father as I would expect my son to serve me: that I

47

have not been able to do. To serve my ruler as I would expect my ministers to serve me: that I have not been able to do. To serve my elder brothers as I would expect my younger brothers to serve me: that I have not been able to do. To be the first to treat friends as I would expect them to treat me: that I have not been able to do.[49]

Confucius' self-criticism, far from being simply a heuristic device, indicates that in assuming ordinary responsibilities there is bound to be room for improvement. Loyalty, filiality, brotherhood, and friendship are common virtues, but the processes of ritualization through which they can be fully realized are long and subtle. Maturity in this sense means both the ability to manifest virtues like these properly and the awareness that one must never cease to make further effort to establish oneself in ritual. The mature person is therefore "earnest and genuine."[50] For he knows that for the realization of true humanity the burden is heavy and the journey is long.

This duty-consciousness is predicated on the Confucian golden rule: "Do not do to others what you would not want others to do to you."[51] The golden rule is always negatively stated because the emphasis is on self-cultivation. Given the centrality of one's own quest for personal knowledge, perhaps it is neither necessary nor desirable to impose on others what one believes to be right for oneself. Underlying the golden rule, then, is the premise that "conscientiousness [*chung*] and altruism [*shu*] are not far from the Way."[52] The inner demand for being truthful to one's humane self is inseparable from the social need to care for others; and the learning for self-realization is also the learning for harmonizing human relations. The real threat to a genuine manifestation of the humane self is not society but one's own selfish desires. Altruism is thus not a consequence of conscientiousness but its inalienable complement. The positive character of this Confucian doctrine is implicit in the assertion that the Way is pursued not by insisting on its abstract universality but by assuring what is best for one's humane self, the self that forms a community with others.

As the transformation from a commitment to learning in the poetic state to an assumption of social responsibilities in the ritual state symbolizes Confucius' maturation as a young adult, "no longer having perplexities" symbolizes Confucius' disposition in the middle years. "No perplexities" first suggests an independence of mind. His will had by then become so firmly set on the Way that wealth and honor were to him like "floating clouds"[53] with no danger of casting any shadow on his mind. This ability to remain disinterested, however, was hardly a recoil from social involvement. It was a form of self-possession, suggesting inner strength and repose: "I have listened in silence and noted what was said. I have never grown tired of learning nor wearied of teaching others what I have learned–these are just natural with me."[54] The unperturbed mind, to borrow from Mencius, is the resultant effect of "righteous deeds."[55] It is a wisdom that, despite active participation in society, perceives the total situation clearly. Thus, only "the wise have no perplexities."[56]

Yet the unperplexed adult is not only intellectually alert but emotionally stable and strong. His independence of mind is as much an indication of moral courage as a sign of wisdom. When Tzu-lu asked what constituted "a complete man" (a truly mature person), Confucius said:

> If anyone had the wisdom of Tsang Wu-chung, the uncovetousness of Meng Kung-ch'o, the valor of P'ien Chuang-tzu, and the artistic talents of Jan Ch'iu, and graced these virtues by the cultivation of ritual and music, then indeed I think we might call him "a complete man."

However, realizing that what he had described was too much an ideal for his disciple to emulate, he continued with Tzu-lu, who was noted for his moral courage, particularly in mind:

> But perhaps today we need not ask all this of the complete man. The man, who in the view of gain thinks of righteousness; who in the view of danger is prepared to give up his life; and who does not forget an old agreement however far back it extends—such a man may be considered "a complete man."[57]

If "beyond perplexities" signifies the wisdom and courage of manhood, "knowing the Mandate of Heaven" points to an even more sophisticated frame of mind in which the coming of old age is confronted squarely both as an inevitable process of maturation and as a greater promise of reconciliation. Indeed, the meaning of the Mandate of Heaven is twofold. It connotes the limitation of one's own fate as well as the fulfillment of a "transcendent" command. At fifty Confucius had experienced many hardships in life, among which the deaths of several of his best disciples and the repeated failures of his hope to set the world in order must have been especially agonizing. By then Confucius had become acutely aware of the inescapable limitation of human efforts to exert lasting influence on the brute realities of life. His personal encounters with dehumanizing forces in social conflicts and in fiercely contested political arenas had totally frustrated his "dream" of returning to the great peace of the Chou dynasty. As his advice and protests time and again fell on heedless ears, he felt that his alienation from the world was complete: "Only Heaven knows me!"[58] Nevertheless, as a confirmed humanist, he refused to forsake the world and herd with birds and beasts: "If I am not to be a man among other men, then what am I to be? If the Way prevailed under Heaven, I should not be trying to alter things."[59] As he was approaching old age he felt more strongly the tension between a profound sense of the finitude of man and an equally profound belief in the perfectibility of human nature. Yet, his own choice of action was clear: recognizing that what he could do to set the world in order was extremely limited, still he could not but do it.

"Knowing the Mandate of Heaven" can therefore be conceived as an expression of Confucius' spiritual crisis. A distinctive character of it is a deeply felt sense of mission. Despite the bitterness of his lot, his concern for the human world became even greater. To be sure, once he conveyed to Tzu-kung his wish not to say anything. When the disciple wondered how the Way could be revealed if the Master chose to remain silent, Confucius responded, "Heaven does not speak; yet the four seasons run their course thereby, the hundred creatures, each after its kind, are born thereby. Heaven does no speaking!"[60] Yet Confucius' tacit understanding of the Mandate of Heaven is not a sign of passivity but of total commitment, a positive effort to carry out a lifelong task. In fact, he made it clear that the Mandate of Heaven is not an object of speculation but a thing to be feared and respected.[61] To know the Mandate of Heaven is therefore more than an attainment of comprehension. At the age of fifty-nine, when his life was seriously threatened by a military officer in the state of Sung, Confucius is recorded to have said "Heaven produced the virtue that is in me; what can Huan T'ui do to me?"[62] This sense of being chosen to fulfill a transcendent command is further illustrated by another incident that had happened three years previously:

When Confucius was in personal danger in K'uang, he said, "Since the death of King Wen, is not the course of culture [wen] in my keeping? If it had been the will of Heaven to destroy this culture, it would not have been given to a mortal [like me]. But if it is the will of Heaven that this culture should not perish, what can the people of K'uang do to me?[63]

Against this background, Confucius' self-definition as a transmitter rather than a maker[64] assumes a shape of meaning seldom understood and appreciated by students of Chinese thought. A transmitter is tradition-bound only in the sense that for the sake of self-knowledge he never ceases to learn from the past. To him, the value of history is judged not only by its usefulness and relevance to the present but also by its uninterrupted affirmation of the authentic possibility of humanness in the world. He does not assume the role of a maker, not because he fails to recognize the power of creativity but because by a conscious choice he refuses to cut himself off from the humanizing processes that have significantly contributed to his own maturation. In fact, as a transmitter, he continuously renews himself by delving deeply into the sources of his chosen heritage. His respect for the ancients does not lead him to a glorification of the past. Rather, his intention is to make sure that the humanity of the former sages always remains a felt presence in the world. His mission, then, is to assure cultural continuity through personal knowledge. In a deeper sense, Confucius' unqualified dedication to the transmission of what has for centuries been called the Sagely Way is not at all in conflict with his acute awareness of the finitude of man. Thus, independence of mind, suggesting both wisdom and courage, is now further refined. To know one's limitation, instead of inhibiting one's determination to forge ahead, actually enhances one's commitment to action. And one's sense of mission, far from suggesting hubris, is based on a realistic appraisal of one's circumscription as well as one's inner strength. The encroachment of old age seems to have given another dimension to Confucius' adulthood.

"I was at ease with whatever I heard" suggests receptivity. The art of listening, especially as contrasted with that of seeing, is neither aggressive nor possessive. It is an affirmation of the world in a spirit of detachment. For it manifests maternal virtues of caring, forgiving, and accepting without at the same time exhibiting an unexamined attachment to a love object. It seems that by then Confucius' inner demand to change the world had been transformed into a silent appreciation of it. In the words of a twelfth-century commentator, "when sound enters, the mind opens up without rejection or resistance; as the art of knowing has reached its ultimate perfection, the mind can have it without reflection."[65] This penetrating responsiveness of the mind was surely the result of a long and strenuous self-examination. Understandably, Confucius, as depicted by his students, had succeeded in freeing himself from four defects of the mind: opinionatedness, dogmatism, obstinacy, and egoism.[66] It is vitally important to note, however, that the spiritual "carefreeness" of Confucius at sixty implies neither eremitism nor asceticism. Rather, it symbolizes self-realization through the experience of unconflicted continuity with the world in all its aspects. The Master did say, "In the morning, hear the Way; in the evening, die content!"[67] But the Way can never be heard by leaving the world. Indeed, the true peace of mind is not attained by deliverance from, but by participation in, the world. And only those who are really in the world are on the Way and thus have a chance of hearing the Way.

"I could follow my heart's desire without transgressing the boundaries of right" implies harmony. This last phase of Confucius' adulthood seems to symbolize the fruition of a long process of maturation. The commitment to learning at fifteen, the establishment of the self in ritual at thirty, the attainment of an unperturbed mind at forty, the knowledge of the will of Heaven at fifty, and the receptive appreciation of the world at sixty all converged into a new stage of realization. As Mencius suggested, "the great man does not lose his childlike heart,"[68] and the joy of unrestrained freedom in the septuagenary Confucius seems to have been an artistically cultivated spontaneity, a second childhood in old age. "Poetry" and "ritual" are no longer fitting descriptions; the degree of integration characterized by a harmonization of what one is and what one ought to be can now be better understood in the symbolism of music as performed in Lu, Confucius' native state: "[I]t began with a strict unison. Soon the musicians were given more liberty; but the tone remained harmonious, brilliant, consistent, right on till the close."[69] The closing with "jade tubes," which produce a deep, euphonic sound, is, in Mencius' words, "the concern of a sage."[70] Only then can we say that the Way is heard and even death is welcome.

However, as already mentioned, the example of Confucius' adulthood does not serve as an absolute norm but as a standard of inspiration in the Confucian tradition. Actually the Master never instructed his students to follow him in order to find the Way. Instead, he inspired them to pursue the Way by realizing humanity— or adulthood, if you will—in themselves. His real strength as an exemplary teacher then came from a persuasive power, which, in the words of his admirers, was as gentle and refreshing as the spring breezes. Yen Hui, who died in his early thirties, never attained the level of adulthood his Master was confident he could have reached, but his description of the Confucian Way is worth quoting:

> The more I strain my gaze upward toward it, the higher it soars. The deeper I bore down into it, the harder it becomes. I see it in front; but suddenly it is behind. Step by step the Master lures me on. He has broadened me with culture, restrained me with ritual. Even if I wanted to stop, I could not. Just when I feel that I have exhausted every resource, something seems to rise up, standing sharp and clear. Yet though I long to pursue it, I can find no way of getting to it at all.[71]

Even among Confucius' closest disciples, the paths of self-realization are varied. Between Yen Hui's premature death and Tseng Tzu's longevity, there are numerous manifestations of adulthood. The case of Confucius is but one of them. It is therefore conceivable that a person in his eighties or nineties might be able to advance further on the Way than Confucius had in his seventies. It is also conceivable that people under new circumstances might choose to pursue the Way in a mode that differs significantly from what traditionally has been sanctioned as authentically Confucian. After all, from the Confucian perspective, the approaches to sagehood are as many as there are sages. And by implication, although adulthood can be recognized, it can never be defined.

NOTES

[1]See the "Nei-tse" chapter in *Li-chi* (1815 edition), 28:20a-21b.

[2]*Analects*, 8.7. See Arthur Waley, trans., *The Analects of Confucius* (London: Allen and Unwin, 1938), p. 134. Also cf. Wing-tsit Chan, trans., *A Source Book in Chinese Philosophy* (Princeton: Princeton University Press, 1963), p. 33, and James Legge, trans., "Confucian Analects" in *The Chinese Classics* (Oxford: Clarendon Press, 1893–95), 1: 210–11. For an inspiring discussion on the Way in the *Analects*, see Herbert Fingarette, *Confucius—The Secular as Sacred* (New York: Harper and Row, 1972), pp. 18–36.

[3]*Analects*, 9.20.

[4]*Analects*, 9.16. See Waley, p. 142. As Waley points out, the extensive discussion on the metaphor of the water in *Mencius* (4B.18) addresses itself to the same idea.

[5]*Chung-yung*, 1.1.

[6]*Analects*, 15.28. See Chan, p. 15.

[7]*Ta-hsüeh*, 2. See Chan, p. 87.

[8]*Analects*, 14.37. The same passage is also found in *Chung-yung*, 14.3. See Chan, p. 101.

[9]*Chung-yung*, 14.5. See Chan, p. 102.

[10]*Chung-yung*, 9. See Chan, p. 99.

[11]*Analects*, 13.21.

[12]*Chung-yung*, 8. See Chan, p. 99.

[13]*Chung-yung*, 12.1–2.

[14]*Analects*, 17.13.

[15]*Mencius*, 7B.37. See D.C. Lau, trans., *Mencius* (Penguin Classics, 1970), p. 203.

[16]Lau, p. 203.

[17]*Ibid.* The term *hsiang-yüan* is rendered by Lau as "village honest man."

[18]*Analects*, 7.6.

[19]*Analects*, 9.10.

[20]*Analects*, 6.28. See Chan, p. 31.

[21]*Analects*, 14.25.

[22]*Analects*, 2.12.

[23]"Duty-consciousness" is here contrasted with "rights-consciousness." While the latter emphasizes one's legitimate claims, the former is concerned about the moral imperative, a sense of commitment, completely independent of outside influence.

[24]*Analects*, 8.3. See Waley, p. 133. A different version of the poem is found in James Legge, trans., *She-king (Book of Poetry)*, in *Chinese Classics*, vol. 4 pt. 2, p. 335.

[25]For a methodological discussion on this, see A. S. Cua, "Confucian Vision and Experience of the World," *Philosophy East and West* 25, no. 3 (July, 1975): 327–28.

[26]*Analects*, 16.7. See Waley, pp. 205–206.

[27]*Mencius*, 2A.2, sec. 16.

[28]*Analects*, 13.21.

[29]*Analects*, 14.25.

[30]*Analects*, 4.2. See Waley, p. 102.

[31]*Analects*, 5.10.

[32]*Analects*, 14.46. See Waley, p. 192.

[33]Waley did not believe that Confucius could have been so rude to an old man; and so he arbitrarily decided that Yüan Jang was in fact a young boy, although he was fully aware that his view contradicted virtually all traditional commentaries. See Waley, p. 192, n. 3. Legge did accept that Yüan Jang was an old man, but he also felt that Confucius' candid remarks were quite unusual. For his apologetic comments, see Legge, trans., *Confucian Analects*, pp. 292–293, n. 46.

[34]*Analects*, 9.22. See Waley, p. 143.

[35]*Analects*, 14.47. See Legge, p. 293.

[36]*Analects*, 9.27. See Waley, p. 144. I am indebted to Joan Erikson for calling my attention to this important dimension of Confucian education.

[37]*Analects*, 8.8.

[38]*Analects*, 7.8. See Waley, p. 124.

[39]*Analects*, 9.17. See Waley, p. 142.

[40]*Analects*, 17.9. See Legge, p. 323.

[41]*Analects*, 17.10. See Waley, p. 212.

[42]*Analects*, 3.3.

[43]*Analects*, 8.2. See Legge, p. 208. *Li* is rendered by Legge as "rules of propriety."

[44]*Analects*, 3.8.

[45]*Analects*, 2.4.

[46]*Analects*, 5.27. See Waley, p. 114.

[47]*Analects*, 6.2; 11.6.

[48]*Analects*, 7.18. See Chan, p. 32. It seems clear that the "something" in "in vigorous pursuit of something" refers to "learning."

[49]*Chung-yung*, 13.4. See Chan, p. 101. This statement seems incompatible with Confucius' remark, "I can claim that at Court I have duly served the Duke and his office; at home, my father and elder brother. As regards matters of mourning, I am conscious of no neglect, nor have I ever been overcome with wine. Concerning these things at any rate my mind is quite at rest." (*Analects*, 9.15; Waley, p. 144.) But the apparent contradiction between the views can easily be resolved, if the whole matter is understood as involving different levels of self-cultivation. Surely, Confucius did not consider himself a failure in carrying out the basic requirements of loyalty and filiality. However, neither was he satisfied with what he was able to accomplish. Although his mind was quite at rest, his effort to improve himself remained persistent.

[50]*Chung-yung*, 13.3.

[51]*Analects*, 15.23. Also see *Chung-yung*, 13.3.

[52]*Chung-yung*, 13.3.

[53]*Analects*, 7.15. The entire statement reads: "He who seeks only coarse food to eat, water to drink, and bent arm for pillow will without looking for it find happiness to boot. Any thought of accepting wealth and rank by means that I know to be wrong is as remote from me as the clouds that float above." See Waley, p. 126.

[54]*Analects*, 7.2. See Waley, p. 123, with minor modifications.

[55]*Mencius*, 2A.2, sec. 15.

[56]*Analects*, 9.28; 14.30.

[57] *Analects*, 14.13. See Waley, p. 183, for the first part and Legge, pp. 279–280, for the second part. It should be noted that the term *ch'eng-jen*, rendered by Waley as "a perfect man," is also the term for "adult" or "adulthood."

[58] *Analects*, 14.37.

[59] *Analects*, 18.6. See Waley, p. 220.

[60] *Analects*, 17.19. See Waley, p. 214.

[61] *Analects*, 16.8.

[62] *Analects*, 7.22. See Chan, p. 32.

[63] *Analects*, 9.5. See Chan, p. 35.

[64] *Analects*, 7.1.

[65] See Chu Hsi's commentary on the *Analects*, in *Ssu-shu chi-chu* (Taipei: Shih-chieh, 1952; reprint), p. 7.

[66] *Analects*, 9.4.

[67] *Analects*, 4.8. See Waley, p. 103.

[68] *Mencius*, 4B.12.

[69] *Analects*, 3.23.

[70] *Mencius*, 5B.1. See Lau, p. 150.

[71] *Analects*, 9.10. See Waley, p. 140.

4. On the Mencian Perception
of Moral Self-Development

Mencius' claim that human nature is good is well-known among students of classical Confucian thought. It has been taken for granted that underlying Mencius' deceptively simple thesis is an appeal to intuition. He offers no explicit argument, other than the insistence that moral propensities, such as the "four germinations," are inherent in human nature. As a corollary, he believes unquestioningly that all human beings have the inner ability to commiserate with others, to feel ashamed of themselves, to have a sense of humbleness, and to differentiate right from wrong. The only example of an attempt to "prove" his thesis by any sort of empirical procedure seems no more than a commonsense observation:

> When I say that men have the mind which cannot bear to see the suffering of others, my meaning may be illustrated thus: Now, when men suddenly see a child about to fall into a well, they all have a feeling of alarm and distress; not to gain friendship with the child's parents, nor to seek the praise of their neighbors and friends, nor because they dislike the reputation [of lack of humanity if they did not rescue the child]. From such a case, we see that a man without the feeling of commiseration is not human. [2A.6]

Understandably even sympathetic interpreters of the Mencian position, such as H.G. Creel, often feel impelled to note that Mencius "offers very sophisticated discussions of the differences between human and animal nature, of the way man's material and sexual needs may override his humane judgment, and of the effects of environment on man's nature," so that his alleged "proof" of the goodness of human nature should not be taken as evidence of Mencius' simplemindedness.

In this essay, I intend to show that the Mencian thesis, far from being an unexamined dogmatic assertion, is an integral part of a coherent and thoughtful defense of a personalist position in philosophical anthropology. Indeed, I believe that if Mencius' subtle appreciation of all the complexities of human life is carefully studied, his view on human nature may very well turn out to be one of the most persuasive articulations on the subject. Of course my immediate concern is not a comprehensive presentation of Mencius' considered opinion on "the innate moral qualities" as bases for the goodness of human nature; rather, I will probe his thesis as a way of understanding what may be called the Mencian perception of moral self-development.

On the surface, it might seem that the best way to determine the meaning of the concept of self in Mencius is to study the cluster of words associated with that concept in the *Book of Mencius*. A linguistic analysis of these related words could then provide us with the parameters by which the values of the self could be fixed, as it were, in Mencius' system of thought. But such a procedure, while useful, cannot account for either the dialogical situation in which Mencius as a speaker articulates his thought in response to concrete questioning or the genetic reasons behind the formulation of the Mencian idea of self, which have actually become inseparable aspects of the idea's internal structure. In addition, while such a procedure ostensibly frees itself from the intentional fallacy, it completely ignores the spiritual direction of Mencius as a living, experiencing, and creating thinker. Needless to say, as an inquiring historian, I cannot afford to overlook ground level philological work as a point of departure. But for me, the interpretive task begins when our encounter with Mencius is as much a demand on our own openness to his challenge as a need to make him meaningful to us.

Quite a few scholars have suggested that underlying the Mencian thesis on human nature is a strong belief in man's perfectibility. However, as some have noticed, the idea of human perfectibility does not specify whether environmental intervention or native endowment plays the key role in the perfecting process. Mencius and Hsün Tzu, a sophisticated critic of the Mencian thesis, share this idea, but their reasons for advocating it are significantly different. For Hsün Tzu, the perfecting process involves a complex interaction between the cognitive functions of the mind and social constraints. Levels of one's perfection are defined in terms of the malleability of one's human nature to communally shared values and norms perceived and understood by the intelligence of one's mind. One's willing participation in the perfecting process thus depends on internal self-cultivation as well as on conformity to societal ideals, but "malleation" according to well-established ritual forms is undoubtedly the focus of Hsün Tzu's educational efforts.

Mencius is also sensitive to environmental influences. It is not difficult to show that he recognizes that economic conditions, political situations, and social relations have a profound impact on a person's ethical life. Furthermore, he insists that improvements be made in those crucial areas of the environment before realistic programs of moral education can be implemented. The concrete examples of learning a language in an unfavorable linguistic world (3B.6), of inculcating a sense of loyalty in ministers without reciprocal benevolence from the king, and of developing a "secure mind" independent of access to "secure livelihood" (1A.7, 20; 3A.3) amply demonstrate that Mencius is acutely aware of the shaping influences of the environment on a person's psychological milieu in which beliefs, motives, and attitudes are formed. Yet, for Mencius, there is something in each human being that, in the ultimate sense, can never be subject to external control. This something is neither learned nor acquired; it is a given reality, endowed by Heaven as the defining characteristic of being human.

As A. C. Graham has pointed out, among Mencius' contemporaries in the fourth century B.C. quite a few philosophers seem to have subscribed to the proposition that human nature is what human beings are born with. The etymological identification of "birth" (*sheng*) and "nature" (*hsing*) in classical Chinese usage has enabled several modern scholars to argue that the view was widely held as an interpretive consensus. Historically there is no reason to doubt the accuracy of this analysis. It seems plausible that an overwhelming majority of Mencius' adversaries actually advocated a naturalist position on human nature. The view that human nature is what human beings are born with, for example, led to the general observation that appetite for food and sex are human nature. Against this background, the Mencian thesis can be viewed as a critique of this interpretive consensus. Mencius' strategy of presenting his position on the matter is best shown in his exchanges with Kao Tzu. Each of these exchanges, most comprising no more than a few lines, is in itself a subtle manifestation of Mencius' overall concern, a clue to his underlying assumptions about human nature. Let us examine one of them:

> Kao Tzu said, "What is inborn is called nature." Mencius said, "When you say that what is inborn is called nature, is that like saying that white is white?" "Yes." "Then is the whiteness of the white feather the same as the whiteness of snow? Or, again, is the whiteness of snow the same as the whiteness of white jade?" "Yes." "Then is the nature of a dog the same as the nature of an ox, and is the nature of an ox the same as the nature of man?" [6A.4]

On the surface, Kao Tzu could have maintained that precisely because what is inborn is called nature, what is inborn in an ox is the nature of an ox and what is inborn in a man is the nature of man, without committing himself to the seeming absurdity that the nature of an ox is the same as the nature of man. But given his naturalist position, which is defined in terms of basic instinctual demands, I am not sure whether Kao Tzu would or could have differentiated human nature from animal nature in general.

To Mencius, the naturalist position is not factually wrong but, as an attempt to arrive at a holistic understanding of the uniqueness of being human, it is deficient and one-sided. In the words of a later passage, which seem to apply here as well, the apparent truism advocated by Kao Tzu is like the man who "takes care of his finger and, without knowing it, neglects his back and shoulders" (6A.14). Mencius continues, however, that if the man "eats and drinks yet without neglecting what is of more importance, how could the nourishment of his mouth and belly be considered as serving merely a few inches of his body?" The point is that since a proper knowledge of man's physical existence necessitates an appreciation of the *gestalt*, the nourishment of one kind of basic need must not be done at the expense of the wellbeing of the whole body. Therefore, as it is simple-minded to reduce one's physical nourishment to a few inches of one's body, so it is deficient and one-sided to reduce human nature merely to appetite for food and sex.

Obviously, in Mencius' opinion, the proposition that human nature is what we, as human beings, are born with cannot fully account for the something that is inherent in each of us as the defining characteristic of our being human. The proposition is too general to appreciate the unique human quality that is not explainable in terms of the animal instincts that we seem to share with oxen and dogs. To be sure, Mencius can subscribe to the view that instinctual demands are themselves neither learned nor acquired and that they are, in a sense, given realities endowed by Heaven. He can perhaps also accept the observation that appetite for food and sex are so fundamental to human life that they ought to be recognized as absolutely basic needs. But the something in each of us that, in the ultimate sense, can never be subject to external control clearly points in a different direction.

An examination of the famous allegory of the Ox Mountain helps us understand the issue in a new light:

> The trees of the Ox Mountain were once beautiful. Being situated, however, in the borders of a large state, they were hewn down with axes and bills—and could they retain their beauty? Still, through the activity of the vegetative life day and night, and the nourishing influence of the rain and dew, they were not without buds and sprouts springing forth, but then came the cattle and goats and browsed upon them. To these things is owing the bare and stripped appearance of the mountain; when people now see it, they think it was never finely wooded. But is this the nature of the mountain? And so also of what properly belongs to man; shall it be said that the mind of any man was without humanity (*jen*) and righteousness (*i*)? The way in which a man loses his proper goodness of mind is like the way in which the trees are denuded by axes and bills. Hewn down day after day, can the mind retain its beauty? [6A.8]

If the mind cannot retain its beauty, it seems apparent that environmental influences are so overwhelming that its original nature can be irredeemably disturbed and destroyed. Mencius' further observation seems to confirm this suspicion: "When there is repeated disturbance, the restorative influence of the night will not be sufficient to preserve [the proper goodness of the mind]. When the influence of the night is not sufficient to preserve it, man becomes not much different from the beast. People see that he acts like an animal, and think that he never had the original endowment [for goodness]." In what sense can we still maintain that there is something in each of us that,

61

in the ultimate sense, can never be subject to external control?

The question seems to have bothered Mencius. In the concluding part of the allegory, he refuses to grant that what one appears to be is necessarily what one really is. Surely he admits that "with proper nourishment and care, everything grows, whereas without proper nourishment and care, everything decays." But it would be misleading to suggest that Mencius actually means to imply that once a man has become not much different from a beast, there is little chance for him to regain his humanity. On the contrary, time and again he stresses the power of the will for self-realization, a power never totally lost, although it is conceivable that it can be forever latent. This is perhaps the main reason that in the last lines of the allegory, Mencius quotes the Confucian saying, "Hold it fast and you preserve it. Let it go and you lose it. It comes in and goes out at no definite time and without anyone's knowing its direction," and comments that this statement refers to the human mind.

In fact, the human mind is such that no matter how disturbed and destroyed it has become, its inner strength for rejuvenation can never be completely suppressed. It is in this sense, I suppose, that Mencius has an unflagging faith in human perfectibility through self-effort. To him, the establishment of the will is all that is needed to preserve the original mind. Therefore, "hold it fast and you preserve it" signifies a self-transforming inner decision, a way of internal healing and nourishing that is both necessary and sufficient for the cultivation of the mind. The healing rest of the days and nights and the nourishing air of the calm morning, by contrast, are merely desirable conditions for normal self-development. Indeed, Mencius even suggests in some cases a difficult personal ordeal may turn out to be a blessing in disguise:

> When Heaven is about to confer a great responsibility on any man, it will exercise his mind with suffering, subject his sinews and bones to hard work, expose his body to hunger, put him to poverty, place obstacles in the paths of his deeds, so as to stimulate his mind, harden his nature, and improve wherever he is incompetent. [6B.15]

However, this must not be construed as evidence of Mencius' advocacy of a particular thesis on challenge and response. For he also feels comfortable with the commonsense observation that "in good years most of the young people behave well. In bad years most of them abandon themselves to evil. This is not due to any difference in the natural capacity endowed by Heaven. The abandonment is due to the fact that the mind is allowed to fall into evil" (6A.7).

That Mencius is absolutely serious about human perfectibility through self-effort is beyond dispute, but the analogical reasoning by which he articulates his interpretive position needs further elaboration. To begin, it should now become obvious that the something in each of us that ultimately can never be subject to external control actually refers to *hsin* (mind and heart). Paradoxically, a realistic appraisal of the nature and function of the mind as being susceptible to environmental influences does not conflict with the view that the mind can always be preserved if one so wills. A constant concern for "losing" the mind and a persistent belief in an innate ability to "preserve" the mind are co-ingredients in Mencius' line of thinking. While Mencius recognizes that we all have in varying degrees lost our minds, and only the sages have preserved theirs, he insists that as "there is a common taste for flavor in all mouths, a common sense for sound in all ears, and a common sense for beauty in all eyes," there is also a commonality in all human minds. And the sage is characterized as someone having already possessed, in the sense of having fully manifested, "what is common in all our minds" (6A.7).

The Mencian version of the allegory of the growing of wheat stresses commonality rather than divergence caused by environmental forces:

> You sow the seeds and cover them with soil. The land is the same and the time of sowing is also the same. In time they all grow up luxuriantly. When the time of harvest comes, they are all ripe. Although there may be a difference between the different stalks of wheat, it is due to differences in the soil, as rich or poor, to the unequal nourishment obtained from the rain and the dew, and to differences in human effort. Therefore all things of the same kind are similar to one another. Why should there be any doubt about human beings? The sage and I are the same in kind. [6A.7]

Commonality means, first of all, that the sage, like us, is a human being endowed with the same nature. Thus the saying of an ancient worthy, Lung Tzu: "If a man makes shoes without knowing the size of people's feet, I know that he will at least not make them to be like baskets" (6A.7) is quoted by Mencius to suggest the underlying compatibility of all human beings. But obviously Mencius is not proposing the leveling notion that the sage is merely human. Rather, he intends to show that inherent in our nature is precisely the same reality that enables ordinary human beings to become sages.

To the rhetorical question, "What is it that we have in common in our minds?" Mencius specifies, "it is the sense of principle and righteousness [*i-li*, moral principles]" (6A.7). This seems to imply that the moral sense in the mind is neither learned nor acquired. It is inborn and can be "lost," but is always recoverable if one wills to "preserve" it. Actually Mencius unequivocally states, "It is not the worthies alone who have this mind. All men have it, but only the worthies have been able to preserve it" (6A.10). And we may add that it is precisely in this context that Mencius characterizes the way of learning as none other than seeking for the lost mind. Once the mind is preserved, the moral sense will be regained and, by implication, the road to being human taken again.

It may seem, at this juncture, that Mencius' "moral sense" is essentially an appeal to intuition. And, recalling the example of suddenly seeing a child about to fall into a well, the appeal also seems directed toward the quest for a kind of physiological foundation of morality. This brings us to a close look at Mencius' thought on the "four germinations."

A man without the feeling of commiseration is not human; a man without the feeling of shame and dislike is not human; a man without the feeling of deference and compliance is not human; and a man without the feeling of right and wrong is not human. The feeling of commiseration is the germination of humanity; the feeling of shame and dislike is the germination of righteousness; the feeling of deference and compliance is the germination of propriety; and the feeling of right and wrong is the germination of wisdom. Men have these four germinations just as they have their four limbs. Having these four germinations, but saying that they cannot develop themselves, is self-destruction. . . . If anyone with these four germinations in him knows how to give them the fullest extension and development, the result will be like fire beginning to burn or a spring beginning to shoot forth. [2A.6]

We can, of course, suppose that in saying a man without the feelings of commiseration, of shame and dislike, of deference and compliance, and of right and wrong is not human, Mencius may simply mean to convey a point of semantics, namely that he refuses to call those who cannot or will not exhibit these feelings human beings. Surely the principle of the rectification of names, which has been extensively used to formulate such critical concepts as that of the king, is applicable here. But the force of Mencius' statement seems to lie elsewhere.

It is true that Mencius clearly states that "humanity, righteousness, propriety, and wisdom are not drilled into us from outside. We originally have them with us. Only we do not think [to find them]" (6A.6); but it is quite possible that what he really intends to convey is not only a matter of semantics but also a reference to the irreducibility of one's moral sense. The difference is subtle but vitally important. A man without those feelings is not human because it is psychologically impossible for a man not to have them. It is not the case that we can and should condemn someone who does not exhibit those feelings as inhuman according to our judgments. Indeed, it is inconceivable that a man, so long as he can still exercise his will, does not have a ready access to his own mind wherein the "germinations" of his basic feelings reside. Needless to say, the irreducibility of one's moral sense, which is rooted in one's nature, does not guarantee a spontaneous self-realization. Mencius is acutely aware of this:

> Therefore it is said, "Seek and you will find it, neglect and you will lose it." [Men differ in the development of their endowments], some twice as much as others, some five times, and some to an incalculable degree, because not one can develop his original endowment to the fullest extent. [6A.6]

The contention that the "four germinations" are always available for moral self-development seems in apparent conflict with the observation that the mind often has to be found and cultivated and that in a practical sense it can never be developed to the fullest extent. A way of resolving the conflict is to recommend a twofold interpretation of the mind as both an ontological reality and an existential process. The manner in which such an interpretation may be justified as well as the far-reaching implications it may have cannot be explored here. Yet the mind so interpreted seems to make good sense in light of the Mencian literature we have examined thus far. The "four germinations" understood in terms of the mind as an ontological reality can be characterized as the mind's original manifestations of its true nature; they are therefore absolutely irreducible. On the other hand, the finding, cultivating, and developing understood in terms of the mind as an existential process can be characterized as the mind's own efforts of self-cultivation. They are therefore necessarily ceaseless.

This is certainly compatible with Mencius' insistence on a conceptual distinction between physiological needs and moral feelings and yet, at the same time, on the importance of recognizing the former not only as legitimate constitutive elements in the structure of human nature but also as integral parts of one's quest for moral self-development. The practical consideration then is not the suppression of instinctual demands, such as appetites for food and sex, but their proper expression in a holistic way in order to be human. And it is precisely in this connection, I suppose, that the differentiation between the "great body" and the "small body" of human nature is made (6A.15). The small body, despite its universality as what is common to each member of the animal kingdom, tends to be fixed on external objects for immediate gratification. As a result, it is easily limited by a rather restricted area of human concern and can be extremely limiting to an inclusive process of self-growth. The great body, by contrast, is the basis for personal identity and for genuine communication, and despite its elusiveness as something often barely present in our ordinary daily existence, it is that by which the uniqueness of our human way is defined.

An example of Mencius' thinking on the divergence of the great body and the small body in self-development is found in the following exchange:

> Kung-tu Tzu asked, "We are all human beings. Why is it that some men become great and others become small?" Mencius said, "Those who follow the great body in their nature become great men and those who follow the small body in their nature become small men." "But we are all human beings. Why is it that some follow their great body and others follow their small body?"

Mencius replied, "When our senses of sight and hearing are used without thought and are thereby obscured by material things, the material things act on the material senses and lead them astray. That is all. The function of the mind is to think. If we think, we will get it (the moral sense). If we do not think, we will not get it. This is what Heaven has given to us. If we first build up the great part of our nature, then the small part cannot overcome it. It is simply this that makes a man great." [6A.15]

The centrality of the idea of "thinking" (*ssu*) may give one the impression that Mencius seems to have subscribed to a kind of rationalist position. With a stretch of the imagination, we may also suppose that "if we think, we will get it" implies the possibility of a transcendental procedure whereby the constitution of the mind itself, as a thinking agent, determines a priori the form, as it were, of moral sense. That such a line of inquiry into the Mencian mode of thought may yield fruitful results is not being questioned here. But it seems unlikely that by his use of the idea of thinking Mencius really intends to advance a formalistic thesis devoid of any specific moral contents. For Mencius notes in analogical terms:

Humanity is man's mind and righteousness is man's path. Pity the man who abandons the path and does not follow it, and who has lost his mind and does not know how to recover it. When people's dogs and fowls are lost, they go to look for them, and yet, when they have lost their minds, they do not go to look for them. The way of learning is none other than finding the lost mind. [6A.11]

The task of being human, according to this interpretive thrust, involves not merely the exercise of universalizable rationality in moral situations but the antecedent commitment to and the actual activity of moral self-development. The paradox of the whole enterprise then is that the concerted effort to find, cultivate, and develop the mind is predicated on the belief that the mind as the defining characteristic of human nature is itself the ultimate basis for such an effort. There is no appeal to either the immortality of the soul or the existence of God. The spontaneity of the mind is, in the last analysis, the necessary and sufficient reason for us to be moral.

Against this background, it may not be far-fetched to suggest that Mencius perceives, in the process of moral self-development, not only a multiplicity of ways to be pursued but, more important perhaps, also a convergence of stages to be perfected. Therefore, while Mencius recognizes several different approaches to sagehood, he maintains that as the usefulness of the five kinds of grain depends on their ripeness, "so the value of humanity depends on its being brought to maturity" (6A.19). In fact, on one occasion at least, Mencius even attempts to characterize a few perfected stages in poetic terms:

He who commands our liking is called good.
He who is sincere with himself is called true.
He who is sufficient and real is called beautiful.
He whose sufficiency and reality shine forth is called great.
He whose greatness transforms itself is called sagely.
He whose sageliness is beyond our comprehension is called spiritual. [7B.25]

Undoubtedly, from the good to the spiritual there are numerous degrees of refinement. Moral self-development so perceived is tantamount to an unceasing process of humanization.

Note: For translations of *Mencius* in this essay, see W.T. Chan, *A Source Book in Chinese Philosophy* (Princeton: Princeton University Press, 1973), pp. 55–83. Minor changes have been made. Also, cf. D.C. Lau, trans., *Mencius* (London: Penguin Classics, 1970) and James Legge, *The Chinese Classics*, vol. 2 (Oxford: Clarendon Press, 1895).

Part Two

Neo-Confucian Modes of Thinking

5. The Neo-Confucian Concept of Man

I

The brilliant sinologist Étienne Balazs once characterized all Chinese philosophy as preeminently social philosophy: "Even when it attempts to detach itself from the temporal world and arrive at some form of pure, transcendental metaphysics there can be no hope of understanding it without recognizing its point of departure to which sooner or later it returns."[1] Confucianism, according to this assertion, is the paradigmatic example of social philosophy. Balazs' description is acceptable if and only if "social philosophy" is defined in a broad sense to include personal commitment to the basic values of humanity. Strictly speaking, the point of departure in Confucianism is self-cultivation (hsiu-shen) rather than social responsibility. It is true that Confucian self-cultivation necessarily leads to social responsibility, and furthermore, the process of self-cultivation in the Confucian sense ought to be carried out in a social context. Still it can be maintained that the perfecting self rather than the corresponding society is really the focus of attention.

Ta-hsüeh (The Great Learning) explicitly remarks that from the Son of Heaven to the commoners all should regard self-cultivation as the root.[2] Underlying this statement is the conviction that man is malleable and indeed perfectible through self-effort. The perfectibility of man through self-effort thus becomes a defining characteristic of Confucian humanism and the real strength of the Neo-Confucian development of the Confucian concept of man.

By the perfectibility of man, however, it is not meant that man can create his own nature at random. It means that man's own strength, rather than the mediation of some supernatural agent, is the source of actualizing his inexhaustible potentiality. It also suggests that the meaning of life is created and experienced internally in man himself. For man is "designed" to perform a great task in life—self-realization, which in its fullest development leads not only to peace in the world but to perfect identification with Heaven (*t'ien*). Man is instructed to fulfill such a "design" by moral imperative. Man's given conditions in the secular world, such as his instinctual demands, his sociopolitical situation, and his natural environment, are all legitimate constituents of this so-called design of man. Therefore, the greatest challenge of man is not to confront what is beyond human possibility, so vividly portrayed in the Greek tragedies, but to bring to pass the message that the ultimate meaning of life is in the ordinary existence of man.

II

In the "T'ai-chi-t'u shuo" (An explanation of the diagram of the Great Ultimate), Chou Tun-i (Lien-hsi, 1017–73) places man in the pivotal position of his metaphysical system. Man, who receives the highest excellence in the creative process of the Great Ultimate, is himself not merely a "creature." He is also a creative agent who participates in the onto-cosmological process that brings about the completion of the Great Ultimate. Man can perform such a function not because of some superhuman guidance, but because he is precisely what he ought to be. Indeed, the sage who "establishes himself as the ultimate standard for man" does not transcend the structure of man; instead he is its very embodiment.[3] In other words, the sage is the most authentic and genuine man. According to Chou Tun-i's quotation from the *Book of Change,* such a man "accords in his virtue with Heaven and Earth; in his brilliancy, with sun and moon; in his orderliness, with the four seasons; and in his good and evil fortunes, with the spiritual beings."[4]

How can a mortal being assume such a cosmic stature? Indeed, how is this concept of man different from that of a subjectivism or anthropocentrism? The answer lies in the uniqueness of the Confucian approach to the problem of humanity. The classical formulation of such an approach can be found in the *Chung-yung (Doctrine of the Mean),* which seems to be a source of inspiration for Chou Tun-i's other important treatise called *T'ung-shu* (Penetrating the *Book of Change*). In the *Chung-yung*, we find the following statement:

> It is only he who has the most *ch'eng* [sincerity] who can develop his nature to the utmost. Able to do this, he is able to do the same to the nature of other men. Able to do this, he is able to do the same to the nature of things. Able to do this, he can assist the transforming and nourishing operations of Heaven and Earth. Being able to do this, he can form a trinity with Heaven and Earth.[5]

The key term in the quoted passage is sincerity (*ch'eng*). Through sincerity man can realize the true nature not only of himself, but of his fellow human beings and indeed of the phenomenal world as a whole. Consistent with this spirit Chou Tun-i says, "Sincerity is the foundation of the sage," and "Sagehood is nothing but sincerity."[6]

As we have already pointed out, the sage in the Neo-Confucian sense is the most authentic and genuine man. We can now add that the sage is also the most sincere man, which means the man who is most truthful to his humanity. Real humanity is of course not confined to the individual self. In fact, unless one can overcome such subjectivistic tendencies as selfishness, one can never be truthful to one's selfhood. Yet, only through concrete self-realization, which means the full manifestation of the most authentic, genuine, and sincere humanity inherent in oneself, can one become a man in the true sense of the word. It is quite understandable that humanity or humanheartedness is thus defined as man (*jen che jen yeh*). This brings us to the famous "Hsi-ming" (Western Inscription) of Chang Tsai (*Heng-ch'ü*, 1020–77), which begins with the following lines:

> Heaven is my father and Earth is my mother, and even such a small creature as I find an intimate place in their midst. Therefore that which fills the universe I regard as my body and that which directs the universe I consider as my nature. All people are my brothers and sisters, and all things are my companions.[7]

This is certainly not a descriptive statement but an articulation of personal commitment. To Chang Tsai, man is the filial son of the universe. He is entrusted, as it were, with the great mission of caring for the myriad things in the world. He does this not by way of con-

73

quering nature but by way of mastering himself. For the true nature of man is the best, some would say the only, vehicle by which the true nature of things can be understood and realized. But to be a man, or rather to become what a man ought to be, signifies an infinite process of self-cultivation. Indeed, "the reason why the man of humanity and the filial son can serve Heaven and be sincere with himself is simply that they are unceasing in their humanity and filial piety."[8]

Chang Tsai's ideal of man as the filial son of the universe who, for the sake of self-fulfillment, serves Heaven and Earth in an unceasing spirit, is further developed by his nephew Ch'eng Hao (Ming-tao, 1032–85). In an essay entitled "Shih-jen" (On understanding humanity), Ch'eng Hao presents the now well-known thesis that "the man of humanity forms one body with all things without any differentiation."[9] Underlying this simple formulation is Ch'eng Hao's deep concern for the *sensitivity* of man. Man as the most sentient being always has the inner urge to penetrate the mystery of the universe and to enter into spiritual communion with nature. The power of sympathy and empathy is so great in man that ideally there is no single thing that lies outside the orbit of human sensitivity. Of course in actuality man often fails to extend his humanity to its utmost capacity. In citing a book on Chinese medicine, which describes paralysis of the four limbs as *pu-jen* (literally "absence of humanity"), Ch'eng Hao argues:

> The man of humanity regards Heaven and Earth and all things as one body. To him there is nothing that is not himself. Since he has recognized all things as himself, can there be any limit to his humanity? If things are not part of the self, naturally they have nothing to do with it. As in the case of paralysis of the four limbs, the *ch'i* (vital force) no longer penetrates them, and therefore they are no longer parts of the self.[10]

Accordingly, to embody all things in one's sensitivity is not only humanly possible but necessarily human. For the scope of humanity as characterized by sensitivity is limitless. If one fails to "extend" one's sensitivity to embrace all things, it is not because of the intrinsic weakness of one's humanity. Rather, it is because one's humanity is somewhere paralyzed and thus falls short of its utmost capacity. The problem of humanity so conceived has some far-reaching implications. For example, being insensitive to the sufferings of others or to the destruction of nature becomes much more serious than a lack of social responsibility or an indifference to ecological conditions. It should be interpreted as an expression of inhumanity.

To Ch'eng Hao, "forming one body with all things" is not merely an intellectual position. It is basically an experiential confirmation. In fact, from the viewpoint of the Neo-Confucianists in general, an intellectual position without the support of experiential confirmation frequently degenerates into "empty talk." Ch'eng Hao, or Chang Tsai, or Chou Tun-i may have arrived at "some form of pure, transcendental metaphysics," but the true message is lost if we do not recognize the whole dimension of self-cultivation as its point of departure.

Ch'eng Hao's younger brother, Ch'eng I (I-ch'uan, 1033–1107), has been credited with a most balanced dictum on this point: "Self-cultivation requires seriousness; the pursuit of learning depends on the extension of knowledge."[11] Following the so-called eight steps of the *Great Learning*, he suggests, "The first thing is to rectify the mind and make the will sincere. The sincerity of the will depends upon the extension of knowledge and the extension of knowledge depends upon the investigation of things."[12] He further suggests that by the investigation of things is meant the investigation of the principle (*li*) inherent in everything. One must investigate one item at a time. And "when one has accumulated much knowledge he will naturally achieve a thorough understanding like a sudden release."[13] To Ch'eng I, self-perfection is a process of gradual inclusion. It begins with problems of the self, then extends to those of the family and of the state, and eventually embraces those of the universe as a whole. Although Ch'eng I always warns his students against "overexpansion," he adheres to his brother's highly idealistic vision of man.

The reason is not difficult to see. Ch'eng I contends that everything has its principle. The task of man is to understand through personal experience the principle that is inherent in everything. Only when one has understood this exhaustively can one be said to have united oneself with all things. To do this one must have the determination, the courage, and the energy to confront as many *things* as

75

one possibly can. Far from being empiricistic, Ch'eng I's doctrine is centered on the conviction that with vigorous self-discipline, a series of encounters with the external world in the form of reading books, discussing historical events, or handling daily affairs will gradually lead to a state of impartiality,[14] which is the basis of a true communion with the universe. To borrow his own words, "Where there is impartiality, there is unity, and where there is partiality, there is multiplicity. The highest truth is always resolved into a unity, and an essential principle is never a duality. If people's minds are as different as their faces are, it is solely due to partiality."[15] In a different context, Ch'eng I explicitly states, "Humanity is universal impartiality; it is the foundation of goodness."[16]

III

In the moral metaphysics of Chu Hsi (Yüan-hui, 1130–1200), the concept of man develops to a new height of intellectual sophistication. It is true that man is perfectible; he is the filial son of the universe and can form one body with all things, but what is the real philosophical basis of this ideal, and how in concrete forms can it be actualized? Chu Hsi's personal experience in confronting, in his late thirties, the issue of "equilibrium and harmony" (*chung-ho*) as presented by the *Doctrine of the Mean* impelled him to reflect realistically on all the fundamental problems in the Neo-Confucian legacy to his time.

According to his interpretation, each individual thing embodies the Great Ultimate and the universe as a whole embodies the same Great Ultimate. The Great Ultimate in the universe as a principle is one and its manifestations are many. The manifested principle, however, is neither a distorted nor a partial fulfillment of the Great Ultimate. Rather, it is the complete concretization of the Great Ultimate. Like the reflection of the moon in the river, it is the same moon in its entirety. Yet the process of concretization involves not only principle but also material force (*ch'i*). And the reality of each individual thing lies in the interdependence of principle and material force.

76

Man as an individual thing also consists of principle and material force. Principle resides in human nature and material force constitutes the physical form. Man, however, is not an ordinary thing. He is endowed with another delicate stuff called mind. Although human mind is inseparable from material force, as an agent of creativity and sensitivity it has the potential of "embracing and penetrating all (things) and leaving nothing to be desired."[17] The mind can therefore transform material force, such as instinctual demands, into a kind of moral energy so as to reveal fully the principle of man in daily life.This is possible only when the mind through strenuous efforts of self-cultivation is completely purified. Commenting on Chang Tsai's statement that "by enlarging one's mind one can enter into all things in the world," Chu Hsi says:

> The expression "enter into" is like saying that humanity enters into all events and is all-pervasive. It means that the operation of the principle of the mind penetrates all as blood circulates and reaches the entire body. If there is a single thing not yet entered, the reaching is not yet complete and there are still things not yet embraced. This shows that the mind still excludes something. For selfishness separates and obstructs, and consequently one and others stand in opposition. This being the case, even those dearest to us may be excluded.[18]

Chu Hsi further suggests that only when the mind has embraced and penetrated all things is humanity fully manifested. Humanity in this connection is both immanent and transcendent. For it is both "the character of the mind and the principle of love."[19] As the character of the mind, it can be realized through internal self-transformation, such as trying to be sincere and serious with oneself; yet, as the principle of love, it can only be realized through learning. And since the principle of love is inherent in human nature, the ultimate goal of learning is to unite the human mind with the principle in human nature. When such a unity is complete, the Great Ultimate is fully revealed. Thereupon man becomes what he ought to be.

Chu Hsi's phenomenal attempt to struggle through the delicate issue of self-realization by a more sophisticated formulation of the concepts of mind and principle presents us with a number of rather perplexing problems, many of which are still enthusiastically discussed and debated among contemporary students of Confucianism. Suffice it now to focus on one example. What is the true relationship between the principle and the mind? Chu Hsi contends that the principle is inherent in human nature, but the conscious effort to actualize the true nature of humanity (its principle) is through the function of the mind. The mind, nevertheless, must go through a strenuous process of self-purification before it can be established as the true agent of human perfection, for the mind is a delicate stuff, composed of the material force rather than of the principle. If it wills to realize the Great Ultimate that is in human nature, it must transform itself from a mere psychophysiological entity to a moral and ontological reality. Such a transformation depends not only on internal cultivation but also on the interiorization of established moral values through continuous and accumulative learning. We are thus confronted with a static principle, which is the true nature of humanity, and a dynamic mind, which can be truly human only when it is purified by self-effort. Of course we may still maintain that Chu Hsi eventually unites the mind and the principle by self-cultivation in a well-structured program of learning. Ontologically, it is undeniable that Chu Hsi departed somewhat from the early Masters by separating the ultimate ground of man's self-realization from its actual source of energy.

As a challenge to Chu Hsi's seemingly dualistic tendency in the dichotomy of mind and principle, Lu Hsiang-shan (Chiu-yüan, 1139–93) advances the thesis that "the mind is one and principle is one. Perfect truth is reduced to a unity; the essential principle is never a duality. The mind and principle can never be separated into two."[20] He further states that principle is inherent in the mind, and the mind of man is the whole universe in its microcosm. Therefore, "the affairs in the universe are my affairs. My own affairs are affairs of the universe."[21] Following the teaching of Mencius that the mind is not only the basis of man's moral perfectibility but also the ground of man's spiritual communion with the universe, Lu Hsiang-shan says: "There is only one mind. My mind, my friends' mind, the mind of the sages thousands of years ago, and the mind of sages thousands of years to come are all the same. The substance of the mind is infinite. If one can completely develop his mind, he will become identified with Heaven."[22]

Unfortunately, Lu Hsiang-shan never developed his experiential insight into a balanced philosophical position. In fact, he had very little interest in philosophical argumentation per se. Understandably the historically significant "Goose Lake" debate failed to establish a lasting rapprochement between Chu Hsi and his junior challenger. Furthermore, with the emotion-charged issue of Ch'an (Zen) in the background, a fruitful dialogue between the two thinkers, which might have altered the general direction of Chinese philosophy in the twelfth century, never came into being.

Yet despite the tension and conflict within the Neo-Confucian tradition, it seems that there is an agreement among virtually all of the Neo-Confucianists: man is a moral being who through self-effort extends his human sensitivity to all the beings of the universe so as to realize himself in the midst of the world and as an integral part of it, in the sense that his self-perfection necessarily embodies the perfection of the universe as a whole. If we view the controversy between Chu and Lu from this perspective, the "tension" and "conflict" actually point to the inner dynamism of the Neo-Confucian concept of man, which in my opinion is best portrayed in the works of Wang Yang-ming (Shou-jen, 1472–1529).

It has been widely accepted by students of Chinese thought that the idealism of Lu Hsiang-shan anticipated that of Wang Yang-ming. Genetically, however, Wang Yang-ming began with the *Problematik* of Chu Hsi and never consciously alienated himself from the philosophy of Master Chu, although he was very much inspired by Lu Hsiang-shan's concept of mind. It should be noted also that since the times of Chu Hsi and Lu Hsiang-shan, there had been three centuries of Neo-Confucian development before the emergence of Wang Yang-ming as its leading spokesman. It may be difficult for us to identify a group of Neo-Confucian thinkers in the Yüan (1260–1368) and early Ming (1368–1644) periods who were comparable in originality to the great Sung (960–1279) masters outlined above. But it is relatively easy to trace a continuous line of exemplary teachers in this Neo-Confucian era. These teachers, as spiritual leaders of their times, all engaged in the cultivation of their ethical lives. Through their lifelong commitments, they bear witness to the Confucian ideal that man is perfectible through self-effort. It is my contention that without the cumulative struggle of these teachers, notably Hsü Heng (1209–1281) and Wu Ch'eng (1249–1333) in the Yüan dynasty, and Hsüeh Hsüan (1393–1464), Wu Yü-pi (1391–1469), Hu Chü-jen (1434–1484), and Ch'en Hsien-chang (1428–1500) in the Ming dynasty, the revitalization of the Neo-Confucian tradition in the "dynamic idealism" of Wang Yang-ming is almost inconceivable.

IV

To conclude the present study, we cannot do better than quote Yang-ming's own words. In the light of the foregoing discussion, it may be suggested that when Yang-ming made the following remarks, he had the support of not only the "psychological reality" of his own inner experience but also the "historical actuality" of a long and continuous cultural heritage:

> The great man regards Heaven and Earth and the myriad things as one body. He regards the world as one family and the country as one person. . . . That the great man can regard Heaven, Earth, and the myriad things as one body is not because he deliberately wants to do so, but because it is natural to the humane nature of his mind that he do so. . . . Even the mind of the small man is no different. Only he himself makes it small. Therefore when he sees a child about to fall into a well, he cannot help a feeling of alarm and commiseration. This shows that his humanity forms one body with the child. It may be objected that the child belongs to the same species. Again, when he observes the pitiful cries and frightened appearance of birds and animals about to be slaughtered, he cannot help feeling an "inability to bear" their suffering. This shows that his humanity forms one body with birds and animals. It may be objected that birds and animals are sentient beings as he is. But when he sees plants broken and destroyed, he cannot help a feeling of pity. This shows that his humanity forms one body with plants. It may be said that plants are living things as he is. Yet even when he sees tiles and stones shattered and crushed, he cannot help a feeling of regret. This shows that his humanity forms one body with tiles and stones. . . .[23]

Yang-ming's "great man" (*ta-jen*) in the present context can very well be rendered as the most authentic, genuine, and sincere man. Such a man is neither fated to be extraordinary nor blessed with some superhuman quality. Essentially he is a common man, living in the everyday world in Heidegger's sense of "being there." But he is truthful to his basic "design" by continuously experiencing and affirming the real humanity that is in him. In so doing he transforms himself into an artistic human reality and becomes the most sentient being of the universe. His uniqueness, to borrow a Mencian expression, lies in the fact that he has been first to obtain the likeness of our human mind. For he is after all a man among men. Indeed, "that the great man can regard Heaven, Earth, and the myriad things as one body is not because he *deliberately* wants to do so, but because it is natural to the humane nature of his mind that he do so." I have emphasized the word "deliberately" to stress the difference Yang-ming implies between a conscious and intentional striving for an unrealizable human ideal and a natural and spontaneous feeling inherent in the very structure of man. The making of a great man is thus more than an event in history and a drama in society. It is fundamentally the act of a silent "yes" to humanity.

NOTES

[1]Cf. Étienne Balazs, "La crise sociale et la philosophie politique à la fin des Han," *T'oung Pao* 39 (1949): 83–131. For an English version, see "Political Philosophy and Social Crisis in the End of Han," in Étienne Balazs, *Chinese Civilization and Bureaucracy; Variations on a Theme*, trans. H. M. Wright, ed. Arthur F. Wright (New Haven: Yale University Press, 1964), p. 195.
[2]*The Great Learning* 1.6. Cf. *The Chinese Classics*, ed. and trans. James Legge, 5 vols. (Oxford: Clarendon Press, 1893–95), 1: 359.
[3]Chou Tun-i, "T'ai-chi-t'u shuo," in *Chou Tzu ch'üan-shu* 1:2. For a standard English version, see Wing-tsit Chan, trans. and comp., *A Source Book in Chinese Philosophy* (hereafter abbreviated as *Source*) (Princeton: Princeton University Press, 1963), p. 463.
[4]*Ibid., Source*, pp. 463–464.
[5]*The Doctrine of the Mean*, chap. 23. For the English version, see Fung Yu-lan, *A Short History of Chinese Philosophy*, ed. Derk Bodde (New York: Macmillan Co., 1948), p. 176.

[6]Chou Tun-i, *T'ung-shu*, chap. 1, pt. 1; chap. 2, pt. 2. *Source*, pp. 465, 466.

[7]Chang Tsai, "Hsi-ming," originally part of chap. 17 of *Cheng-meng* in *Chang Tzu ch'üan-shu* 1:1. *Source*, p. 497.

[8]Chang Tsai, *Cheng-meng*, chap. 6. *Source*, p. 508.

[9]Ch'eng Hao, *Erh-Ch'eng i-shu* 2A:3a. *Source*, p. 523.

[10]*Ibid.*, 2A: 2a-b. *Source*, p. 530.

[11]Ch'eng I, *Erh-Ch'eng i-shu* 18:5b. *Source*, p. 562.

[12]*Ibid. Source*, pp. 560–561.

[13]*Ibid.*

[14]*Ibid.*

[15]*Ibid.*, 15:1b. *Source*, p. 553.

[16]Ch'eng I, *Wai-shu* 2:34a. *Source*, p. 571.

[17]Chu Hsi, "Jen-shuo," in *Chu Tzu wen-chi* 67:20. *Source*, p. 593.

[18]Chu Hsi, *Chu Tzu ch'üan-shu* 44:12b. *Source*, p. 629.

[19]Chu Hsi, *Lun-yü chi-chu*, chap. 1, commentary on the *Analects*, 1:2.

[20]Lu Hsiang-shan, *Hsiang-shan ch'üan-chi* 1:3b. *Source*, p. 574.

[21]*Ibid.*, 22:5a. *Source*, p. 580.

[22]*Ibid.*, 35:10a. *Source*, p. 585.

[23]Wang Yang-ming, "Ta-hsüeh wen," in *Wang Wen-ch'eng Kung ch'üan-shu* 26:1b. *Source*, pp. 659–660.

6. The Unity of Knowing and Acting— From a Neo-Confucian Perspective

I

Philosophy as a natural function of the mind is an independent, irreducible, and self-sufficient realm of human activity.[1] It gives its own laws, develops its own methods, and chooses its own subjects. Yet as a fundamental inquiry into the underlying structures of being, philosophy must come into contact with the total reality of human experience. For it is the function of philosophy to increase man's wisdom by creating new, and deepening old, insights into all dimensions of human consciousness. Philosophy so conceived is more than a critical investigation; it is a spiritual quest for truth through meditative thinking as well as logical reasoning.

Such a quest involves man's whole being rather than merely his cognitive faculty. Indeed, in the mainstream of Eastern thought, there has been the realization that doing philosophy is in itself a religious act. It necessarily leads to the creation of values such as an integrated personality, a heightened social conscience, and a deepened moral commitment. The act of philosophizing is therefore a form of spiritual self-cultivation. To philosophize is not only to examine the foundations of one's being, but also to strengthen one's spirituality.

Actually, a similar orientation can be found in the mystic elements of Plato, the writings of St. Augustine, the Stoics, the medieval saints, Pascal, Kierkegaard, and the works of modern philosophers such as Martin Buber, Gabriel Marcel, and Martin Heidegger. In light of the experience in the East, be it Hinduism, Buddhism, Taoism, or Confucianism, the above-mentioned thinkers seem to symbolize a global search for philosophical wisdom, which, according to

Marcel, "is to be found wherever man tries not to organize his life around a center; instead he strives to organize it with respect to everything that has to do with the business of keeping oneself in existence; all else he regards as peripheral and subordinate."[2]

To be sure, this is not the only way to philosophize. In fact, in the majority of academic centers for the professional study of philosophy in England and the United States, this specific kind of approach has for many years been relegated to the background, if not altogether ostracized from departments of philosophy.[3] Thus it seems advisable to leave open the question, What is the most authentic way of doing philosophy? Unless the modern philosopher consciously chooses to remain insensitive to the great spiritual traditions in human history, it does make sense to stress the importance of man's age-long heritage as a basis for creative thinking, rather than merely as material for critical analysis.

If it is accepted that the great spiritual traditions in the world today have a prominent role to perform in the *pensée pensante* ("the thinking thought," to borrow a term coined by Blondel[4]) of modern philosophy, it becomes imperative that we study the creative thoughts in these traditions for the sake not only of a critical appreciation of historical wisdom, but also of our own way of doing philosophy. Since this form of philosophizing involves a kind of religious commitment, to distinguish it from the philosophical study of religion we shall call it "religiophilosophy," a tentative definition of which is: the inquiry into human insights by disciplined reflection, for the primary purpose of spiritual self-transformation. Religiophilosophy thus defined characterizes the nature and function of philosophizing in all the major historical traditions of the East. In addition, it truthfully represents theological thinking in Judaism, Christianity, and Islam. It may even be suggested that religiophilosophy, as a way of doing philosophy, is a new message being delivered by some of the leading thinkers in modern Europe.[5]

II

Confucianism as a religiophilosophy seeks to "establish the ultimacy of man."[6] Its primary concern is to study the uniqueness of man to understand his morality, sociality, and religiosity. Although this kind of study necessarily involves a critical understanding of issues such as the mind and human nature, its fundamental task is centered on the question of how to become the most authentic man or the sage. From the Confucian point of view, it is inconceivable that one be seriously engaged in the study of how to become the most authentic man purely as a detached inquirer, without involving any personal commitment. For the Confucian approach to sagehood rests on the belief that man is perfectible through his own effort. To know oneself as a form of self-cultivation is therefore deemed simultaneously an act of internal self-transformation. Indeed, self-knowledge and self-transformation are not only closely interrelated, they are also fully integrated. My attempt here is to reflect on this insight in the light of Neo-Confucian thinking.

Historically Neo-Confucianism is a spiritual tradition in China dating from the eleventh century to the seventeenth.[7] It can be considered an intellectual response to the challenges of Ch'an (Zen) Buddhism and religious Taoism in a predominantly Confucian value-oriented society. In a long and strenuous process of searching for a new spiritual identity following the decline of Confucian thinking over a period of centuries, the Neo-Confucianists appropriated many Buddhist and Taoist values. It is beyond the scope of this article to specify the nature of their appropriation, but it is important to point out that, despite its efforts to absorb inspiration from other spiritual systems, Neo-Confucianism is a creative adaptation of classical Confucian insights, rather than a syncretic culmination of the "Three Teachings."

Scholars of Chinese thought, nevertheless, have raised several questions about the validity of the Neo-Confucian masters' claims to be in the mainstream of Confucian thinking. Some of the issues that are still seriously debated include: How deeply was Chou Tun-i (Lien-hsi, 1017–73) influenced by Taoist cosmogony? How much was the universalism of Chang Tsai (Heng-ch'ü, 1020–77) derived from the Mahayana Buddhist idea of compassion? How closely related are the quietism of Ch'eng Hao (Ming-tao, 1032–85) and the practice of quiet-sitting in Taoism and Ch'an Buddhism? How Ch'an-like was Lu Chiu-yüan (Hsiang-shan, 1132–93)? And how Buddhistic or Taoistic was Wang Shou-jen (Yang-ming, 1472–1529)?

85

Even in the cases of Ch'eng I (I-ch'uan, 1033–1107) and Chu Hsi (Yuan-hui, 1130–1200), the approach to Confucianism has frequently been considered a departure from rather than a fulfillment of the ancient wisdom in classical Confucian thought.

My primary aim here is not to judge the authenticity of Neo-Confucianism in the light of the spiritual orientation in classical Confucianism, but to probe the intrinsic value of Neo-Confucian thinking itself. Since the issue of authenticity is relevant to a general understanding of the problems to be discussed, it seems useful to make clear my own position in this matter at the outset. This necessitates a brief discussion of the basic *Problematik* of classical Confucianism.

Philosophically, as well as historically, Confucianism symbolizes a very complex spiritual phenomenon. The scope of its involvement defies simple categorization. Even broad terms such as *religion, social philosophy,* and *ethical system* are too narrow to encompass the diversity of Confucian concerns, especially if the terms are used in a restrictive sense. For example, if Confucianism is described as a religion and by religion is meant a kind of spiritualism purportedly detached from the secular world, the whole dimension of sociality in Confucianism will be left out. If Confucianism is described as a social philosophy, its central concern of relating the self to the most generalized level of universality, or *t'ien* (heaven), will be ignored. If the spiritual aspect of Confucian self-cultivation is emphasized exclusively, its intention of complete self-fulfillment, which must also embrace the whole area of corporality, will be misunderstood. On the other hand, if the Confucian insistence on man as a sociopolitical being is overstated, its ideal of self-transcendence in the form of being one with Heaven and Earth will become incomprehensible.

Therefore it is of paramount importance that we grasp the underlying structure of Confucian intentionality. Undoubtedly the primary concern of the Confucianist is to become a sage, and as already mentioned, the Confucian sage symbolizes the most authentic, genuine, and sincere man. From the Confucian point of view, the ultimate basis of and actual strength for becoming a sage are located in the very nature of man, which is imparted, but not created, by Heaven. The path to sagehood is therefore an unceasing process of self-transformation, with the existential situation of man here and now as its point of departure. The process is one of gradual inclusion, a process that seeks to integrate the structure of the self with that of man, with that of nature, and eventually with that of the cosmos. In a deeper sense, the process of integration is concomitantly that of authentication. The self becomes truer to its original structure when it is ultimately identified with the cosmos, or the great self.

It is misleading to describe this process merely as an expansion of human consciousness or as a development of the spiritual self. According to Mencius (371?–289? B.C.), the process of *chien-hsing* (realization of the bodily design) is a holistic one, involving both the *ta-t'i* (the great body) and the *hsiao-t'i* (the small body). *Ta-t'i* refers to the intrinsic moral feelings that make man uniquely human; *hsiao-t'i* refers to the basic instinctual demands that make man a part of the animal kingdom. The word "great" is used to desciibe *ta-t'i*, for although the "budlike" beginnings of intrinsic moral feelings are delicate, when they are fully cultivated they become all-embracing human sensitivity. The word *small* describes *hsiao-t'i*; although the "floodlike" forces of the basic instinctual demands are strong, if they are properly channeled they constitute the irreducible reality of the individual self. Therefore, self-transformation denies or slights neither spirituality nor corporality. As a holistic process of realizing the bodily design, self-transformation helps man to become a whole being in his lived concreteness. In the last analysis, it is none other than the process of humanization.[8]

In Confucianism the true meaning of man must be sought beyond his anthropological structure. A classical formulation of such a position may be found in the sayings of Mencius: "For a man to give full realization to his mind is for him to understand his own nature, and a man who knows his own nature will know Heaven."[9] The word *chih* ("know") in the present context connotes not only cognitive knowing but also affective identifying, or experiential "embodying." The message implicit in the above quotation points to a "concrete-universal" approach to the ontology of man. Specifically, the concrete path of self-knowledge is considered the most authentic way of entering into universal communion with the cosmos. To use a Mencian analogy, this is like the sinking of a well: the deeper one goes into the ground of one's own being, the closer

87

one gets to the spring of common humanity and the source of cosmic creativity, a point to be developed later.[10] Indeed, unless man transcends not only his egoistic structure but also his anthropological structure, he can never fully realize the ontological meaning of humanity.

If this is accepted as a basic *Problematik* of classical Confucianism, the philosophical task of the Neo-Confucianists can be interpreted as a systematic reflection on what may be called the "inner dimension" of classical Confucianism. The primary method used is not logical reasoning or analytical argumentation, but a series of experiential encounters with the basic literature so as to understand its original insight. Philosophical creativity in this connection is not demonstrated in the ability to construct a conceptual edifice based on a limited number of premises. Rather, it is shown in the ability to relate a comprehensive ontological insight to immediate daily affairs so as to integrate in a dynamic way one's concrete existence here and now with one's most generalized perception of the universe as a whole. To be sure, underlying this interpretation is the assumption that the mystic elements in *Mencius*, the *Doctrine of the Mean,* and the *Book of Change* are all authentic texts in classical Confucian thinking. I am well aware that this assumption is not irrefutable, but so far as existing scholarly research on this specific point is concerned, there does not seem to be enough evidence to prove otherwise. Therefore, in response to the questions about the validity of the Neo-Confucian masters' claims to be in the mainstream of Confucian thinking, I suggest that we deepen our own understanding and broaden our awareness of the key issues in the classical Confucian tradition by maintaining a constant dialogue with the leading philosophers in the Neo-Confucian period. If we must pass judgment on their "authenticity," we cannot afford to misread their intentionality.[11]

To reflect on this particular insight of Confucianism in the light of Neo-Confucian thinking, I shall address myself to three basic problem areas: (1) the structure of *li-chih* (to establish the will or to make an existential decision), (2) the notion of *chih-hsing ho-i* (the unity of knowing and acting), and (3) the concept of *ch'eng* (sincerity, completeness, truth, reality, or creativity). It is hoped that such discussion will throw light on the inner dimension of

88

Confucian thinking as a possible approach to the complicated phenomena of religiophilosophy.

III

The structure of *li-chih* is analogous to that of existential decision in the Kierkegaardian sense: it is a fundamental choice that requires an ultimate commitment; it is a qualitative change that affects the entire dimension of one's being; and it is an unceasing process that demands constant reaffirmation. Yet since there is a basic difference in orientation between the Confucian way to sagehood and the Christian approach to salvation, the analogy must not be carried too far.

For the Confucianists, the fundamental choice is directed inward toward human nature. If man is not merely a conglomeration of externalizable physiological, psychological, and sociological states, a conscious choice is required to establish his spiritual identity. This is why Mencius advocated the primacy of establishing that which is great, or the *ta-che*, in each human being, and why the Neo-Confucianists—notably Chou Tun-i and Lu Chiu-yüan—insist on the centrality of "establishing the ultimacy of man."

The qualitative change in Confucianism, unlike its counterpart in Christianity, is not an either-or leap of faith, but a both-and return to the self. When Confucius says in the *Analects*, "At fifteen, I set my heart on learning,"[12] he is describing his early commitment to self-transformation. The decision to learn, which in the classical sense means to be engaged in self-enlightenment,[13] thus symbolizes a qualitative change in the orientation of one's life. As Hsün Tzu (fl 298–238 B.C.) dramatically put it: "the art of learning occupies the whole of life; to arrive at its purpose, you cannot stop for an instant. To do this is to be a man; to stop is to be a beast."[14] Learning so conceived is a conscious attempt to change oneself from being in a state of mere psychophysiological growth to that of ethicoreligious existence. Such a change is a qualitative one, for it seeks to change from the natural growth of the partial man, or the "small body," to the meaningful existence of the fully integrated whole man, or the "great body." To reiterate an earlier point, in the Confucian sense an ethicoreligious existence necessarily entails the realization of one's psychophysiological growth, for it is a return to the true self, which comprises *both* the large *and* the small body.

Paradoxically, neither the fundamental choice nor the qualitative change appears as merely a discrete moment in one's life history. Since Confucianism is not a revealed religion, the "establishment of the will" is not so much a mystic experience of the transcendent Absolute as it is an enlightening experience of the immanent Self. Therefore the never-ending process it entails does not take the form of a dialogical relationship with the "wholly other;" rather, it takes the form of a dialectical development of the Self. The inscription on the washing vessel of King T'ang (r. 1751?–1739? B.C.), which is quoted in the *Great Learning*, says: "If you can renew yourself one day, then you can renew yourself every day, and keep renewing yourself day after day."[15] Thus the establishment of the will is both a single act and a continuous process. As a single act, it so shakes the foundation of one's temporal existence as to enable one to arrive at a deeper dimension of self-awareness. As a continuous process it reaffirms the bedrock of one's being in an unending effort of self-realization.

Furthermore, the structure of *li-chih* involves what may be called a spatiotemporal dimension, symbolized by the ineffable Confucian concept of *shih* (timeliness or timeousness). In Confucianism, to establish the will or to make an existential decision is not to "deliver" oneself from one's concrete situation; rather it is a continually renewed effort to relate oneself meaningfully to one's lived concreteness. Sociopolitical conditions such as one's family affairs, communal responsibilities, or societal obligations are legitimate elements of one's true existence here and now, for only in the context of one's fundamental human relations can one, in experiential terms, decide to engage in the humanizing task of self-realization. One does not depart from the human situation; instead one begins with and eventually returns to the human situation.

As an integral part of the humanizing task, *li-chih* signifies a future action of realizing the self, an action that depends on the past and is within one's present power. The future aspect of *li-chih* is not an undefined or undefinable project conditioned primarily by the unknown, or even by the unknowable. It is not a process of self-denial, but one of self-fulfillment. It is a movement not of alienation from, but of reconciliation with, the reality of man. Similarly, in the structure of *li-chih*, the "past"—namely, the irreducible human conditions—does not necessarily impose a set of meaningless restrictions on one's actions. It provides the means for concrete integration and realization of human values within one's present power. As a result, the establishment of the will is an act of the present that links the "experienced necessity" of the past with the creative freedom of the future.

IV

As Mencius points out, the will is the directionality of the mind.[16] When the mind *directs*, a "bodily energy" follows. To be sure, Mencius warns us that since the direction of the mind may also be influenced by a psychosomatic disposition, it is essential that we cultivate our bodily energy for the service of the mind. Yet the interaction of the will and the bodily energy actually implies that the directionality of the mind has inner strength of its own. It is inconceivable that when the mind directs, the whole bodily constitution is not in some way affected by it. Therefore the establishment of the will involves both cognitive and affective dimensions. This leads us to the notion of *chih-hsing ho-i*.

Etymologically, *chih* refers to the faculty of knowing, *hsing* refers to the function of acting, and *ho-i* means either unity or identity. Although the "unity of knowing and acting" was formulated by Wang Yang-ming in 1509, as the result of his experiential encounter with Chu Hsi's doctrine of *ko-wu* (the investigation of things),[17] it may very well be accepted as a central concern in Confucianism as a whole. According to Chu Hsi, the road to sagehood involves a perception of the underlying *li* (ordering principle)[18] in the totality of things (including intellectual ideas, natural phenomena, and human affairs). Theoretically, if the mind is completely purified, one can fully understand the *li* inherent in one's own nature. Practically, however, it is necessary for each to go through a gradual, strenuous, and persistent process of spiritual appropriation before his mind is able to arrive at a sudden comprehension of the *li* as the "ground of being" of all things. Yang-ming agrees with Chu Hsi that self-transformation requires learning, but he casts doubt on the separability of *hsin* (the mind) and *li*. If the human mind's understanding of the *li* of man does not take the form of an apperception, man's self-knowledge has to make a detour in order to search for objective truths from the outside. Yet Yang-ming asks: Can we really derive a guiding principle for action by investigating the anatomy of a bamboo tree? Must we search for internal self-identity in the midst of natural phenomena? Is the structure of man, in the last analysis, somewhat inadequate for self-knowledge, thereby necessitating the interiorization of external elements in order to make up for it?

Through a long and painful struggle with these kinds of issues—the process was described by Yang-ming as "a hundred deaths and a thousand hardships"[19]—he came to to the realization that the decision to become a sage (the most authentic, genuine, and sincere man) is itself the *pen* (root) of sagehood. Ultimately it is both the necessary and sufficient basis for becoming a sage. Indeed, if man is conceived as a self-transforming and self-realizing agent, the decision to become a sage is precisely what each man ought to make prior to any form of learning. This is in essence comparable to the Mencian position of establishing first what is great in each of us. To seek greatness as a prior condition to learning is by no means a denial or depreciation of the importance of empirical study. To do so, however, does suggest that the route to sagehood begins with an inner decision, without which learning is not relevant to the task of self-realization.

I have already mentioned that the establishment of the will as an inner decision involves both cognitive and affective dimensions. Certainly it is *knowing* that projects into the ideal state of what one ought to be in the future. But it is more than a mere cognitive knowing. As a form of introspective examination, knowing simultaneously transforms one's present existence into a state of being projected toward the future ideal. Indeed, the decision is knowing only in the sense that it is a transforming self-reflection. Similarly, the decision is *acting*, which reorders one's existential situation and affects the whole dimension of one's life. Yet as an actualization of reflective thinking, it is not a random act. Thus the decision is acting only in the sense that it is an intentional self-affirmation. A speculative thought without much experiential significance, or an ephemeral act without much intellectual value, can never become a part of the inner decision. Knowing, which causes fundamental changes in one's existence, and acting, which brings new depth to one's perception, form a unity in the structure of inner decision.

The unity of knowing and acting so conceived is neither an achieved state nor a desired ideal. As Wang Yang-ming says, the unity is the "original nature" of both knowing and acting in the process of man's inner decision to transform and perfect himself. In Yang-ming's words, "Knowing is the beginning of acting; acting is the completion of knowing."[20] Indeed, "Knowing is the crystallization of the will to act and acting is the task of carrying out that knowledge."[21] The inseparability of knowing and acting is thus more than a corrective measure; it is a description of their true nature. If we investigate the *pen-t'i* (original structure) of knowing and acting, we are compelled to recognize that "without knowing, acting is impossible; without acting, knowing is impossible."[22] The real nature of knowing in this respect is to be found in the actual transforming effects it has exerted on behavior. Similarly, the real nature of acting is to be found in the actual deepening effects it contributes to self-knowledge. Therefore, to know human nature is not merely to gain some objective knowledge about it, but to act accordingly. To act, then, is not only to change the external world but also to deepen and broaden self-knowledge.

The inseparability of knowing and acting does not imply a closed system. The inner decision, as both an act and a process, is always dynamically interrelated with the life situations one personally encounters. Self-knowledge can never be authenticated if one is isolated from the ethicosocial context in which he becomes aware of the true self. The Confucianist further contends that the true self can never be fully realized except in the network of human-relatedness. As the *Great Learning* maintains, self-cultivation has to lead to communal values such as harmony in the family, order in the state, and peace in the world.[23] Implicit in this approach is Wang Yang-stimng's atement: "The great man regards Heaven, Earth, and the myriad things as one body."[24] He is able to do so not by any deliberate effort, but by being himself. If one fails to attain this, he should follow the example of the great archer: "When he misses the center of the target, he turns around and seeks the cause of failure within himself."[25]

Although this does not mean that one is "fated" to travel the concrete path of self-realization alone, it at least means the burden of the journey rests on the individual. One of Confucius's most devoted disciples, Tseng Tzu, was so concerned with his heavy charge that he described his way of life as walking on the edge of a deep valley or as treading thin ice.[26] Each step necessitates an inner decision, which, as both knowing and acting, is the only access to the ontology of man.

Thus we come to the crucial issue of communication.

V

In Section II, I described *chien-hsing* as a holistic process, involving both the *ta-t'i* and the *hsiao-t'i*. I also stated that self-transformation in this connection denies, or slights, neither spirituality nor corporality. Mencius says: "If a man who cares about food and drink can do so without neglecting any part of his person, then his mouth and belly are much more than just a foot or an inch of his skin."[27] If the *hsiao-t'i* embraces the whole structure of the bodily constitution, how much more so must be the embracing quality of the *ta-t'i*. Again, Mencius states that the cultivation of mind necessarily "manifests itself in the face, giving it a sleek appearance. It also shows in the back and extends to the limbs, rendering their message intelligible without words."[28] It is only in this sense that Mencius suggests further: "Our body and complexion are given to us by Heaven. Only a sage can give his body complete fulfillment."[29]

It should be pointed out, however, that *chien-hsing,* as the complete fulfillment of one's body, must not be confined to the anthropological structure. Paradoxically, unless one goes beyond the restrictions of anthropology, one can never fully realize his nature as a man. This brings us to a highly controversial statement in Mencius: "All the ten thousand things are there in me. There is no greater joy for me than to find, on self-examination, that I am sincere (*ch'eng*) to myself."[30] To illustrate this point, I shall present an inquiry into the concept of *ch'eng* in the *Doctrine of the Mean* as understood by Neo-Confucian thinkers such as Chou Tun-i and Liu Tsung-chou (Nien-t'ai, 1578–1645).

94

It should be mentioned at the beginning that "sincerity" is a poor approximation of the Chinese character *ch'eng*, which etymologically also connotes *completion, actualization,* or *perfection.* Such connotations of the English word "sincerity" as *honesty, genuineness,* and *truth* are also included in *ch'eng.* However, since *ch'eng* conveys only good implications, it cannot be used in a negative sense, to mean, for example, a firm belief in the validity of one's own opinions ("He is an entirely sincere and cruel tyrant"). For the sake of convenience, I will use—sometimes misuse—the word "sincerity" in this specific context to present the Confucian viewpoint.

Since the Confucianist believes that both the ultimate ground and the actual strength of becoming a sage lie in the very nature of man, the act of establishing the will is ultimately an internal self-transformation. A defining characteristic of man is thus his possession of the need and power for transforming himself from the existence of an ordinary man into that of a sage. Furthermore, since internal self-transformation is actually a process of self-purification and self-authentication, one fulfills one's highest obligations as man, in the words of Chang Tsai, simply by being unceasing in one's humanity.[31] Similarly, once the process of self-transformation is stopped, one gradually ceases to be human. To use Ch'eng Hao's analogy, this is like paralysis of the four limbs. When the sensitivity to further self-realization becomes numb, the scope and depth of one's humanity are bound to be restricted.[32] An extreme form of such a restriction is described in the Chinese vernacular as "walking corpse and running fresh." This seemingly naive position is based on an ontological insight into the nature of man.

According to the *Doctrine of the Mean,* man's sincere nature is imparted by Heaven; to follow the truth of human nature is the authentic Way, and to cultivate the Way is the original meaning of teaching.[33] Man's fundamental approach to Heaven is therefore to be sought in the structure of man itself. A transcendent reality completely outside the structure of man is either inconceivable or irrelevant to man's ultimate concern. Paradoxically, the only way man can transcend himself is through a process of "humanization," which in this specific context means a return to one's sincere nature. One may, of course, raise the objection, Why should man try to transcend himself in the first place? The answer lies in the basic *Problematik* of Confucianism: if man does not transcend his anthropological structure, he cannot fulfill his design as a man in the most sincere sense of the word. Indeed, "Sincerity is the Way of Heaven. To learn how to be sincere is the Way of man."[34] The sage, as the most sincere man, is "naturally and easily in harmony with the Way,"[35] for he is identified with Heaven. When one is not yet completely united with Heaven, he must try to be sincere by "choosing the good and holding fast to it,"[36] to develop fully his own humanity.

The *Doctrine of the Mean* further suggests that sincerity entails *ming*, "enlightening insights," and the primary function of teaching is to see to it that enlightening insights lead eventually to sincerity.[37] For the enlightening insight, as basically a form of cognitive understanding, must find its resting place, as it were, in the transforming power of sincerity. That transforming power is inherent in sincerity can be shown by the following statement:

> Only he who is absolutely sincere can realize his nature to the utmost. Able to do this, he is able to do the same to the nature of other men. Able to do this, he is able to do the same to the nature of things. Able to do this, he can assist the transforming and nourishing of Heaven and Earth. Being able to do this, he can form a trinity with Heaven and Earth.[38]

Implicit in this quotation is the assertion that the man who is absolutely sincere is the same man who has completely realized himself through internal self-transformation. Such a man is thought to have the power of extending the task of self-realization to the cosmos in general. For being absolutely sincere (genuine, truthful, and honest) entails the ability to actualize, complete, and perfect one's true nature, which ontologically means the nature of other men, of things, and of the universe.

It is interesting to note in this context that the act of self-transformation and the state of sincerity are thought to be inseparable. To be sincere is to realize oneself through self-transformation; to engage oneself in self-transformation is simultaneously a necessary expression of being sincere. Since self-transformation is a process of becoming, and sincerity is usually thought to be a state of being, it means that the ordinary distinction of becoming and being is no

96

longer applicable in this case. To define man as a self-transforming and self-realizing agent is to characterize him in terms of his becoming process.

This Confucian position can be labelled as humanist only in a very special sense. The man of humanity, being the most sincere manifestation of human nature, must also be able to realize the nature of the "myriad things" and assist Heaven and Earth in their transforming and nourishing functions. If one cannot transcend one's anthropological structure, let alone egoistic structure, one's self-transformation is still in the initial stage. Unless one can realize the nature of all things to form a trinity with Heaven and Earth, one's self-realization cannot be complete. In this sense, humanity implies a profound care for and deep commitment to the well-being of the natural world—indeed, to the cosmos.

In light of the foregoing, sincerity seems to have dynamism of its own. It seeks to reorder the external world in such a way as to bring about its own realization. Sincerity thus conceived symbolizes the mystic working of creativity itself. The *Doctrine of the the Mean* states:

> Sincerity necessarily leads to visibility. From visibility it leads to manifestation. From manifestation, it leads to illumination (or enlightenment). Illumination entails activity. Activity entails change. And change leads to transformation. Only he who is absolutely sincere can eventually transform.[39]

To be sure, this may very well be interpreted as the mystic experience of the absolutely sincere sage. Yet the *Mean* further says: "Sincerity means self-completing, and the Way is self-directing. Sincerity is the beginning and end of things. Without sincerity there can be nothing."[40] Sincerity in this sense is both the creative process by which the existence of things becomes possible, and the ground of being on which the things as they really are ultimately rests.

Actually, the mystic experience of the sage is itself a manifestation of sincerity. For sincerity as a transcendent reality is the "Way of Heaven," which is actualizable through man's conscious effort to be sincere, that is, through the "Way of man." The sage, being completely unified or identified with Heaven, thus transcends anthropological restrictions, embodies the most authentic humanity, and participates in the great cosmic transformation itself. In the words of the *Mean:*

> One who is absolutely sincere can regulate and attune the great relations of mankind, establish the great foundations of humanity, and understand the transforming and nourishing process of Heaven and Earth. Does he depend on anything else? How pure and genuine—he is humanity. How deep and unfathomable—he is ocean. How vast and great—he is heaven. How can he comprehend this, if he does not have intelligence, perception, sageliness, and wisdom to carry out the virtue of Heaven.[41]

The sage can perform such a task, not because of some superhuman endowment, but because he is absolutely truthful to his own humanity. Although sincerity is a transcendent reality, its creative power never ceases to function in the inner dimensions of humanity. Since man's nature is imparted by Heaven, the creative power of sincerity is inherent in the very structure of man. To learn how to be sincere is ultimately an attempt to become truly human. For humanity in its ultimate sense is the fullest manifestation of sincerity. Accordingly the sage participates in cosmic creativity simply by his humaneness. Being absolutely sincere, the sage humanizes in the spirit of cosmic creativity. That humanity can assume such a creative dimension again lies in the nature of sincerity itself:

> Therefore absolute sincerity is ceaseless. Being ceaseless, it is lasting. Being lasting, it is evident. Being evident, it is infinite. Being infinite, it is broad and deep. Being broad and deep, it is high and illuminating. Because it is broad and deep it is laden with all things. Because it is high and illuminating it shines on all things. Because it is infinite and lasting it completes all things. In being broad and deep, it identifies with Earth. In being high and illuminating, it identifies with Heaven. In being infinite, it is limitless. Such being its nature, it manifests without trace, changes without motion, and completes without any effort.[42]

The "concrete-universal" approach in Confucianism may be summarized as follows: If one intends to become an authentic man, one must establish the will to become a whole man, which means the fulfillment of both human corporality and spirituality. The establishment of the will as an inner decision is itself both *knowing* and *acting*. Only in the unity of knowing and acting can the true nature of inner decision be found, because the root of self-realization is inherent in the very structure of man. Self-realization, however, is not a process of individuation; it is primarily a course of universal communion. The more one sinks into the depth of one's being, the more he transcends his anthropological restriction. Underlying this paradox is the Confucian belief that the true nature of man and the real creativity of the cosmos are both "grounded" in *sincerity*. When one, through self-cultivation, becomes absolutely sincere, one is the most authentic man and simultaneously participates in the transforming and nourishing process of the cosmos. To do so is to fulfill one's human nature.

NOTES

[1]See Stuart Hampshire, "Freedom of Mind," in his *Freedom of Mind and Other Essays* (Princeton: Princeton University Press, 1971), pp. 3–20.

[2]Gabriel Marcel, *Searchings* (New York: Newman Press, 1967), p. 39.

[3]Of course it can be suggested that doing philosophy in the form of analyzing ordinary language may also have a profound religious import. It is quite conceivable that many philosophers are engaged in the task of linguistic analysis as a form of mental discipline, if not of spiritual self-transformation.

[4]Quoted in Marcel, p. 31.

[5]If religiophilosophy is used in a broad sense, it may also include the philosophies of Merleau-Ponty and Jean-Paul Sartre. For the kind of sociopolitical totalization they envision is in the last analysis a spiritual transformation of the greatest magnitude.

[6]Cf. the original formulation of this concept in *I-ching* (the *Book of Change*), commentary on hexagram no. 1, *ch'ien* (Heaven) and its Neo-Confucian development in the "T'ai-chi t'u-shuo" of Chou Tun-i (*Chou Tzu ch'üan-shu*, chaps. 1–2, pp. 4–32). For a brief discussion on this issue, see Tu Wei-ming, "The Neo-Confucian Concept of Man," in *Philosophy East and West* 21, no. 1 (Jan. 1971): 80. (Above, p. 81.)

[7]Since the revival of Neo-Confucian thinking by modern Chinese philosophers such as Hsiung Shih-li (1885–1968), Liang Shu-ming (1893–), and Fung Yu-lan (1895–), there has been a continuous effort to reconstruct Chinese philosophy in the spirit of Confucianism. The works of T'ang Chün-i, Mou Tsung-san, and Hsü Fu-kuan are paradigmatic examples of such an effort. Unfortunately, their writings are little known outside of Hong Kong and Taiwan. An introductory account of the early development of this school can be found in Wing-tsit Chan's *Religious Trends in Modern China* (New York: Columbia University Press, 1953).

[8]Cf. *Mencius*, 6A.15. For an English translation, see *Mencius*, trans. by D. C. Lau

(London: Penguin Books, 1970), p. 168. Lau's Introduction gives an excellent summary of Mencius' spiritual orientation.

[9] *Mencius*, 7A. 1. For the translation, see Lau, p. 182.

[10] The classical formulation of such a position is to be found in *Chung-yung* (the *Doctrine of the Mean*), chap. 23. For an English translation, see Fung Yu-lan, *A Short History of Chinese Philosophy*, ed. Derk Bodde (New York: Macmillan Co., 1948), p. 176.

[11] In the last few decades many serious attempts have been made to study the "true spirit" of classical Confucianism. Textual analyses have been used to find out the original meanings of the sayings of Confucius and Mencius. However, the conscious effort to arrive at an objective understanding of Chinese thought in its formative years has frequently been influenced by the ethos of Ch'ing learning and European sinological scholasticism. If we must pass judgment on the authenticity of the Neo-Confucian interpretation of classical Confucianism, it is important that we arrive at a higher level of intellectual sophistication. Only then will we be able to analyze critically the philosophical presuppositions of the Neo-Confucianists.

[12] *Analects*, 2:4.

[13] It seems very likely that the Neo-Confucian interpretation was influenced by Buddhism, but in Hsü Shen's *Shuo-wen* (Explanation of characters), a first century dictionary, *chüeh* (enlightening) is used to explain *hsüeh* (learning). This may only indicate phonetic and etymological similarities between the two characters, but there is also a strong indication that a semantic link does exist between them as well.

[14] *Hsün Tzu*, chap. 1, "Ch'üan-hsüeh" (An encouragement to study).

[15] *Ta-hsüeh* (the *Great Learning*), chap. 2.

[16] *Mencius*, 2A.2. Lau, pp. 76–78.

[17] Cf. *Nien-p'u* in *Yang-ming ch'üan-shu*, 32: 7a–8b (*Ssu-pu pei-yao* edition).

[18] For a general discussion of the concept, see Wing-tsit Chan, "The Evolution of the Neo-Confucian Concept of Li as Principle," in *Tsing-hua Journal of Chinese Studies*, n.s., 4, no. 2 (February, 1964): 123–148.

[19] Cf. *Yang-ming ch'üan-shu*, 33:16b.

[20] *Ibid.*, 1: 3a–b. For an English translation of Wang Yang-ming's *Ch'uan-hsi lu*, see Wing-tsit Chan, *Instructions for Practical Living and Other Neo-Confucian Writings by Wang Yang-ming* (New York: Columbia University Press, 1963), pp. 11 and 30.

[21] Cf. Wing-tsit Chan, p. 11.

[22] *Ibid.*

[23] *Ta-hsüeh*, chap. 1.

[24] *Yang-ming ch'üan-shu*, 26:1b.

[25] *Chung-yung*, chap. 14.

[26] *Analects*, 8.3. Actually Tseng Tzu was quoting the *Book of Poetry* to illustrate his point:

> In fear and trembling,
> With caution and care,
> As though on the brink of a chasm,
> As though treading thin ice.

For the translation, cf. *The Analects of Confucius*, trans. by Arthur Waley (London: Allen and Unwin, 1938), p. 133.

[27]*Mencius*, 6A. 14. Lau, 168.

[28]*Ibid.*, 7A. 21. Lau, 186.

[29]*Ibid.*, 7A. 38. Lau, 191. I believe that if Heaven is not misunderstood as anthropomorphic, it conveys the meaning of the Chinese word *t'ien* quite well.

[30]*Ibid.*, 7A. 4. Lau, 182. I have changed the word "true" to "sincere."

[31]Chang Tsai, *Cheng-meng*, chap. 6.

[32]Ch'eng Hao, *Erh-Ch'eng i-shu*, 2A: 2a-b.

[33]*Chung-yung*, chap. 1.

[34]*Ibid.*, chap. 20.

[35]*Ibid.*

[36]*Ibid.*

[37]*Ibid.*, chap. 21.

[38]*Ibid.*, chap. 22.

[39]*Ibid.*, chap. 23.

[40]*Ibid.*. chap. 25.

[41]*Ibid.*, chap. 32.

[42]*Ibid.*, chap. 26.

7. 'Inner Experience':
The Basis of Creativity
in Neo-Confucian Thinking

Writing in *Creative Fidelity*, Gabriel Marcel asserts:

The problem now was not so much one of building as of digging; philosophical activity was now definable as a drilling rather than a construction. The further I went in the examination of *my experience*, and into the hidden meaning of these two words, the more unacceptable became the idea of a particular body of thoughts which was my system, one I could call my own; the presumption that the universe could be encapsuled in a more or less rigorously related set of formulas, seemed absurd.[1]

To be sure, Marcel's rebellion against the construction of a disinterestedly argued system of ideas as a legitimate form of philosophical inquiry must be understood in terms of his self-image as a "Neo-Socratic" and in the context of religious existentialism.[2] But his singleminded effort to underline the primacy of inner experience, as a challenge to the main stream of Western philosophy, has a profound meaning for our attempt to apprehend the Neo-Confucian mode of thinking. Indeed, the direction of his questioning, especially his declaration that "philosophy is experience *transmuted* into thought," will help us to appreciate more fully the "central datum" in the Neo-Confucian tradition. Since our immediate concern is not to raise an issue in comparative philosophy, the viewpoint of the brilliant Christian philosopher is mentioned here merely as a way of introducing the subject of the present study.

The need for the construction of a general theory of metaphysics or ethics for its own sake never occurs to the Neo-Confucianist as a major concern in his quest for self-realization. Either by conscious choice or by default, he does not pose theoretical questions about the what and the why of man from an objective point of view. He neither seeks nor establishes logical systems to demonstrate his philosophy of life. He resists the temptation to abstract a set of encapsulated formulas from his spiritual awareness. And he refuses to subject his moral feelings to an externalized pattern of intellectual argumentation. Instead he focuses on the cultivation of the inner experience, both as a way of self-knowledge and as a method of true communion with the other.

The term *inner experience* is employed here to signify a cluster of Neo-Confucian ideas. For the sake of expediency, I shall limit this part of the discussion to only one of the several relevant key concepts, *t'i*, which literally means "to embody." Since *t'i* as a noun denotes the body in terms of both its form and substance, when it is used as a verb or an adjective it frequently conveys the meaning of involving the whole person. It should be pointed out that *t'i* in a derivative sense may also refer to the structure and essence of reality. But in the present context it has little connection with the highly controversial problem of the *t'i-yung* ("substance-function") dichotomy in Chinese philosophy. Rather, it forms compounds with words such as *ch'a* ("examination"), *wei* ("taste"), *jen* ("comprehension"), *hui* ("understanding"), *cheng* ("confirmation"), and *yen* ("verification"). Sometimes it is simply used as a verb by being attached to the final particle *chih*.[3]

Underlying the meaning of these divergent compounds is the concerted theme of total commitment, involving the entire "body and mind." Thus *t'i-ch'a* in its original meaning refers to a deep examination of one's being rather than a thorough investigation of some external thing. Similarly *t'i-wei* in a strict sense is not applied to any sensory perception of a transient nature. Its usage is limited to the kind of "taste" or "flavor" that can be developed only through a long and strenuous process of self-cultivation. *T'i-jen* certainly entails the mental activity of cognition, but it involves more than the comprehension of something out there. Since the act of comprehending in this particular connection requires a continuous process of interiorization, it is inconceivable that one can have *t'i-jen* in the true sense of the term without undergoing a significant transformation of one's way of life.

T'i-hui therefore means to understand experientially, as if one has "encountered" or "met" in person, that which is to be understood. To know an objective truth in passing without deepening one's self-knowledge is certainly not to understand in the form of *t'i-hui*. Accordingly *t'i-cheng* does not mean to confirm the validity of a theorem by a set of empirically tested criteria. It points to a kind of "confirmation" in which the truthfulness of an idea cannot be demonstrated by logical argument but must be lived by concrete experience. However, such an experience is neither mysterious nor subjective, although its meaning can be readily acknowledged only by those who have tuned their minds and bodies to appreciate it. In the same way, *t'i-yen* implies the willingness to devote one's whole being to an ideal or a truth. Indeed, the term connotes such a deep and lasting commitment that its usage is restricted to "great ideas" such as life, love, and beauty. As a result, when the Neo-Confucian master suggests to his students that the only way to take hold of a certain dimension of his teaching is to "embody it" (*t'i-chih*), he is absolutely serious. The absence of a clearly articulated position on such matters is not a result of the teacher's deliberate attempt to remain silent as a pedagogical device, but of his sincere determination to be truthful to the very nature of such a teaching.

In the consciousness of the Neo-Confucian thinker, the main task is neither to build an ethical system nor to analyze a metaphysical theory. To teach is a way of manifesting what one has learned through self-cultivation, and to learn is a method of crystallizing what one has taught by personal example. It is in this connection that "teaching and learning are mutually encouraging" (*chiao-hsüeh hsiang-chang*), and "exemplary teaching" (*shen-chiao*), as against teaching by word (*yen-chiao*), is considered a better avenue to learning. Consequently, the Neo-Confucian thinker characterizes his knowledge as the "learning of the body and mind" (*shen-hsin chih hsüeh*); which is also understood as the way of becoming a genuine person.

The decision to focus on the problem of *how* rather than the cognitive issues of *what* and *why* certainly has many far-reaching implications. The basic concern, however, is to refrain from converting issues of profound human significance into mere objects of speculation. Understandably, the majority of Neo-Confucian writings are neither expositions of ideas *qua* ideas nor treatises on purely contemplative issues; they are rather records of spiritual quests and events. They mainly take the form of dialogues, aphorisms, reflections, anecdotes, letters, and poetry. Even in some of the highly sophisticated essays on "humanity" (*jen*), emphasis is still on experiential understanding rather than the art of argumentation. This emphasis on the personality behind the mode of articulation impels the Neo-Confucian to think not only with his head but with his entire "body and mind."

To think with one's whole being is not to cogitate on some external truth. It is a way of examining, tasting, comprehending, understanding, confirming, and verifying the quality of one's life. Underlying this kind of reflection is a process of digging and drilling that necessarily leads to an awareness of the self not as a mental construct but as an experienced reality. Wang Yang-ming (1472–1529) states that his ideas become empty words if they are detached from the concrete experiential bases on which they are meaningfully organized:

> I have come to the realization of the teaching of *liang-chih* . . . [innate knowledge] through a hundred deaths and a thousand hardships. It is with utmost reluctance that I have articulated [the totality of my inner experience] in a single breath. I strongly fear that the student might easily grasp [this simple formulation of] it, treat it as a circumstantial notion, and play with it, without solidly dwelling in it and strenuously working at it. This would certainly turn his back upon [the real meaning of] such knowledge.[4]

To be sure, Yang-ming's "dynamic idealism" is not representative of the dominant trend of Sung learning. Nor is it necessarily in line with the philosophical orientation of the early Ming masters, who can be legitimately characterized as followers of the Chu Hsi (1130–1200) and Ch'eng I (1033–1107) school. But Yang-ming's concern in this particular connection seems to have been shared by virtually all major thinkers in the Neo-Confucian tradition. In fact, many less famous scholars in this period seem also to have internalized this aspect of exemplary teaching. Hsüeh Hsüan (1393–

105

1464), the early Ming master, delineates his approach to knowledge as *shih* (literally, "solid").[5] For, as a process of self-fulfillment rather than an accumulation of empirical data, the knowledge obtained must be "solidly" sealed to one's whole existence. This emphasis on experiential learning is reminiscent of Ch'eng I's characterization of the entire tradition of Confucian teaching as *shih-hsüeh* ("solid learning").[6] Indeed, Ts'ao Tuan's (1376–1434) instruction on the cultivation of the *hsin* ("mind-heart"),[7] Wu Yü-pi's (1392–1469) insistence on self-discipline,[8] and Hu Chü-jen's (1434–1484) devotion to the practice of reverence[9] all point to the central concern that inner experience is a prerequisite for appropriating the meaning of their teaching. They can well appreciate Lu Hsiang-shan's (1139–1193) command that his students make an existential decision as a precondition for taking up learning with him.[10]

We may tentatively define this approach to philosophical thinking as "concrete-universal."[11] It is commonly accepted that universal principles can only be obtained by transcending the particular. To achieve a high level of generality, thought has to be detached from the concrete. To construct a theorem that can have some universal claim necessitates a process of abstraction. In the present case, however, the inner experience of a concrete person serves as the real basis of generalization. And only through a total immersion in one's own being can the source of universality be reached. Mencius' statement that "he who has completely realized his mind knows his nature; knowing his nature, he knows Heaven"[12] is therefore a classical formulation of such an orientation. Commenting on this passage, Lu Hsiang-shan advances his idealistic thesis: "Mind is only one mind. My own mind, or that of my friend, or that of a sage of a thousand generations hence–their minds are all only [one] like this. The extent of the mind is very great. If I can completely realize my mind, I thereby become identified with Heaven. Study consists of nothing more than to apprehend this."[13]

Implicit in the above statement is the belief that one's inner experience is the real ground of communication. It is not only the ultimate basis of human relationships but also the foundation on which man, according to the *Doctrine of the Mean*, "participates in the transforming and nourishing operations of Heaven and Earth."[14] Therefore, the "inner experience" we have been talking about is neither a kind of intuitionism nor a solipsistic state. It is not even a spark of inspiration. Actually, the apparent emphasis on "subjectivity" is not at all in conflict with the view that "to conquer oneself and return to propriety is humanity."[15] Indeed, the ego has to be transcended and sometimes even denied for the sake of realizing the genuine self. For self-control, overcoming the ego, is the authentic way to gain inner experience. This path is universally open to every human being, but it ought to be traveled concretely by each person.

The cultivation of an inner experience is consequently a search for self-identity. Yet in Neo-Confucian thinking this process of looking into oneself does not at all alienate one from society. It actually impels one to enter into what may be called "the community of the like-minded" or even "the community of selfhood." In such a community one not only befriends one's contemporaries, but one also establishes an immediate relationship with the ancients. Wang P'in (Hsin-po, 1082–1153), a relatively unknown thinker of the Sung dynasty, captures this spirit well in his remarkable statement:

> The former sages and the later sages are in perfect harmony. It is because they do not transmit the Tao of the sage but the mind of the sage. Actually they do not transmit the mind of the sage but their own minds. Indeed my mind is not different from that of the sage. It is vast and infinite. It embraces myriad goods. To expand this mind is thus the way to transmit the Tao of the sages.[16]

To appreciate the Way of the Sages is not only to study its external manifestations, such as in the Classics, but to understand the "intentionality" (*i*) behind the spoken word. Actually, the intentionality of the Sages can never be grasped as merely an external phenomenon. It must be savored in one's own mind. Indeed, only in cultivating an inner experience of the mind can the Way of the Sages be fully "compassed." When one establishes a "spiritual communion" (*shen-hui*) with the ancients, one emerges as their spokesman and delegate. One bridges the gap between one's spiritual contemporaries and one's temporal colleagues in performing the creative act of a living transmitter.

What one tries to transmit is of course not the form or even the content of the ancients but their minds. To imitate their form would be to behave like Wang Ken (1483–1540), whose effort to dress like

107

an ancient sage merely credited him with the reputation of being *ku-kuai*, "archaic and weird."[17] Only through a constantly active process of "internalization"—in the present context tantamount to self-realization—is one capable of transmitting the intentionality of the ancients. In a deeper sense, the intentionality of the ancients is really an experienced reality of one's inner self, but with the challenge of the ancients, one can more fully "witness" the subtle meaning of it.

Since the mind of the ancients can never be reproduced, transmission in a real sense always implies an act of creativity—not creating something out of nothing, to be sure, but deepening one's self-awareness to the extent that its quality is comparable to that of the ancients. Each transmission, in this connection, is itself a unique event that can be located in a specific spatiotemporal sequence. It is the cumulative achievement of these events that constitutes the so-called Great Tradition. To be an integral part of such a tradition requires creative adaptation and spiritual metamorphosis, which in the Neo-Confucian terminology is commonly known as *pien-hua ch'i-chih*, "transforming one's concrete being."[18]

When "inner experience" is conceived as the basis of creativity, the art of constructing some philosophical system *ex nihilo*, no matter how "ingenious" (*ch'iao*) it may be, cannot be accepted as profound. Great moments in thought are those in which some perennial concerns of man are perceptively articulated, not by a reflection on abstract principles but by an insightful grasp of concrete human situations. Profundity in thought is thus understood in terms of one's ability to penetrate the bedrock of one's given tradition, which necessarily involves a strong sense of history. However, far from being bound to the past as fixed entity, to have a historical consciousness is to develop the power of creativity not in isolation but in a dialogue with those great historical personalities by whom one's own work is meaningfully judged and properly appreciated. To the Neo-Confucian thinker, what happens here and now is more than the demonstration of a single individual genius; it is the fulfillment of a historical mission and the vivification of an accumulative tradition. The success of a creative act does not signify a departure from the past.

Rather it is a new realization of what has long been intended by the seminal minds of one's chosen transmission. To pursue antiquity therefore means to dig and drill into that historicity which symbolizes the most significant landmarks of human achievement in the past. The individual talent does not go through a process of depersonalization in order to become an integral part of his tradition, for the basis on which he can embody the essence of the ancients and generate his source of creativity is his true self.

NOTES

[1]Trans. Robert Rosthal (New York: Farrar, Strauss & Co., 1964), p. 14.

[2]Although Marcel is better known in America as a leading Christian existentialist, he has repeatedly rejected such a label. He prefers to be called a "Neo-Socratic." In a broad sense, however, Marcel, together with Paul Tillich and Martin Buber, may be referred to as an important architect of religious existentialism in the twentieth century.

[3]Virtually all of the terms used in the present context have appeared in Neo-Confucian writings. In fact, this particular usage of *t'i* can also be found in the *Doctrine of the Mean*. Suggestively, Wing-tsit Chan has rendered the phrase *t'i ch'ün-ch'en* as "identifying oneself with the welfare of the whole body of officers." See his *A Source Book in Chinese Philosophy* (Princeton, N.J.: Princeton University Press, 1963), p. 105. For the original source see the *Doctrine of the Mean*, trans. James Legge (Oxford: Clarendon Press, 1893), ch. 20.

[4]See his *Nien-p'u*, under 50 *sui*, first month, in *Yang-ming ch'üan-shu* (*Ssu-pu pei-yao* ed.), 33:16b.

[5]The concept occurs quite frequently in Hsüeh Hsüan's writings. For example, see his *Tu-shu lu* (1751 ed.), 2:8, 4:7.

[6]Ch'eng I's statement is quoted by Chu Hsi in his introductory note to the *Doctrine of the Mean* in his *Ssu-shu chi-chu*.

[7]For an example of Ts'ao Tuan's emphasis on *hsin*, see the following statement: "In everything one must devote one's effort to the exercise of the mind, and that is the main road of entering into the gate of Confucian teaching." Huang Tsung-hsi, *Ming-ju hsüeh-an* (*Ssu-pu pei-yao* ed.), xliv/1b.

[8]His dedication to self-discipline is vividly demonstrated in his *Jih-lu*. See the first *chüan* of *K'ang-chai hsien-sheng chi*.

[9]See his *Chü-yeh lu* (*Cheng-i t'ang* ed.), 8:4–5.

[10]Although Lu Hsiang-shan has been credited with the notion of *li-chih* (to establish one's will, or simply to make an existential decision), Chu Hsi has also put much emphasis on the importance of making up one's mind to become a sage as a precondition for Confucian learning. See Ch'ien Mu, *Chu Tzu hsin hsüeh-an* (Tai-

pei: San-min Book Co., 1971), 2:364–78.

[11] In my opinion, the best analysis of this kind of approach to date is in Mou Tsung-san's *Hsin-t'i yü hsing-t'i* (Taipei: San-min Book Co., 1968), 1:1–10.

[12] *Mencius* 7A.1.

[13] *Hsiang-shan ch'üan-chi* (*Ssu-pu pei-yao* ed.), 35:10a. For this translation, see Chan, *Source Book*, p. 585.

[14] Ch. 22.

[15] *Analects* 12.1.

[16] The statement is found in Wang P'in's memorial to Emperor Kao Tsung, which is included in the "Chen-che hsüeh-an" section of the *Sung-Yüan hsüeh-an* (*Ssu-pu pei-yao* ed.), 19:1b. This statement has been wrongly attributed to the famous Sung thinker Ch'eng Hao (1032–1085) ever since Huang Tsung-hsi mistakenly identified the statements as contained in Ch'eng Hao's memorial to Emperor Shen Tsung, in his contribution to the *Sung-Yüan hsüeh-an* (see 13:15). Several important anthologies of Neo-Confucian sayings have also attributed the statement to Ch'eng Hao. For a general discussion on this issue, see Ch'ien Mu, *Chu Tzu hsin hsüeh-an*, 3:300–301 and 540–42.

[17] *Ming-ju hsüeh-an*, 32:6.

[18] *Ch'i-chih* is a difficult concept to translate. In the Neo-Confucian literature, it is frequently used in conjunction with *i-li*. For example, *i-li chih-hsing* refers to man's moral nature, whereas *ch'i-chih chih hsing* refers to his physical nature. According to Chu Hsi, Chang Tsai (1020–1077), an uncle of the Ch'eng brothers, made a great contribution to Confucian learning by stressing the importance of understanding man's *ch'i-chih chih-hsing*.

8. Mind and Human Nature
(Review Article)*

One of the most fundamental concerns of Confucian humanism is how to become a sage through self-effort. Since the emphasis is on the experiential how rather than on the cognitive why, the road to sagehood is basically a matter of spiritual quest and not merely of intellectual argumentation. Yet since the time of Mencius, the problems of mind (*hsin*) and human nature (*hsing*) have become prominent, for the commitment to attain sagehood (the most authentic, genuine, and sincere humanity) rests on an ontological understanding of true humanity. Such an understanding probes the being of man, not only as a social reality but also as an ethicoreligious agent.

Indeed, man is more than the sum of genes, plus psychic energy, plus sociological forces. He is also a creative participant in the cosmic process. And, according to Confucian philosophy, it is in this very process that the ultimate meaning of human existence really lies. Therefore one of the pivotal notions in Confucian symbolism is "the establishment of the ultimacy of man" (*li jen-chi*). The notion, which presupposes an appreciation of man's metaphysical status, is according to Professor Mou Tsung-san first conceived in the classical Confucian writings such as *Mencius*, the *Doctrine of the Mean* (*Chung-yung*), and the *Book of Change* (*I-ching*). Professor Mou further contends that these three classics together with the *Analects* constitute the most authentic manifestation of Confucian philosophy.

In such a philosophy human nature is understood to be good, for the ultimate basis of man's self-perfection lies in the very structure of man. Indeed, man can become what he ought to be not by the interference of any transcendent reality, or the "wholly other," but by the process of self-transformation, which is an incessant process

***Hsin-t'i yü hsing-t'i* (The substance of the mind and the substance of human nature), by Mou Tsung-san. Taipei: Cheng-chung Book Co., 1969. 3 vols.

111

of spiritual "appropriation." This is not in any sense an argument for anthropocentrism, because the process of spiritual appropriation necessarily involves the creative process of Heaven and Earth, which form a triad with the ontology of man. Thus, man is that being who through self-transformation, a kind of inner illumination, realizes not only the moral goodness that is intrinsic to his nature but also the cosmic creativity that embraces the universe in its entirety.

Professor Mou maintains that such a philosophical formulation of the notion of man in Confucianism is due to a primordial insight into the mind as both an ontological being and a cosmological activity. Since the mind is what makes man uniquely human, it is in Mencian terminology the "great self" (*ta-t'i*), or the true human nature. Similarly, Confucian God-terms such as *tao* (the Way), *jen* (Humanity), *ch'eng* (Sincerity) and *chung* (the Mean) all point to that human reality which is both ontological and cosmological. Professor Mou suggests that the philosophical heritage in classical Confucianism has already pointed to the way of constructing a "moral metaphysics," an intellectual enterprise that Kant failed to develop in his metaphysics of morals. This suggestion, which is only briefly discussed in Professor Mou's Prolegomenon (*tsung-lun*), becomes the central theme of another book entitled, *Chih te chih-chüeh yü Chung-kuo che-hsüeh* (Intellectual intuition and Chinese philosophy), published in 1971 in Taipei by the Shang-wu Book Company.

In light of the above, Professor Mou describes the Neo-Confucian development as both a natural fruition of the germinal wisdom first conceived in the Mencian tradition of Confucianism, and an ingenious departure from the same spiritual orientation just mentioned. The former refers to what may be called the "authentic line" of Neo-Confucian philosophy, which is further divided into two complementary streams: (1) Chou Tuni-i (Lien-hsi, 1017–1073)— Chang Tsai (Heng-ch'ü, 1020–1077)—Ch'eng Hao (Ming-tao, 1032–1085)—Hu Hung (Wu-feng, 1100–1155)—Liu Tsung-chou (Chi-shan, 1578–1645), and (2) Lu Hsiang-shan (Chiu-yüan, 1139–1193)—Wang Yang-ming (Shou-jen, 1472–1529). The latter refers to what may be called the "actual line" of Neo-Confucian philosophy which mainly consists of Ch'eng I (I-ch'uan, 1033–1107) and Chu Hsi (Yüan-hui, 1130–1200). Contrary to the commonly accepted dichotomous categorization of the Neo-Confucian tradition into the

Ch'eng-Chu School (the Rationalist School or the School of Principle) and the Lu-Wang School (the Idealist School or the School of
Mind), Neo-Confucianism is here divided into three, clearly distin-
guishable trends.

What is the nature of this interpretation, and what kind of
justification is there to hold such a view? Of course, the inadequacy of
the dichotomous categorization has been recognized by other scholars
as well. Professor Wing-tsit Chan in *A Source Book in Chinese Philosophy*
carefully transcends such a classificatory scheme by employing
concepts appropriate to the thought-contents themselves. Professor
T'ang Chün-i, in a series of philosophical treatises on Chu Hsi, Lu
Hsiang-shan, and Wang Yang-ming, also seeks to go beyond the conventional demarcation of Ch'eng-Chu on the one hand and Lu-Wang
on the other. (Cf. his most recent article on this issue in *Hsin-ya
hsüeh-pao,* 9:1, 1969.) Furthermore, as A. C. Graham has shown in
his critical study on the key concepts of the two Ch'eng brothers,
their philosophical orientations are essentially different. (See
Graham's *Two Chinese Philosophers,* London: Lund Humphries,
1958.) This may be cited to support the prevalent view that Ch'eng
I was the originator of the Ch'eng-Chu School and his elder brother
Ch'eng Hao was closer in spirit to the Lu-Wang School. Where then
does the originality of Professor Mou Tsung-san's formulation really
lie?

According to Mou, although the Lu-Wang School truly trans-
mitted the germinal wisdom of classical Confucianism, and the
Ch'eng-Chu School, despite its departure from the basic intention of
the Mencian tradition, made original contributions to Confucian
thought, the most remarkable and significant line of development in
the Neo-Confucian period was from Chou Tun-i to Liu Tsung-chou
by way of Chang Tsai, Ch'eng Hao, and Hu Hung. Professor Mou
remarked in his private letter to the reviewer that he was impelled to
take this provocative position by more than a decade of painstaking
philosophical inquiry and scholarly research. The central concern of
his decade-long intellectual pursuit was to understand Chu Hsi and
the philosophical import, not merely the genetic development, of
his ideas. Only after Mou believed that he had truthfully comprehended the hierarchical structure of Chu Hsi's philosophical system
did he feel confident to "relocate" Chu Hsi, as it were, and to reorder

113

the entire tradition of Neo-Confucianism.

It is commonly accepted that despite Chu Hsi's conscious efforts to understand Mencius, due to his own metaphysical presuppositions he failed to apprehend some of the most crucial issues in Mencian moral philosophy. It is also widely known that despite Lu Hsiang-shan's Ch'an-like demonstration in the "Goose Lake Debate" with Chu Hsi (1175), he captured the basic intention of Mencius, whom he regarded as his main source of inspiration. We may add that it is also generally understood that despite tension and conflict between the two Ch'eng brothers in terms of basic philosophical orientations, Chu Hsi accepted Ch'eng I as the legitimate interpreter of his brother's ideas. Professor Mou takes these opinions seriously and engages in a careful analysis of the original texts to substantiate the philosophical meaning of these assertions.

Professor Wing-tsit Chan has stated, "No one has exercised greater influence on Chinese thought than Chu Hsi, except Confucius, Mencius, Lao Tzu, and Chuang Tzu. He gave Confucianism new meaning and for centuries dominated not only Chinese thought but the thought of Korea and Japan as well" (*Source Book,* p. 588). To argue that Chu Hsi was not authentically Confucian is to invite criticism, or at least to incite polemics. Professor Mou seems to be fully aware of the grave consequences of his position. In fact it may very well be said that the kernel of his three-volume study is to present a critique of Chu Hsi in order to put the true Confucian message, as he sees it, in a proper perspective. We may even go so far as to characterize his work as a search for the reality of Chu Hsi's philosophy, if only for the sake of refuting it. What is the matter with Chu Hsi, or rather what is Professor Mou's real *Problematik?*

From the viewpoint of Chinese intellectual history, it was Chu Hsi who selected and grouped together the *Analects,* the *Book of Mencius,* the *Great Learning,* and the *Doctrine of the Mean* (the latter two are chapters of the *Book of Rites*), known to this date as the Four Books. It was also he who first established the "orthodox" line of Confucian transmission from Confucius through Mencius, Chou Tun-i, Chang Tsai, Ch'eng Hao, and Ch'eng I. As the greatest philosophical synthesizer in China for the last millennium, Master Chu was instrumental in providing a philosophical framework for the concept of *tao-t'ung.* However, it is undeniable that in addition to his abortive attempt to understand Mencius, Chu Hsi relegated the *Book of Change* to a work on divination, a position radically different from his predecessors who relied heavily on it for much of their philosophical inspiration. His single-minded devotion to the *Great Learning* further separated him from his spiritual fathers, except Ch'eng I, to whom he owed the initial formulations of many of his major theses. Therefore, it seems understandable that Professor Mou depicts Chu Hsi as an intellectual genius who by his own philosophical strength not only created a novel tradition within Neo-Confucianism but also assumed the de facto leadership for the Neo-Confucian tradition as a whole.

From the viewpoint of the "typology of ideas," however, Chu Hsi's philosophical approach cannot veritably accommodate the intention of the early Sung masters. On the contrary, his ingenious appropriation of many of the great themes of his precursors mainly contributes to the resourcefulness of his own system, which is a departure from, rather than a fulfillment of, the germinal wisdom mentioned above. Professor Mou takes pain to show in concrete terms how the ontological insight into the structure of the mind as both being and activity undergoes a fundamental change in Chu Hsi's thinking. To be sure, Chu Hsi also maintains that human nature is good, but he insists that human nature is good because it itself is *li* (principle). Since *li* as the ultimate ground of existence is being and not activity, the energy of cosmic activity is assigned to the concept of *ch'i* (material or vital force). When *li* and *ch'i* are described as two mutually interacting and yet discrete realities, the ultimate ground of existence (being) no longer identifies with the principle of actualization (activity). As a result, despite its having the potentiality of conforming itself to *li*, the mind is essentially the delicate stuff, *ch'i*.

Chu Hsi's dualistic tendency to separate static being from dynamic activity on the metaphysical level necessarily brings about a variety of binary structures such as *li-ch'i, hsin-li, hsin-hsing*, and *hsing-ch'ing* (feeling). Consequently, the dynamic process of internal self-transformation is de-emphasized and a set of new moral disciplines centering around Ch'eng I's saying that "self-cultivation requires seriousness; the pursuit of learning depends on the extension of knowledge" becomes the *sine qua non* of Confucian self-identity. It

115

is only natural that the concept of *ko-wu* (investigation of things and affairs) in the *Great Learning* occupies a pivotal position in Chu Hsi's philosophy. To be sure, Chu Hsi's main concern is still how to become a sage through self-effort, for his concept of *ko-wu* is ethical-religious rather than empirical-scientific. Yet it seems advisable to describe his road to sagehood as different not only from that of Mencius but also from those of the early Sung masters.

To argue his case in the concrete Professor Mou devotes his volume 3 entirely to Chu Hsi. Based on the Ch'ing scholar Wang Mou-hung's authoritative account of Master Chu's intellectual biography (*Chu Tzu nien-p'u*), Professor Mou studies the development of Chu Hsi's philosophy in chronological order. Especially notable are his penetrating analyses of Chu Hsi's intellectual maturation under the guidance of his teacher Li T'ung (Yen-p'ing, 1088–1163), Chu Hsi's philosophical debate with Chang Shih (Nan-hsien, 1133–1180) and his associates in a series of letters written in his late thirties, Chu Hsi's meditative thinking on the issue of *chung-ho* (centrality and harmony, key concepts in the *Doctrine of the Mean*) in his early forties, Chu Hsi's original insights as shown in his prominent treatise on humanity ("Jen-shuo"), Chu Hsi's cosmological ideas as presented in his tripartite demarcation of *hsin, hsing,* and *ch'ing,* Chu Hsi's completion of his metaphysics in the systematic treatment of the binary structure of *li* and *ch'i,* and Chu Hsi's views on learning, on his own spiritual attainment, and on methodology in his later years.

Although the study of Chu Hsi is sequentially the last of the three-volume work, genetically it seems to have been Professor Mou's first concern. In fact, he published an early version of Chu Hsi's encounter with the issue of *chung-ho* almost a decade ago. (Cf. his article on "Chu Tzu k'u-ts'an chung-ho te ching-kuo" in *Hsin-ya shu-yüan hsüeh-shu nien-k'an,* 1961.) Actually, only against the background of Chu Hsi's debate with Chang Shih can we appreciate Professor Mou's insistence on the importance of Hu Hung, Chang Shih's intellectual master, as a key figure in the Neo-Confucian transmission. Indeed, one of the unique features of volume 2 is a series of detailed analyses of excerpts from Hu Hung's *Understanding Words (Chih-yen),* a much neglected work by a relatively unknown philosopher. According to Professor Mou, the decline of the Hu

116

School of Neo-Confucianism, which was founded by Hu An-kuo (Wen-ting, 1073–1138) and expounded by his son Hu Hung, was due mainly to the inability of Chang Shih and his Hunan-based associates to face squarely the challenge of Chu Hsi. Yet in terms of philosophical orientation as such, the position of the Hu school is very much in line with that of the early Sung masters. Thus we are told that in the writings of Hu Hung it is not difficult to point out his conscious attempts to digest the central ideas of Chou Tun-i, Chang Tsai, and Ch'eng Hao. Especially remarkable is his experiential appropriation of Mencius' concept of mind and Ch'eng Hao's concept of humanity into his own philosophy. It is in this sense that Professor Mou characterizes Hu Hung's approach as *"nei-tsai te ni-chüeh t'i-cheng"* (an experiential verification through immanent retrospective enlightening, Vol. 2, p. 430), which is reminiscent of the germinal wisdom in Mencian Confucianism.

Therefore, Professor Mou presents us in a systematic way with a series of highly original inquiries into Neo-Confucian philosophy. Although the scope of his involvement is rather extensive, the quality of his analysis remains at a very high level of intellectual sophistication. His ability to strike a balance between comprehensiveness and depth of analysis is mainly due to a very perceptive selection from a large quantity of unpunctuated texts of only those key passages that will reveal the "true faces," so to speak, of the great Sung masters. Indisputable landmarks in Neo-Confucian philosophy are carefully brooded over, sometimes line by line. Works that receive such treatments include: Chou Tun-i's "T'ai-chi t'u-shuo" (An explanation of the Diagram of the Great Ultimate) and *T'ung-shu* (Penetrating the *Book of Change*), Chang Tsai's "Hsi-ming" (the Western Inscription) and *Cheng-meng* (Correcting youthful ignorance) in volume 1; Ch'eng Hao's "Shih-jen p'ien" (On understanding humanity) and "Ta Chang Heng-ch'ü ting-hsing shu" (Reply to Master Heng-ch'ü's letter on calming human nature), Ch'eng I's sayings on issues such as *hsing-ch'ing, li-ch'i,* and *chung-ho,* Hu Hung's *Chih-yen,* in volume 2; and Chu Hsi's "Jen-shuo" (A treatise on humanity) in volume 3.

In a deeper sense, however, Professor Mou's work represents only an important stage in his continuous reflection on Chinese philosophy in general. As one of the most brilliant modern Chinese thinkers, his study is more than an intellectual exercise; it symbolizes a series of experiential "dialogues" with those great historical masters who made his own way of thinking meaningful. It should be pointed out, nevertheless, that in the present study Professor Mou completes his investigation with Chu Hsi. The development from Lu Hsiang-shan to Wang Yang-ming has only been highlighted in the context of the Sung philosophers. (For his early views on Wang Yang-ming, see *Wang Yang-ming chih-liang-chih chiao*, Taipei: Chung-yang wen-wu Kung-ying she, 1954.) We thus look forward to a fourth volume on the philosophical transformation in Ming China (1368–1644). We would also like to know how he proposes to relate his approach —a critical analysis of types of ideas as integral parts of discrete philosophical systems—to that of Professor T'ang Chün-i, who has engaged himself in a serious attempt to probe the interpenetration and complementarity of ideas belonging to seemingly incompatible philosophical systems.

In conclusion, it can confidently be said that throughout this three-volume work Professor Mou delights us with penetrating insights and abashes us with new and crucial information. What has been accomplished is not merely an inspiring interpretation of a great cultural phenomenon by a creative scholar, but also the record of a genuine quest for a deep understanding of human reality by a seminal mind.

9. Reconstituting the Confucian Tradition (Review Article)*

Wing-tsit Chan suggests in his source book in Chinese philosophy that the influence Chu Hsi has exercised on Chinese thought measures up to that of Confucius.[1] He was the most authoritative interpreter of the Confucian tradition in the last eight centuries, and the effects of Chu Hsi's intellectual message still echo throughout East Asia. Indeed it may be claimed that prior to the impact of the West the predominant value-orientation in East Asian society and politics was Confucianism of the Chu Hsi tradition. Chu Hsi's ideas were not only intellectually appropriated, but also practically implemented by the governments in Ming-Ch'ing China, Tokugawa Japan, and Yi Dynasty Korea. Without stretching the truth, it may be said that Chu Hsi's world view was a commanding ideology of the East Asian world in the premodern era.

Unfortunately no substantial translation of Chu Hsi's collected works into English has appeared since the publication of J. P. Bruce's free rendition of Chu Hsi's remarks on the human condition in 1922.[2] Bruce's other book, a descriptive account of *Chu Hsi and His Masters*, inadequate as it is, has remained a "standard reference" for more that half a century.[3] However, modern research on the Sung thinker has been growing steadily for decades in Hong Kong and Taiwan. With the publication of a series of original reflections on Chu Hsi's philosophical ideas by Fan Shou-k'ang, T'ang Chun-i, and Mou Tsung-san in the last ten years,[4] the discourse on the subject among Chinese scholars has been elevated to a level of sophistication unprecedented in the study of Neo-Confucianism. Ch'ien Mu's comprehensive presentation of Chu Hsi's thought (*ssu-hsiang*) and scholarship (*hsüeh-shu*) adds a new dimension to this already impressive intellectual heritage.

Chu Tzu hsin hsüeh-an (A new scholarly record on Chu Hsi), by Ch'ien Mu. Taipei: San-min Book Co., 1971. 5 vols.

Ch'ien Mu's systematic inquiry into Neo-Confucianism seems to have begun in the 1920's. His highly acclaimed short survey of Wang Yang-ming's (1472–1529) thought published in 1930[5] contains a chapter on some of the key problem areas in Sung Learning, among which Chu Hsi's method of self-cultivation stands out as a defining characteristic of Neo-Confucian thought. In general, however, Ch'ien Mu has been noted for his works on cultural history rather than on the history of ideas. In a lecture published in 1940 on the occasion of the fortieth anniversary of the founding of Peking University, he presents a general survey of intellectual trends in the Sung-Yüan-Ming period (960–1644). The focus is on the social and cultural significance of the rise of Neo-Confucianism. This is also his main interest in the highly influential *Kuo-shih ta-kang* (Outline of Chinese history; Shanghai: Commercial Press, 1948). Even in his more specialized studies such as *Sung-Ming li-hsüeh kai-shu* (Survey of Sung-Ming Neo-Confucianism; Taipei: Chung-hua Wen-hua Publishing Co., 1957) and *Chung-kuo chin san-pei nien hsüeh-shu shih* (A history of Chinese scholarship in the last three hundred years; Chungking: Commercial Press, 1945), the central concern is still with the social function of ideas. His purely academic analyses in *Hsien-Ch'in chu-tzu hsi-nien* (Chronology of pre-Ch'in philosophers; Shanghai: Commercial, Press, 1936) and *Liu Hsiang Hsin fu-tzu nien-p'u* (Chronological biographies of Liu Hsiang and Liu Hsin; Chungking: Commercial Press, 1947) give further evidence of this particular predilection. Therefore, his decision to undertake a comprehensive inquiry into Chu Hsi's thought and scholarship seems to be a new venture, marking a significant departure from his career of almost four decades as a cultural historian.

According to his preface, Ch'ien Mu committed himself to the task of writing a comprehensive work on Chu Hsi in the summer of 1964 after he had resigned from the presidency of New Asia College in Hong Kong. He began his project by reading the *Collection of Literary Works by Master Chu (Chu Tzu wen-chi)*. After he had completed the 121 *chüan* in a ten-month period of intensive study, he continued to work on the *Classified Conversations of Master Chu (Chu Tzu yü-lei)* which consists of 140 *chüan*. To facilitate his research, he launched into an extensive note-taking that eventually led to the classification of more than three thousand items of "essential points" *(yao-chih)*. Having determined his major categories on the basis of primary sources, he proceeded to consult a massive number of secondary sources and interpretive literature. The bulk of the manuscript was completed in November 1969. In the following year, he wrote a long introductory essay trying to summarize the study of fifty-eight chapters and over a million words.

Ch'ien Mu's five-volume study on Chu Hsi consists of two major parts. The part on thought (Vols. 1 and 2) is further divided into sections on *li-ch'i* (principle-material force) and *hsin-hsing* (mind-human nature), and the part on scholarship (Vols. 4 and 5) is further divided into sections on classics, history, and literature. Within the section on classics, special chapters are assigned to *I (Book of Change)*, *Shih (Book of Poetry)*, *Shu (Book of History)*, *Ch'un-ch'iu (Spring and Autumn Annals)*, *Li (Book of Rites)*, and *Ssu-shu* (Four Books: *Analects*, *Book of Mencius*, *Great Learning*, and *Doctrine of the Mean*).

Furthermore, a chapter each on *chiao-k'an* (textual verification), *pien-wei* (textual authentication), and *k'ao-chü* (empirical research) has been added. The study concludes with a chapter on Chu Hsi's miscellaneous reflections on divination, medicine, music, calligraphy, painting, and sciences. In addition to the parts on thought and scholarship, the entire Volume 3 is devoted to a study of Chu Hsi's intellectual development, and consists of a series of monographic studies on his pattern of spiritual maturation, his appropriation of philosophical insights from the early Sung masters, his critique of his contemporaries, notably Lu Hsiang-shan (1139–1193), and his attack on Ch'an Buddhism.

Suggestively Ch'ien Mu designates his study as a *hsüeh-an*, which can be roughly rendered as a scholarly record intended to map out the intellectual biography and philosophical ideas of a thinker. The paradigmatic example of this genre is Huang Tsung-hsi's (1610–1695) *Ming-ju hsüeh-an* (A scholarly record of the Ming Confucians), which has been widely acclaimed as "the first notable attempt in China at systematic and critical intellectual history."[6] A salient feature of such a study is its professed intention to be representative. A *hsüeh-an* usually includes a biographic sketch of the thinker and a selection of his writings and sayings. The author's appreciation or criticism is frequently expressed indirectly in the succinct biographic remarks and in the method of selecting original sources. Ch'ien Mu's

121

approach to Chu Hsi departs significantly from the *hsüeh-an* style in terms of its comprehensive coverage and elaborate organization, but his insistence on including many direct, sometimes lengthy, quotations from original sources and on making his judgments implicit in descriptive accounts is very much in the spirit of the *hsüeh-an* tradition.

Ch'ien Mu asserts in the very beginning of his study that Chu Hsi was not only the great synthesizer of all the major intellectual trends in the Neo-Confucian revival of the Northern Sung but the chief architect of the structure that Confucian thought has assumed ever since the thirteenth century. Accordingly, it is inadequate to study him mainly as a Southern Sung philosopher. Ch'ien Mu contends that just as the emergence of classical Confucianism resulted from a conscious response to the decline and fall of the feudal order of the Chou dynasty and led to a courageous struggle against dehumanizing forces in the Spring and Autumn period (722–481 B.C.), the rise of Neo-Confucianism should be conceived as the "awakening" (*chüeh-hsing*) of the Chinese literati as they confronted the disintegration of the Chinese Empire and the challenge of Buddhism. Understandably the Neo-Confucian intellectuals were acutely aware of affairs of state and deeply committed to the preservation of what they believed to be the authentic classical and historical traditions. The reform movements of Fan Chung-yen (989–1052) and Wang An-shih (1021–1086), the classical scholarship of Hu Yuan (993–1059), Sun Fu (992–1057), and Li Kou (1009–1050), the historiography of Ou-yang Hsiu (1007–1070) and Ssu-ma Kuang (1019–1086), and the literary writings of virtually all of them therefore constituted part of the heritage wherein Chu Hsi found his role and function in society.

However, it would be misleading to characterize Chu Hsi as essentially either a political philosopher or a man of letters. Despite his profound influence in shaping the general direction of what may be called the official ideology of the later empires in China, Chu, Hsi was never wholly engaged in matters of politics. To be sure, classics and history absorbed much of his time, and he could well qualify as the leading classicist and historian of his generation. Scholarship, no matter how broadly it is conceived, was not his central concern. Rather, as a student of Li T'ung (1093–1163), who in turn had followed the teaching of Ch'eng I (1033–1107), Chu Hsi dedicated himself to the transmission and interpretation of the Neo-Confucian Way. It should be pointed out that, in his perception at the time, the Neo-Confucian Way, far from being a new creation of the Sung scholars, was the true representation of the teaching of Confucius and Mencius. The teaching, both an intellectual tradition and a spiritual message, was thought to have been distorted for more than a millenium before it began to be rectified in the vocations of Chou Tun-i (1027–1073), Chang Tsai (1020–1077), Ch'eng Hao (1032–1085), and Ch'eng I. Chu Hsi's self-image as a "transmitter" and "interpreter" of the Confucian Way was therefore defined in terms of the ethicoreligious orientation of the Northern Sung masters. Since Chu Hsi himself was instrumental in formulating the pattern of transmission and the method of interpretation, he was in a sense the maker of his own heritage.

Philosophically Chu Hsi was instrumental in establishing the "orthodox" line of Confucian transmission in the early Sung from Chou Tun-i through Chang Tsai, Ch'eng Hao, and Ch'eng I. His intention to harmonize the ideas of the Four Masters, however, gave the Confucian tradition a new complexion that seems hardly recognizable purely in terms of the Norfhern Sung revival. This is of course not to suggest that Chu Hsi had drastically departed from the teachings of his predecessors. In fact his originality lay in his ability to integrate particular insights into a comprehensive structure, recapitulating all the major concepts in Neo-Confucianism up to his time. And this was not done by constructing an abstract system based on the available ideas of the early Sung thinkers but by "digging" deeply into their problem areas, sharing their agonies, and living through the pitfalls they had encountered. Chu Hsi's intellectual endeavor was not a painless appropriation of the insights of other men but a continuous quest for experiential understanding of the best minds in his chosen tradition. This becomes most evident in a series of dialogues he had with his students over a period of almost thirty years. Ch'ien Mu is absolutely correct in maintaining that the *Classified Conversations* must be consulted in any serious attempt to study Chu Hsi, the philosopher, in action. Thus in his analysis of Chu Hsi's thought the *Conversations* are extensively quoted.

The part on thought mainly consists of selections from the

original sources arranged according to subject matter. The author's comments are interspersed with direct quotations, in a manner reminiscent of the format in traditional scholarship. The study is organized around a number of topical ideas. On the surface, they seem to be no more than labels under which relevant issues are glued. The first reading does give one the impression that the headings are used simply for identification. An examination of the table of contents seems to confirm the suspicion that the development from one chapter to the other is often haphazard and the sequential order in general is not apparent. One at first wonders why Ch'ien Mu did not choose to improve his overall design by arranging his material in categories such as psychology, society, polity, religion, and philosophy. One could further suggest that he divide his category of philosophy, for example, into discrete units such as metaphysics, epistemology, ethics, aesthetics, and the like. However, the imposition of a modern classification of knowledge on a body of literature in Neo-Confucian China is hardly justifiable. In fact the issue lies deeper than simply the problem of taxonomy.

Ch'ien Mu's comments on the key concepts that structure his presentation are not textual studies but heuristic devices that guide the reader to appreciate Chu Hsi's thought in a spirit of discovery. Although no easily recognizable design is apparent, his method does help to map out the major areas of concern in Chu Hsi's philosophy. Of course the reader may want to use the work simply as a reference book, for it contains a wealth of data on a variety of subjects, and it is certainly the most comprehensive study on Chu Hsi's thought in the Chinese language to this date. As a research tool, however, it seems unyieldingly difficult to use. For example, there is little attempt at cross reference. Even the index at the end is helpful only to those who are familiar with the material. The book is certainly not intended to be an encyclopedic account of Chu Hsi's thought. As the author's experiential understanding of Chu Hsi, it is based on judgments of personal knowledge rather than on a set of preconceived objective criteria. Therefore, it is quite remarkable that underlying the thirty-five chapters involving Ch'ien Mu's reflections on more than fifty key concepts selected from the Master's *Collected Literary Works* and *Classified Conversations* is a sense of unity very much in the mode of Neo-Confucian thinking.

124

Actually Ch'ien Mu's approach in this section is quite compatible with Chu Hsi's own task of compiling an anthology of the writings and sayings of the four Northern Sung masters in *Chin-ssu lu* (*Reflections on Things at Hand*). The two basic categories, *li-ch'i* and *hsin-hsing*, are often rendered by modern scholars and by Ch'ien in his preface as metaphysics and philosophy of life; the former includes ontological and cosmological issues whereas the latter is primarily concerned with moral problems. It should be noted, however, that these categories are used generically to distinguish two mutually complementary spheres of thought. Apparently Ch'ien Mu is not exact about their technical meanings. To be sure, issues such as *yin-yang* (female and male principles) and *kuei-shen* (negative and positive spiritual forces) are naturally classified under metaphysics. But with the inclusion of concepts such as *t'ien-li* and *jen-yü* (Heavenly principle and human desires), *shan-o* (good and evil), and *sheng-hsien* (sage and worthy), the classificatory scheme does appear to be arbitrary. Fortunately, in the main text, Ch'ien follows Chu Hsi's precedent and designates the two sections on thought as principle-material force and mind-human nature. It is therefore legitimate to consider *tao-ch'i* (general principle and concrete thing), *t'i-yung* (substance and function), and even *ming* (destiny) as integral parts of the discussions on principle and material force. Similarly it makes sense to take into account problems such as *chung-shu* (truthfulness and considerateness), *chih-hsing* (knowledge and action), and *ch'eng-ssu* (sincerity and cogitation) in a general study of mind and human nature. Since Chu Hsi's interests were never purely speculative, even overt cosmological issues such as *yin* and *yang* necessarily lead to moral considerations. It is only for the sake of expediency that discrete categories are assigned.

A salient feature of Ch'ien Mu's study on Chu Hsi's thought is his insistence on the centrality of the concept of mind. In his general discussion of Chu Hsi's views on mind and principle, he notes that the emphasis clearly seems to have been placed on the former. Contrary to the prevalent opinion that Chu Hsi, as a true heir of Ch'eng I, was mainly concerned with the dimension of principle, Ch'ien Mu suggests that Chu Hsi's teaching can even be characterized as a form of *hsin-hsüeh* (school of mind). Thus in addition to the chapter on the relationship between mind and principle, Ch'ien Mu devotes no

125

fewer than seven chapters exclusively to the discussion of mind. The issue of mind plays a predominant role in many other chapters as well. Ch'ien Mu's interpretation certainly has far-reaching implications. For one thing, it presents a serious challenge to the firm belief, held by such eminent scholars as Fung Yu-lan, that the Neo-Confucian tradition can be meaningfully divided into *Li-hsüeh* (School of Principle) and *Hsin-hsüeh*. According to Fung's interpretation, Chu Hsi was the greatest architect of *Li-hsüeh* whereas his rival, Lu Hsiang-shan, was the most formidable defender of *Hsin-hsüeh*. Ch'ien Mu argues rather convincingly that the dichotomy of mind and principle in this particular connection may be helpful to understand the spiritual thrust of Lu Hsiang-shan, but it is totally inadequate as an attempt to appreciate Chu Hsi. In the light of recent studies by Mou Tsung-san and T'ang Chün-i, the conventional division of the Neo-Confucian tradition into the Ch'eng-Chu School and Lu-Wang School appears not only simple-minded but dangerously misleading. Ch'ien Mu further demonstrates that to differentiate Chu Hsi and Lu Hsiang-shan in terms of the distinction between principle and mind is factually incorrect and theoretically unsound. Of course this is not intended to blur the fundamental differences between Chu and Lu. It simply rejects the conventional explanation of such differences.

Ch'ien Mu shows in his careful study that throughout his life Chu Hsi was deeply immersed in understanding the divergent aspects of the mind. Ever since his meditative thinking on the problem of the mind in his late twenties, Chu Hsi had been continuously engaged in the task of developing a comprehensive vision of the mind. He first sought to grasp the essence of the mind through inner experience. After a bitter struggle to free himself from the subtle influences of Ch'an, he made clear analytical distinctions between the Confucian perception of mind and the Buddhist approach to mind. He maintained that the Confucian Tao is in the last analysis transmitting the minds of the sages. However, unlike the transmission of the mind in Ch'an the sagely mind has both a transcendent reference and a cultural dimension. In his discussion of the human mind (*jen-hsin*) and ontological mind (*tao-hsin*), he signified that the human mind, conditioned by the "self-centeredness of the material being" (*hsing-ch'i chih ssu*), can be transformed through moral cultivation to become identified with the ontological mind. Such an identification enables the ontological mind, which is the true basis of humanity, to manifest

126

the "Heavenly principle" in human affairs. It is therefore important for one to cultivate the mind so that, despite the inherent limitation of the physical self, it can "embody" principle, which is the ultimate ground of human nature. It was in this connection that Chu Hsi emphasized the "manifested" (*i-fa*) and "unmanifested" (*wei-fa*) states of the mind, and "spiritual nourishment" (*han-yang*) and "reflective examination" (*hsing-ch'a*) of the mind. Indeed, his reflections on "seriousness" (*ching*), "quietude" (*ching*), and "self-control" (*k'e-chi*) are also to be understood in reference to his concept of mind.

Accordingly, the famous debate between Chu Hsi and Lu Hsiang-shan at the Goose Lake Temple in 1175 was not on the choice between mind and principle. Rather, it was a debate on the two different perceptions of mind. To Lu, mind is principle. Moral cultivation involves no more than the "simple and easy" (*i-chien*) effort of recovering one's original mind. The process of becoming a sage can be carried out by making an inner decision to establish what is great in each human being. To honor the irreducible humanity in one's own nature is the direct and fundamental way of self-realization. Chu, on the other hand, contended that although the ontological mind embodies the principle, the human mind is precariously prone to wrongdoing. While he agreed with Lu that human nature is good, he insisted that the principle inherent in human nature is not identical with the mind. When the human mind is imbued with selfish desires, it can easily render one's inner goodness inoperative. The cultivation of the mind, which includes systematic study and continuous inquiry, is therefore an unceasing process of self-transformation. Specifically, through efforts such as the "investigation of things" (*ko-wu*), a human being can fundamentally transform his physical self and become one not only with his fellow men but also with the "Ultimate Reality" (*t'ai-chi*).

By making subtle, analytical distinctions in the concept of mind, Chu Hsi developed a sophisticated theory of human nature without alienating himself from the Mencian image of man. Particularly notable was his ingenious appropriation of the idea of *ch'i-chih chih hsing* (physical nature) into his highly integrated system of philosophical anthropology. The idea, first formulated by Chang Tsai and brought to fruition by the Ch'eng brothers, seeks to establish the thesis that material force, such as physical endowments and human desires, is existentially inseparable from principle. Although the original nature of man manifests itself in principle, the human mind is necessarily an integral part of material force. It is therefore incomplete to stress the goodness of man as an ontological basis for self-realization. Unless the actual *condition humaine*, a mixture of moral propensity and egoistic demands, is thoroughly taken into account, an idealistic attachment to man's inner greatness can easily lead one astray. As Ch'ien Mu points out, this is the main reason why Chu Hsi put so much emphasis on the concept of the "investigation of things." Without the persistent effort of learning, Chu Hsi would argue, man cannot in a truly experiential sense become what he ought to be. For the difficulty lies not in the "oneness of the fundamental principle" (*li-i*) but in the "multiplicity of its concrete manifestations" (*fen-shu*).

To demonstrate that Chu Hsi was indeed the great synthesizer who masterfully orchestrated all the major philosophical motifs of the Northern Sung masters and created an awe-inspiring composition of his own, Ch'ien Mu first takes pains to delineate the intellectual genealogy that provided Chu Hsi with a unique access to the Northern Sung tradition as a whole. In addition to the Four Masters, we should also note Chu Hsi's relationship to Shao Yung (1011–1077) and Ssu-ma Kuang. Although Chu Hsi's philosophical system was mainly inspired by Chou Tun-i, Chang Tsai, and the Ch'eng brothers, for his comprehensive view of Sung cosmology and historiography he was indebted to Shao and Ssu-ma. Thus in his veneration of his intellectual forefathers he never failed to pay special tribute to the "Six Teachers" (*liu hsien-sheng*). Nevertheless, Chu Hsi's primary commitment seems to have been to Ch'eng I. This was partly due to the connection through his teacher Li T'ung. Thus in his *Conversations*, Chu Hsi makes many extensive comments not only on Ch'eng I but also on his disciples. Since the *Conversations* include records only after Chu Hsi was forty years old and the majority of them consist of post-sixty sayings, they very much reflect his mature thoughts. As Ch'ien Mu points out, Chu Hsi was sometimes highly critical of Ch'eng I's followers, such as Yu Tso (1053–1132), Yang Shih (1053–1135), and Hsieh Liang-tso (1050–1103). This is certainly true in his advanced age. The fact that Chu Hsi was deeply concerned about their interpretations of Master Ch'eng's teaching, however, seems also to indicate that he had seriously studied each of them in his formative years.

128

Although the formation of Chu Hsi's great synthesis can be perceived as a series of conscious responses to the root concepts of the Northern Sung masters, his intellectual dynamics owed much to his intense dialogues with contemporary thinkers as well. Especially noteworthy was his association with Chang Nan-hsien (1133–1180) and his associates. Chang, a prominent disciple of Hu Wu-feng (1105–1155), was instrumental in bringing on one of the most significant philosophical exchanges in Southern Sung. The exchange centered around Hu's treatise on *Understanding Words (Chih-yen)*, which expounds, among other theses, the unity of mind and human nature. After many discussions with Chang Nan-hsien and continuous correspondence with Chang's followers afterwards, Chu Hsi was able to argue in the tradition of Ch'eng I that human nature is the same as principle but not identical with mind. Chu Hsi's final triumph in bringing over the Hunan scholars to his philosophical position marked an important stage in his intellectual growth. Equally important was his friendship with Lü Tsu-ch'ien (1137–1181), cocompiler of *Reflections on Things at Hand*. As the leader of one of the outstanding currents of thought at this time, Lü advocated a form of "practical learning," which later featured prominently in the Chekiang School of Neo-Confucianism. As James T.C. Liu has pointed out in a recent monograph, Lü's students played a key role in persuading the court to accept Neo-Confucianism as the state orthodoxy.[7] A direct result of this policy was the canonization of Chu Hsi as the last and only Southern Sung thinker in the line of transmission of the Confucian Tao. Lü was also responsible for arranging the famous debate between Chu Hsi and Lu Hsiang-shan at the Goose Lake Temple.

Chu Hsi's short but intense personal confrontation with Lu Hsiang-shan has been recognized by intellectual historians as one of the most significant landmarks in the development of Neo-Confucian thought. It has also been taken as the basis for the assertion that Sung Learning can be meaningfully divided into the Chu Hsi School of Principle and the Lu Hsiang-shan School of Mind. Even though we consider the dichotomy, as a scheme of classification, both simplistic and misleading, the issues involved in the confrontation undoubtedly have many far-reaching implications. An examination of the fundamental points of contention has thus become a popular subject of study among students of Chinese philosophy. Indeed, as one of the most seriously researched topics in Neo-Confucianism, the "dissimilarity and compatibility between Chu and Lu" (*Chu-Lu i-t'ung*) features prominently in virtually all general surveys on Sung Learning. In Ch'ien Mu's work, more than a quarter of Volume 3 is concerned exclusively with this problem.

Lu accused Chu of having committed the fallacy of putting too much emphasis on book learning, which leads to a fragmentary understanding of the mind. Chu responded that a gradual process of self-cultivation is essential to a real appreciation of the mind. Underlying the difference, however, is more than the conflict between sudden enlightenment and gradual enlightenment. It is also the conflict between the perception of mind as the authentic manifestation of principle and thus the ultimate ground as well as the actual faculty of self-realization, and the perception of mind as the synthesis of human nature and human feelings (a mixture of principle and material force) and thus the actual faculty but not the ultimate ground of self-realization. While Lu insisted on the self-sufficiency of the human mind, Chu Hsi had serious doubts about the claim that since every human mind is identical with the mind of the sage, self-realization involves no more than a simple and direct process of inner spiritual transformation.

At the time of the Goose Lake Temple debate, Chu Hsi was already in his late forties, whereas Lu Hsiang-shan was only thirty-six years old. As Ch'ien Mu points out, by then Chu had completed more than a dozen books on Confucian classics and on early Sung Confucianism; he had also gone through years of intellectual struggle with the Hunan and Chekiang scholars. Although he was well disposed to accommodate Lu's position, he was quite taken aback by the arrogance and the uncompromising attitude of the young thinker, who was to become the leader of the Kiangsi School. However, Chu and Lu maintained a long and cordial friendship after the debate. Their intellectual discussions through correspondence also continued for many years. In 1181, Chu Hsi invited Lu Hsiang-shan to present a lecture at his famous White Deer Grotto Academy. Lu's talk on the distinction between righteous decisions and utilitarian motives was an important event in the Academy and received high praise from Chu. Then a series of accidental events adversely affected their friendship. Their relation deteriorated seriously over the quarrel on Chou Tun-i's "T'ai-chi-t'u shuo" (Explanation of the Diagram of the Great Ultimate) in 1188, almost fourteen years after the debate. Four years later Lu Hsiang-shan died. The alleged animosity between Chu and Lu was later intensified by a continuous feud between their disciples. However, Chu's intellectual influence was so pervasive that subsequent generations of Confucian thinkers were overwhelmed by his subtly constructed and freshly invigorated philosophy. As a result, Lu's teaching failed to make an important impact on the minds of either the Yüan (1260–1368) or the early Ming (1368–1644) scholars.

Our perception of the phenomenon is somewhat confounded by the emergence of Wang Yang-ming as a brilliant spokesman for Confucianism in the sixteenth century. His conscious choice to revitalize the thought of Lu Hsiang-shan again ignited the debate, which led to a substantial reformulation of the pattern of intellectual development in China in the premodern period. Wang Yang-ming, however, fully acknowledged that it was really Chu Hsi's intellectual challenge that prompted his rethinking on Confucianism. In fact, he was himself so much persuaded by the power of Chu Hsi's thought that for quite awhile he strongly believed that, despite apparent incongruence, his philosophical orientation was in genuine agreement with Chu Hsi's "final words." It is, therefore, fitting for Ch'ien Mu to include a critical analysis of Wang Yang-ming's highly controversial compilation of the so-called *Chu Tzu wan-nien ting-lun* (Chu Hsi's final words in later years). Although some philosophical issues remain unanswered, Ch'ien has certainly dispelled for us a great deal of historical and textual confusion.

Ch'ien Mu's discussion of Chu Hsi's scholarship (Volumes 4 and 5) contains many marvellous observations. Especially remarkable are his thoughtful assertion that Chu Hsi's commentaries on the classics are significantly different from those of the Ch'eng brothers and his detailed analysis of Chu Hsi's historical vision. The former seriously challenges the conventional belief that Chu, as a faithful follower of Ch'eng I, rarely departed from the *Surviving Works* (*I-shu*) of the two Ch'engs. The latter substantiates a claim by recent scholars, such as Yü Ying-shin, that Chu Hsi's historiography profoundly influenced not only historians in the Ming but also Han scholars in the Ch'ing (1644–1912).[8] In addition, Ch'ien Mu argues rather convincingly against the prevalent opinion that Chu Hsi, unlike his predecessors, regarded the *Book of Change* as primarily for divination. Actually Chu Hsi criticized Ch'eng I's attempt to study the *Change* purely as a philosophical treatise, because he believed that since the book originated as a set of prognostic practices, it was important to appreciate its philosophical import in the light of its divinatory structure. Therefore, Chu Hsi took the "Judgments" of the hexagrams seriously as bases for rediscovering the "original meanings" (*pen-i*) of the ancient authors. Chu Hsi might have failed to combine the two dimensions in a manner satisfactory to himself, but it seems clear that his intention was to arrive at a synthesis of the *hsiang-shu* (images and numbers, divinatory) and the *i-li* (meaning and principle, philosophical) traditions of the *Book of Change*.

Chu Hsi's vigorous attempt to study the *Book of Poetry* as a reservoir of aesthetic insights as well as a treasury of moral lessons is brought to life by Ch'ien Mu's skillful selection of pertinent quotations and anecdotes to illustrate his point. For Master Chu, poetry must be read and experienced before it can be objectively analyzed. To enable the commentator to see a poem as a highly condensed form of articulation, he suggested that it be recited forty to fifty times as a prerequisite for launching any critical study of it. Recitation in this connection is not at all unreasoned rote learning; it is intended to cultivate a sensitivity, to appreciate the nuance between lines, and to apprehend the inner structure of the poem. After some personal knowledge of the poem has been acquired, Chu Hsi then recommended comparative study of available commentaries. Such a study should be followed by another thirty to forty recitative exercises. An experiential understanding of the "flow" of a poem can be attained only by a constant interplay between these two types of learning. Thus, Chu Hsi was able to chart a new course for the study of the *Poetry* by transcending the moralism of centuries of traditional scholarship on the subject. His independence of mind was further evidenced by a series of critical remarks on the *Book of History* and *Spring and Autumn Annals*. To him they both contain a great deal of outmoded and cryptic material. He even warned his students not to waste too much time on them.

Ch'ien Mu shows, in a masterful treatment of original sources, that Chu Hsi's lifelong commitment to the *Book of Rites* was diametrically opposed to his ambivalent attitudes toward the other two classics. According to a statement in the *Classified Conversations*. Chu Hsi began his study of *Chia-li* (family rituals) when he was not yet twenty years old. His interest in this area remained strong throughout his life, and intensified after the death of his mother in the winter of 1175, several months after the Goose Lake Temple debate. However, concern for family rituals was only a part of his overall interest in *Rites*. To him the study of rituals involved much more than a reconstruction of ceremonial practices in the Confucian tradition. It was also an attempt to provide a comprehensive guide for social behavior. Ritualization in this connection was thought to be the actualization of personality ideals through the transforming powers of moral persuasion. In 1194, Chu Hsi memorialized the throne to have an institute established for the exclusive study of the *Rites*. He was prepared, with the help of a dozen former students, to assume the responsibility for such a task. The purpose was to assist the scholar-officials in fostering a sense of "real learning" (*shih-hsüeh*) that could eventually be applied to political affairs. Although Chu Hsi's proposal was never acted on by the court, he continued to work on his own. As Ch'ien Mu points out, Chu Hsi wrote three letters on the day before his death, and two of them were instructions to his students concerning the continuation of his work on the *Rites*.

By identifying important pieces of evidence hitherto unrecognized by scholars in the field, Ch'ien Mu persuasively argues that the later controversy on the so-called *Chu Tzu chia-li* (Master Chu's family rituals), which prompted thinkers such as Yen Yüan (1635–1704) to attack the ritualism of the Ch'eng-Chu School, was mainly due to the posthumous publication of an incomplete text of this work. It was, therefore, not so much a reflection of Chu Hsi's mature thought as an indication of what he might have done in youth. Of course we cannot be sure about the story that the manuscript had been lost for years, only to be found shortly after the Master died. But Ch'ien Mu's explanation seems more convincing than Wang Mou-hung's (1668–1741) suggestion that the whole thing was a fabrication.[9] For Chu Hsi not only mentioned this particular project to his friends and students but also alluded to its format in several of his letters. What Chu Hsi really had in mind was not a new compilation of family rituals but a collaborative anthology based on the works by Ssu-ma Kuang and Ch'eng I. This is reminiscent of Chu Hsi's other joint ventures such as *T'ung-chien kang-mu* (Outline and digest of the *General Mirror*). However, unlike his works in history, Chu Hsi's reflections on the *Rites* significantly departed from the main thrust of classical scholarship in Northern Sung. Of the three major texts on Confucian rituals, known as the *san-li* (three books on rites), he regarded *I-li* as the root, *Li-chi* as the branches, and *Chou-li* as a self-sufficient monograph on ancient institutions. This further testifies to the fact that Chu Hsi's judgment was often based on his own perception of the given tradition and not necessarily on the established authority of his time. Had he followed the instructions of the Northern Sung scholars, he would have focused his attention on *Chou-li* and *Li-chi* rather than on the more obscure text of *I-li*.

Therefore, Chu Hsi's serious efforts to revitalize the tradition involved creative adaptation as well as faithful interpretation. His relationship to Confucianism in general and Northern Sung Learning in particular was a dialectic one. Although his self-image, like that of Confucius, was to be a transmitter rather than a maker, his conscious attempt to "continue" (*chi*) the "transmission of the Way" *tao-t'ung*) frequently led to a fundamental restructuring of the tradition. However, it only scratches the surface to suggest that Chu Hsi had inadvertently formed a tradition of his own, while ostensibly allying himself with the past. For what he really "created" was the cumulative result of a series of penetrating inquiries into the leading minds of the Confucian tradition as a whole. Indeed, his immersion in the tradition was so profound and his impact on it so great that it is extremely difficult to make subtle distinctions between the original direction of the tradition before the "immersion" and its newly assumed orientation after the "impact." For Chu Hsi's creativity was inseparable from his traditionality.

An example of this phenomenon is found in Chu Hsi's conscientious studies of the Four Books. As Ch'ien Mu points out, discussions of the Four Books constitute more than one third of the entire *Classified Conversations*, whereas references to the Five Classics are numbered fewer than half of those to the Four Books. Actually Chu Hsi was instrumental in the formation of the Four Books. Wing-tsit Chan characterizes this particular undertaking as Chu Hsi's "most radical innovation."[10] In brief, what he did was to select the *Great Learning* and the *Doctrine of the Mean* (two chapters of the *Book of Rites*), and group them together with the *Analects* and the *Book of Mencius*, as the Four Books. He then wrote thoughtful commentaries on them, interpreted them as an integrated philosophy, and made them the core of Confucian teaching. Since the Four Books, together with Chu Hsi's commentaries, were accepted by the government as the basis of the civil service examinations from 1313 to 1905, "they have exercised far greater influence on Chinese life and thought in the last six hundred years than any other Classic."[11] It was mainly through institutional support of this kind that Chu Hsi's fame also spread to Korea, Japan, and Vietnam. In the light of the above, what Chu Hsi actually brought about was no less than *reconstitution of the Confucian tradition*.

Nevertheless, Chu Hsi's radical innovation was not at all intended to depart from the tradition. On the contrary, he was dedicated to the continuation of the authentic line of transmission and absolutely serious about understanding the true teaching of the sages. His commentaries were thus designed to elicit the inner meanings of the original texts. In Chu Hsi's own perception, they were records of his continuous struggle to understand word by word what the sages really tried to convey. Writing a commentary in this connection was much more than a scholarly enterprise; it demanded the participation of the entire body and mind. Chu Hsi repeatedly remarked that the strenuous task sapped much of his "bitter strength." His commentaries were to him serious "dialogues" with Confucius and Mencius: "The sage utters a word as a word, I weigh and measure it with a completely impartial mind. Without any trace of subjective imposition, I simply follow its drift." This state of selfless appreciation of the words of the sages was by no means easy to attain. After numerous attempts to revise his commentaries on the Four Books, which represented almost three decades of intensive study so that "not a single character can be added or subtracted," Chu Hsi stated, "Only now, at sixty-one, have I arrived at an experiential understanding [of the Four Books]. Had I died last year, I would have had all my pains for nothing." Even then, Ch'ien Mu notes, Chu Hsi did not cease to improve his work. It is well-known that his last attempt, a change of three characters in his commentary on the

135

Great Learning, was made only three days before his death.

Ch'ien Mu has certainly made a significant contribution to interpretive scholarship on Chu Hsi. Not since the publication of Wang Mou-hung's *Chu Tzu nien-p'u* (Chronological biography of Chu Hsi) in the eighteenth century, have Chu Hsi's thought and scholarship been studied so comprehensively and conscientiously in the Chinese language. The image of Chu Hsi, as presented in the five-volume study, has an integrity rarely found in sinological literature. Ch'ien Mu's holistic vision will undoubtedly provide criteria for judging a variety of partial views on Chu Hsi for years to come. To be sure, Chu Hsi's philosophy is more perceptively analyzed in Mou Tsung-san's *Hsin-t'i yü hsing-t'i* (Mind and human nature), and his life history is more vividly presented in Wang Mou-hung's *Chronological Biography,* but it is in Ch'ien Mu that we find the entire texture of Chu Hsi's great synthesis. What has been achieved in Ch'ien Mu's work is an exhibition of Chu Hsi's major concerns in the context of the Confucian tradition as a whole. In conclusion, however, it must be maintained that there is no short cut to Chu Hsi's world of ideas. Ch'ien Mu's *hsin hsüeh-an* on Chu Hsi, like Huang Tsung-hsi's *hsüeh-an* on Wang Yang-ming, is inevitably a contrivance, notwithstanding its seriousness of purpose and perspicuity of presentation. And no matter how sophisticated the design is, it is no substitute for the wonder, indeed the delight, of reading Chu Hsi's poems, letters, commentaries, and philosophical reflections themselves. The willingness and courage to confront the many "fruitful ambiguities" in the *Literary Works* and *Classified Conversations* is still the closest approximation to meeting Chu Hsi face to face.

NOTES

[1] Wing-tsit Chan, *A Source Book in Chinese Philosophy* (Princeton: Princeton University Press, 1963), p. 588.

[2] J. P. Bruce, trans., *The Philosophy of Human Nature by Chu Hsi* (London: Probsthain, 1922).

[3] J. P. Bruce, *Chu Hsi and His Masters* (London: Probsthain, 1923). Charles O. Hucker notes that it is "a standard reference on the development of Neo-Confucianism in Sung times and its culmination in the synthesis of Chu Hsi." See his

China: A Critical Bibliography (Tucson: University of Arizona Press, 1962). To my knowledge, the only other substantial monographic study on Chu Hsi in English is Conrad M. Schirokauer's unpublished dissertation on the political thought and behavior of Chu Hsi (Stanford University, 1960). See Mr. Schirokauer's "Chu Hsi's Political Career," in *Confucian Personalities*, edited by Arthur Wright and Denis Twitchett (Stanford: Stanford University Press, 1962), pp. 162–188.

[4]Fan Shou-k'ang, *Chu Tzu chi ch'i che-hsüeh* (Chu Hsi and his philosophy; Taipei: K'ai-ming Press, 1964). T'ang Chün-i, *Chung-kuo che-hsüeh yüan-lun* (An original exposition of Chinese philosophy), 2 vols. (Hong Kong: Young-sun Press, 1965–68). Mou Tsung-san, *Hsin-t'i yü hsing-t'i* (Mind and human nature), 3 vols. (Taipei: Cheng-chung Press, 1968).

[5]Ch'ien Mu, *Yang-ming hsüeh shu-yao* (A summary of Yang-ming's learning; reprint; Taipei: Cheng-chung Press, 1954).

[6]Wm. T. de Bary, comp., *Sources of Chinese Tradition* (New York: Columbia University Press, 1960), pp. 585–586.

[7]James T. C. Liu, "How Did a Neo-Confucian School Become the State Orthodoxy?" in *Philosophy East and West* 23, no. 4 (October 1973): 483–505.

[8]Yü Ying-shih, "Ts'ung Sung-Ming ju-hsüeh ti fa-chan lun Ch'ing-tai ssu-hsiang shih" ("Ch'ing Thought as Seen Through the Development of Sung-Ming Confucianism,") in *Chung-kuo hsüeh-jen* (Chinese Scholar) 2 (September 1970): 19–41. This is the first part of a two-part article. The subtitle is "Sung-Ming ju-hsüeh chung chih-shih chu-i ti ch'uan-t'ung" ("The Tradition of Intellectualism in Sung-Ming Confucianism.")

[9]Wang Mou-hung, *Chu Tzu nien-p'u k'ao-i* (A critical examination of Chu Hsi's chronological biography; *Ts'ung-shu chi-ch'eng* edition, 1937), pp. 263–268.

[10]Wing-tsit Chan, p. 589.

[11]*Ibid.*

10. Subjectivity and Ontological Reality—
An Interpretation of Wang Yang-ming's
Mode of Thinking

I

To resist the temptation to tie up loose ends prematurely is most difficult in the task of expounding Wang Yang-ming's mode of thinking. His precepts such as *chih-hsing ho-i* (the unity of knowing and acting), *ts'un t'ien-li ch'ü jen-yü* (to preserve the Heavenly principle and to extirpate human desires), and *chih liang-chih* (to extend innate knowledge) are so familiar to the student of Chinese thought that an attempt to construct a cogent philosophical system for Wang Yang-ming, as compared to that for a Chu Hsi (1130–1200) or a Wang Fu-chih (1619–1692), seems relatively simple. It is not to be wondered that there exist many constructions of Wang Yang-ming's philosophy. One is easily led to believe that the data are of such a plastic nature that without much artificial effort they can be shaped into a variety of designs according to the intentions of the designers. How much this is attributable to Yang-ming's own decision to discourage any systematization of his ideas remains an open question. But the act of constructing a philosophical edifice for Yang-ming cannot be justified merely on grounds that such an intellectual game has been widely and continuously practiced.

Of course Yang-ming's conscious choice not to present his ideas in a systematically developed form does not at all rule out the possibility of laying out the structure of his philosophy by making explicit the "inner logic" of his teaching. In fact, it is our responsibility to see to it that the hidden meaning of Yang-ming's teaching be unfolded. At issue, however, is not the desirability of reconstructing the philosophy of one of the most original and influential architects of the Chinese intellectual tradition, but the precise method of reconstruction.

I am increasingly suspicious of the claim that the reconstruction

138

of Yang-ming's philosophy involves no more than the procedure of integrating his basic precepts into a rational system. Nor do I accept the presumption that the content of Yang-ming's thought can be encapsulated in a more or less rigorously related set of formulas. For I cannot endorse the optimistic view that, once the blueprint of Yang-ming's philosophical edifice is dissected and analyzed, the task of reconstruction can be painlessly accomplished by a group of professional builders.

To borrow from Gabriel Marcel: "The problem now was not so much one of building as of digging; philosophical activity was now definable as a drilling rather than a construction."[1] What does "digging or drilling" mean as a methodological approach to Yang-ming's thinking? Unlike the act of constructing, it does not presuppose the availability of an existing blueprint. It is directed more by a spirit of discovery than by the need to impose a system on the primary sources extant on the subject. Of course, it is hoped that through continuous efforts of discovery, the inner structure of Yang-ming's thought will be revealed. But before the time is ripe, it seems more productive to retain the fruitful ambiguities in his philosophy than to force them into a neat but superficial synthesis.

II

Wang Yang-ming once characterized his learning as the "learning of the body and mind" (*shen-hsin chih hsüeh*).[2] If we take this characterization seriously, we cannot afford to ignore the experiential dimension of Yang-ming's learning in an interpretation of his thinking. This gives rise to a fairly complicated methodological issue: How can we talk systematically about an approach to learning that has flatly rejected the validity of intellectual argumentation as an adequate means of communicating this type of knowledge? Indeed, Yang-ming, time and again, refused to subject his learning to a written form for fear that a "conceptual understanding" (*chih-chieh*) would abstract it from its experiential basis, which is its real "content." If the experiential basis is absent, an intellectual understanding is at best a formalistic attempt to approximate what can only be manifested through practical efforts. Intellectual understanding is inevitably one-sided, for the exemplary teacher, unlike the teacher of words, must try to transmit the content of the learning ot his students through his entire body and mind. He prefers verbal expressions to written instructions because the former are situational suggestions, which can be responsive to both the specificity of the occasion and the peculiarity of the student, whereas the latter are fixed instructions, which may be inadequate to suit either the occasion or the student.

We must hasten to point out that Yang-ming's emphasis on experience and situation is intended neither to denounce intellectuality nor to advocate a situational ethic. Rather, it is based on a belief that the process of real learning involves the whole person in his concrete, daily existence. This kind of learning is not to appropriate something external to the body and mind. Nor is it to acquire a skill alien to the self. It constitutes none other than the learning of how to become a person, which in the Neo-Confucian terminology means how to cultivate one's own body and mind and how to realize the universal humanity in oneself. If this is the main concern, Yang-ming's fear lies not so much in the exercise of the intellect per se as in an intellectual projection and/or objectification of the subject matter, which must be experienced as a precondition for cognitive reflection. Once the learning of how to become a person is treated *merely* as an intellectual topic, the affective needs that may have prompted the discussion in the first place will be neutralized, and, as a result, the experiential basis on which the topic presents itself will also be lost. It is true that intellectual argumentation frequently clarifies our ways of thinking, but in this connection it must be applied with an awareness of its intrinsic weakness in grasping this type of learning.

The central concern of Yang-ming's learning is the problem of man. However, its main purpose is not to present an objective study of human beings but to point to the way of becoming a genuine person. Since the complete manifestation of humanity is that of the sage, the purpose seems to be to emulate the sagely way. But following the Mencian tradition, Yang-ming believes that every person *can* become a sage simply by willing to be one, for sagehood is realizable by self-learning. Even the emulation of the sage is predicated on an inner decision that can never be imposed from the outside. This

140

SUBJECTIVITY AND ONTOLOGICAL REALITY

gives rise to a familiar paradox: To learn to become a sage I must begin with an awareness that sagehood is inherently in me. If I am truly aware of it, what is there that has to be learned? An anecdote in the *Instruction for Practical Living* may be helpful in this connection:

> Wang Yü-chung, Tsou Ch'ien-chih, and I were in attendance together in Ch'ien-chou. The Teacher said, "There is the sage in everyone. Only because one falls short of self-confidence the sage (inherent in oneself) is being buried." Thereupon he looked at Yü-chung and said, "Originally there is a sage in your bosom." Yü-chung rose and said that he did not deserve it. The Teacher said, "This is what you yourself own. Why decline?" Yü-chung said again, "I do not deserve it." The Teacher said, "Everyone has it. How much more is that true of you, Yü-chung! Why Should you be modest? It won't do even if you are modest." Whereupon Yü-chung smiled and accepted (the compliment).[3]

According to this anecdote the sage that is inherent in everyone is a reality that can never be lost. Indeed, Yang-ming further discourses that no matter what one does, the inner sage can never be destroyed. Even a thief realizes in himself that he should not be a thief. If you call him a thief, he will still blush.

On the other hand, Yang-ming's lifelong struggle to manifest the sage in himself, so to speak, bears witness to the fact that to become what one *ought to be*, far from being "simple and easy" (*chien-i*), is a strenuous and unceasing process of self-realization. If Yang-ming had to suffer "a hundred deaths and a thousand hardships"[4] before he was able to remark confidently that he was indeed responsive to the demands of his inner sage, the psychological agony and the moral courage that are required of each of us to realize the sage in ourselves must be incredibly great. In fact, the legacy of Yang-ming's learning, including a few of his own writings, the verbatim records of his instructions, and dialogues reconstructed by his disciples, does not smack of the arrogance of an accomplished teacher. An important reason for his reluctance to put his ideas in a written form seems to be the awareness that his learning is meaningful only to those who have made a prior commitment to the unique patterns of realizing the sage in themselves. It may very well become a source of confusion for those who lack inner experiences of their own and purport to search for the truth of sagehood through the intellectual appropriation of the contextual teachings of others. Implicit in this method of learning is the acknowledgment that the teacher does not necessarily have privileged access to the sagely truth. Like his students, he is in the process of becoming what he ought to be. The inner sage so conceived is a potentiality which can never be fully realized.

To say that the sage inherent in each of us is both a reality that can never be lost, and a potentiality that can never be fully realized, is a way of introducing Yang-ming's perception. For the sake of expediency, I propose to approach this type of perception from two complementary points of view. When we say that every person can be a sage because sagehood is inherent in each of us, we talk about man's structure of being: what man is ontologically and what he ought to be existentially. When we say that no one is in fact a sage because inner sagehood can never be fully realized, we talk about man's process of becoming: what ontologically he is not and what existentially he ought not to be. From the point of view of being, I am what I ought to be and what I ought to be is none other than what I really am. From the point of view of becoming, I am not what I ought to be and what I ought to be is qualitatively different from what I really am. When Yang-ming says that every person is a sage, he refers to the "original substance" (*pen-t'i*) of man's being. When he implies that no one can fully realize his sagehood, he refers to the "practical effort" (*kung-fu*) of man's becoming. The former is the ground of self-realization and the latter is its concrete process. Since man is not an abstract concept but a live reality, he should not be understood merely in terms of his "original face." Similarly, it is difficult to accept the view that the reality of man constitutes no more than the totality of his concrete acts.

We have already suggested that man's structure of being and man's process of becoming are two complementary points of view. Indeed, if I interpret Yang-ming's perception correctly, they actually represent two inseparable dimensions of human reality. Therefore, we must recognize that man is both a given structure and an indeterminate process. To say that I am a given structure is not to deny the freedom of choice, for I alone can make the inner decision to become what I ought to be. And such a decision necessarily transforms the restrictive ties of my given structure into a set of instrumentaria for self-realization. To say that I am an indeterminate process is not to undermine my inner identity. No matter how I choose to act, I do so in the context of my being a meaningful entity. Therefore, a measure of freedom is an integral part of the given structure, and a sense of identity is an integral part of the indeterminate process. Although the structure is given, for the sake of self-realization it must undergo a process of transformation. By the same token, the indeterminate process constantly assumes a temporal structure because of its self-identity. Consequently man's *being* what he is must be sought in his *becoming* what he ought to be, and vice versa.

We can work out the main thrust of the argument as follows: What man existentially is differs from what he ontologically is and existentially can become. But his state of existence neither denies what he ontologically is nor inhibits what he existentially can become. To say that every man can become a sage is to say that every man can existentially become what he ought to be. He can become what he ought to be by self-effort, as differentiated from the intervention of an agent separable from his own structure as a human being, because the ultimate ground of his self-realization rests on what he is ontologically. However, man's being (the sage that is in him) may be "buried," even though it can never be totally "lost." And when it is buried for an extended period of time, a man who is, to be sure, a potential sage may, in fact, like the Ox Mountain in *Mencius*, appear to be completely "defaced." Therefore, despite his intrinsic sagehood, man must learn how to become a sage in his daily existence. The learning involves an unceasing process of self-realization, which in this connection means the process of manifesting the sage that is in each of us.

We must recognize in our preliminary consideration that the unity of the original substance, as the ultimate ground of man's being, and practical efforts, as the concrete process of man's becoming, is not an assertion of belief, nor is it merely an argument of logic. Rather it is a certitude of experience. Understandably the "learning of the body and mind" revolves around man's daily existence as the primary datum. Rational analysis and intellectual discourse are greatly valued in this approach, but they must be based on the inner experience of the inquirer. For the main task is not to

143

search for objective truths but to deepen and broaden self-knowledge. Philosophy, so conceived, is teaching by personal example. If we follow this line of thought, we cannot philosophize merely as a disinterested analyst, because to do philosophy necessarily entails the act of self-transformation. Although this mode of thinking appears to be in some disagreement with the conventional academic characterization of philosophy as pure analysis, it is not at all in conflict with the Socratic vision, "Know thyself." However, if the inner experience of the self is the basis of philosophical inquiry, how can we transcend the various invidious forms of subjectivism? This brings us to one of the foci of Yang-ming's philosophy: the problem of the self.

The learning of the body and mind can also be understood as a form of self-learning: an attempt to manifest the genuine humanity inherent in the self. Actually this type of learning is also interpreted as the learning of how to become a sage. Sagehood, in the present context, means genuine humanity, which can also be characterized as true selfhood. To become a sage is therefore to be truthful to oneself. Understandably the three basic precepts of Yang-ming's teaching, mentioned at the beginning of this article, are all centered around the issue of self-realization. This evokes several intriguing problems in Yang-ming's mature philosophy. What is the ultimate reality of the self? Is there any necessity for the self to enter into communication with another? How is the self connected with the myriad things? Since Yang-ming has been identified for centuries with what may be called the "subjective" position, it is of paramount importance that we note as a *point d'appui* the fundamental distinction between his philosophy of subjectivity and the fallacy of subjectivism.

III

Chih-hsing ho-i is Yang-ming's first philosophical formulation in his career as an exemplary teacher of the "learning of body and mind." The only instruction that seems to have preceded this formulation is his insistence that the student must be willing to make a prior commitment to the vocation of becoming a sage before taking

144

up any formal study with him. Genetically *chih-hsing ho-i* is the crystallization of Yang-ming's years of agonizing strife to arrive at an experiential understanding of Chu Hsi's pedagogical method, *ko-wu* (investigation of things). In light of two famous anecdotes—namely, the seven-day spiritual confrontation with the precept of *ko-wu* in front of a bamboo grove in 1492,[5] and the life-and-death struggle to attain internal peace by reverting to *ko-wu* from the search for external *li* (principle or reason) to rectify the mind in 1508[6]—Yang-ming's *chih-hsing ho-i* in 1509 symbolizes an important triumph of his repeated attempts to understand himself. Since the road to complete self-knowledge never ends, *chih-hsing ho-i* marks only the beginning of a long and dedicated quest for self-realization. However, even in this early formulation, Yang-ming already demonstrates a great insight into the principle of subjectivity, as a concrete and yet universally applicable way of the sage. Such a way seems to depart from Chu Hsi's *ko-wu* in several aspects.

First, *ko-wu* perceives the subject and object as two independent entities; they come into contact when the subject makes conscious efforts to approach the object. *Chih-hsing ho-i* rejects such an artificial dichotomy and points to a dynamic process of self-realization in which man's subjectivity becomes a real experience rather than an abstract concept. Second, *ko-wu* puts too much stress on the tangible forms of self-cultivation, which tends to objectify moral decision into a "goal" of self-efforts. However, *chih-hsing ho-i* "bridges" the gap between the inner and outer by focusing on the linkage between thought and practice. Third, *ko-wu* inclines to quantify morality into a series of discrete deeds; as a result, external manifestations take precedence over inner transformations. *Chih-hsing ho-i*, on the other hand, keeps moral consciousness awake in all situations so that even the motion of the "incipient activation" (*chi*) of the mind will not be overlooked. Fourth, *ko-wu* tends to subsume moral principles under the rubric of empirical knowledge, whereas *chih-hsing ho-i*, by centering around intentionality, underscores the inner dimension of ethicoreligious cultivation. Finally, it seems that a sense of urgency is lacking in *ko-wu*, for it assumes that the process of self-realization is necessarily a gradual one. By focusing on the directionality of the will, *chih-hsing ho-i* speaks to moral self-cultivation in a sense of immediacy. The question of the gradual versus the sudden process of self-realization becomes secondary, for the central concern is *how* to manifest the inner sage here and now, rather than by *what* process the inner sage will eventually be manifested.

It must be pointed out that in Yang-ming's own perception, although *chih-hsing ho-i* fundamentally transforms Chu Hsi's interpretation of *ko-wu*, it is intended neither to reject the method of *ko-wu* nor to disparage its importance. Rather, the purpose is to restore *ko-wu* its original position in the *Great Learning*. Whether Yang-ming's attempt to return to the so-called ancient edition of the *Great Learning* can be supported on textual grounds should not concern us here. But we must bear in mind that Yang-ming's critique of Chu Hsi lies not so much in the method of *ko-wu* per se as in the philosophical foundation on which such a method is advocated. If I believe that self-knowledge is obtainable only through a gradual process of intellectually appropriating the *li* inherent in external things, I inadvertently subscribe to the position that *li* in myself lacks both self-sufficiency and creativity. If I must internalize *li* from the outside, the ultimate basis of my self-realization cannot be located within my human nature. Thus I must be taught to become what I ought to be. And teaching so conceived is not self-discovery but is imposing a set of established social values on the self. As a result the *li* that is the ground of my being is not necessarily an integral part of my existence. This is why Yang-ming asserts that in Chu Hsi's philosophy there is a rupture between *hsin* (heart-mind) and *li*.

In terms of practical efforts, Yang-ming also feels that Chu Hsi's precept of *ko-wu* lacks a central focus. The expression he uses is *t'ou-nao* (literally, head-brain).[7] If the learning of the body and mind revolves around the main purpose of becoming a sage, *ko-wu* as a method of self-realization must pivot on an inner decision. If such a decision is absent, no matter how many items of things and affairs are carefully investigated and studied, they cannot contribute to self-knowledge at all. Yang-ming is absolutely serious in maintaining that the student must first make an existential decision about his life before he is allowed to take up learning with him.[8] He is quite aware that unless the threshold of commitment is crossed, empirical knowledge can never be translated into self-knowledge. However, once the *t'ou-nao* is obtained, the method of *ko-wu* is not only beneficial but indispensable to self-knowledge. *Ko-wu* so understood is not

146

merely investigating external phenomena but rectifying natural things and human affairs in accordance with the overarching concern of self-realization.

It is in this sense that to know (*chih*) is not a purely cognitive function without involving the whole existence of the knower, and to act (*hsing*) cannot be an isolated performance devoid of the broad context of the self. The unity (*ho-i*) of knowing and acting so conceived should not be interpreted as a general statement about the relationship between theory and praxis, although it certainly is pregnant with such far-reaching implications. What Yang-ming has in mind, however, seems to be inseparably linked with this ultimate concern of how to become a sage. It may seem presumptuous to argue that he propounds the unity of knowing and acting in the capacity of a sage. It is certainly legitimate to suggest that the precept is advocated in the spirit of someone who has actively been engaged in the process of trying to become a sage. I am aware that such a qualification inevitably restricts the epistemological scope of *chih-hsing ho-i*. One may very well wonder how it is to be applied to areas other than ethicoreligious philosophy. My immediate task, however, is not to expound its general applicability but to see to it that its core meaning is preserved.

If *chih-hsing ho-i* is to be comprehended in terms of the process of self-realization, it is inconceivable that to know does not necessarily lead to a transforming action and to act does not entail a deepening and broadening effect on the existing knowledge. Indeed, to know is not merely to engage in a disinterested mental activity of apprehending something out there. It is to see to it that the perception of what should be done is fully actualized in concrete behavior. For knowing to be genuine it must evoke the whole process whereby that which is known is simultaneously manifested in daily conduct: "Knowledge is the beginning of action."[9] To borrow Yang-ming's own example, knowing that I should practice filial love is not merely to know some abstract principle but to manifest a dimension of my inner experience in concrete action here and now. I cannot be said to know filial love if I simply subscribe to the proposition that filial love is desirable because it is a feeling inherent in my human nature. If I endorse such a position on intellectual grounds alone, I do it in bad faith; for I do not have any experiential basis to support my

147

endorsement. Knowing, in this connection, is not restricted to a cognitive function. It is in essence the "clear awareness (*ming-chüeh*) and refined reconnaissance (*ching-ch'a*) of action."[10]

What then is a genuine action? The idea that praxis must have a tangible impact on the existing constellation of affairs is too narrow a definition to accommodate Yang-ming's concept of *hsing*. Action begins when a thought has assumed a directionality and becomes an intention (*i*). To intend is already to act. For an action to be genuine it must be an integral part of the whole process whereby what is acted on is meaningfully identified in the context of self-awareness: "Action is the completion of knowledge."[11] Returning to Yang-ming's example, to act in accordance with filial love is not to follow a set of accepted rituals but to fulfill a basic human feeling. It should be added that if the feeling of filiality is expressed in a conventionally recognized form, it is only dictated by an inner urge to manifest a general feeling in a way communicable to those involved. It is therefore quite conceivable that when a well-established ritual fails to suit a particular circumstance it can be modified and even rejected. Yang-ming's deliberate attempt to make some changes in the mourning ceremony for his father is a case in point. Although his action drew severe criticism from his best friend, Chan Jo-shui (1466–1560), it was by no means in conflict with his own teaching.[12] A genuine action is thus the concretization of an experiential knowing. It is in essence the "real immediacy (*chen-ch'ieh*) and true reality (*tu-shih*)"[13] of knowledge.

Chih-hsing ho-i so conceived denotes the identity of a dynamic process rather than the unity of two static concepts. Specifically it refers to the creative way of becoming a sage. As Yang-ming clearly remarks, the "basic principle" (*tsung-chih*) of this precept is to teach the student to eliminate selfish desires and to manifest the original substance of knowing and acting in daily affairs. It is not intended to argue in the abstract what the nature of knowledge and action should be. If inner sagehood is the central concern, the practical effort commences as soon as a thought presents itself as an intention. On the other side of the same reality, conscious reflection never ceases to function as a guide as long as the actualizing process remains incomplete. Truly, "knowledge is the intentional direction of action and action is the practical effort of knowledge."[14] Yang-ming further contends, "Learning to be a sage involves only uniform effort. Knowledge and action must not be separated."[15]

Underlying the above discussion is the awareness that the way of the sage is to be found in the structure of the self, because *li* is not only inherent in human nature but also embodied in the mind. The identity of *hsin* and *li*, a precept Yang-ming shares with Lu Hsiang-shan (1139–1193), provides a philosophical basis for the contention that the road to sagehood involves nothing other than the whole process of internal self-transformation. *Chih-hsing ho-i* as a response to Chu Hsi's interpretation of *ko-wu* thus can be understood as an experiential confirmation of the validity of such a process. This insistence on subjectivity as a unifying and creating principle inevitably leads to the question of subjectivism, which brings us to Yang-ming's second important heuristic precept, *ts'un t'ien-li ch'ü jen-yü*.

IV

Shortly after Yang-ming advocated *chih-hsing ho-i*, he suggested "quiet sitting" as a method of probing the "substance of human nature" (*hsing-t'i*), which is comparable to the Ch'an practice of manifesting the inner buddhahood through a direct experience of self-awareness. However, it did not take him long to alter his teaching. He later regretted that, for a while, he had put too much emphasis on the quietist approach to self-cultivation. By the spring of 1514, he had fundamentally reoriented his pedagogical efforts and had focused his attention on the precept *ts'un t'ien-li ch'ü jen-yü*.[16] This gives rise to a crucial question: Why is quiet sitting, a form of inner spiritual self-cultivation, not accepted as a highly desirable method of learning to become a sage? In other words, if the structure of the self is sufficient for the actualization of the inner sage, what else is needed to manifest what is inherent in human nature? If we leave aside explanations of a social, political, or psychological nature, the answer seems to lie in Yang-ming's vision of the self.

We have already pointed out that in Yang-ming's philosophy the ontological being of man is reciprocally attached to his existential becoming, and they actually represent two inseparable dimensions of human reality. Therefore, the proposition that ontologically the

149

self is sufficient for the actualization of the inner sage does not necessarily imply that even without practical efforts man can, in an existential sense, automatically become what he ought to be. In fact for the inner sage to be manifested as an experienced reality, continuous self-cultivation is required. Of course, quiet sitting is itself a form of self-cultivation. The point at issue is then the specific kind of self-cultivation that is most congenial to the realization of the self.

To recapitulate an earlier discussion, although *chih-hsing ho-i* is formulated as a critique of Chu Hsi's interpretation of *ko-wu*, Yang-ming never intends to abandon the whole practice of *ko-wu*. Instead, he spends much effort on restoring the true meaning of *ko-wu*, as he understands it, in the perspective of the so-called eight items of the *Great Learning*. What Yang-ming attempts to do is to replace Chu Hsi's conception of *ko-wu* as the investigation of things with his own interpretation that *ko-wu* be construed as the "regulation" or "rectification" (*cheng*) of human affairs. On the surface, this is no more than a different philological rendering of the ancient text. Underlying the change, however, is the introduction of a new vision of the self. To Yang-ming the five developmental stages of self-realization in the *Great Learning*, which constitute the "inner dimension" of the eight items, symbolize one uniform process rather than a series of discrete steps of learning. The focus of his attention, unlike that of Chu Hsi's, is not the specific techniques involved but the quality of one's existential self as perceived by a process of inner reflection. It is in this connection that he considers "the examination of one's subtle thoughts and deliberations" a much more profound undertaking than other kinds of self-cultivation instructed by Chu Hsi.[17]

It would be misleading to suggest that since Yang-ming puts much emphasis on inner reflection, quiet sitting must be accepted as an important method of *ko-wu*. Actually in Yang-ming's new vision whether or not one engages in quiet sitting is inconsequential. The real issue lies in the "sincerity of the will" (*ch'eng-i*). So long as a person's will is sincere, which means that he is truthful to his genuine self, the quality of his being will be preserved, even without the practice of quiet sitting. On the other hand, if he has not yet made a decision to be honest with the original intentions of his inner sage, such a practice cannot in itself bring about a fundamental transformation. A close examination of a key passage in Yang-ming's teaching is in order: "The master of the body (*shen*) is the mind. What emanates from the mind is the intention. The original substance of the intention is knowledge, and wherever the intention is directed is a thing (*wu*)."[18]

The inner structure of this teaching is a set of four correlations. Each of them characterizes an important aspect of the self. They are (1) the correlation of body and mind, (2) the correlation of mind and intention, (3) the correlation of intention and knowledge and, (4) the correlation of intention and thing. It is not difficult to recognize the centrality of intention in this formulation of the self. This is the fundamental reason Yang-ming insists on returning to the alleged ancient edition of the *Great Learning*, in which intentionality seems to occupy a much more prominent position than in Chu Hsi's revised edition. Yang-ming's perception may be worked out diagrammatically:

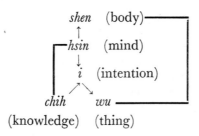

(1) The body is not external to the mind, for it is where the mind resides. Yet, since the mind is the master of the body, the body can be intended as a thing by the mind. (2) The directionality of the mind is the intention, which is the manifestation of the mind. (3) Knowledge in this connection refers to the original consciousness of the mind. Based on the preceding statement, it is the original substance of the intention. (4) The thing is not external to the mind either, for it is that on which the directionality of the mind is fixed.

To paraphrase Yang-ming's own words, the four kinds of correlations actually point to the uniform process of self-cultivation. The ears, eyes, mouth, nose, and four limbs are parts of the body. But only in reference to the mind can they see, hear, speak, or act.

151

Simultaneously the mind depends on the functions of the sensory organs to satisfy its own demands for seeing, hearing, speaking, or acting. The body as a physical existence is where the mind dwells, but the mind gives commands to the body. The intention is the function of the mind. As the directionality of the mind, it provides a link between its original substance (knowledge) and its intended object (a thing).

In the light of the preceding, sincerity of the will refers to a process through which the intention becomes truthful to the genuine directionality of the mind. Such a process inevitably involves the rectification of the intended object and the penetration of the original substance of the mind. It is therefore identical with the process of cultivating the body and with that of regulating the mind. This is why Yang-ming continues with the remark, "They are all one. The intention never exists in a vacuum. It is always connected with some thing. Therefore sincerity of the will entails rectifying it in the thing to which the will (the intention) is directed."[19]

By focusing on sincerity of the will, Yang-ming perceives *ko-wu* as a dynamic process through which man's ontological being is manifested in his existential becoming. Specifically the process is understood as a twofold procedure, practiced simultaneously on two fronts: *ts'un t'ien-li* (the preservation of the Heavenly principle) on the one hand, and *ch'ü jen-yü* (the extirpation of human desires) on the other.

T'ien-li, a term that Yang-ming inherited from Ch'eng Hao[20] (1032–1085), refers to the ultimate basis on which man can become what he ought to be. Rendered as Heavenly principle or Heavenly reason, *t'ien-li* conveys the idea that the ontological reality of human nature and the inner sage in the mind is "naturally so." To preserve *ts'un* Heavenly principle, a person should see to it that his "original face" be "saved." If the Heavenly principle is naturally his, what actually causes his concern for preserving it? From what should he try to save it? This leads us to the problematics of human desires.

In addition to the frequently used *jen-yü*, a host of other terms are employed to designate this area of concern: *ssu-yü* (selfish desires), *wu-yü* (material desires), and *ssu-i* (selfish ideas), just to mention a few. Given Yang-ming's vision of man, human desires

152

should first be understood as those forces which tend to obstruct and distort man's becoming what he ought to be. Obstruction in this connection means a passive limitation, and distortion means an active falsification. To extirpate (*ch'ü*) human desires is therefore to eliminate those processes that have not only limited the full development of a person's genuine self but also falsified the true nature of his original intention.

A comprehensive analysis of Yang-ming's theory of human desires requires an exposition of the Neo-Confucian concept of evil, which is certainly beyond our immediate concern. Suffice it now to focus our attention on two aspects of the general issue: bad habits (*ch'i-hsi*) and selfishness (*tzu-ssu*). The former implies both an inertia and a decreased power of resistance, and the latter signifies a serious paralysis of human sensitivity. When a person is tied down by habitual forces, his ability to exercise the creative power for self-growth will be greatly limited. Despite his inner sage, his will to be sincere and genuine may become so weak that his state of existence has actually become as involuntary as "wood and stone." The danger of being selfish is more devastating. It is not only a form of pathological isolation. Even within the isolated self, it recognizes merely a small area of basic human needs. To use an example from the *Mencius*, this is like taking care of one's finger at the expense of the whole body.

In Yang-ming's teaching, the extirpation of human desires and the preservation of the heavenly principle represent two inseparable aspects of the same process. To preserve the Heavenly principle is to "establish sincerity" (*li-ch'eng*),[21] which means to protect the genuineness of one's ontological being. Such acts depend on one's ability to conquer human desires. When one is really in control of oneself, to use a Yang-ming analogy, the incipient tendencies of human desires will be like a drop of snow in a burning furnace. Similarly, to extirpate human desires is not just a means to an end. It is a continuous process of self-purification. Yang-ming says that *ko-wu*, as a way of rectifying one's intention, must be practiced from the commencement of learning to the completion of sagehood. Since sagehoood can never be completed in an existential sense, *ko-wu* is in fact an unceasing process of self-cultivation. Such a process is not a departure from human nature but a return to it, for the real source of man's ability to eliminate the obstructing and distorting forces of bad habits and selfishness lies in his own mind.

Ontologically the mind is the affective manifestation of the Heavenly principle, and the Heavenly principle is the original substance of the mind. They are absolutely indivisible. Existentially, however, when the mind encounters a thing, it faces the danger of being fixated in its intended object. If such a fixation is prolonged, the mind is gradually "materialized" (wu-hua) by the inertia of the thing. When this occurs, the Heavenly principle becomes functionally neutralized. Consequently the dynamism and creativity essential to self-realization will not be generated, and the original substance of the mind is "buried." The ontological identification of the mind and the heavenly principle notwithstanding, in the conduct of daily affairs the mind may existentially be controlled by human desires. As a result, its normal functions are obstructed and distorted. To extirpate human desires is therefore to restore the substance and to rectify the function of the mind. Such an effort is indistinguishable from the preservation of the Heavenly principle. It is in this sense that Yang-ming puts much emphasis on the incompatibility of the Heavenly principle and human desires. The preservation of the former necessitates the exclusion of the latter.

Yang-ming's insistence on the contradiction of the Heavenly principle and human desires is comparable to the classical demarcation of tao-hsin (the mind of the Way) and jen-hsin (the mind of the limited man).[22] The former is broad in extension and genuine in quality, whereas the latter is a limited and false representation of the original substance of the mind. In a paradoxical sense human desires are not at all human; for as selfish expressions of the mind, they have already obstructed and distorted its true intentions, which means that the mind is existentially alienated from its original substance. When the mind ceases to function in accordance with its original substance, in the terminology of Ch'eng Hao, the humanity that is inherent in it may be "paralyzed." As we have already mentioned, human desires are selfish desires; instead of fulfilling the self, they tend to destroy it. Viewed from this perspective, to extirpate human desires and to preserve the Heavenly principle is to aim at the elimination of selfishness so that the genuine self can be secured.

V

In 1521, Yang-ming formally advocated the precept of *liang-chih* (innate knowledge, conscientious wisdom, intuitive knowledge of the good, conscientious consciousness, or simply good conscience),[23] more than six years after he had formulated the instructional method of *ts'un t'ien-li ch'ü jen-yü*. What is the relation between *liang-chih* and his teaching on the preservation of the Heavenly principle and the extirpation of human desires? Indeed what is the significance of *liang-chih* in the light of his thinking on subjectivity? According to Yang-ming's chronological biography, his advocacy of *liang-chih* was predicated on an "experiential realization" (*t'i-jen*) that the Heavenly principle is none other than the *liang-chih* inherent in the mind. Prior to his experiential realization, Yang-ming had repeatedly instructed his students to appreciate the meaning of the Heavenly principle through personal confirmation. However, when a student asked him what the Heavenly principle really denotes, Yang-ming was at a loss for the precise word to pinpoint its specific reference. Therefore, when he actually identified the Heavenly principle as *liang-chih,* he remarked in great spiritual delight that for a number of years the word had been there, as if on the tip of his tongue, and yet he was unable to articulate it.[24] It seems that once the word was uttered and the precise identification made, the experience was like the sudden release of a flood. The flow was so powerful that it was absolutely unstoppable. Of course, the point is not the verbal identification but its experiential basis. Nevertheless, what does it signify when the Heavenly principle is understood as *liang-chih?*

We have already stated that *chih-hsing ho-i* is predicated on the identity of the mind and the principle. We have also noted that *ts'un t'ien-li ch'ü jen-yü* is based on the belief that the principle is the original substance of the mind. By employing the classical Mencian concept of *liang-chih* to characterize the Heavenly principle, Yang-ming certainly does not intend to depart from the two precepts mentioned above. How much can we claim that his idea of *liang-chih* actually symbolizes a new vision of subjectivity? To be sure many epistemological and ontological issues are involved, but suffice it now to focus our attention on two interrelated areas of concern, namely, its internality and its universality.

Although *liang-chih* is closely connected with the senses and the intellect, it is reducible neither to sensory perception nor to conceptual understanding. And yet, as Yang-ming has pointed out, *liang-chih* is the "clear illumination" (*chao-ming*) and "spiritual awareness" (*ling-chüeh*) of the Heavenly principle. Since the Heavenly principle is the original substance of the mind, *liang-chih* manifests both the affective and cognitive dimensions of the mind. As clear illumination, *liang-chih* is the penetrative insight that grasps the ultimate reality by a self-generative "intellectual intuition."[25] As a spiritual awareness, *liang-chih* is an all-embracing sensibility that embodies the whole universe by a self-sufficient "anthropocosmic feeling." Hence, *liang-chih* is not an internalized value. It is not something that can be learned. Neither does *liang-chih* originate from a source of mystery, such as the "wholly other," which is completely beyond the structure of man. It is true that *liang-chih* cannot be totally devoid of empirical knowledge, but it is absolutely independent of what the Neo-Confucian commonly refers to as the "knowledge of hearing and seeing" (*wen-chien chih chih*). Therefore, in Yang-ming's philosophy, *liang-chih* should be understood as the innermost and indissoluble reality of man. It is also the ultimate reason why the inner sage in each human being can never be completely lost.

Nevertheless, despite its internality, which is in sharp conflict with any form of subjectivism, *liang-chih* must be "extended." The extension of *liang-chih* is actually for the sake of its own self-realization. This line of thinking needs some clarification. Although *liang-chih* is said to be the innermost reality of man, it is not confined to human beings, or even to animate beings. For it is the ultimate reality of Heaven, Earth, and the myriad things. In fact *liang-chih* as a concept is not localizable. Its flexibility is vividly shown in the following statement: "*Liang-chih* is oneness. From the point of view of its wondrous function, it is called *shen* (spirituality). From the point of view of its transformation, it is called *ch'i* (material force, ether, or existence in process). From the point of view of its crystallization, it is called *ching* (essence)."[26] This brings us to its universality:

The *liang-chih* of man is the same as that of plants and trees, tiles and stones. Without the *liang-chih* inherent in man, there cannot be plants and trees, tiles and stones. This is not true of them only.

Even Heaven and Earth cannot exist without the *liang-chih* that is inherent in man. For at bottom Heaven, Earth, the myriad things, and man form one body. The point at which this unity is manifested in its most refined and excellent form is the clear intelligence of the human mind.[27]

It is in this sense that the uniqueness of man is defined not merely by his possession of *liang-chih* but also by his ability to extend his *liang-chih* to embody the universe as a whole. In his "Inquiry on the *Great Learning*," Yang-ming defines human nature in terms of a series of empathetic communions between man and all other beings in the universe. Man's nature is such that his spiritual sensibility and loving care link him in an organismic unity with the cosmos as a whole. To manifest his humanity, or to actualize the sage that is in him, is to experience the inseparability of his own being from his fellow human beings, from the beings in the animal kingdom, from animate beings such as trees and grass, and even from inanimate beings such as tiles and stones. According to Yang-ming's perception, man's primordial unity with all beings in the universe is neither an achieved state nor a desirable ideal. It is essentially an experienced and lived reality. This is what man ontologically is. Hence the distinction between the great man who manifests his humanity to a great extent and the limited man who manifests his humanity only to a limited extent lies not in man's being but in what he existentially has become. To reiterate an earlier point, the limited man has become small not because the limitation of the sage that is in him, but because the sage has been "buried" in selfish desires. When man's humanity is neutralized, despite his being, existentially he may become an expression of inhumanity.

It is precisely in this sense that Yang-ming's instructional efforts have centered around the problem of *how* to become a sage in the context of what man existentially is here and now. He seldom engages himself in a systematic exposition of his teaching, for he is aware that conceptual understanding detached from the immediacy of self-transformation may turn out to be a form of subjectivism. Real manifestation of humanity is impossible if selfish desires are not extirpated. To the extent that selfish desires are eliminated, the *liang-chih* in man will be revealed naturally. We are thus confronted

157

with an exceedingly interesting conception of the human situation. Man is ontologically one with "Heaven, Earth, and the myriad things," and yet in his concrete experience he is aware that the existential process through which he can become what he ought to be must follow a differentiated structure of relationship. Although such a relationship gives a concrete manifestation to the organismic unity of his being, it can intellectually, as well as experientially, limit or even falsify his self-realization. For example, caring for oneself is a concrete manifestation of one's being, but if one's self-care becomes fixated in the subjective structure of the self, it may easily turn into egocentrism, which is a paralyzing limitation of one's humanity. By the same token, filial love may become an expression of nepotism, the love for one's fellow countrymen may become a form of ethnocentrism, and even the love for mankind cannot escape the danger of anthropocentrism. The extirpation of selfish desires is therefore to free man from being fixated in a limited and falsified version of humanity. It is true that man's sensibility and care cannot but be manifested in a form of relationship. But at a specific juncture of human existence, one's relationship can be either a form of subjective attachment or a manifestation of self-fulfillment. The function of *liang-chih* is to differentiate selfish desires from the Heavenly principle. Once such a differentiation is made, it naturally acts in accordance with its own perception. Subjective attachment as a falsification of the original intention of the mind must be eliminated. Only then can the wish of the inner sage be fulfilled.

To conclude, man can form a spiritual communion with all the beings in the universe because ontologically he is in an organismic unity with Heaven, Earth, and the myriad things. However, to manifest the sage that is inherent in him, he must travel the concrete path of self-realization. Such a path involves the correlation of a differentiated relationship, on the one hand, and a manifold structure of sensibility and care, on the other. The main task then is to fulfill such a relationship without being fixated in any of its limited expressions. To the extent man is able to free himself from selfish desires, his humanity will be "expanded" to its full potential. And the ultimate ground of his ability to transcend the obstructing and distorting forces of subjectivism is his own *liang-chih*.

It is instructive to note that as early as 1505, when Yang-ming was still in his early thirties, he entered into a "covenant" with Chan Jo-shui to spread the Confucian Tao. According to a reference made in the poem dedicated to him by Chan in the following year, both of them at the time adhered to Ch'eng Hao's teaching: "The man of humanity forms one body with all things in the universe."[28] It may therefore be suggested that the identification of subjectivity (*liang-chih*) and ontological reality (*t'ien-li*), as a defining characteristic of Yang-ming's mode of thinking, seems to have been deeply rooted in a unique type of anthropocosmic experience.

In such an experience, subjectivity is fundamentally different from subjectivism. A series of assumptions are involved: (1) As the inner sagehood and true selfhood, subjectivity symbolizes genuine humanity. (2) Although existentially its concrete manifestations can be obstructed and distorted, genuine humanity is in an ontological sense an irreducible reality. (3) Despite its self-sufficiency, the irreducible reality can always generate dynamism and creativity. (4) Even though the dynamic and creative power does not produce something *ex nihilo*, it entails a process of self-realization. (5) Practical difficulties notwithstanding, the process of self-realization ultimately leads to the complete manifestation of the Heavenly principle. (6) In the last analysis, the Heavenly principle as an ontological reality is the original substance of the mind. And the original substance of the mind as pure subjectivity must be extended to manifest the Heavenly principle.

NOTES

[1]*Creative Fidelity*, Robert Rosthal, trans. (New York: Farrar, Straus, and Co., 1964), p. 14.

[2]See his *Nien-p'u* (Chronological biography) under 34 *sui*, in *Wang Yang-ming ch'üan-shu* (The complete works of Wang Yang-ming; Taipei: Cheng-chung Book Co., 1955) vol. 4, p. 82 (hereafter cited as *WYMCS*).

[3]*Ch'uan-hsi lu* (*Instructions for Practical Living*; hereafter cited as *CHL*) 3, in *WYMCS*, vol. 1, p. 77. See Wing-tsit Chan, trans., *Instructions for Practical Living and Other Neo-Confucian Writings by Wang Yang-ming* (New York: Columbia University Press, 1963), pp. 193–194.

[4]*Nien-p'u* under 50 *sui*, *WYMCS*, vol. 4, p. 125.

[5]*Nien-p'u* under 21 *sui*, *WYMCS*, vol. 4, p. 80. See also, *CHL* 3, *WYMCS*, vol. 1, p. 100.

[6]*Nien-p'u* under 37 *sui*, *WYMCS*, vol. 4, p. 84.

[7]*CHL* 3, *WYMCS*, vol. 1, p. 82.

[8]*Nien-p'u* under 34 *sui*, *WYMCS*, vol. 4, p. 82.

[9]*CHL* 1, *WYMCS*, vol. 1, p. 11.

[10]*CHL* 2, *WYMCS*, vol. 1, p. 35.

[11]*CHL* 1, *WYMCS*, vol. 1, p. 11.

[12]*Nien-p'u* under 51 *sui*, second month, *WYMCS*, vol. 4, p. 129.

[13]*CHL* 2, *WYMCS*, vol. 1, p. 35.

[14]*CHL* 1, *WYMCS*, vol. 1, p. 4.

[15]*Ibid.* See also *CHL* 1, *WYMCS*, vol. 1, p. 11.

[16]*Nien-p'u* under 43 *sui*, fifth month, *WYMCS*, vol. 4, p. 91.

[17]Yang-ming states, "In his doctrine of *ko-wu*, Chu Hsi lacked a basis (*t'ou-nao*). For instance, he said (that part of the method of investigating things) is 'the examination of one's subtle thoughts and deliberations.' (Being the most fundamental,) this should not be grouped together with 'searching for the principles of things in books,' 'testing them in one's conspicuous activities,' and 'finding them out in discussion.' He lacked a sense of relative importance." The above statement is found in *CHL* 3, *WYMCS*, vol. 1, p. 82. For the translation, see Wing-tsit Chan, *Instructions for Practical Living*, p. 204. A brief account on this issue can be found in Yang-ming's "Ta yu-jen wen" (A reply to a friend's query), in *WYMCS*, vol. 2, pp. 48–50. For a critique of Yang-ming's attack on Chu Hsi, see T'ang Chün-i, *Chung-kuo che-hsüeh yüan-lun* (An original exposition of Chinese philosophy; Hong Kong: Young-sun Publishing Co., 1966), vol. 1, pp. 321–323. Chu Hsi's statement appears in his *Ta-hsüeh ching-yen chiang-i* (Official lectures on the *Great Learning*), *Chu Tzu ta-ch'üan* (Complete literary works of Master Chu), 15:16a-b.

[18]*CHL* 1, *WYMCS*, vol. 1, p. 5.

[19]*CHL* 3, *WYMCS*, vol. 1, pp. 75–76.

[20]See his letter to Ma Tzu-hsin in *WYMCS*, vol. 2, p. 55.

[21]See his fifth letter to Huang Tsung-hsien in *WYMCS*, vol. 2, p. 7.

[22]*Jen-hsin*, literally, should be rendered as "the mind of man" or "the human mind." However, in the present context it is extremely misleading to use the word "human" without any qualification. Actually the translation I have used in this particular case is not at all in conflict with the original meaning of the word. In fact it is the *tao-hsin* that really denotes the ontological being of man. *Jen-hsin*, as differentiated from *tao-hsin*, refers to the selfish mind, hence the mind of the limited man.

[23]The practical difficulty in grasping the meaning of *liang-chih* is reflected in the following translations of the term: "innate knowledge" (Wing-tsit Chan), "conscientious wisdom" (Thomé H. Fang), "intuitive knowledge of good" (David S. Nivison), and "conscientious consciousness" (T'ang Chün-i). Occasionally the term "good conscience" is also suggested. In fact *liang-hsin*, which literally means good conscience, is sometimes used interchangeably with *liang-chih*.

[24]*Nien-p'u* under 50 *sui*, *WYMCS*, v. 14, p. 125.

[25]The term is borrowed from Mou Tsung-san. See his highly original work on *Chih te chih-chüeh yü Chung-kuo che-hsüeh* (Intellectual intuition and Chinese philos-

ophy; Taipei: Commercial Press, 1972).

[26]*CHL* 2, *WYMCS*, vol. 1, p. 51.

[27]*CHL* 3, *WYMCS*, vol. 1. pp. 89–90.

[28]See Ch'eng Hao, "Shih jen" (On understanding humanity), in *Erh-Ch'eng i-shu* (The surviving works of the two Ch'engs), 2A:3. For the historical account, see Chan Jo-shui, "Yang-ming hsien-sheng mu-chih-ming" (Master Yang-ming's epitaph), in *WYMCS*, vol. 4, p. 224.

11. An Inquiry into Wang Yang-ming's Four-Sentence Teaching

In this exploratory essay, I would like to argue that Wang Yang-ming's (Shou-jen, 1472–1529) Four-Sentence Teaching, as interpreted by one of his immediate successors, comes very close to the spirit of Ch'an (Zen). This certainly raises the intriguing question, "How Buddhistic is Wang Yang-ming?" Instead of addressing myself to a general interpretation of Yang-ming's spiritual orientation, however, I will confine my efforts to an analysis of the philosophical import of the Four-Sentence Teaching. Although I still maintain that Yang-ming by a conscious choice clearly identified himself with the Confucian Way, I am now convinced that a sophisticated appreciation of his mode of thinking also requires an investigation of its relationship to Ch'an. Without such an investigation, I would contend, it is impossible to probe the subtleness of Yang-ming's teachings, especially those just prior to his departure for Ssu-en and T'ien-chou in 1527. Of course by focusing my attention on this aspect of Yang-ming's religiophilosophy, I do not mean to rule out the possibility that in other aspects he might have been influenced more deeply by Taoism. My central concern here is simply to present an inquiry into one of his most significant attempts at the formulation of his ideas, which, in my opinion, particularly illustrates his Ch'anlike wisdom.

The question whether the mind-in-itself (*hsin-t'i*), intention (*i*), *liang-chih*, and thing (*wu*) are all beyond the distinction of good and evil is a basic ground of contention between Yang-ming's two prominent disciples, Ch'ien Te-hung (Hsü-shan, 1496–1574) and Wang Chi (Lung-hsi 1489–1583). The whole issue centers around Yang-ming's famous Four-Sentence Teaching:[1]

There is neither good nor evil in the mind-in-itself.

There are both good and evil in the activation of intentions.

Knowing good and evil is the [faculty] of *liang-chih*.

Doing good and removing evil is the rectification of things.

While Ch'ien Te-hung accepts the Teaching as the Master's doctrine in four axioms, Lung-hsi doubts that it is the ultimate formulation of Yang-ming's view on the matter. He argues that if the mind-in-itself is without good and evil, then intention, knowledge, and thing should all be without good and evil. On the other hand, if intention is not devoid of good and evil, there must be good and evil in the mind-in-itself. Lung-hsi's argument points to a fundamental problem in Yang-ming's religiophilosophy.

It should be noted that underlying the Four-Sentence Teaching is a set of assumptions that first appeared in the *Great Learning* (*Ta-hsüeh*). Actually the four sentences are structurally comparable to the first four "steps" of the eightfold process in the *Great Learning*.[2] In a separate study, I have characterized them as the "inner dimension" of self-cultivation (*hsiu-shen*), as contrasted with its "outer manifestations," such as regulating the family (*ch'i-chia*), ordering the state (*chih-kuo*), and bringing peace throughout the world (*p'ing t'ien-hsia*). The first four steps consist of (1) investigation of things (*ko-wu*), (2) extension of knowledge (*chih-chih*), (3) sincerity of the will (*ch'eng-i*), and (4) rectification of the mind (*cheng-hsin*). If we focus our attention on the wording of the Chinese text, it is clear that the key concepts are identical to those of the Four-Sentence Teaching: *hsin* (mind), *i* (will, intention), *chih* (knowledge), and *wu* (thing). Since Yang-ming perceives *ko-wu* (investigation of things) as the rectification of things and *chih-chih* (extension of knowledge) as the extension of *liang-chih*, the interpreted meanings of the four steps in the *Great Learning* and those of the Four-Sentence Teaching are virtually the same. It should also be noted that historically the formulation of the Four-Sentence Teaching occurred within months of Yang-ming's "Inquiry into the *Great Learning*" (*Ta-hsüeh wen*);[3] this further suggests that there must be a close affinity between them.

To put the discussion in its original context, it is essential that we focus more sharply on Lung-hsi's interpretive position. The following quotation seems particularly relevant:

The Master [Yang-ming] sets up his teaching in response to contingent situations. This is called expedience (*ch'üan-fa*). We must not be attached to its fixed formulation. Substance, function,

163

manifestation, and subtlety are the same incipience (*chi*). The mind, the intention, *liang-chih*, and the thing are all one event. If we realize that the mind is the mind without good and evil, then the intention is the intention without good and evil, the knowing [of *liang-chih*] is the knowing without good and evil, and the thing is the thing without good and evil. For the mind without mindfulness is concealed in profundity, the intention without intentness is round and perfect in its response, the knowing without knowledge is tranquil in its substance, and the thing without thingness is unfathomable in its function.[4]

Lung-hsi's argument can be understood through an inquiry into the mind-in-itself. If we take the concept of mind as our point of departure, we are bound to have some definite ideas about the meanings of intention, *liang-chih*, and thing. The term *hsin-chih-t'i* is often rendered as "the substance of the mind." Professor Mou Tsung-san of New Asia College suggests that it is better translated as "mind-in-itself."[5] The reason should become clear later.

To say that the mind-in-itself is beyond good and evil is to maintain that concepts such as good and evil are simply inapplicable to the "reality" of the mind because as such the mind cannot be differentiated into discrete entities and then subsumed under a relative category. It is certainly legitimate, and not only in the tradition of Chu Hsi (1130–1200), to describe the human mind (*jen-hsin*) as laden with selfish desires and so dangerously prone to evildoing; but to designate the mind-in-itself as either good or evil is to negate the basic assumption that it is "supremely good" (*chih-shan*).[6] To characterize supreme goodness as a form of good is to relativize an ultimate concept by a dichotomous scheme. This may not be as absurd as the idea of the "evil mind-in-itself" but it is equally misleading.

For the sake of expedience, we may define this approach to the mind as a "negative" method: clothing it in the state of nothingness. To say that the mind is clothed in the state of nothingness is, however, not to suggest that the mind is defined in terms of an ontological nonreality. The question whether the mind-in-itself is an ultimate reality or is, in the final analysis, a nonbeing should not concern us here. The issue is, given the transcendental nature of the mind-in-itself, what mode of comprehension is most suitable? Suppose the mind-in-itself is an ultimate reality rather than a nonbeing, does it necessarily follow that it is good, evil, or simply neutral? According to Lung-hsi's contention, which in this connection is in complete agreement with the first line of the Four-Sentence Teaching, it is senseless to describe the mind-in-itself in such terms; for as soon as this is done the mind-in-itself is inadequately understood as an empirical mind.

While the empirical mind manifests itself in concrete form, the mind-in-itself, as a substantial being, never manifests itself in concrete form. To the mind-in-itself, concrete forms are unnecessary attachments; they signify neither what it is nor how it really functions. It is in this sense that Lung-hsi defines the mind-in-itself as the mind that can manifest itself without the form of the mind. Of course *wu-hsin chih hsin* can be grammatically rendered as "the mind of no-mind."[7] But it is vitally important to note that "no-mind" here specifically refers to the ability of the mind to function without "mindful" traces of its functioning. Understandably such a mind is beyond the distinction of good and evil.

The mind-in-itself so perceived is, I believe, in perfect accord with the thrust of Yang-ming's other teachings. The Master once remarked:

> However, if one does not realize that the mind-in-itself is devoid of all things [that is, completely pure and open], and focuses his mind solely on loving good and hating evil, he will merely add to his mind this much of his own intention and therefore his mind will not be broad and impartial. Only when one does not make any special effort whatsoever to like or dislike, as described in the *Book of History*, can the mind be in its original substance.[8]

There are other comparable examples in which the mind-in-itself is also approached by the Master in terms of the "negative" method. Yang-ming once used an analogy to illustrate his point. He stated that like the eye, the mind-in-itself is absolutely intolerant of the slightest presence of dust. It matters very little what the quality of the dust is. As gold dust is as disturbing to the eye as any other kind of dust, so good and evil intentions are equally disturbing to the mind-in-itself.[9] In short, Yang-ming maintains that the mind-in-itself is without any trace of good or evil. Only then can it be understood as "supremely good."

Comparably *liang-chih* can also be understood as beyond good and evil. In Yang-ming's thinking, *liang-chih* is not only the ultimate ground of self-realization but also the primordial strength for self-cultivation. It is not simply knowing as a form of cognitive understanding but acting in the sense of experiential enlightening that necessarily brings about self-transformation at the deepest level. Knowing so conceived is certainly not restricted to empirical knowledge. It is not just to know an object, no matter how comprehensive the sensory perception is meant to be. To know an object presupposes a spatial distance between the knower and the object under investigation and a temporal gap between the commencement and the completion of the investigating procedure. It requires analytical methods and experimental skills. To be sure, it can also affect one's way of life. But the knowing of *liang-chih* is in itself a creative act. It is the basis on which genuine action can be completed. Similarly, acting in this connection is not merely praxis. It is neither the practice of an external art nor the conduct of an acquired habit. The acting of *liang-chih* necessarily involves a profound self-awareness. For only with it can true intellectual self-definition be realized. The unity of knowing and acting is a defining characteristic of *liang-chih*.

This leads us to the corollary that *liang-chih* is both a substantial being and a transforming activity. It is on the one hand the innermost core of sensibility and on the other the most profound source of strength for self-cultivation. Far from being an external, abstract idea, it manifests itself as an internal, concrete reality, indeed as the center of creativity. To be sure, *liang-chih* is not separate from sensory perceptions, but neither can it be fully appreciated in terms of ordinary experiences alone. Its "integrity," so to speak, can never be reduced to what the Neo-Confucian scholars called "the knowledge of hearing and seeing." It is probably in this sense that Yang-ming characterized *liang-chih* as "the refined spirituality of creative transformation" (*tsao-hua chih ching-ling*).[10] Actually, *liang-chih* is not only an anthropological concept, restricted to the definition of human beings; it is the ultimate reality of the myriad things (*wan-wu*) as well. Indeed, *liang-chih* makes it possible for Heaven and Earth to become intelligible and meaningful processes of existence. Accordingly *liang-chih* was designated by Yang-ming as the "original substance"

166

(*pen-t'i*) of the mind; it is, in the last analysis, a different mode of expressing the mind-in-itself. Understandably *liang-chih* must not be conceived as either good or evil, for like the mind-in-itself it is supremely good.

If the mind-in-itself is beyond good and evil, how can intention be considered as having good and evil? In what sense is Lung-hsi justified in claiming that "if we realize that the mind is the mind without good and evil, then the intention is the intention without good and evil"? The underlying question is of course that of the relationship between the mind and intention. One way of answering the question is to define intention as the directionality of the mind. Intention so defined is an activation pointing toward a concrete manifestation of the mind. The inseparability of intention and the mind thus resembles that of waves and the ocean. If the ocean is beyond good and evil, it seems quite misleading to suggest that the waves themselves, as natural activities of the ocean, are either good or evil. Thus intention is, like the mind-in-itself, also a transcendental concept, and Lung-hsi is therefore justified in asserting that intention is neither good nor evil. Correspondingly, if *liang-chih* is beyond good and evil, how can the thing be considered as having good and evil? This raises the question of the specific relationship between the thing and *liang-chih*. If the thing originates from *liang-chih*, it is inconceivable that the thing of *liang-chih* is not also supremely good. This line of reasoning seems in perfect accord with Yang-ming's teaching.

In fact Yang-ming often conceptualizes a thing in terms of the self-expression of *liang-chih*. Comparable to the inseparability of the mind-in-itself and its intention, the thing as a concrete manifestation of *liang-chih* is necessarily an integral part of *liang-chih's* self-definition. As a result, Lung-hsi's insistence that if the mind is without good and evil, then the thing is without good and evil, is not at all in conflict with what the Master himself clearly advocates. The following formulation by Yang-ming is singularly pertinent:

Principle (*li*) is one and no more. In terms of its condensation and concentration [in the individual] it is called the nature (*hsing*). In terms of the master of this condensation and concentration it is called the mind. In terms of the manifestation and activation of

167

this master it is called the intention. In terms of the enlightening awareness of this manifestation and activation it is called knowledge. In terms of the stimulus and response of this enlightening awareness it is called the thing.[11]

The whole discussion here is obviously at the transcendental level. In the light of Lung-hsi's insights, it can be easily argued that "the mind without the forms of mind" signifies the manner in which the mind masters human nature; it is precisely because the condensed and concentrated principle is deeply preserved in human nature that the mind can be said to have been "concealed in profundity." Similarly, "intention without the form of intention" signifies the manner in which intention manifests and activates the mind; since intention, like the waves of the ocean, emerges naturally as the inner demand of the mind itself, its response can be said to be "round and perfect." "Knowing without the form of knowing" thus signifies the manner in which intention becomes acutely aware of its own orientation; if intention is understood as the directionality of the mind, knowledge pertaining to the self-awareness of the mind can therefore be described as "tranquil in itself." Accordingly, the "thing without the form of thing" signifies the manner in which *liang-chih* acts in concrete situations; not being a fixed object, the thing as the affection of *liang-chih* is indeed "unfathomable in its function."

Lung-hsi's approach to the Four-Sentence Teaching has been characterized as "fourfold nothingness" (*ssu-wu*). In other words, the four root concepts are all perceived as in a state of nothing. It is vitally important to note that the term *nothing* in this particular connection is functionally defined. It actually means, in a transcendental sense, that mind-in-itself, *liang-chih*, intention, and thing are all freed from attachments. Cultivation of the mind can be fully realized only when the effort is not being "mindfully" attached. Likewise, intention is truly genuine when it is manifested as if with no intentness. Just as the most profound knowing has no trace of knowledge, the perfect thing completely delivers itself from thingness.

However, a crucial distinction must be made. While the mind-in-itself and *liang-chih* are absolutely beyond good and evil, intention and the thing can very well be analyzed in terms of good and evil. Although it makes sense to say that the intention of the mind-in-

168

itself and the thing of *liang-chih* are supremely good, it is difficult to maintain that intentions and things are always beyond good and evil. Even in a state of nothing, the level at which the mind-in-itself transcends mindfulness is fundamentally different from the level at which intention is said to be without intentness. Correspondingly, the "unknowingness" of *liang-chih* in no way resembles the "nothingness" of the thing. While *liang-chih* always knows without the form of knowledge, only when the thing is conceived as the affection of *liang-chih* can it be characterized as a thing without thingness.

In the actual process of self-cultivation, however, the thing is often perceived as an intended object, locatable in a concrete situation. It is neither contentless nor formless. The tangibility of a thing is so central to self-cultivation that to deny it is to undermine the very basis on which the conscious effort of self-cultivation is focused. In this context, to deprive a thing of its thingness, as it were, is tantamount to relinquishing the whole enterprise of self-cultivation.

This brings us back to the basic question, "What is a thing?" If it is conceptualized as an inseparable manifestation of *liang-chih*, it can very well be conceived as a kind of "transcendental affection," completely beyond the dichotomy of good and evil. As a transcendental affection, the thing is, in the last analysis, without thingness. How, then, can the effort of rectification be applied? To rectify a thing certainly does not mean to "rectify" the transcendental affection of *liang-chih*. It is neither desirable nor possible to exert moral effort on *liang-chih* itself. To be sure, *liang-chih* can and should be "extended" (*chih*), which in essence implies a process of self-manifestation. But it is misleading to suggest that the extension or manifestation of *liang-chih* must also be subjected to a rectifying procedure.

However, if the thing is conceptualized as an intended object, it cannot avoid the judgments of good and evil. Nor can it be exempted from any moral scrutiny. It is in this sense that the effort of self-cultivation, known as the rectification of things, becomes relevant. From this perspective, *liang-chih*, which functions as the basis for rectifying the mind's intended objects, must itself make clear differentiations between right and wrong. The thing that needs to be rectified inevitably has the form of a thing; and the *liang-chih* that evaluates human affairs cannot eliminate the form of knowledge.

169

Thus, in a state of being, neither the thing nor *liang-chih* is beyond good and evil, for both of them are "located" in concrete relationships.

Analogously, when intention is conceptualized as the directionality of the mind-in-itself, it is inconceivable that it can be further refined. Indeed, how can the effort of making intention genuine be applied, if the intention in question is, in the last analysis, without intentness? However, if intention is thought to be aroused by an object, it becomes imperative that the aroused intention be judged in reference to its intended object. Self-cultivation, as the effort of making the will (intention) sincere, immediately becomes pertinent. To make the intention sincere is to exert a conscious effort whereby the intention can eventually become true to the original substance of the mind. From this perspective, the mind itself is not necessarily devoid of good and evil either. The mind with the form of the mind must choose to ally with the good so that intention, despite its attachment to the thing, can remain sincere, truthful and genuine.

In contrast with the fourfold nothingness, this approach to the Four-Sentence Teaching is known as the "fourfold beingness" (*ssu-yu*). In other words, the four root concepts are all perceived as in a state of being. Since the thing, having a concrete structure of its own, is not necessarily in the right place, it has to be rectified. Moral effort is then the prerequisite for "removing evil and doing good" so that the intended object can be properly situated. This is predicated on the ability of *liang-chih* to differentiate good from evil. Having the form of knowing, *liang-chih* is itself inevitably fixed in a definite function. If we pursue this line of inquiry, as soon as intention is activated, good or evil unavoidably comes into being. Despite the assertion that the mind-in-itself is supremely good, so far as actual moral practice is concerned, the mind also needs to be constantly "cultivated."

If we commence self-cultivation by a rectification of things, we can conceptualize the Four-Sentence Teaching as a process toward a deepened subjectivity. The first step, from the rectification of things to *liang-chih*, is to synthesize discrete events of self-cultivation in order to arrive at a comprehensive understanding of the "intellectual intuition" on which all moral efforts are based. Next, while *liang-chih* as a form of knowing is a reflection on accomplished facts, intention signifies an incipient tendency toward a concrete action. To be aware of the good and evil inherent in the activation of intention is therefore a more subtle mode of self-cultivation. Finally, it is the "substance" of the mind that ultimately determines the quality of one's being. Unless moral effort can eventually penetrate, so to speak, the deepest layer of human sensitivity, self-cultivation is still incomplete. Since, in a practical sense, there is always latitude for a further refinement of one's inner sensitivity, the process toward an ever-deepened subjectivity is therefore unceasing.

Does this emphasis on self-cultivation as a lifelong commitment signify a gradual, piecemeal teaching on enlightenment? The answer must be in the negative. For the ultimate ground as well as the actual faculty of self-cultivation is *liang-chih*. If self-cultivation commences with the rectification of things, it is because *liang-chih* by knowing good and evil can exert moral effort to do good and remove evil. There is neither external principle to guide nor outside power to initiate moral practice. Both the ontological basis and the real strength of self-cultivation are inherent in *liang-chih*. Furthermore, if self-cultivation commences with the activation of intention, the ultimate ground and the actual faculty of making intention genuine are both located in the mind-in-itself. Indeed, the only possibility of asserting moral effort to redirect intention's incipient tendency is by the self-awakening of the mind. Without this, intention as it is activated by the thing will escape the moral scrutiny of one's inner sensibility. As a result, intention is no longer a genuine expression of the mind but an attachment to an external object.

The Four-Sentence Teaching so conceived can thus be interpreted as indicating two parallel processes: (1) from the thing to *liang-chih*, and (2) from intention to the mind-in-itself. In either case, the central concern is sharply focused on the subtle manifestations of the mind. It is in this sense that to rectify things, to extend *liang-chih*, and to make intention genuine are all modes of cultivating the mind. In Yang-ming's own expression, this is an attempt at "pulling up the root and stopping up the source" (*pa-pen sai-yüan*).[12] If we take this approach seriously, Lung-hsi's critique of the so-called fourfold being-ness becomes readily comprehensible:

The nature ordained by Heaven is purely and supremely good. Wonderfully affecting and responding, its incipient manifestation is

171

naturally unceasing. There is no good to be named. Of course there is originally no evil, but even good cannot dwell in it. Therefore it is called beyond good and evil. If there is either good or evil, it is because the intention is activated by the thing. Without being a "self-so flow" (*tzu-jan liu-hsing*), it becomes attached to a state of being. That which is "self-so flow" moves without motion. That which is attached to a state of being moves with motion. Intention is what the mind manifests. If the intention is the intention of good and evil, *liang-chih* and the thing are simultaneously in the state of being. Neither can the mind be said to be in the state of nothing.[13]

It should be pointed out that Yang-ming himself has made similar claims: "The state of having neither good nor evil is that of principle in tranquillity. Good and evil appear when the vital force (*ch'i*) is perturbed. If the vital force is not perturbed, there is neither good evil, and this is called the supremely good."[14] An exceedingly interesting exchange between Yang-ming and Lung-hsi recorded by Ch'ien Te-hung further illustrates that this must have been a position on which both were agreed:

Our Teacher had already embarked on his journey of military campaign to Ssu-en and T'ien-chou. Ju-chung [the courtesy name of Lung-hsi] and I [Ch'ien Te-hung] followed after him and finally bade him farewell at Yen-t'an. Ju-chung raised the question of the Buddhist teaching on the reality and illusion of *dharmas*. The Teacher said, "With the mind, all is reality (*shih*); without the mind, all is illusion (*huan*). With the mind, all is illusion; without the mind, all is reality." Ju-chung remarked, " 'With the mind, all is reality; without the mind, all is illusion' refers to conscious effort (*kung-fu*) from the viewpoint of original substance (*pen-t'i*). 'With the mind, all is illusion; without the mind, all is reality' refers to original substance from the viewpoint of conscious effort." The Teacher approved his interpretation. At the time I was not yet able to comprehend its meaning. After several years of endeavor, I have now come to the belief that original substance and conscious effort are one. However, our Teacher uttered those words at that time incidentally in answer to a question. There is no need for us Confucians in our instructional efforts to formulate our doctrines by relying on this [Buddhist insight].[15]

Lung-hsi's perceptive grasp of Yang-ming's insight is really phenomenal. The remarkable rapport between them, which is also borne out by numerous other examples in the *Instructions for Practical Living (Ch'üan-hsi lu)*, seems somewhat beyond the comprehension of even Ch'ien Te-hung, one of Yang-ming's most trusted and respected disciples. To be sure, what Yang-ming and Lung-hsi shared as an inner experience was the absolute unity of original substance and conscious effort. But that unity can be perceived from two significantly different viewpoints. If self-cultivation commences with the mind-in-itself, original substance entails conscious effort. This is known as a form of a priori learning (*hsien-t'ien chih hsüeh*). For the "rectification" of the mind, as a holistic attempt at sudden enlightenment, is not empirically definable. The concept of rectification in this connection is fundamentally different from that in the "rectification of things." To rectify a thing is to exert conscious effort on an intended object, but to "rectify" the mind is simply to manifest the original substance of it. Since the mind, as the innermost subjectivity, can never be "rectified" as an object, the rectification of the mind actually means the self-awakening of the mind. Once the mind-in-itself is fully awakened, intention becomes a "self-so flow" and the thing, where intention dwells, becomes properly situated. This certainly is not empirical learning; in a strict sense, it is not even learnable. "With the mind, all is reality; without the mind, all is illusion" thus signifies the self-awakening of the mind.

On the other hand, if self-cultivation commences with intention, conscious effort is an indispensable but not a sufficient ground for recovering the original substance of the mind. This is known as a form of a posteriori learning (*hou-t'ien chih hsüeh*). For intention, as activated by the thing, must be made sincere by empirically verifiable moral decisions. As Lung-hsi has pointed out, when intention is no longer a "self-so flow," it becomes attached to a state of being. As a result, it cannot transcend the dichotomy of good and evil. Moral decisions are thus required to free intention from being fixed in the thing; only then can it again become a genuine manifestation of the mind-in-itself. This necessitates efforts such as the rectification of things. Actually doing good and removing evil is a concrete way of making intention sincere. In a deeper sense, however, unless the mind is "rectified," there is no assurance that intention can remain sincere. To say that sincerity of intention depends on the rectification of the

173

mind implies that moral efforts can be exerted on the mind. On the surface, this seems diametrically opposed to our previous assertion that the mind can never be rectified as an object. To be sure, in a priori learning, it is meaningless to speak of rectification of the mind. But in a posteriori learning, since the mind is in a state of being, it cannot be devoid of forms. In fact, what is rectified is not the mind-in-itself but the form of the mind. "With the mind, all is illusion; without the mind, all is reality" thus signifies the conscious attempt of the mind to liberate itself from its own form.

Of course, Lung-hsi was disposed to practice a priori learning. He strongly believed that the ultimate meaning of the Four-Sentence Teaching is to be sought in the mind without the form of the mind. Indeed, the mind but not the mind of mindfulness is the mind-in-itself. This comes close to the idea that *"prajñā* but not *prajñā* is called *prajñā.*" It may not be farfetched to suggest that Lung-hsi, through an experiential understanding of his Master's spiritual orientation, was able to push Yang-ming's Four-Sentence Teaching to its logical conclusion. It should be noted that Yang-ming himself fully endorsed Lung-hsi's interpretation, although he still insisted on the validity of the four axioms in their original formulation. It seems also that Yang-ming was quite aware of the Buddhist implications of Lung-hsi's attempt to put the four root concepts in a state of nothing. Yang-ming's willingness to answer Lung-hsi's questions about the reality or illusion of dharma and the manner in which he actually dealt with the issue further indicate that he was not at all reluctant to confront Buddhist ideas. Indeed, Yang-ming seems to have taken a great delight in formulating religiophilosophical insights in Buddhist terminology.

Therefore I would not object to the assertion that Yang-ming, despite his early intellectual self-definition as a Confucian, was throughout his life deeply inspired by Buddhist ideas. His Four-Sentence Teaching and many of his encounters with Lung-hsi point to a dimension of his religiophilosophy that can well be explored in the context of Ch'an. Nor would I insist on calling Lung-hsi a "Confucian," simply because he was true to Yang-ming's spiritual orientation. Although I cannot be certain that Lung-hsi's "Ch'anlike" wisdom was necessarily a reflection of his specific predilection for Buddhism, I am absolutely sure that he, like his Master, never felt at home with the scholar-officials in Ming society who jealously defended the Confucian Tao against Buddhist heterodoxy for the wrong reasons. Ch'ien Te-hung was obviously concerned about Confucian appropriation of Buddhist insights. Had he mastered the drift of Yang-ming's teaching as perceptively as Lung-hsi, he might have enthusiastically lent himself to such a creative adaptation.

NOTES

[1] A very vivid account of the original controversy over the Four-Sentence Teaching is found in the *Instructions for Practical Living (Ch'uan-hsi lu)* recorded by Ch'ien Te-hung. Since the main focus of my analysis in the present study is on the interpretive position of Wang Lung-hsi, it seems appropriate to quote in full what Ch'ien believed to have transpired in the discussion. The following translation is taken from Professor Wing-tsit Chan's pioneering work:

> In the ninth month of the sixth year of Chia-ching [1527] our Teacher had been called from retirement and appointed to subdue once more the rebellion in Ssu-en and T'ien-chou [when the earlier expedition under another official had failed]. As he was about to start, Ju-chung [Wang Chi] and I [Ch'ien Te-hung] discussed learning. He repeated the words of the Teacher's instructions as follows:
> "In the original substance of the mind there is no distinction of good and evil.
> When the will becomes active, however, such distinction exists.
> The faculty of innate knowledge is to know good and evil.
> The investigation of things is to do good and remove evil."
> I asked, "What do you think this means?"
> Ju-chung said, "This is perhaps not the final conclusion. If we say that in the original substance of the mind there is no distinction between good and evil, then there must be no such distinction in the will, in knowledge, and in things. If we say that there is a distinction between good and evil in the will, then in the final analysis there must also be such a distinction in the substance of the mind."
> I said, "The substance of the mind is the nature endowed in us by Heaven, and is originally neither good nor evil. But because we have a mind dominated by habits, we see in our thoughts a distinction between good and evil. The work of the investigation of things, the extension of knowledge, the sincerity of the will, the rectification of the mind, and the cultivation of the personal life is aimed precisely at recovering that original nature and substance. If there were no good or evil to start with, what would be the necessity of such effort?"

That evening we sat down beside the Teacher at the T'ien-ch'üan Bridge. Each stated his view and asked to be corrected. The Teacher said, "I am going to leave now. I wanted to have you come and talk this matter through. You two gentlemen complement each other very well, and should not hold on to one side. Here I deal with two types of people. The man of sharp intelligence apprehends straight from the source. The original substance of the human mind is in fact crystal-clear without any impediment and is the equilibrium before the feelings are aroused. The man of sharp intelligence has accomplished his task as soon as he has apprehended the original substance, penetrating the self, other people, and things internal and things external all at the same time. On the other hand, there are inevitably those whose minds are dominated by habits so that the original substance of the mind is obstructed. I therefore teach them definitely and sincerely to do good and remove evil in their will and thoughts. When they become expert at the task and the impurities of the mind are completely eliminated, the original substance of the mind will become wholly clear. Ju-chung's view is the one I use in dealing with the man of sharp intelligence. Te-hung's view is for the second type. If you two gentlemen use your views interchangeably, you will be able to lead all people—of the highest, average, and lowest intelligence—to the truth. If each of you holds on to one side, right here you will err in handling properly the different types of man and each in his own way will fail to understand fully the substance of the Way."

After a while he said again, "From now on whenever you discuss learning with friends be sure not to lose sight of my basic purpose.

In the original substance of the mind there is no distinction of good and evil.

When the will becomes active, however, such distinction exists.

The faculty of innate knowledge is to know good and evil.

The investigation of things is to do good and remove evil.

Just keep to these words of mine and instruct people according to their types, and there will not be any defect. This is indeed a task that penetrates both the higher and the lower levels. It is not easy to find people of sharp intelligence in the world. Even Yen Hui and Ming-tao [Ch'eng Hao] dared not assume that they could fully realize the original substance of the mind as soon as they apprehended the task. How can we lightly expect this from people? People's minds are dominated by habits. If we do not teach them concretely and sincerely to devote themselves to the task of doing good and removing evil right in their innate knowledge rather than merely imagining an original substance in a vacuum, all that they do will not be genuine and they will do no more than cultivate a mind of vacuity and quietness [like that of the Buddhists and Taoists]. This defect is not a small matter and must be exposed as early as possible." On that day both Ju-chung and I attained some enlightenment.

See Wing-tsit Chan, trans., *Instructions for Practical Living and Other Neo-Confucian Writings by Wang Yang-ming* (New York: Columbia University Press, 1963), pp.

243-245. It should be noted that for reasons of internal consistency, the Four-Sentence Teaching is rendered differently in my presentation.

[2]The eightfold process of the *Great Learning* appears as follows: "The ancients who wished to manifest their clear character to the world would first bring order to their states. Those who wished to bring order to their states would first regulate their families. Those who wished to regulate their families would first cultivate their personal lives. Those who wished to cultivate their personal lives would first rectify their minds. Those who wished to rectify their minds would first make their wills sincere. Those who wished to make their wills sincere would first extend their knowledge. The extension of knowledge consists in the investigation of things." See Wing-tsit Chan, *A Source Book in Chinese Philosophy* (Princeton: Princeton University Press, 1963), p. 86.

[3]According to Ch'ien Te-hung's preface to the *Great Learning*, it was recorded by Yang-ming at the request of his students before his departure for the military campaign in Ssu-T'ien. Since the imperial order arrived in the fifth month of 1527 and Yang-ming embarked on the journey in the ninth month of the same year, it must have occurred within months of the historical debate on the Four-Sentence Teaching. See his *Nien-p'u* in *Yang-ming ch'üan-shu* (*Ssu-pu pei-yao*), 34: 16b-18b.

[4]*Wang Lung-hsi yü-lu* (reprint; Taipei: Kuang-wen Book Co., 1960), 1: 1a.

[5]Mou Tsung-san, "The Immediate Successor of Wang Yang-ming: Wang Lung-hsi and His Theory of *ssu-wu*," *Philosophy East and West* 23, nos. 1 and 2 (January and April, 1973): 104, n.2. For a more extensive analysis of the same issue, see his "Wang-hsüeh ti fen-hua yü fa-chan," in *Hsin-ya Shu-yüan hsüeh-shu nien-k'an*, 14 (1972): 93-94.

[6]The term was actually used by Yang-ming himself; see *Ch'uan-hsi lu*, in *Yang-ming ch'üan-shu*, 1: 2b.

[7]The term has been rendered as "the mind of no-mind" by Chang Chung-yuan, " 'The Essential Source of Identity' in Wang Lung-hsi's Philosophy," *Philosophy East and West* 23 (1973): 37.

[8]See Wing-tsit Chan, trans., *Instruction for Practical Living*, p. 77. Some changes have been made.

[9]See *Ch'uan-hsi lu*, 3: 26a.

[10]The same term is translated by Wing-tsit Chan as "the spirit of creation." See Chan, *Instructions*, p. 216, and *Ch'uan-hsi lu*, 3: 26a-b.

[11]See Yang-ming's letter in reply to Lo Cheng-an, in *Ch'uan-hsi lu*, 2: 28a. Cf. Chan, *Instructions*, p. 161.

[12]*Ibid.*, p. 117.

[13]This is actually a continuation of Lung-hsi's statement mentioned in note 4. See *Wang Lung-hsi yü-lu*, 1: 1a-b.

[14]*Ch'uan-hsi lu*, 1: 22a. See Chan's translation in *Instructions*, pp. 63–64.

[15]*Ch'uan-hsi lu*, 3: 26b. Cf. Chan's translation in *Instructions*, p. 258. In Lung-hsi's biography, the following statement is recorded in reference to this particular exchange:

The mind is neither being nor nonbeing; *dharmas* are neither real nor illusory. As soon as one is attached to being, nonbeing, reality, or illusion, one has already fallen into the trap of a "fragmented routine" (*tuan-ch'ang*). This is like juggling with balls. They are neither attached nor departed from any one place. Therefore it is called the "primordial unity" (*yüan-t'ung*).

See "Wang Lung-hsi hsien-sheng chuan," in *Wang Lung-hsi yü-lu*, p. 1.

12. Transformational Thinking as Philosophy (Review Article)*

Ronald G. Dimberg, in his well-researched and sys-tematically presented monograph on the sixteenth-century Chinese intellectual Ho Hsin-yin, defines the Confucian *Problematik* in terms of a threefold concern: "the individual in relation to society, his ultimate potential as a human being, and how best to fulfill that potential" (p. 1). After a brief analysis of the perennial tension be-tween the preservation of personal integrity and the demand for social responsibility in the Confucian tradition as a whole, Dimberg argues quite convincingly that while the Neo-Confucian approach to the problem of the individual was essentially in accord with that of classical Confucianism, the single-minded quest of the Neo-Con-fucian masters for "identity with all things by affirming one's hu-manity, in this way to overcome selfishness" (p. 11) fundamentally transformed the meaning of "being Confucian" in Sung-Ming China. To be sure, under the influence of the political culture at the time, it was extremely difficult for a concerned intellectual to forgo involve-ment in the government and pursue learning for the sake of spiritual self-cultivation. But by mid-Ming the balance had notably shifted away from the age-long belief that entering officialdom through the examination system was a necessary and a desirable way of realizing the Confucian ideal.

An outstanding example of this shift of balance, signifying an increasing importance of "subjectivity" in the sixteenth century, was the rise of the T'ai-chou School, named after the native place in modern Kiangsu of Wang Ken, the famous disciple of Wang Yang-ming. Intent on manifesting Wang Yang-ming's precept of "innate knowledge" in the everydayness of the common people, Wang Ken

* *The Sage and Society: The Life and Thought of Ho Hsin-Yin*, by Ronald G. Dimberg. Monographs of the Society for Asian and Comparative Philosophy, No. 1. Honolulu: University Press of Hawaii, 1974. pp. x + 175.

179

argued that education, far from being the accumulation of empirical knowledge, was aimed at preserving what is most authentic in each individual. Since every human being is endowed with the "clear wisdom" to intuit what is most fitting for self-realization, the individual person regardless of social background is best qualified for the task of "nourishing his own body." Learning so conceived is a process of self-authentication amid a variety of depersonalizing forces. Yet Wang Ken's fidelity to the Confucian tradition compelled him to seek inner truth in the context of human-relatedness. His conscious choice not to participate directly in governmental service did not at all lessen his engagement in the task of social welfare. To be sure, he suffered from a profound sense of political alienation. But, as long as his teaching remained socially relevant, his seemingly apolitical message was laden with far-reaching political implications. Indeed, contrary to many familiar forms of adjustment to the world, what he endeavored to accomplish was not only a radical critique of the status quo but also a basic restructuring of the established rules for judging political worth. Thus it is understandable, *pace* Dimberg (p. 26), that without formulating concrete programs of social or economic reform he was nevertheless able to make significant changes in the grammar of the then prevalent political language.

It may not be farfetched to suggest that "forming one body with all things" as the highest ideal of self-realization is a defining characteristic of this "new" language. To be sure, when Yen Chün, a teacher of Ho Hsin-yin, expressed his "uninhibited self-assertion" (p. 41) in terms of such an ideal, he was on the surface merely recapitulating a dictum in the famous "Western Inscription" of Chang Tsai. However, by reiterating the centrality of this particular dictum of the Sung Master, Yen Chün, perhaps inadvertently, accentuated an aspect of Sung learning that certainly had been an integral part of Neo-Confucian symbolism but never the single most important feature of it. Of course this by no means implies that Yen Chün, or for that matter the founder of the T'ai-chou school Wang Ken, was instrumental in gaining currency for this unique idiom. The question of genetic reasons is probably unanswerable. But Dimberg's strategy of presenting the case of Ho Hsin-yin in the context of the symbolic structure of the T'ai-chou school is justified. Without a familiarity with the intellectual struggles of Hsü Yüeh as well as those of the aforementioned Wang Ken and Yen Chün, it would be difficult to understand why Ho was fully convinced that his attack on the then prevalent notion of family welfare as a form of parochialism (p. 43) was an accurate representation of the philosophical intention of the *Great Learning*. Similarly, under the influence of the same intellectual ethos he strongly believed that the concept of private ownership of land was incompatible with the Confucian spirit of impartiality (p. 44) and that the promulgation of a universalizable program of education was an effective measure for combating nepotism (p. 46).

Actually, if I may be permitted to advance a tentative interpretation, it was also this new mode of perception that prompted Ho to engage in such activities as forming a coterie of scholar-officials to discuss the teachings of Wang Ken, and organizing an "intellectual hostel," a kind of a Neo-Confucian salon, in Peking in the fateful year of 1560 when he was alleged to have experienced a confrontation with Chang Chü-cheng (pp. 48–49). If we take seriously Dimberg's characterization of a salient feature of Ho's personality as "the inquisitiveness of the free thinker" (p. 43), it is quite conceivable that Ho in fact later became a "target" of Chang Chü-cheng's campaign against independent academies and intellectual associations. Even though "there is no evidence to suggest a direct link between the suppression of the academies in 1579 and Ho's arrest in the same year," (p. 53), Ho seemed to know what he was talking about when with his last breath he held Chang responsible for his death. Of course, "in fairness to Chang Chü-cheng it should be emphasized that evidence against him, particularly in the matter of Ho's death, is circumstantial at best" (p. 53). Yet the issue involved is not a matter of legality. And a brief analysis of what Ho considered to be the message of his magnum opus, *Yüan-hsüeh yüan-chiang* (rendered by Dimberg as *On Study and Discussion*) may help to put the issue in a proper perspective.

The importance of "study and discussion" in the Wang Yang-ming tradition as a whole needs little elaboration. Yang-ming himself had time and again defined his lifelong commitment to Confucianism in terms of teaching (*chiang-hsüeh*, literally "discourse and learning"). Accordingly it was in "study and discussion" that Yang-ming found his intellectual self-definition. In a strict sense, however, Yang-ming's "study and discussion" was intended not merely to appropriate objective truths but to transform one's own "body and mind." The primary concern of teaching is, therefore, to inspire students to a quest for self-knowledge. Since ontologically as well as anthropologically human communication is based on an in-depth manifestation of selfhood, the authentic path leading toward true mutuality is through a process of digging into one's own ground of existence. It is in this sense that "forming one body with all things" is not a form of universalization that necessitates the negation of the self. Rather, it is in subjectivity, as an experienced reality, that the basis of universalism really lies. To transcend parochialism, or any other kind of subjectivism, is not to deny subjectivity but to bring it to complete fruition. Education so conceived is not simply a program of transmitting the knowledge of "hearing and seeing"; it is a holistic way of learning to be human.

In a political culture where learning to be human was viewed as one of the most important tasks of the "benevolent" state, it is quite understandable that education was laden with far-reaching political implications. If the followers of the T'ai-chou school were consciously trying to promulgate a mode of education fundamentally different from that of the governmental authorities, their decision was bound to be interpreted by the officials as a political as well as an ideological protest against the imperial leadership. Even without taking the whole issue of influencing "public opinion" into consideration, it is not unthinkable that Ho's consistent effort to assume the role of "teacher" inevitably led him to direct confrontation with the state. Accordingly, notwithstanding the circumstantiality of the evidence, Ho was not groundless when he asserted that Chang was responsible for his death.

What is the *philosophical* meaning of Ho's life and thought then? Before an answer can be attempted, it may be useful to note that the question presupposes an insight that has not yet been systematically reflected on in the study of Chinese philosophy. It is certainly beyond our present concern to speculate on what some of the fruitful inquiries in this regard might turn out to be. Suffice it now to say that the Heideggerian notion of freeing "thinking" from professionalized philosophy is particularly relevant. If we take seriously Ho's perception that Confucianism is a way of life rather than an academic discipline (p. 132), Ho's mode of philosophizing can very well be

182

characterized as "man thinking." Indeed, philosophy so understood cannot be reduced to either pure analysis or to system building, as if such an enterprise was the privilege of academically trained professionals. On the contrary, to philosophize is to free the human spirit from all forms of constraints including the unexamined assumption that philosophy is but an intellectual exercise. Specifically the thinking man must simultaneously be a "sensitive person" in his everydayness. He cannot choose to philosophize in a definite place and at a specific time, for philosophizing is a defining characteristic of his existence. It is therefore quite misleading to suggest that the distinctive feature of a philosopher is that he is disciplined to think more analytically than the majority of his fellow human beings. To be sure, a philosopher is often methodical in his thought process and systematic in his linguistic presentation. But his ultimate concern is not simply to reflect on reality so that it can be consistently described. Unless he can transform reality through thinking, what he does is no more than scratching the surface of experienced truth.

Ho's precepts on human nature (pp. 60–70) may, to the critical mind, appear to be no more than a series of assertions of belief rather than a freshly argued position on humanity. However, Ho's inner logic is readily comprehensible, if we do not impose on it an alien structure of interpretation or reduce it to a set of psychosociological reasons. The force of his argument, as it were, is generated from an absolute seriousness of purpose and a complete dedication of the body and mind. For he not only philosophized with his head but also with his heart and his physical strength. It is too simple, indeed unjustifiable, to declare that after all Ho was more religious than philosophical, as if a total commitment to one's intellectual perception necessarily depreciates one's philosophical sophistication. In fact the inseparability of Ho's life and thought is itself philosophically as well as religiously significant. Without digressing into an entirely different plane of discourse, it may be helpful to note that the mode of philosophizing that can completely detach itself from the "religious" commitment of the philosopher is rare, if not impossible, in any intellectual heritage no matter how narrowly defined. Therefore, when Ho discussed the physical self as the prime mover in man's behavior (p. 60), he was not only advocating a program of self-cultivation but also expressing, in his idiosyncratic manner, the way to be human through conscious self-reflection. Only in this sense was he able to bridge the gap between what is (nature) and what ought to be (morality). Likewise, he was able to make the exceedingly interesting remark that the intellectual (the thinker) is not a different sort of human being but a more refined manifestation of humanity. His suggestive description of Confucius as the "concealed dragon" (p. 71) should also be understood and appreciated in this connection, and so, I would further maintain, should his theory of proper interpersonal relationships (p. 79) and his analyses of family, friendship, and self.

Intellectual historians are particularly fascinated by what may be called the "radical universalism" in Ho's Confucian thought. His innovative attempt to reorder the priority of Confucian ethics—elevating friendship and comradeship above filiality, for example—certainly raised serious doubts about his fidelity to the Sagely Way in the minds of his contemporaries. It is not to be wondered that issues such as "orthodoxy" have attracted a great deal of attention among students of Chinese philosophy. Admittedly Ho, like his T'ai-chou colleagues, significantly restructured Confucian values to the extent that his interpretation of the Confucian Tao was incompatible in a fundamental way with that of many avowed Confucians of his time. The conflict and tension between Ho's claim to Confucian truth and that of his adversaries, such as Chang Chü-cheng, was much more serious than, say, the confrontation between the Confucians and the Buddhists in general. Of course this is as much a historical as a philosophical issue. But for students of Neo-Confucian philosophy, two problem areas seem to merit further attention. The first can probably be called linguistic. It seems that the time is ripe for a more sophisticated inquiry into the Neo-Confucian language of which Ho's critical self-reflection is a part. We need to know not only the grammatical rules but also the actual practices of the Neo-Confucian language. Philosophically the task involves concrete (technical, if you wish) studies of the modes of expression of key figures in the Neo-Confucian tradition so that we can rethink their thought processes without damaging too much the integrity of their "philosophy." It is on the basis of such a symbolic analysis that the second step of re-presenting Ho's philosophical anthropology can be fruitfully conducted. As far as thinking is concerned, Ho is probably

184

not the best choice in the T'ai-chou school and Dimberg's admirable study, as a pioneering work on the subject, may not be the best introduction to Neo-Confucian philosophy. But just as Ho refused to remain merely "a loyal, meritorious and resolute official" (p. 110), Dimberg's monograph is a great step beyond the overworked thesis that the traditional Confucian scholar-official, as a member of the ruling elite, was either by choice or by default a supporter of the existing sociopolitical order. I am fully convinced by Dimberg's study that to understand and to bring understanding to Neo-Confucian thought, it is neither necessary nor desirable to "prove" that it can be made philosophically meaningful in terms of currently familiar structures of thinking. I am quite aware that to arrive at the meaning of Neo-Confucianism it is not enough to indulge in an analysis of personalities, because Neo-Confucian symbolism is not reducible to practical considerations of its spokesmen. However, without a familiarity with the Neo-Confucian style of life and its instructions on practical living, there is no chance of understanding its philosophical intention—a continuous, indeed, daily reflection on things at hand. It is in this sense that even though "Ho lived apart from his family for the last twenty years of his life, and became an outspoken critic of the bureaucratic establishment and some of its members" (p. 143), he was in his own way a creative interpreter of the Confucian heritage. And it is probably not far-fetched to suggest that Ho's emphasis on practicality anticipated the intellectual transformation of Yen Yüan, that his vision on the physical self foreshadowed the new philosophy of Tai Chen, and that his courage to launch a frontal attack on the notion of the "three bonds" even provided a symbolic possibility for the "radical universalism" of T'an Ssu-t'ung.

13. Yen Yüan: From Inner Experience to Lived Concreteness

As the study of Chinese thought becomes more sophisticated, some of Joseph Levenson's dichotomous interpretations of the cultural transformation of modern China may have to be substantially revised. In the meantime, however, his insight into the dilemma of the modern Chinese literatus who tries to justify his emotional attachment to traditional ideas by an apologetic appeal to a system of values imported from the West is useful. Levenson has pointed out that in so doing, the Chinese literatus both sacrifices the organismic integrity of the traditional ideas and fails to grasp the contextual variations of the imported values. As a result, neither the ideas that were historically significant in shaping the lives of the great personalities in traditional China, nor the values that are currently instrumental in orienting the thoughts of the great minds of the modern West can take root in the Chinese scholarly soil.[1]

One of the saddest consequences of this maladjustment is the conscious and unconscious distortion of more than eight centuries of Chinese thought, commonly known as the Neo-Confucian era. Scholars since Liang Ch'i-ch'ao have been impelled by a sense of cultural urgency to look for Westernlike values in the body of traditional ideas.[2] Their search was concentrated mostly in the ancient period. The technological ingenuity in Mo Ti, the art of logic in Kung-sun Lung, the spirit of science in Hsün Tzu and Wang Ch'ung—all these and others supported their image of what the new China should be. By comparison, Sui-T'ang Buddhism and Sung-Ming Confucianism, with the possible exception of the abortive attempt to see Chu Hsi's *ko-wu* as scientifically respectable, seemed to have no relevance. Only very near the end of the Ming dynasty did scholars find something comparable to scientism and pragmatism.[3] Their enthusiasm was later continued by the Marxian historians' attempt to characterize this period as the culmination of the early

Chinese enlightenment, from a materialist point of view.[4]

Any effort to study and interpret the Neo-Confucian tradition in general and seventeenth-century Chinese thought in particular is therefore confronted with the double difficulty of insufficient objective knowledge and inflated subjective judgments.

Yen Yüan (Hsi-chai, 1635–1704), one of the most original thinkers of this period, is a case in point. The difficulty is further compounded by his reluctance to commit his own ideas to writing and by modern scholars' willingness to manipulate the limited data on him for various ideological purposes. It thus seems advisable first to examine some of the "established" views on Yen Yüan.

Ironically, Yen Yüan, who was relatively unknown in his own time because he lived far from the centers of influence, gained in reputation in the early 1920s among a group of prominent intellectual activists precisely because of a well-organized campaign by those in power. The leader of the campaign was none other than the president of the Republic of China, Hsü Shih-ch'ang. Under his leadership a scholastic society in honor of Yen Yüan, with the suggestive name *Ssu-ts'un* (Four Preservations),[5] was organized in 1920. According to the records of the society, within three years the membership rose to a surprising eight hundred. In 1923 a complete and punctuated edition of the collected works of Yen Yüan and of his best disciple, Li Kung (Shu-ku, 1659–1733), was published and widely circulated as an official undertaking of the society. In 1925 a high school bearing the name of the society was opened in Peking. In addition, a monthly journal dedicated to the study and promulgation of Yen Yüan's thought began publication.[6]

To go into the reasons behind Hsü's efforts would lead to all sorts of ramifications. Suffice it to say here that regional power— specifically, the Chih-li faction—was primarily responsible for the movement. Hsü's attempt to revitalize the Pei-hsüeh (Northern learning) was definitely influenced by the demand of his Hopei intellectuals to formulate a new ideology to lead the nation.[7] Of course, it was not unusual that the rise of a regional power in China should lead to a search for justification beyond the sheer force of politics. Similar cases can be found in Wang Yang-ming's appeal to the Chekiang group and to a lesser degree in Ch'en Po-sha's appeal to the Cantonese. Even Wang Fu-chih's recent rise to prominence in the genealogy of the great materialists, whatever the articulated rationale of the Party ideologues, owed much to his Hunanese origin.[8]

To be sure, if Yen Yüan had had no relevant message for modern China, he would not have been chosen simply because of his regional affiliation. The intellectual occasion for the sudden popularity of Yen Yüan, again with a touch of irony, lies in the timely visit of John Dewey from May 1919 to July 1921. The American philosopher, whose thought, unlike that of William James and Josiah Royce, was very much an indigenous response to a particular situation in the United States, was greatly honored in China as the patron saint of science, the very source of wealth and power. The rediscovery of Yen Yüan as the result of Dewey's intrusion into China is best revealed in the words of Liang Ch'i-ch'ao:

> Since Dewey's lecture tour in China, pragmatism has become a fashionable teaching in our educational circles. This cannot but be said to be a welcome phenomenon. Three hundred years ago in our country there were a Mr. Yen Hsi-chai and his disciple, Mr. Li Shu-ku. They established a school, commonly known as the Yen-Li School. Their ideas were similar to those of Dewey and his colleagues. And in certain ways their ideas were more penetrating than those of Dewey and his colleagues.[9]

One of the most important events in the promotion of Yen Yüan's ideas was Liang's lecture on Ch'ing thought in 1923.[10] Liang characterized Yen's thought as "practical utilitarianism" (*shih-chien shih-yung chu-i*) and dramatically announced that Yen and Li, in essence, had launched an "extremely violent but sincere great revolutionary movement"[11] against all other modes of thinking in the last two thousand years of Chinese thought. Liang was especially impressed with Yen's action-philosophy, which in his judgment was precisely what Chinese youth needed. Liang was equally impressed by Yen Yüan's concern for practicality, which he interpreted as the spirit of experimental science. He declared further that if Yen had been born in the twentieth century, he would certainly have become a great scientist and would have advocated the "omnicompetence of science"[12] (*k'o hsüeh wan-neng*).

Liang's enthusiasm aroused the interest of many other scholars, including the nationalist, Chang Ping-lin, the moderate essayist,

Chou Tso-jen, and the liberal, Hu Shih.[13] Their views, however, were not so much scholarly inquiries into the thought of an original thinker as educated speculations on the relevance of Yen's approach to the solutions of many serious problems confronting China at the time. Mansfield Freeman, following in the footsteps of both Hsü Shih-ch'ang and Liang Ch'i-ch'ao, contributed an article entitled "Yen Hsi-chai, a 17th Century Philosopher" to the *Journal of the North China Branch of the Royal Asiatic Society* as early as 1926. After citing laudatory remarks about Yen Yüan from Hsü's introduction to his work on Yen-Li philosophy and Liang's *History of Chinese Thought of the Last Three Hundred Years*, Freeman confidently stated that the seventeenth-century "Chinese pragmatist" held a high place in the thought of contemporary Chinese scholars, and his philosophy of education had real significance for modern China.[14]

It was in the 1930s, however, with the publication of Fung Yu-lan's *History of Chinese Philosophy*, Ch'ien Mu's *History of Chinese Thought of the Last Three Hundred Years,* and Ch'en Teng-yüan's *Survey of the Philosophical Thought of Yen Hsi-chai*, that Yen Yüan's ideas took root in the scholarly world. It seems remarkable that, owing to Fung's new realism, in his highly selective study of Chinese philosophy, Yen Yüan occupies a conspicuous position, whereas Ch'en Po-sha, Chan Kan-ch'üan, Liu Tsung-chou, and Huang Tsung-hsi merit only passing reference.[15] Ch'ien Mu further suggests that Yen Yüan's unprecedented act of "smashing" the whole Neo-Confucian tradition surpassed southern scholars such as Huang Tsung-hsi, Wang Fu-chih, and Ku Yen-wu in courage and decisiveness.[16] To support his point, Ch'ien even quotes Wang K'un-shen's tribute to Yen Yüan in the form of a couplet: "He opened his mouth to utter the words that for two thousand years none was able to speak, and he put down on paper the thoughts that for two thousand years none dared to write."[17]

The rise of Marxism-Leninism in China again put Yen Yüan in a new light. A systematic effort was made by Chinese Communist historians to "restore" the true place of Yen Yüan in the development of dialectical materialism in China. Hou Wai-lu, in his comprehensive study of Chinese thought, denounces the bourgeois fallacy of equating "classical utilitarianism" with "capitalistic pragmatism."[18] He calls for an overall reevaluation of the seventeenth-century Chinese philosophy and arrives at the conclusion that Yen Yüan's major contribution lies in his new world view.[19] After a rather ingenuous and somewhat distorted textual analysis, Hou implicitly labels Yen's thought as a kind of materialist realism. Although Hou also criticizes Yen's residual antiquarianism, he praises him as a progressive fighter for the truth of materialism.[20]

What, then, is the authentic image of Yen Yüan? Was he a great revolutionary, an embodiment of the spirit of science, a man of action, a confirmed pragmatist, and a progressive realist? Paradoxically, there is some truth in all of the above designations, but it seems ill-advised to accept any of them as a serious attempt to understand Yen Yüan the man. To expose, at least in part, the motivation behind these "established" views is not to brush them aside as inconsequential, but to use them as possible channels toward a more objective study of the *Problematik* of Yen Yüan.

My present concern, therefore, is not to grasp the historical Yen Yüan as such or to understand his times in terms of what actually happened. Neither the life history of Yen Yüan nor the sociocultural milieu in which he lived is our main concern. Instead, the focus will be on the intellectual mode of Yen Yüan's response to one of the major issues of his time, an issue that not only had *historical* significance, but was one that continued to beset Confucian thinkers for many generations to come. Perhaps a study of this kind will throw some light on the internal development of Confucianism in the seventeenth century, especially in reference to the perennial problem of *hsiu-shen* (self-cultivation) in the Confucian tradition as a whole.

When Yen Yüan was born in 1635 (the eighth year of the reign of the last Ming emperor, Ch'ung-chen), the first generation of Neo-Confucian thinkers in the seventeenth century was already well on its way to national prominence: Huang Tsung-hsi (1610–95), Chang Lü-hsiang (1611–74), Ku Yen-wu (1613–82), and Lu Lung-ch'i (1630–93).[21] Yen Yüan's reputation, on the other hand, was not to go beyond a small circle of scholars during his lifetime. His native village, halfway between Peking and Tientsin, had never stood out as an intellectual center. His poverty-stricken father had been adopted by a Chu family in another district. When Yen Yüan was only three years old his father disappeared, allegedly captured by the Manchus during their invasion of the capital in 1638. As a result, he was raised by the Chu family and given the surname Chu.[22]

At the age of seven, Yen Yüan began his formal education with a private tutor. His mother remarried when he was eleven. A marriage was arranged for him when he was only fourteen, but under the pretext of practicing the art of Taoist self-cultivation, he managed to keep his wife at a distance. It seems obvious that Yen Yüan's education and marriage were imposed on him for utilitarian reasons by his "grandfather," the man who had adopted his father. At fifteen, when his grandfather resorted to bribery to obtain for him the first-degree status, Yen Yüan was said to have burst into tears and refused to take any food, saying, "I would rather be an authentic illiterate than a fake literatus."[23]

At eighteen (1653), he passed the first-degree examination. Two years later he decided against any further attempts to enter government service, although he was still going through the motions of practicing literary writing and taking examinations simply to please his grandparents. His attention then focused on reading Ssu-ma Kuang's *Tzu-chih t'ung-chien* (Comprehensive Mirror for the Aid of Government). His involvement in the study of history and statecraft prompted him to dip into a variety of military books. He also practiced swordsmanship and self-defense. His deviation from the main course of social advancement reached a high point when he seriously engaged himself in the study of medicine with a view to making a living from it.[24]

However, in 1658, at the age of twenty-three Yen Yüan began a career as a teacher. He named his study "*Ssu-ku* (Remembering the Ancients) *chai*" and himself "*Ssu-ku jen.*" He wrote a treatise entitled "The Kingly Way" (*Wang-tao lun*), which was based on his rather romantic ideas about the golden age of the "three sagely dynasties." Speculating on issues such as the adaptation of the well-field system, the strength of the feudal order, the contents of education in ancient times, the possible revitalization of the procedures of recommendation and election of the Han dynasty, the urgency of suppressing heterodox teachings, and reforms in land taxation, what he did was no more than an intellectual exercise in the realm of state affairs.[25] To be sure, even in this brief work he demonstrated a high level of sophistication and originality, but it was still indicative of the concerns of an idealistic young man. Unfortunately this work has been studied and analyzed by some modern scholars as a record of Yen Yüan's subtle proposal for revolutionary social reforms. One of the reasons is probably that the work was later given a new title, *Ts'un-chih pien* (The preservation of statecraft), and printed together with three of Yen Yüan's mature works.[26]

In 1659, after almost a decade of married life, his wife gave birth to a son whom he named Fu-k'ao (literally, "en route to examination"). Again under heavy pressures from his grandfather, he decided to take the annual examination in Peking. But his trip to the capital was unfruitful. He failed not only to pass the examination but also to avail himself of the literary talent in Peking. The Manchu court severely prohibited any form of gathering by the candidates.[27] Yen Yüan's abortive attempts to enter government service and the literary societies reinforced his reluctance to commit himself to sociopolitical activities. By then he had assumed the main responsibility for supporting his family. He spent most of his time tilling the land; occasionally he also practiced medicine. It was during this period that he encountered the writings of the Neo-Confucian philosophers, especially those of the Ch'eng-Chu school. His serious, careful study of the *Hsing-li ta-ch'üan* (An Anthology of Works on Human Nature and the Universal Principle) had a profound impact on both his intellectual outlook and his way of life.[28]

In 1661, Yen Yüan established an altar to the *tao-t'ung* (the "genealogy of the Way," or "orthodox succession"). His sacred line began with the legendary cultural hero, Fu-hsi, and was handed down from the Duke of Chou to Confucius. After Confucius, he singled out Yen Hui, Tseng Tzu, Tzu-ssu, Mencius, Chou Tun-i, Ch'eng Hao, Ch'eng I, Chang Tsai, Shao Yung, and Chu Hsi for daily worship. In addition, he put his own preference, two legendary physicians, on the altar. His existential—and indeed religious—commitment to Neo-Confucian teachings shaped his spiritual direction for at least the next seven years.[29] To discipline himself, he practiced daily quiet-sitting, worked in the fields, and studied the classics and history until midnight. He also organized a literary club mainly for the purpose of mutual exhortation on moral conduct. He made scholarly tours to nearby villages to visit well-known teachers. Through a series of dialogues with these learned men, he tried to broaden and deepen his understanding of the basic Neo-Confucian ideas. Further, with the help of an intimate friend, Wang Fa-ch'ien, as his "mirror," he kept a diary to record his own self-criticism.

Viewed objectively and detachedly, Yen Yüan's method seems somewhat mechanical. He reflected on the state of his mind—his critical self-awareness—several times a day. If his mind was "purely present" (absolutely attentive) for a given period he would mark a circle in the space designated for that period. If his mind was completely absent he would mark a cross. If its presence exceeded its absence he would leave the main part of the circle in white; otherwise he left the main part of the circle in black. In 1669, three years after he had initiated the method, he added additional symbols to represent control of his speech and temper. If he made one superfluous remark he would add a line to the circle $\bigcirc$. If his superfluous remarks passed five he would cross off the circle $\otimes$. If he lost his temper once he would add a T to the circle $\overline{\smile}$. If he lost his temper more than five times he would cancel the circle with three lines $\otimes$.[30]

This was a rather rigid application of Mencius' instruction that true learning consists of nothing but the search for the lost mind. The concentration of energy and the focus of attention in such a practice, however, required the total devotion of the practitioner. When Yen Yüan applied this rigorous self-control to his daily affairs, his mode of living became highly ritualized. Indeed, he was so ritualistic about the way he dressed, ate, walked, and talked that every transgression was faithfully recorded as a warning for future action. He even insisted on putting down his evil thoughts before they materialized. He contended that if every mistake was recorded in ink as a reminder, although the diary would be filled with black marks, there would eventually be a day for reform; if nothing was recorded, a hundred mistakes might be let off and the chances for repentance thereby diminished.[31]

Only in the light of his ritualization can we understand how the simple act of mourning the death of his "grandmother" at the age of thirty-three could inflict so much damage on his health that he never fully recovered from it. This dramatic event occurred in 1668. On the death of his grandmother he decided to assume the re-

193

sponsibility of the principal mourner in place of his father. Without yet knowing that his father had been adopted by the Chu family, he went into mourning with the dual role of an unfilial son (due to his father's absence) and of a gratifying grandson. The mourning period started on the fourteenth day of the second month. For the first three days, he ate nothing, and yielded to sobbing and shedding tears at least three times a day. He resisted the convention of hiring musicians, nor did he invite a monk or Taoist priest to help with the ritual. On the fourth day he ate porridge, but only once in the morning and once in the evening. He refused to bury the body until the twenty-fourth day of the second month. During the burial ceremony he cried in such an uncontrollable manner that he bumped his head on the coffin and lost consciousness.

On the sixth day of the fourth month, he built himself a small hut near the tomb. By then he had been wearing a rough hemp-cloth garment day and night for about two months, which resulted in his arms and legs swelling with lumps. He did not change into a plain nightgown in the evenings until the third day of the sixth month. By the tenth month he was critically ill. Had he not been told the story of his father's adoption by a sympathetic old man of the Chu family, which was later verified by his remarried mother, Yen might have continued with his ritualized self-torture for three years.[32]

Although Yen Yüan physically survived the traumatic experience, his spiritual orientation was profoundly altered by it. He became dissatisfied with Chu Hsi's *Chia-li*, a treatise on family rituals that he had followed in minute detail during the period of mourning. He also questioned the whole Neo-Confucian emphasis on quiet-sitting and book reading.[33] In 1669, two months after his bitter experience, he completed a treatise on human nature entitled *Ts'un-hsing pien* (On the preservation of human nature).[34] His arguments against Chu Hsi's dualistic interpretation of human nature and in favor of returning to Mencius' insistence on the original goodness of man anticipated Tai Chen's philosophical inquiry into the concept of the good. As a symbolic act, he changed the name of his study from *Ssu-ku chai* to *Hsi-chai* (The Studio of Practice).[35] Toward the end of the same year, he completed another important treatise entitled *Ts'un-hsüeh pien* (On the preservation of learning), in which he severely criticized the teachings of Ch'eng I and Chu Hsi and

194

advocated a return to the educational programs of the Duke of Chou and Confucius.[36]

Yen Yüan's attack on Ch'eng I and Chu Hsi marked a fundamental change in his spiritual orientation. Quiet-sitting and book reading were relegated to secondary importance. Activism in the form of moral practice became his central concern. The word *hsi,* which he used to rename his study, best symbolized this new direction. Etymologically *hsi* depicts a bird learning to fly. In the first line of the *Analects,* it is used to indicate the process through which one's learning becomes fully interiorized. To focus on *hsi* rather on quiet-sitting or book reading is to emphasize the realm of concrete activities. It should be noted, however, that Yen Yüan's departure from the Ch'eng-Chu school did not constitute a rejection of its ritualism. On the contrary, after his painful experience in 1668 he became even more convinced that the most authentic approach to self-cultivation was through the practice of rituals (*hsi-li*).[37]

In 1670 he learned that his father came from the Yen family of Po-yeh, and he made a special visit to his ancestral home in Hopei. To his happy surprise, his own grandmother, née Chang, was still alive in her eighties. When he returned home he mixed some of his blood with ink and wrote a tablet in honor of his father. He performed salutory bows in front of the tablet day and night as if his father were still present. In 1673, when his "grandfather" died, he formally reverted to the surname Yen. In 1679 he lost the sight of his left eye as the result of an infection. But this did not prevent him from completing another important treatise, originally entitled *Huan mi-t'u* (Calling for those who have lost the way), but later changed to *Ts'un-jen pien* (On the preservation of humanity). Nor did the blindness in his left eye stop him from making an extensive journey to Manchuria in search of his father's whereabouts. When he arrived in Feng-t'ien fu, he kneeled down by the side of the road and distributed pamphlets describing his father. After about a year his sincere efforts produced some result: his half-sister, whom he had never met before, came to him from Manchuria with the sad news that their father had died. Thus ended Yen's long struggle to determine for himself his true origins.

In 1689 he formally accepted Li Kung as his disciple. Two years later he made his only journey to the central part of China. The entire trip lasted about six and a half months. Thereafter, except for his short-lived mastership of Chang-nan Academy, which was destroyed by flood in 1696, Yen spent the rest of his life studying, teaching, and occasionally writing. In 1701, when Li Kung was about to leave for the capital, Yen bade farewell to him, saying that to preserve the Tao on a thousand rolls (*chüan*) of paper is less meaningful than to entrust it to a few men of some understanding; the first order of concern in Li's trip to the north should be to rouse the students to an experiential grasp of the Confucian truth.

Yen Yüan died in 1704 at the age of sixty-nine. His last words to his beloved students were: "The world is still improvable. You should cultivate your learning and prepare yourselves for some useful task."[38]

Yen Yüan's life presents us with a number of puzzling questions. How can he be characterized as an activist when for the most part he lived like a recluse in a small village? Is there any justification for propagandizing his revolutionary spirit, as some modern scholars do, when he constantly ritualized his way of life into a conventional mode? How could he reconcile his emphasis on practical involvement in sociopolitical affairs with his own role as a teacher in an isolated environment? Indeed, how could he criticize Chu Hsi's family rituals as being too demanding when his own self-discipline was even more difficult to follow?

To answer these questions we must go beyond Yen Yüan's life and study his intellectual commitments. This cannot be done, however, without a proper understanding of the kinds of problems he confronted. The fall of the Ming dynasty had a profound impact on virtually all mid-seventeenth-century Chinese thinkers. The Confucian response to the decline and final collapse of the great Chinese empire was certainly one of the most important dimensions of seventeenth-century Chinese thought. Wang Fu-chih's advocacy of ethnoculturalism, Huang Tsung-hsi's critique of despotism, and Ku Yen-wu's advocacy of the decentralization of authority and the strengthening of provincial powers should all be understood against the background of this important event. Yen Yüan's "The Kingly Way," a treatise on statecraft, thus reflected a common concern of his generation.

However, as I have already pointed out, Yen Yüan's work of

1658, written in his early twenties, was not indicative of his mature views. A brief survey of his life reveals that, unlike Wang Fu-chih, Huang Tsung-hsi, and Ku Yen-wu, he did not have a broad perspective on dynastic and institutional history; unlike Huang he did not have an intimate knowledge of contemporary politics, and unlike Ku he did not have a comprehensive understanding of local conditions. Since Yen was intellectually isolated from the major issues of his time and politically detached from the centers of power and influence, one could hardly expect his contribution to be made in what is called political thought. Yet his failure to develop a profound historical consciousness, to come to grips with the political realities of the court, or to delve deeply into the socioeconomic conditions of the provinces did not deprive him of an essential position in seventeenth-century Chinese thought. Where then was his strength?

In response to the fall of the Ming dynasty, Yen Yüan made an often-quoted criticism of the Confucian literati: "In times of leisure they discussed with folded hands the lofty ideas of mind and human nature; when they were confronted with a crucial situation they could repay their prince only by committing suicide."[39] This may well serve as a key to Yen Yüan's *Problematik*. Yet if one takes the quotation seriously, one cannot but wonder why those who actually sacrificed their lives should be singled out as targets of attack. The very decision to commit suicide required tremendous resolution; the willingness to fulfill a deep commitment by sacrificing one's own life was far from a trifling matter. Also, Yen Yüan was himself very much concerned with the issues of mind and human nature; he could not have objected to any serious discussion of these ideas. Why, then, was he so unsparing in his evaluation of the late Ming Confucian literati?

One way of answering the question is to stress Yen's "pragmatism." He did not criticize the act of committing suicide itself, nor did he attack philosophical discussion per se. He was dissatisfied with the absence of pragmatic value in both cases. It is easy to cite examples in Yen Yüan's teachings to illustrate his pragmatic concerns. His attacks on the Neo-Confucianists after his traumatic experience in 1668 is one example. Yen maintained that extensive reading or writing was damaging to one's health and ridiculed those Confucian scholars who spent most of their times on books as "shamefully acquiring the appearance of women."[40] He even found an analogy between those widowed women who wasted their lives in mourning the dead and the Neo-Confucianists who buried themselves in books. Two vivid accounts of those effete scholars are found in Yen Yüan's *Ts'un-hsüeh*. One derives from his personal observation:

> My friend Chang Shih-ch'ing was well versed in books. He said that he had almost completed reading the histories of the last two thousand years from the Ch'in-Han period onward. He explained the meanings of those books to his students. When his strength was exhausted he rested on the bed, panting. After a long while, he would get up and lecture again. When his strength was exhausted he would again lie down. This was indeed unusual exertion; it not only ruined his health but also failed to produce any talent. Under that kind of condition how could any of his students study the "six arts?"[41]

The other had to do with his own teacher, a scholar in Ch'i-yang:

> Tiao Meng-chi of Ch'i-yang expended his strength in the learning of quiet-sitting and book reading. He read by day, contemplated by night, and wrote down his ideas in one hundred *chüan*. But every day he was run down in health, spitting and coughing. Three months before his death he even lost his voice.[42]

After a survey of such cases Yen Yüan concluded that those who sat motionless for hours and spent most of their time reading books were invariably weak and useless; they became the laughing-stock of soldiers and farmers.[43] He thus advocated a new form of learning called *shih-hsüeh* (literally, "real learning"). It should be pointed out, however, that the concept of *shih* had long been used by Confucian scholars to describe their approaches to learning. Since the main concern of Confucianism was self-realization through moral cultivation, experiential knowledge was always considered superior to speculative theory. It is in this sense that teaching by words, in the eyes of the Confucianists, is far less effective than teaching by example. The early Ming Confucian master, Hsüeh Hsüan (Wen-ch'ing, 1389–1464), also called his approach to learning "real" (*shih-hsüeh*) because it was not an accumulation of empirical facts but a process of self-fulfillment through a series of experiential encounters with the ideas presented in the books.[44] The existential dimension of learning was so crucial to Confucianism that none of the Sung-Ming masters ever separated book reading from the actual practice of self-cultivation. What, then, was "new" in Yen Yüan's *shih-hsüeh?*

In the accounts of Yen Yüan's life it seems evident that he had never questioned the prominence of self-cultivation in the Confucian hierarchy of values. Even after he had become disillusioned with the Ch'eng-Chu school, he still followed a rigorous plan of self-dicipline. Ironically, his ritualized life style could have been praised by the Ch'eng-Chu Confucianists as an excellent example of self-control. It is true that Yen Yüan severely reprehended the Sung-Yüan Confucian emphasis on tranquillity and passivity, but he faithfully adhered to its methods of "internal self-transformation." In one important sense, though, Yen Yüan substantially departed from the Ch'eng-Chu school, a departure that has been characterized by a few modern scholars as a "philosophy of dynamism." Essentially it differs little from Wang Yang-ming's advocacy of "constant practice in the midst of concrete affairs."[45] This is probably one of the reasons why Yang P'ei-chih and others maintain that Yen Yüan was deeply influenced by this great mid-Ming thinker. To illustrate this point there is a rather elaborate example of learning to play the lute given us by Yen Yüan:

> The *Book of Poetry* and the *Book of History* are like an instruction book for the lute. Thoroughly mastering the instruction book and being able to explain it in detail—can this be called the actual study of the lute? This is why I said that to search for the efficacy of the Tao by way of discussing and reading is to be a thousand *li* from the truth. It is worse still if an absurd person points to the instruction book and says, "This is the lute." . . . Only when one has learned to sing the score, to master the fingering, to tune the string, to follow the rhythm, and to play in harmony, can one be said to have studied the lute.[46]

He continued to describe the state of being "versed" (*hsi*) in the lute and the state of being "competent" (*neng*) in it.

Through this analogy Yen's message seems apparent. One can never learn to play the lute by reading the instruction book, no mat-

199

ter how diligently and conscientiously one reads it. The art of playing the lute cannot be mastered through a mental process of internalization; it can be learned only by practice.

Yen Yüan's emphasis on practice again reminds us of Wang Yang-ming's "unity of knowledge and action."[47] Knowledge is merely empty talk if it cannot be put to use. Genuine knowledge is simultaneously a form of acting that must make a practical difference in the world, for practicality is an essential criterion of true knowledge. To *know* how to play the lute and yet not be able actually to play it is an example of misusing the word *know* to describe a state of being ignorant. It is inconceivable that one can say that one knows how to play the lute when he has merely intellectually comprehended the instruction book. But the compatibility of Yen and Wang must not be overstressed. After all, Yang-ming's activism presupposes that the ultimate basis for man's moral self-realization is a completely self-sufficient process of internal transformation, whereas Yen Yüan's dynamism insists that self-cultivation has to be carried out in the concrete world amid its practical affairs.[48]

Yen Yüan's insight into the complexity of actual practice requires further explanation. To him the real challenge of self-cultivation is not only to make a qualitative "leap" from knowing to acting, but also to continue the process of practice in a constant or even routine way. To have mastered the basic techniques of the lute is merely the beginning. Only through years of practice can one become proficient in the art. Even if one has learned all the skills of playing the music by heart, one is still far from being a virtuoso. To arrive at a state where "one's heart forgets about one's hands and one's hands no longer feel the strings,"[49] one must practice diligently and unceasingly.

Similarly, ritual practice involves an incessant commitment to self-perfection. It is a daily, indeed hourly, affair, and by necessity it has to assume a concrete form. Of course there is little excitement in such trifling acts as rising early, dressing properly, eating moderately, refraining from superfluous talking, walking at an unhurried pace, sitting straight, and keeping a diary consistently. But like the training of a lute virtuoso, to integrate all these seemingly fragmentary acts into a holistic expression of the ritualized personality requires a lifelong commitment.

The act of a specific ritual practice is not only a record but also a self-revealing gesture. It in a sense offers a solution to the perennial Confucian problem of "inner and outer" (*nei-wai*), for it bridges the gap between an inner effort of self-cultivation and its outer manifestation in the family, the state, and, indeed, the entire universe. A ritualized act, in the true sense of the word, always involves both inner and outer dimensions. It is neither an unexternalizable experience nor a contentless form. On the one hand, it records the attained level of self-cultivation; on the other it reveals the spiritual strength in the sociopolitical realm. Yen Yüan was especially sensitive to the symbolic meanings of ritualized acts; he insisted on the perfect execution of virtually every one of them. For example he never left his room without being properly dressed, even late in the evening when he simply got up from the bed to go to the toilet. He contended that the act of leaving the room provided an important opportunity for practicing moral self-cultivation.[50]

After all, to study the lute is to acquire a skill, but to engage in ritual practice is to master oneself. The art one must learn in mastering oneself is that of self-cultivation. Unlike the study of the lute, one cannot for a minute lay down one's instrument and rest. The moment one forsakes ritual practice, one has already deviated from the course of self-cultivation. Constant practice does not guarantee a competent performance. Yen Yüan was thus frequently in a state of "fear and trembling." He was frightened, to be sure, neither by the presence of a transcendent reality nor by the thought of retribution. Like Confucius's disciple, Tseng Tzu, he felt he was always "standing on the edge of a chasm or walking on thin ice" for fear of failing the task of self-cultivation. And this brings us to the *Problematik* of Yen Yüan.

It is true that Yen Yüan never questioned the centrality of self-cultivation in the value system of Confucianism. He nevertheless challenged the workability of the Ch'eng-Chu version of it. He established the criterion of practicality to differentiate what he called the authentic Confucian self-cultivation from other non-Confucian methods of spiritual self-discipline. To him, quiet-sitting never produced truly practical values. The mysterious experiences of the Ch'an masters were merely flowers in the mirror or the moon in the water:

201

One can only in time of idleness amuse oneself with these delusions. If one attempts to use the light or to carry the beauty, one is bound to fail. . . . The flower and the moon are gone when the mirror and the water are taken away. When the effort of quiet-sitting continues without cessation throughout one's whole lifetime, the delusions may become more wonderful and the void may become more profound. However, that is just like the man who day after day for a lifetime sits in front of the mirror or the water, amusing himself with the flowers or the moon. He only deceives himself through his whole lifetime.[51]

Yen Yüan maintained that true self-cultivation is designed "to change the world" (chuan-shih). The aim is to strengthen one's internal self-identity so that one can change the world instead of "being changed by the world" (shih-chuan).[52] To have a tangible impact on the concrete realities of one's environment becomes an inseparable dimension of one's self-cultivation. If the new experience resulting from one's self-cultivation cannot be converted into some form of energy for the improvement of the world, it is both useless and worthless. Yen Yüan confidently stated that no matter how profound the Sung masters were philosophically, their conviction that the cult of quietude would yield the fruit of enlightenment was a fiction.[53] He was certain that values could be created only by a dynamic encounter with the realities of life. It is thus understandable why Yen Yüan went out of his way to defend the Confucian states-man, Wang An-shih (1021–86). Wang was courageous enough to confront the "brute facts" of his times, and it is also in this sense that Yen Yüan praised the activism of other Sung scholar officials.[54]

Yen Yüan's central concern thus became how to translate the spiritual strength of self-cultivation into sociopolitical forces in order to shape the world according to the Confucian ideal. To him, use-fulness was the key to Confucian truth. Being useful in a modest sense means that the aim of one's private effort is not merely to attain a state of internal peace but to make a tangible contribution to one's immediate environment and to set a living example for one's folks at home. To dwell in spiritual quietude as an end in itself is a luxury no true Confucianist can afford. In fact, all Confucian sages in history were men of action. According to Yen Yüan, it is inconceivable that a Confucianist, as differentiated from a Taoist or a Ch'an Buddhist, could live up to his true image by cultivating his spiritual self in complete isolation. The level of self-realization, in the Confucian context, is measured by the degree of its usefulness. As the sage extends his practical value to the universe in general, so the ordinary Confucianist exerts his moral influence at home. The true follower of Confucian teachings never fails to share his "inner light" with the people around him.[55]

To return to my earlier point, Yen Yüan did not object to the discussion of such fundamental issues as mind and human nature. As I shall explain later, he was himself devoted to their study. Nor did he show any disrespect for those who sacrificed their lives to symbolize their deep commitments. He remarked once: "In reading Chia-shen hsün-nan lu (A record on the loyalist deaths of 1644), whenever I encountered the saying, 'Shamefully I am at a loss to find any means to meet the critical situation; all I have left is to repay my debt of gratitude to the emperor by dying,' I was always mournfully moved to tears."[56] Yen Yüan was well aware that it was not the intrinsic weakness of discussing the lofty ideas of mind and human nature that led to the downfall of the Ming dynasty. The fundamental issue was the inability of the best Confucianists to translate their efforts at internal self-cultivation into useful energy to meet the crisis of the state. He was so impressed with the heroic sacrifices of those Confucian loyalists, yet so disheartened by their powerlessness, that he felt it necessary to conclude that, judging by the criterion of practicality, they all died meaningless deaths.

Instead of abandoning the practice of self-cultivation and concentrating on the instrumental values of statecraft exclusively, which would seem to many of us to be the natural alternative, Yen Yüan made a series of inquiries into the "roots" of man's self-realization. Contrary to the common belief that Yen Yüan was a pragmatist, his Problematik compelled him to examine some of the most fundamental philosophical concepts in Neo-Confucianism, rather than pursue the course of "scientific empiricism." His originality actually lies in the critique of the Ch'eng-Chu concept of human nature and the formulation of a new Confucian concept of man. We shall therefore proceed to an examination of Yen Yüan's inquiry into human nature.

One of the essential concerns of Confucianism is the uniqueness of man. Since the time of Mencius, when the problem of differentiating human beings from other animals became philosophically significant, Confucian thinkers have always been involved in reflection on man's self-image. With the beginning of the Confucian revival in the Sung dynasty, they again centered on the issue of how "to establish the ultimacy of man" (*li jen-chi*). It may be said that human reality is the point of departure for virtually all serious works by Confucian scholars and that human nature is the recurring theme in the Confucian tradition as a whole. Yen Yüan's inquiry into the nature of man therefore placed him contextually in the mainstream of Confucian thinking.

Methodologically, Yen Yüan presented his views on human nature in a series of critical comments on the sayings of Chu Hsi.[57] His main purpose was not so much to expose the weakness of the great Sung philosopher as to put his own ideas in proper perspective. It seems appropriate, therefore, to characterize his "critical comments" as sincere attempts to enter into a "dialogue" with Chu Hsi, that is, to think sympathetically with the Neo-Confucian master so as to come to grips with his real difficulties.

Yen Yüan was aware that Chu Hsi's approach to human nature had been deeply influenced by Chang Tsai's notion of *ch'i* (material force or vital breath), especially the more restrictive concept of *ch'i-chih chih hsing* (physical nature). While Chu Hsi believed that Chang, by adding the "physical" dimension to the Mencian idea of man, had made a tremendous contribution to the formulation of a more balanced and more comprehensive view of human nature in the Confucian tradition, Yen Yüan felt that Chang had actually confused the issue. The thrust of his critique of Chu Hsi in this connection thus centered around Chu Hsi's attempt to incorporate Chang's concept of physical nature into the Mencian idea of man. He argued that such an attempt led to some unnecessary complications, and that Chu Hsi had failed to come to grips with Mencius' insight that man is intrinsically perfectible despite his weakness.

Yen Yüan agreed with Chu Hsi that, as a general principle, in the discussion of man, merely talking about physical nature without reference to moral nature is to commit the fallacy of obscurity, and merely talking about moral nature without reference to physical nature is to commit the fallacy of incompleteness.[58] He could not, however, agree with Chu Hsi that Mencius' views on man considered as a whole were still "incomplete." He felt that Chu Hsi had actually misinterpreted Mencius in his attempt to develop a more satisfactory concept of human nature. By forcing Chang Tsai's idea on Mencius, Chu Hsi had to accept the position that "evil must also be understood as part of human nature,"[59] which was indeed a major departure from Mencius' insistence on man's inner goodness.

It should be mentioned in passing that Yen Yüan found an affinity between his role as a critic and that of Mencius: neither of them had any strong liking for argument, but both were impelled by moral indignation to take issue with the established view of their times.[60] Mencius insisted that human nature is good, so as to provide an ultimate basis for man's perfectibility through self-cultivation. He contended that the beginnings, or rather the "budding potentials" (*tuan*), of the four cardinal virtues (human-heartedness, righteousness, propriety, and wisdom) are inherent in the mind. Moral self-cultivation centers on the reflective and introspective functions of the mind. It is because of the unique ability of the human mind to transform itself into a higher order of perfection for the sake of self-realization that human nature is defined as good. It is this particular nature of man that creates moral values and distinguishes man from the rest of the animals—indeed, from any other kind of being.[61]

To say that human nature is good is thus to characterize man by his unique endowment. This is basically consistent with Confucius' teaching that the attainment of moral perfection depends on an inner decision: "Is humanity something remote? If I want to be humane, behold, humanity has arrived."[62] To be sure, Mencius' emphasis on the goodness of man does not overlook the physical side of man's nature, such as the instinctual demands of sex and appetite. On the contrary, he regarded these demands as a legitimate part of man. Yen Yüan was especially delighted to learn that both feeling (*ch'ing*) and ability (*ts'ai*), two important aspects of the physical nature, were designated by Mencius as good.[63] How did Mencius reconcile the apparent incongruity between the unique attributes of man and those which he shares with other animals, if he tried to label both as good? This leads us to the theory of "great body" (*ta-t'i*) and "small body" (*hsiac-t'i*).

For the sake of convenience, it may be useful to discuss Mencius' theory in terms of the deep-structure and surface-structure of human nature. The "great body" refers to the ultimate basis of man's being—his uniqueness. It is the deep-structure of human nature. The "small body" refers to the physical existence of man, or his corporeality. It is the surface-structure of human nature. Paradoxically, the deep-structure, described by Mencius as "great," is that tiny "bud" special to man; whereas the surface-structure, described by Mencius as "small," is that large "stuff" common to all animals. Self-cultivation, however, is not to develop the inherent "buds" of virtue at the expense of man's physical nature. Rather, it is to cultivate the deep-structure so that the surface-structure can also be properly "nourished." As the saying goes, "Virtue can foster the body" (*te jun-shen*).[64] Yen Yüan pointed out that Mencius emphasized *chien-hsing* (realizing the bodily design) as the authentic way of self-cultivation. Only when the deep-structure is fully manifested can the physical nature be truly developed. If merely the surface-structure is manifest, it will never reveal the unique nature of man. It may even bring about its own destruction and thus ruin the corporeality as well.[65] Therefore the important message is to cultivate the deep-structure so that the surface-structure is also cultivated.

Underlying this approach to human nature is a respect for the complete man. To use the above terminology, the deep- and surface-structures are both respected, and self-cultivation is to see to it that both are fully integrated into a holistic structure. Chu Hsi's attempt to assign all human values to the deep-structure and all human evils to the surface-structure therefore created an unnecessary tension in the holistic structure of man. In so doing, he destroyed the unity between man's great and small bodies. If the development of the great body inevitably leads to the suppression of the small body, how can anyone "realize the bodily design" by way of self-cultivation? If the surface-structure has to be relinquished before man can become what he ought to be, how can a full manifestation of the deep-structure help the physical nature to develop itself? By formulating the concept of *ch'i-chih chih hsing* as the main source of evil, Chu Hsi replaced Mencius' complete man with his own version—a partial man who sacrifices his physical nature for an unreal self-fulfillment.

206

Yen Yüan further maintained that since self-cultivation has to be carried out in a concrete disciplinary process, the physical nature is actually the "instrumentality" for the realization of the true self. To deny the importance of human corporeality is to detach man from the very context of his existence. Chu Hsi criticized *ch'ing* (feelings) as dangerous because strong passion frequently inflicts damage on the true nature of man. Yen Yüan contended that strong passion itself is not to be blamed. In fact, filial sons and loyal ministers are all passionate human beings. Chu Hsi followed Ch'eng I in condemning *ts'ai* (powers, drives). Yen Yüan contended that since *ts'ai*, as a constituent element of the physical nature, is one of the concrete bases of man's goodness, it is certainly not to be belittled.[66]

In addition, Yen Yüan argued that *ch'ing* is the manifestation of the inherent moral propensity of man; *ts'ai* is the means by which such a propensity reveals itself in concrete affairs. Without *ch'ing* and *ts'ai* the true nature of man cannot present itself; without the physical nature there is no point of talking about *ch'ing* and *ts'ai*. Without either, the true nature of man is also absent. Therefore *ch'ing* is none other than the manifestation (*hsien*) of true human nature, and *ts'ai* is none other than the ability (*neng*) of true human nature. The so-called *ch'i-chih* (literally, the stuff of material force, referring to that which constitutes the physical nature) is, after all, that of *ch'ing*, of *ts'ai*, and of man's true nature.[67]

Yen Yüan might have used Mencius to strengthen his case, but the message he wanted to deliver seems quite convincing. The central question can be stated as follows: whether the ideal man is a denial of his actual existence or the actual man is the very basis of his ideal manifestation. From Chu Hsi's viewpoint, what a man ought to be is attainable only when the moral agent, through a long process of self-purification, has succeeded in changing the direction of what he actually is. For example, his instinctive need for sex and food has to be sublimated or suppressed. Yen Yüan, on the other hand, suggested that what a man ought to be is rooted in the very structure of what he actually is. To attain self-realization one must be truthful to both the deep- and surface-structures of human nature. For example, to him it is basically immoral to practice celibacy as a means to attain a higher level of spirituality.

It should be mentioned in this connection that Yen Yüan's principal criticism of Buddhism was its practice of celibacy. Yen Yüan declared that the relationship between husband and wife is not only the most primordial but also the most fundamental of all human relations. He stated, "Only after there have been husband and wife are there father and son; only after there have been father and son are there elder and younger brothers; only after there have been elder and younger brothers are there friends; and only after there have been friends are there lord and minister."[68] Since the sagely way begins with husband and wife, to deny the value of sexuality is to nip in the bud the basic Confucian relationships. Chu Hsi's failure to understand that the physical nature is also morally good was indicative of Buddhist influence,[69] Yen argues.

As we have already pointed out, Yen Yüan maintained that the physical nature is really the instrumentality of self-realization. Without it, man is merely an abstract concept. Only by the instrumentality of the physical nature can man become a concrete reality. To become a spiritual being completely outside the bodily form is at most a figment of the imagination.[70] It is true that his physical nature restricts man's freedom, but it is also through his physical nature that man's true potential is understood and expressed.[71] If a human being is a concrete manifestation rather than an abstract approximation, then man's physical nature is not only a work of art that demands appreciation but also a creative agent that constantly gives birth to new human realities.

In the light of the above, it seems less puzzling that Yen Yüan should have launched an attack on Chu Hsi's concept of reverence (*ching*), while his own life-style seems to have borne witness to its applicability. He remarked that there is nothing wrong with the concept itself. But when it is abstracted from the daily affairs of the concrete world and converted into a state of mind, its original dynamism of "carefully attending to a variety of details" is lost. Yen Yüan said:

> The ancients taught men to do housework, and while doing housework to practice reverence. They taught the proper ways of dealing with people, and in these to practice reverence. They taught rituals, music, archery, riding, reading, and mathematics, but in arranging the order of the rituals, in the laws of the notes,

in steadying the bow, in control of the horse, in punctuation, and in calculation, there was nothing without the practice of reverence. Therefore it is said, "Be reverent in handling public affairs," "Be reverent in your daily affairs," and "Be truly reverent in your action." All these emphasize the constant practice of reverence by the complete devotion of both the body and mind. If the traditional methods of the ancients are being laid aside and the practice of reverence is sought in quiet-sitting, meditative self-control, slow-walking, and soft-talking, it is like using the empty form of a Confucian term to do the real work of Buddhism.[72]

The fundamental issue, then, is the choice between a dynamic and active process of self-cultivation that will eventually lead to the realization of a complete and concrete man, and a static and passive course of self-control that at best leads merely to the fulfillment of a partial and abstract man. Yen Yüan contended that the most authentic method of self-cultivation is to *do* rather than to *be*. Man becomes what he should be by engaging in daily affairs. To confront the realities of the world at the moment of internal self-cultivation is, to use Mencius' words, always to be doing something (*pi-yu-shih yen*).

To do something is to make an impact on the existing order of things. No matter how small the impact is, it makes a useful difference. Every man can exert an influence on the world by "doing something," by being active in the affairs of the world. When such deeds have accumulated sufficiently, the direction of the world is bound to change. The true value of man lies in his ability to change the world toward the good. If the Confucianists refuse to do things and insist on simply being themselves, they can never change the world; nor can they escape the fate of being passively changed, or rather destroyed, by the world under the control of others.

Yen Yüan realized that for generations many of the great personalities in the Confucian tradition had devoted themselves to the cultivation of a kind of "inner experience." They might have gained some profound insight into themselves, but they had no useful role to play in the sociopolitical realm. The very fact that they were powerless to perform a useful function in a crucial situation was an indication of the impotence of their existence. Like the helpless screams of widowed women, their sound and fury signified nothing in a world of hard reality. Even when they were determined to change the world by sacrificing their own lives, they still had no practical experience to guide them. Consequently many Confucianists died meaningless deaths.

A fundamental change in the direction of self-cultivation was called for. Yen Yüan pleaded that quiet-sitting, meditation, and book reading be replaced by active participation in the world of daily affairs, or to use my earlier description, by a concrete process of ritualization. For man becomes what he ought to be by doing, practicing, and acting. Human beings never really develop themselves by sitting in meditation. The Confucianist must accordingly transform himself from the abstract state of being a partial, passive, and useless man of words to the concrete reality of being a complete, active, and useful man of deeds. If the Confucianist wants to restore his sense of mission, and indeed his right to survive, he must labor strenuously in what may be called "lived concreteness."

Finally, it must be pointed out that although Yen Yüan's central concern was not self-cultivation so much as the search for inner truth, his serious attempt to redefine the spiritual tradition of Confucianism and to reformulate what he considered essential to Confucian intentionality can be better appreciated in the light of his bitter struggle to discipline himself by an active participation in Confucian rituals. To be sure, his ideal of the complete and concrete man, which is predicated on the Mencian view of human nature, stands in tension with his almost compulsive emphasis on ritualism. He might have failed to develop a philosophy of "human community as holy rite," to borrow the title of Herbert Fingarette's study on Confucian ritualism.[73] But his insistence on an ethicoreligious commitment as a condition prior to any form of sociopolitical activism symbolizes a defining characteristic of the humanistic world view propounded by virtually all great Neo-Confucian thinkers.

At the beginning of this discussion, I raised the question of Yen Yüan's authentic image. I am still far from providing a satisfactory answer. However, I may tentatively suggest that Yen Yüan was a "revolutionary" only in the sense that he attacked the influential Ch'eng-Chu tradition so that he could revitalize the true Confucian approach to self-cultivation. He was an "embodiment of the spirit of science" only in the sense that he detached himself from the fallacy of speculation and returned to the world of concrete objects to discipline himself morally. He was a "man of action" only in the sense that he denounced passivity and advocated a kind of participatory ritualism. He was a "confirmed pragmatist" only in the sense that he emphasized practicality and demanded that all human actions be useful. Finally he was a "realist" only in the sense that he upheld the view that the physical nature of man is an indispensable instrumentality for self-realization.

Unless we are willing to confine our terms to the specific designations stated above, we must conclude that Yen Yüan was not a revolutionary, for he remained faithful to virtually all the basic spiritual values in the Confucian tradition. He was not a scientist, for he never wanted to investigate or study natural phenomena, nor indeed any other phenomena, to obtain a purely intellectual understanding of the external world. He was not an activist either, for his ritualized acts were not ends in themselves but means to a higher goal of self-realization. He was neither a pragmatist nor a realist, for his moral concern was idealistic in orientation and his sense of mission was religious in character.

Yen Yüan's authentic image would have disappointed his modern admirers. His ideas might have also seemed remote from the urgent problems of contemporary China. Nevertheless, he was not only an original thinker of the seventeenth century, but one of the great Confucian intellectuals of all time. The *Problematik* with which he struggled throughout his life comes down to the bedrock of Confucian thinking, and the inquiry to which he devoted his entire intellectual effort penetrates into one of the most profound dimensions of human reality. To study Yen Yüan's *Problematik* and follow his inquiry is not to see his relevance to us, but to appreciate the intrinsic value of his thought in order to cultivate our own sense of relevance.

NOTES

The best edition of Yen Yüan's collected works is the *Yen-Li ts'ung-shu*, edited by Ssu-ts'un hsüeh-hui. The work, which was prefaced in 1923, includes more items (those listed below) than the collected works of Yen Yüan in the *Chi-fu ts'ung-shu.*

(Page numbers refer to the photographic reprint by the Kuang-wen Book Co. of Taiwan.)

Yen Hsi-chai hsien-sheng nien-p'u, pp. 4–46.

Ssu-shu cheng-wu, pp. 47–87.

Yen Hsi-chai hsien-sheng yen-hsing lu, pp. 90–117.

Yen Hsi-chai hsien-sheng p'i-i lu, pp. 119–24.

Ts'un-hsüeh pien, pp. 127–55.

Ts'un-hsing pien, pp. 156–71.

Ts'un-chih pien, pp. 173–80.

Ts'un-jen pien, pp. 181–97.

Chu Tzu yü-lei p'ing, pp. 199–225.

Li-wen shou-ch'ao, pp. 227–53.

Hsi-chai chi-yü, pp. 255–46.

[1]Joseph R. Levenson's three-volume study, *Confucian China and Its Modern Fate* (Berkeley: University of California Press, 1968), vol. 1, pp. xxvii–xxxiii.

[2]Levenson's pioneering study on Liang Ch'i-ch'ao in the context of the predicament of modern Chinese intellectuals can be found in his *Liang Ch'i-ch'ao and the Mind of Modern China* (Cambridge: Harvard University Press, 1953).

[3]Liang Ch'i-ch'ao, *Chung-kuo chin san-pai nien hsüeh-shu shih* (Shanghai: Commercial Press, 1935; hereafter referred to as Liang, *Hsüeh-shu shih*), pp. 1–10, 104–49.

[4]Hou Wai-lu, *Chung-kuo tsao-ch'i ch'i-meng ssu-hsiang shih* (Shanghai: Commercial Press, 1956; hereafter referred to as Hou, *Ssu-hsiang shih*), pp. 3–36.

[5]Four of Yen Yüan's most prominent works were: *Ts'un-chih pien* (On the preservation of statecraft), *Ts'un-hsüeh pien* (On the preservation of learning), *Ts'un-jen pien* (On the preservation of humanity), and *Ts'un-hsing pien* (On the preservation of human nature). All include the word *ts'un*. *Ssu-ts'un* is therefore used here to refer to Yen Yüan's teaching in general.

[6]The story of the revival of interest in Yen Yüan in the 1920s can be reconstructed only from fragmentary information. See Chin Hsü-ju, *Yen Yüan yü Li Kung* (Shanghai: Commercial Press, 1935), pp. 1–3; and Ch'en Teng-yuan, *Yen Hsi-chai che-hsüeh ssu-hsiang shu* (Nanking: Chung-kuo wen-hua yen-chiu-so, prefaced in 1934), vol. 2.

[7]See Chao Heng's preface to *Yen-Li ts'ung-shu* (Peking: Ssu-ts'un hsüeh-hui, 1923).

[8]It may be farfetched to correlate intellectual attachment to great personalities in the past with the politics of regionalism, but the emotional subtlety in regional pride is so important a factor in modern China that any serious study of the formulation of modern Chinese political ideologies must take into consideration the territorial origins of the leaders. Of course, in most cases intellectual ideas were used merely to justify political aims. Frequently the very use of a specific kind of justification, however, shaped the directions of the political aims themselves.

[9]Liang Ch'i-ch'ao, "Yen-Li hsüeh-p'ai yü hsien-tai chiao-yü ssu-ch'ao" (The Yen-Li school and the modern stream of educational thought), included in the appendix of Ch'en Teng-yüan's *Yen Hsi-chai*, vol. 2, p. 331.

[10]Liang gave a series of lectures on Ch'ing thought to the students of Tsing-hua University in 1923. His *Hsüeh-shu shih* was originally written as a series of "instruction notes" (*chiang-i*).

[11]Liang, *Hsüeh-shu shih*, p. 105.

[12]*Ibid.*, p. 123.

[13]For Chang Ping-lin's article see "Cheng Yen" (The rectification of Yen Yüan), in his *Chien-lun*, 4:19–22 (*Chang-shih ts'ung-shu* edition). It should be pointed out that Chang's approach to Yen is basically critical. Yet, through a critical appraisal of Yen's thought, he tried to show that Yen's relevance to modern China by far surpassed the Han Learning of Chi Yün and the Sung Learning of Weng Fang-kang. Chou Tso-jen's article appeared in the literary supplement to the *Ta-kung pao* on October 25, 1933. The article was a reflection on Tai Wang's *Yen-shih hsüeh-chi*. It was the fourth installment of his *K'u-ch'a sui-pi*. Chou's article is sarcastic. It is especially revealing to see his criticism of those who attempted to use Yen Yüan for political purposes. Both Chang's and Chou's articles are included in the appendix of Ch'en's *Yen Hsi-chai*, vol. 2, pp. 358–67.

[14]Mansfield Freeman, "Yen Hsi-chai, a 17th Century Philosopher," in *Journal of the North China Branch of the Royal Asiatic Society* 57 (1926): 70–91.

[15]Fung Yu-lan, *Chung-kuo che-hsüeh shih* (Shanghai: Commercial Press, 1931), vol. 2, pp. 946–48, 974–90. The reason Fung resorted to such an apparent "imbalance" seems to lie in his own commitment to philosophical realism at that time. See Fung Yu-lan, *A History of Chinese Philosophy*, translated by Derk Bodde (Princeton: Princeton University Press, 1952–53), vol. 2.

[16]Ch'ien Mu, *Chung-kuo chin san-pei nien hsüeh-shu shih* (reprint; Taipei: Commercial Press, 1937), p. 159.

[17]*Ibid.*, p. 179.

[18]Hou, *Ssu-hsiang shih*, p. 33.

[19]*Ibid.*, pp. 324–49.

[20]*Ibid.*, pp. 349–75.

[21]Ch'en, *Yen Hsi-chai*, vol. 1, p. 45.

[22]*Yen Hsi-chai hsien-sheng nien p'u*, compiled by Li Kung and edited by Wang Yüan (hereafter referred to as NP), 1:1.

[23]*Ibid.*, 1:3.

[24]*Ibid.*, 1:3b-5.

[25]Yen Yüan's *Wang-tao-lun* was later changed to *Ts'un-chih pien* and included in his collected works as one of the *ssu-ts'un* presentations. See note 5 above.

[26]Cf. Yen Yüan, *Ssu-ts'un pien*, punctuated by Wang Hsing-hsien (Peking: Ssu-ts'un hsüeh-hui, 1923), pp. 1–3.

[27]NP, 1:5b-6. Cf. Kuo Ai-ch'un, *Yen Hsi-chai hsüeh-p'u* (Shanghai: Commercial Press, 1957), p. 4.

[28]NP, 1:6.

[29]*Ibid.*, 1:6b–7.

[30]*Ibid.*, 1:14b–15b.

[31]*Ibid.*, 1:24a–b.

[32]*Ibid.*, 1:16–17b.

33Yen Yüan, *Ts'un-hsing pien*, 2:2a–b. The controversy over whether the *Chia-li* was written by Chu Hsi or not should not concern us here.

34NP, 1:17a.

35*Ibid.*

36Yen Yüan, *Ts'un-hsüeh pien*, 1:8. According to his observation, the main program of the ancient Confucian sages involved the *liu-hsing* (Six Conducts) and *liu-i* (Six Arts). The former consisted of *hsiao* (filial piety), *yu* (friendship), *mu* (kindness), *yin* (compatibility), *jen* (forbearance), and *hsü* (charity); the latter consisted of *li* (rituals), *yüeh* (music), *she* (archery), *yü* (charioteering), *shu* (writing), and *shu* (mathematics).

37NP, 1:18b–21b.

38*Ibid.*, 2:35.

39*Ts'un-hsüeh pien*, 1:11.

40*Ibid.*

41*Ibid.*, 3:1b.

42*Ibid.*

43*Ibid.*, 3:2.

44See Hsüeh Hsüan's *Tu-shu lu* (Records on reading; 1751 edition), 10:11b. In Chu Hsi's commentary on *Chung-yung* (*The Doctrine of the Mean*), Confucianism itself is characterized as *shih-hsüeh*. See his *Ssu-shu chi-chu* (Collected commentaries on the Four Books), preface to *Chung-yung*.

45For a discussion of Wang Yang-ming's inflence on Yen Yüan, see Yang Pei-chih, *Yen Hsi-chai yü Li Shu-ku* (Wuhan: Hubei People's Publishing Co., 1956), pp. 243–58.

46*Ts'un-hsüeh pien*, 3:6b–7.

47Cf. Wang Yang-ming, *Ch'uan-hsi lu* in *Yang-ming ch'üan-shu*, 1:3a–b (SPPY edition).

48Wang's theory is much more profound, but the fact that many of his disciples failed to combine an active life with practical affairs indicates that in his philosophy there is room for those with a tendency toward quietism and passivity. Cf. Hsiung Shih-li, *Shih-li yü-yao ch'u-hsü* (Hong Kong: Tung-sheng Press, 1949), p. 3.

49*Ts'un-hsüeh pien*, 3:7.

50NP, 1:22a–b.

51*Ibid.*, 2:14a–b.

52Yen Yüan, *Hsi-chai hsien-sheng yen-hsing lu*, edited by Chung Ling, 3:4b–5.

53*Ts'un-hsüeh pien*, 2:14b.

54NP, 2:22–23b. At the age of sixty-one, Yen Yüan wrote a general critique of Sung history. He defended Wang An-shih and Han T'o-chou for their activism. His appreciation of Ch'en Liang should also be understood in the light of his defense of these two men.

55For a discussion of Yen Yüan's emphasis on usefulness, see Ch'en, *Yen Hsi-chai*, vol. 1, p. 124.

56*Ts'un-hsüeh pien*, 2:7.

57Yen Yüan attacked Ch'eng I, Chang Tsai, Li Yen-p'ing, and many other thinkers, but his attention was concentrated mainly on Chu Hsi. See *Ts'un-hsing pien*, 1:2a–b.

214

[58]*Ibid.*, 1:13b.
[59]*Chu Tzu ch'üan-shu*, 42:15a.
[60]*Ts'un-hsing pien*, 1:1b.
[61]*Mencius*, 4A.28; 6A.8.
[62]*Analects*, 7.29.
[63]*Ts'un-hsing pien*, 1:12b–13b.
[64]*Ta-hsüeh* (*The Great Learning*), ch. 6.
[65]For a discussion of *ta-t'i* and *hsiao-t'i*. See *Mencius*, 6A.14–15.
[66]*Ts'un-hsing pien*, 2:1b.
[67]*Ibid.*, 2:8b–9.
[68]*Ts'un-jen pien*, 1:7.
[69]For Yen Yüan's criticism of Chu Hsi's concept of evil, see *Ts'un-hsing pien*, 1:7–10.
[70]*Ibid.*, 1:11a–b.
[71]*Ibid.*, 1:10; 2:14.
[72]*Ts'un-hsüeh pien*, 4:3b–4.
[73]Herbert Fingarette, "Human Community as Holy Rite," *Harvard Theological Review* 59, no. 1 (January, 1966): 53–67, and Confucius—The Secular as Sacred (New York: Harper and Row, 1972), ch. 1.

Part Three

Modern Confucian Symbolism

14. Hsiung Shih-li's Quest for Authentic Existence

Confucianism in Modern China

One of the pitfalls in studying Confucianism in general and its modern transformation in particular is that of oversimplification. This may take the form of a conscious attempt to impose a preconceived category on a vast body of Confucian literature or of an indiscriminate use of the word *Confucian* to cover a large group of unknown entities in Chinese cultural history. The two tendencies are equally disturbing. The former approach tends to ignore the whole area of human experience concerned with spiritual values; the latter tends to explain complicated motivational structures in terms of unrefined sociopsychological models. Genetically, Confucianism has been closely associated with an agriculture-based economy, a patrimonial bureaucracy, and a family-centered society; but to reduce the Confucian point of view to an expression of agrarianism, familialism, or bureaucratism is to overlook its ethicoreligious character.

To be sure, as the mainstream of Chinese thought in the last millenium, Confucianism has deep economic, political, and social roots in traditional China. However, even if those roots are completely destroyed, we cannot conclude that Confucianism has thereby lost all of its human relevance. Indeed, it is not inconceivable that some contemporary Chinese intellectuals find in Confucianism not a fixity of past wisdom but a reservoir of humanistic insights, meaningful to their own existence and relevant to their perceptions of the vital issues of the modern world.

Joseph Levenson in his *Trilogy* pronounces the fate of Confucianism as follows:

The orthodox Confucianists, standing still, had been moving

towards oblivion. In the beginning, their idea was a force, the product and the intellectual prop of a living society. In the end it was a shade, living only in the minds of many, treasured in the mind for its own sake after the society which had produced it and which needed it had begun to dissolve away.[1]

This line of thinking does not begin and end with Levenson; it is often followed by students of modern Chinese intellectual history. The decline and fall of Confucian China is now no longer debatable; it is a historical reality. Only the specific event that best symbolized the end has yet to be determined. Some scholars would consider the abolition of the examination system in 1905 the single most important blow to the Confucian tradition. Others would choose the collapse of the Yüan Shih-k'ai regime in 1916, the May Fourth movement in 1919, or the debate on science and metaphysics in 1923. At any rate, since the Confucian tradition definitely ended before the emergence of the republican era, any attempt to salvage it afterwards is usually labeled neotraditional.

If we follow this practice, we inadvertently subscribe to the belief that the modern world, presumably dominated by the rationality of science, and Confucian humanism are incompatible. The rise of one entails the decline of the other. To be sure, Levenson warns us that the dichotomies he offers are not "stark confrontations really 'there' in history," but "heuristic devices for explaining (not conforming to) the life situation." He further contends that his categories are used to explain "the overlapping, intermingling, noncategorical quality of minds, situations, and events." He is quite aware that "antitheses are abstractions, proposed only to let us see how, and why, their starkness in definition is mitigated in history."[2] In his analysis of the fate of Confucianism in modern China, however, the "starkness" of his dichotomy seems to resist even the possibility of historical mitigation. The incompatibility of the traditional, humanistic Confucian China on the one hand and the modern, scientific West (no matter how narrowly defined) on the other is considered such an absolute that even the rise of scientism in China fails to lessen the fundamental conflict.

"What was weak about China," Levenson states, "was not just the paucity of science which the scientism coterie detected. It was what the scientism reflected, as something ostensibly universal, but merely historically significant in the end: too banal as disembodied *thought* to be anything more than an index to Chinese *thinking*."[3] As a result, "cosmopolitan in the Chinese imperial world, Confucianists struck a provincial note in the wider world of the nations, and they passed out of history, into history."[4] Levenson is said to have bled for the decline and fall of the Confucian tradition. The source of his agony seems to lie in his conviction that "the way back" is never "the way out." And yet when Confucian humanism enters the modern world, it cannot but suffer the fate of being alienated from its sociopolitical roots.

Levenson's lament for Confucian China is reflected in his vision of the plight of those modern Chinese intellectuals who are emotionally attached to their *history* but intellectually committed to imported *values*. In other words, their emotional identification with Confucian humanism is a futile, nostalgic longing for the past; their intellectual identification with Western scientific values is merely a cognitive understanding of the necessity of the present. In their identification with the past an intellectual justification is absent, and their identification with the present is devoid of an affective strength. These intellectuals seem to accept the notion that truly original insight in the philosophical sense cannot be generated from within themselves, but must be stimulated from outside. In other words, great ideas in contemporary China must be delivered by a midwife from the Western world.

While in the seventeenth century "a syncretism was necessary to western thought to effect its entrance into the Chinese mind," since the time of Liang Ch'i-ch'ao in the 1890s, "a syncretism [has been] necessary to the Chinese mind to soften the blow of the irresistible entrance of western thought." Levenson continues, "In the first case, the Chinese tradition was standing firm, and the western intruders sought admission by cloaking themselves in the trappings of that tradition; in the second case, the Chinese tradition was disintegrating, and its heirs, to save the fragments, had to interpret them in the spirit of the western intrusion."[5]

In the terminology of *t'i-yung*, once the "substance" is alienated from the "function," the former becomes a useless identity and the latter a groundless adaptation. What actually happened to Chinese intellectuals, in Levenson's view, was that they were gradually persuaded to shift from an unquestioning loyalty to China's cultural identity, which was at the time dynamic enough to accept foreign ideas in terms of its own inner logic, to a complete betrayal of the Confucian tradition, which was neutralized to the extent that it became totally subordinated to the urgent need for adaptation.

However, Levenson's perceptive analysis of the plight of the Chinese intellectual in the world dominated by values alien to Chinese culture was never intended to exclude the possibility that an original thinker in modern China might still find meaning in the Confucian tradition not only for emotional gratification but also for intellectual identification. Liang Shu-ming's (1893–) ability to "champion Confucian moral values and to arouse the Chinese to a degree seldom seen in the contemporary world"[6] in 1921 was not just an isolated instance. Nor should it be understood purely as an expression of nationalist sentiment. The generation of Fung Yu-lan (1895–), Ma I-fu, and Chang Tung-sun (1886–) shared with Liang a level of intellectual sophistication hardly explainable in psychosocial terms alone.

However, the question is not whether or not a creative minority existed but what kind of cultural resources they tapped to formulate their intellectual orientation. If a significant number of them professed to be Confucian in their approach, the answer seems to entail not only the availability of Confucian symbols for imaginative adaptation but also the continuing validity of Confucian ideas as a vehicle for original thinking. On this basis, the notion that the Confucian tradition has passed out of history into history[7] must be reconsidered.

If the tradition is thought to have been inseparably linked with the imperial state, or a residue of that system, then Confucianism as a political ideology must either have totally lost its efficacy or fundamentally altered its power base. From this perspective, its great moment appears to be over and its political message seems an archaic irrelevance.[8] Similarly, if the tradition is thought to have been indivisible from either the agriculture-based economy or the family-centered society, the inexorable changes in the social and economic structures of modern China must inevitably have led to the disintegration of the Confucian value system.

An alternative position envisions Confucianism not merely as a form of political ideology or a kind of socioeconomic ethic, but primarily as a tradition of religious philosophy. Confucianism so conceived is a way of life that demands an existential commitment on the part of Confucians no less intensive and comprehensive than that demanded of the followers of other spiritual traditions, such as Judaism, Christianity, Islam, Buddhism, or Hinduism. The suggestion may seem innocuous, but actually it is still problematical to characterize Confucianism as either a religion or a philosophy, for the Confucian *tao* is a secular way par excellence.[9] And the degree to which Confucianism has been intertwined with the Chinese polity is a phenomenon rare in any other cultural tradition. Many students of Chinese intellectual history have been led to believe that since Confucianism was so intimately a part of imperial China, the fall of the latter must necessarily have brought about the decline of the former. To a large number of social critics of the May Fourth generation, their attack on "Confucius and Sons" was an integral part of their struggle against the remnants of the ruling elite in imperial China.[10]

In the light of the above, it is understandable that any discussion of Confucian personality in modern China seems to smack of antiquarianism. While there is no compelling reason to characterize a Martin Buber, a Paul Tillich, a Suzuki Daisetz, or an S. Radhakrishnan as "neotraditional" in their respective cultures, a modern Confucian, no matter how creative and innovative he or she may be, is likely to be labeled "conservative" or "reactionary" with more or less negative connotations. We have yet to develop a new (and much needed) vocabulary to account for the emergence of a small coterie of sophisticated thinkers in the post-May Fourth generation, Confucian in character, alienated from centers of political power, relatively limited in immediate social influence, but pregnant with ideas of far-reaching implication. Similarly, we have yet to study their ideas in an ethicoreligious dimension. Consequently, they are apt to be called "cultural conservatives."

As Benjamin Schwartz has pointed out, while in the West "conservatism as a conscious doctrine emerges as an inseparable component of the triad conservatism/liberalism/radicalism," the issues raised by those called conservatives in China are "problems of such an order of generality that they transcend the "conservative/liberal/

223

radical" trichotomy.[11] However, he notes that a comparative analysis has given him the impression that the "nationalist component of the conservative syndrome is unusually powerful and the other components weak."[12] This leads us to the question whether nationalist sentiment is also a defining characteristic of cultural conservatism in China. Since "the enormous identity crisis of the articulate classes in modern China caused by the loss of cultural confidence added a sharp edge of intensity to nationalism in China,"[13] one can easily observe that nationalist sentiment was so ubiquitous that it underlay all forms of political persuasion, from ultraconservatism to extreme radicalism. Even the most liberal-minded intellectuals, stung by the burning desire to save China from total disintegration, were in a sense nationalistic, while the cultural conservatives, intent on stressing the importance of preserving or rediscovering a sense of spiritual identity with China's past, added a strong layer of ethnocultural pride to their way of attaining the common goal, namely, arousing the nationalist sentiment of the people. However, the cultural conservatives further believed that the task of saving China involved much more than a quest for wealth and power. Any attempt to manipulate cultural symbols merely for the sake of political integration could neither revive the glory of the past nor create a sense of pride in the present. What could be achieved by this one-dimensional approach would be no more than an emotional attachment to a system of values without a social base, indeed "a shade, living in the minds of many . . . after the society which had produced it and which needed it had begun to dissolve away."[14]

Admittedly many of the cultural conservatives themselves were involved in a romanticization of China's past. Their efforts to universalize Chinese cultural traits such as the monosyllabic language, the bureaucratic state, and the family-centered society were sometimes grotesque. But their approach to national survival was not confined to the political arena. Despite their nationalist sentiment, they raised issues of such magnitude that they must be appreciated as sharing in the concerns of modern individuals generally, and not merely as Chinese responding to the specificities of the Chinese situation.

To some of the cultural conservatives, notably Liang Shu-ming and Hsiung Shih-li (1885–1968), the search for wealth and power as a prerequisite for national survival had to be predicated on a sense of community, which in turn could only result from the fiduciary commitments of the people involved. Accordingly, the most urgent task of the educated elite in China was to sensitize the people and to raise their level of cultural awareness. This could be done only if the intellectuals themselves were resolved to face the challenge of the West not only as a clash of economic strength and military might but also as a confrontation of basic human values. Therefore, the way to save China as a sociopolitical entity was not to imitate slavishly what was believed to be the obvious superiority of the West. To deliver China from its miserable state of inertia, the intellectuals must first try to overcome the false belief that its internal cultural resources had dried up, and that the saving grace had to come from outside.

In this light it is understandable that what really struck Hsiung Shih-li in the Confucian tradition was not its historicism, its holism, its sociologism, or "culturalism," but its ontological vision and its philosophical anthropology. To be sure, Hsiung philosophized from a Confucian perspective, but he did it with a universal intent. He responded to the pressing issues of his time not only as an agonized Chinese intellectual but also as a concerned thinker dedicated to the quest for authentic existence. His cultural conservatism involved an ethicoreligious dimension that both transcended narrowly defined nationalism and informed his national concerns. Thus, at a time when the search for spiritual ideas was thought to be of limited significance, Hsiung perceived that the survival of China as a national community could not bypass the route of cultural reconstruction. While the majority of his contemporaries were obsessed with China's weaknesses, Hsiung opened a new line of inquiry by examining the philosophical basis on which the modern world as well as the future of China was to be judged. To be sure, his value orientation was Confucian in character, but the issues to which he addressed himself were of such a level of relevance that they must be recognized as perennial problems of human existence.

Hsiung's Career as Teacher and Scholar

To study Hsiung Shih-li the man, as reflected in his career as a teacher, is to confront a number of seemingly incompatible images.

225

When the news arrived in Hong Kong of his death in the early summer of 1968 at the age of eighty-four, he was unanimously hailed by Chinese scholars outside of mainland China as one of the most original thinkers in the last century.[15] But his lonely demise seems to have had little impact on the intellectual scene in the People's Republic. He is said to have been one of the most dynamic teachers at Peking University in the late 1920s, but the record seems to show that because of poor health he could not handle more than one lecture course per semester, and he never attained the rank of professor there.[16] Although he is considered one of the most consistent and persistent critics of Chinese communism, he was probably the only eminent idealist who never experienced the humiliation of self-criticism and public confession in the last two decades of his life.[17]

All evidence shows that he led a fairly secluded life throughout his career as a teacher, and his association with the academic community did not begin until he was in his forties. Nevertheless, his followers in Hong Kong and Taiwan outnumbered those of Fung Yu-lan and Liang Shu-ming. Partly because of his self-imposed intellectual isolation and partly because of his uncompromising character, Hsiung never gained a wide reputation in his lifetime; yet his views carried tremendous weight among a group of highly respected scholars, including the logician Shen Yu-ting, the metaphysician Chang Tung-sun, the historian Ho Ch'ang-ch'ün, the Buddhologist Jen Chi-yü, and the Confucian master Ma I-fu.[18]

To study Hsiung Shih-li as embodied in his philosophical treatises is to witness the unfolding of a profound vision, deeply rooted in the Chinese tradition and yet singularly relevant to some of the vital issues of the modern world. Even in a brief survey of his major works one is struck by the perspicacity of his observations and the originality of his ideas. Although his ideas have far-reaching implications, they are centered around a single concern: to live authentically as a Confucian thinker amidst depersonalizing forces in contemporary China.

A brief comparison of Hsiung's public image with that of Hu Shih (1891–1962), probably the most well-known intellectual of the May Fourth generation,[19] is instructive, for these two symbolized two basically different modes of thought in contemporary China. While Hu attempted to conceptualize Chinese problems in terms of categories he had acquired from the West, Hsiung tried to appreciate what he believed to be the strength of Western learning from the perspective of Confucian humanism. And though many of Hu's provocative ideas have long become outmoded in the intellectual world, Hsiung's imaginative vision only now begins to find a sympathetic echo in the minds of professional philosophers.[20]

Hu came from a fairly affluent scholar-official family. He was a cosmopolitan scholar with a broad educational background, a wide intellectual horizon, a high reputation, and an influential position. Hsiung came from a poverty-stricken family. It is doubtful whether he had been exposed to any formal education at all. His scholarly background was limited to the Three Teachings (Confucianism, Taoism, and Buddhism), and his knowledge of Western learning came from translated works. He led a marginal existence as a part-time lecturer, and his social influence was negligible. Hu as the champion of democratic liberalism and pragmatic scientism was the center of attention for more than a decade. He was urbane, eloquent, and gregarious. The large halls where he lectured were constantly filled to capacity. In sharp contrast, Hsiung was a lonely fighter for his own vision of the Confucian *tao*. He was earthy, arrogant, and even eccentric. He had only a small but dedicated following. Others occasionally drifted into his lectures mainly out of curiosity. Hu was closely in touch with the mainstream of ideas. His teacher, John Dewey, during his two-year visit in China (May 1919–July 1921), aroused wide interest in pragmatism. Hsiung, on the other hand, limited his teaching either by choice or by default to an extremely small coterie of scholars. Their concern for the great spiritual traditions of the East was like that of the Indian poet Rabindranath Tagore, whose message of universal human kinship in 1924 generated little enthusiasm among the young.

On the intellectual plane, Hu, despite his early training in the classics, was a great supporter of the campaign to overthrow Confucius and Sons. He advocated the scientific method and a piecemeal solution to well-defined problems, and was intellectually committed to Western learning. With the possible exception of Chu Hsi's notion of *ko-wu* (the investigation of things), he saw very little contemporary significance in the entire tradition of Neo-Confucianism. He believed that the Indianization of China in the spread of

Buddhism had made only negative contributions to the rationality of the Chinese mind. His involvement in the study of ancient Chinese logic, vernacular literature, Moism, and Ch'ing scholarship was intended to demonstrate the applicability of his new method of investigation. Hsiung, by contrast, devoted himself to the creative reformulation of the Confucian position. He propounded a philosophical inquiry into the ontological basis of the Chinese tradition and a complete reexamination of the value system existing at the time. He was deeply committed to the Confucian personality ideal and his involvement in the study of Buddhism was profound. In fact, contrary to Hu's rational, pragmatic approach to restructuring Chinese society, Hsiung was so much an integral part of it that he could only feel his way from within. While Hu was able to look at China's major problems in a relatively disinterested manner, Hsiung totally identified with and felt victimized by them. While Hu achieved a measure of detachment in examining some of the specific social and intellectual issues confronting China at the time, Hsiung was deeply agonized and totally overwhelmed by the spiritual bankruptcy of the Chinese value system.

It is not surprising that their conflicting perceptions actually led to some personal animosity between them. As Hu Shih's associates, presumably members of the credentials committee, began to wonder why and how Hsiung had been hired as a college teacher in the first place, Hsiung and his three or four disciples became so disgusted by the "superficiality and vulgarity" of the so-called *ming-liu hsüeh-che* (famed scholars)[21] that Peking University seemed to them a place full of sound and fury signifying nothing.

In fact, one of Hsiung's most serious campaigns was to expose the insubstantiality of the famed scholars. They might spend hours debating on a philological point or the true authorship of the *Dream of the Red Chabmer*, which to Hsiung only added a bizarre aspect to the spiritual disintegration of the Chinese intelligentsia. Issues of profound ethicoreligious significance seldom crossed their minds. Their claim that the scientific method could open new horizons in classical learning Hsiung regarded as irresponsible. What they actually accomplished, he felt, was no more than a continuation of the least creative Ch'ing scholarship,[22] and under their influence, students had no inclination to establish an experiential link with their own cultural heritage and no interest in probing the intellectual foundations of Western thought. In his view, the marriage of scientism and scholasticism blocked the way to either scientific thought or classical learning and deterred a sophisticated formulation of fruitful ideas.

Challenging the general view that the two decades following the outbreak of the May Fourth movement (1919) had fostered a great release of creative energy in appropriating new ideas, Hsiung criticized the fragmented approach to Western learning as a series of short-lived fads. He remarked that new literature, pragmatic philosophy, and applied science had each in turn become fashionable. When new literature was in vogue the students all wanted to become writers. Then philosophy became their favored field. Later they believed that only applied science could satisfy their dedication to real learning. Hsiung charged that despite massive translation of works by Spencer, J. S. Mill, Huxley, Darwin, Schopenhauer, Nietzsche, Bergson, Dewey, and Russell, and despite the tremendous potential for introducing new insights and visions into China, philosophical ideas from the West had produced little impact on the Chinese mind. Instead, impressionistic notions about them had actually caused obscuration, confusion, superficiality, and other problems in the intellectual world.[23]

While most historians would explain the phenomenon as inevitable in an early phase of cultural assimilation, Hsiung charged that the scholars who assumed the role of transmitters of Western learning had failed to appreciate the complexity of their self-assigned task. Although they were motivated to render some of those fascinating ideas into Chinese, they were not prepared to present a systematic treatment of any of them. Hsiung contended that the only way to absorb the insights of a philosophy that had become a dominant intellectual force in the West was to make a continuous effort to understand its root concepts. Only then could one really enter into the tradition and develop it as an integral part of one's "own thing" (chi-wu). However, Hsiung noted, the pursuit of Western learning as it had been carried on in modern China, like the aimless searching for strange smells on the sea by the eccentric in Lü-shih ch'un-ch'iu, was not only futile, but also damaging to the visions China already had.[24]

Hsiung argued that a more serious attempt to understand the West required a willingness to probe deeply into the philosophical bases of Western ideas. If those who advocated new ideas did it only for propagandist purposes and those who followed the fashion made no effort to comprehend the ideas, "how could the spirit of the [Western] philosophers ever set foot in China?"[25] Hsiung seems to suggest that Western learning, far from being what the westernizers in China professed it to be, involved a profound ethicoreligious dimension that could only be apprehended by a systematic inquiry into its philosophical import. Any sporadic effort to encapsulate it in a simple-minded formulation would seriously inhibit further attempts to study Western ideas. Dewey's lecture tour in China was probably just the kind of phenomenon Hsiung had in mind. Even though Dewey's pragmatism took the intellectual world in China by storm, Hsiung might have argued, as long as his propagators, such as Hu Shih, failed to form an integrated vision of pragmatic philosophy, the possibility for Dewey's ideas to take firm root in China was slim.

Underlying Hsiung's argument was the conviction that genuine learning from the West required a particular kind of intellectual disposition, a willingness to go beyond the apparent manifestations of wealth and power, and a courage to confront issues at the deepest level of human existence. In keeping with this line of reasoning, Hsiung devoted himself to philosophical inquiries with a profound sense of urgency. To him the real choice that was thrust on each Chinese intellectual at the time was whether to live by values created through experiential learning or merely exist by timidly following ideas to which there was no way to relate meaningfully. It was a choice between a creative process of self-assertion and a static prolongation of identity diffusion.

Philosophical inquiries so conceived are much more than pure analyses. They are aimed at the establishment of a structure of meaning in which human activities can be accounted for not as fragmented occurrences but as an integrated process of transformation. However, Hsiung made it clear that his route to philosophy was not a speculative one. Instead of being a series of painless reflections on existing

230

insights, Hsiung's philosophical journey was an agonizing quest for authentic existence. This quest was most intimately revealed in his *Dialogues*.

Hsiung's Self-Image

Although the complete version of Hsiung's *Dialogues* did not appear until 1947, the first part of it was published in 1935 and most of the rest had been completed by 1939. The book contains short articles, essays, lecture notes, recorded sayings, and letters to friends, acquaintances, students, and relatives. Comparable in style to some of the *yü-lu* (recorded sayings) of the Sung-Ming Confucian masters, the book is a series of reflections on a variety of life situations. The bulk of the book involves what Hsiung frequently refers to as *chiang-hsüeh*, or philosophical inquiry in the Neo-Confucian sense. Occasionally we find glimpses of his worries, frustrations, anger, and despair and indeed an autobiographic account of his life history.[26]

We learn that he was born in a poverty-stricken family in the Huang-kang area of Hupei. His father, a follower of the Ch'eng-Chu school, was a village teacher who died of tuberculosis when Hsiung was only ten years old. By then Hsiung had read the *Three-Character Classic* and the Four Books. His father's death forced him to support the family by serving as a cowherd for his neighbor. From then on the only formal teacher he had was a certain Ho Shen-mu, who taught him parts of the Five Classics. Ho was said to have been active in the revolutionary movement toward the end of the Ch'ing dynasty; and having been influenced by the ideas of the Reform movement, he advocated the establishment of local schools and the liberation of women. When Hsiung was in his early twenties, he became fascinated by the new subject of science. At that time, his only access to the world of ideas was to borrow books from a member of the local gentry in a neighboring district. Later he managed to read articles and memorials of the Reformists and became aware of the impending revolutionary change. He then chose Fan Chung-yen's (984–1052) maxim, "To be concerned (*yu*) before the whole world becomes concerned," as his own motto (*tso-yu ming*).[27]

231

Hsiung confessed that as a young man he was utterly unrestrained. In the summer, he would frequently live in a deserted temple, hike nude in hills, and smash Buddhist icons as a pastime. By then he had read some of the works of the late Ming loyalists such as Ku Yen-wu (1613–1682) and Wang Fu-chih (1619–1692). Deeply touched by their cultural loyalism he decided to take part in the revolution. He first joined the army in Wu-ch'ang as an infantryman. Later he entered a special army training school. His revolutionary activities aroused the suspicion of the commander, Chang Piao. Although he escaped before the order for his arrest arrived, an award was offered for information leading to his capture. After the 1911 Revolution and a sojourn back home, he joined an expeditionary team to cultivate the land in the northwestern frontier of Te-an. This move was prompted not so much by a yen for adventure as by the necessity of earning a living for himself; however, because of an intense fear of accidental death, he withdrew from the expedition. In 1918 he joined the Kwangsi army, but again soon changed his mind, and went with a friend to Canton. He reported that it was in 1920 that he finally set his mind on learning. He described this existential decision at the age of thirty-six as a "great transformation" and a "rebirth" in his life.[28]

His first period of concentrated training in rigorous thinking and spiritual cultivation was at the Nanking Institute of Buddhism under the directorship of Ou-yang Ching-wu (1871–1943). However, after he thought he had grasped the philosophical position of the Wei-shih (Consciousness-only) doctrine, he found himself much more in sympathy with the Confucian "learning of mind and human nature" (*hsin-hsing chih hsüeh*).[29] In retrospect he remarked that he suffered from a serious illness in his late thirties, and it was then that he vowed to devote his life to the study of the Way of the sages. The only two books he wrote and published in the last two decades of his life, *Yüan-ju* (On the essence of Confucianism) and *Ch'ien-k'un yen* (An exposition of the two primordial hexagrams), together with all of his works printed before the founding of the People's Republic of China, seem to bear out the seriousness of his decision.

What was the nature of Hsiung Shih-li's decision? Was it an emotional attachment to a traditional ideal that had long since faded away? Was it an apologetic assertion of his cultural identity as a

232

desperate attempt to meet the challenge of the West? Was it his idiosyncratic way of creating an area of meaning for his own existence regardless of the main thrust of the intellectual momentum of the time? Or was it merely a belated manifestation of Chinese culturalism?

To answer any of the above questions presupposes an analysis of Hsiung Shih-li's philosophical argumentation and his underlying intention. Hsiung made it clear that his intention to become a true Confucian was predicated on an inner decision, which he described as the "effort of self-reflection and self-mastery" (*fan-shen k'e-chi chih kung*).[30] The nature of his philosophy is thus linked with his self-image as a Confucian thinker.

Violently reacting against what Levenson calls "syncretism" and Munro terms "token integrationism,"[31] Hsiung believed that the gravest danger confronting modern Chinese intellectuals was their willingness to adapt themselves to forces from outside, while lacking the courage to face squarely the intrinsic problems of their existence here and now. What he saw in modern China was the collapse of the value system, the disintegration of the meaning structure, and more seriously, the loss of the self—not the self as a psychological ego but what is, in the Mencian terminology, the real basis of human existence.[32] Once that sense of the self is lost, we may add, human beings are no more than an aggregate of biological, physiological, and psychological processes. To become a true Confucian in this connection means to be an authentic person, which entails a genuine awareness of the true self.

This explanation is loaded with ambiguous terms that require some elucidation. Hsiung's concept of the self is reminiscent of the Mencian line of Confucianism and especially of the Wang Yang-ming school in the Neo-Confucian tradition. Indeed, the self so conceived is not only an irreducible reality but also the ontological basis for the attainment of sagehood. It should be pointed out that sagehood in this sense refers to true selfhood, which means the full manifestation or complete realization of the humanity (*jen*) inherent in each human being. The tendency toward a subjective point of view is quite obvious, but Hsiung, and for that matter his spiritual predecessors, clearly differentiate self-mastery from self-centeredness and true self from selfishness. Leaving aside technical issues in

233

Hsiung's thought, such as the egocentric predicament and the problem of intersubjectivity, it should be clear in the present context that Hsiung's emphasis on self-realization as a precondition for human communicability is not a form of intuitionism, and it is in basic conflict with, if not diametrically opposed to, many familiar forms of subjectivism.[33]

Although Hsiung Shih-li repeatedly stated that his philosophical intention was in complete agreement with that of Wang Yang-ming, as a situational response to the challenges of his time he departed from Yang-ming's teaching in a fundamental way. While the Ming philosopher refused to put his ideas in a systematically developed form for fear that the experiential dimension would be relegated to the background, Hsiung devoted years of his life to a rigorously constructed presentation of his philosophical position. His deep commitment to self-realization was thus manifested in his intellectual passion to deliver the Confucian message in a systematically reasoned form.

Ordinarily a Confucian by moral conviction must serve the state and assume the burden of social responsibility as an official. Such a person's spirit of *engagement* is commonly reflected in political participation. However, the lives of many historical personalities point to another possibility, which has also been fully accepted as a legitimate demonstration of the Confucian Way, namely the purification of the self in a time of chaos. Hsiung's role as a philosopher dedicated to the task of systematic inquiry is thus compatible with Confucian teaching. In a deeper sense, however, the purification of the self in Confucianism is never conceived as an isolated act or a self-imposed political moratorium, because a transformation in the meaning structure is thought to entail a reshaping of the existing state of affairs. After all, in the Confucian perception, political participation is always predicated on a structure of meaning, which is considered an independent variable. It can be further argued that politics is here viewed as a function of moral education rather than as a system of bureaucratic control. Therefore, the Confucian enters into politics for the purpose of what the *Doctrine of the Mean,* one of Hsiung's favorite classics, calls "realizing one's own human nature as a way of helping others to realize theirs."[34]

Confucians believe that self-realization, inasmuch as it conveys an ethicoreligious meaning, necessarily affects the course of action in the world, even though it should not be seen simply as a means to a social end. It is precisely in this sense that Mencius defines the role of the moral leader (*chün-tzu*) as the guardian of the cosmic process as well as of the social order.[35]

It would not be far-fetched to suggest that Hsiung actually tried to philosophize in the capacity of a *chün-tzu*. Of course he appreciated Liang Shu-ming's efforts to actualize Confucian values in village reforms and Fung Yu-lan's efforts to incorporate Confucian values in a new political ideology, but he believed that his own philosophical efforts to revitalize the Confucian persuasion as an integral part of his quest for a new ontological vision were more fundamental. He felt justified in exploring his ontological vision purely as a concerned thinker, devoid of any direct involvement in political and social action. To a majority of Chinese intellectuals under the spell of scientism, his struggle might appear as rather distant from the burning issues of his times, but he was convinced that doing philosophy as a form of ontological inquiry was intrinsically meaningful to himself and demonstrably significant to his generation.

Implicit in Hsiung's writings, therefore, is an awareness that one's temporal existence is closely linked with a structure of meaning that transcends the immediate historical present. This awareness is predicated on the belief that a person is not a self-sufficient entity isolatable from his or her historical roots, but a center of relationships derived from the past but continuously relevant to the present. Intellectuals, as reflective persons who are consciously responding to the situations of their times, cannot afford to ignore the processes that have conditioned their ways of thinking, molded their patterns of behavior, and shaped the directions of their spirituality. For the sake of self-realization they must penetrate deeply into the nature of those forces that have contributed significantly to their being what they are. According to this line of thinking, even if one is absolutely convinced that the tradition is on the verge of fading away, a sophisticated understanding of it is still necessary as a precondition for creative adaptation. Hsiung's perception of the problem was not apologetic; an intellectual appreciation of Confucianism, he felt, especially its ontological vision, was a fruitful way of restoring self-respect among modern Chinese intellectuals. However, a critical

235

examination of the fundamental discrepancies in terms of value-orientation between China and the West was absolutely essential for the absorption of new values and the preservation of old ones.[36] From this perspective, the greatest fault of the intelligentsia was their unwillingness and inability to probe deeply into the underlying structures of ideas they espoused or rejected. Superficial denunciation of traditional China and wishful appropriation from the modern West had only led the intellectuals to fickleness.

Alienated from the predominant intellectual trends of the time, Hsiung had to be content with a limited circle of friends and a very small group of followers. It was probably this hostile intellectual environment that prompted him to write in an extremely forceful style. Although, as Hsü Fu-kuan has pointed out, elegant phrasing and felicitous diction give a classical tenor to his language, a salient feature of his works is the virility of his presentation—an urgent, sometimes indignant tone.[37] To those familiar with the prose style of the Confucian classics, whether his philosophical followers or not, his literary strength is all but overpowering.[38]

Hsiung the Thinker

It is true that the majority of the May Fourth intellectuals never felt that China's ability to westernize actually depended on a willingness to abandon its cultural burden in total. Even the most ardent supporters of Western learning recognized the need to make China's past relevant to the urgent concerns of the present. But since they all felt that the survival of China was at stake, many were absolutely convinced that strengthening the nation had to take precedence over any other consideration; and problems of meaning, such as the search for spiritual values, were deliberately suspended. Few perceived that ethicoreligious ideas might be essential to nation building.

As a member of the post-May Fourth generation, Hsiung shared in the general desire of the Chinese intelligentsia to "save the nation" (*chiu-kuo*). He was acutely aware of the seriousness of the intellectual task and the urgency of trying to appreciate and internalize the dynamism of the West. However, he insisted that such an attempt must be based on a high level of self-knowledge. He argued that the appropriation of Western insights must be made correlative to the reconstructing of Chinese values.[39] Hsiung believed that drilling deeply into the bedrock of the Chinese mind was not only of intrinsic value; it was functionally necessary for the successful absorption of new ideas. Hsiung's uneasiness with the May Fourth mentality arose not so much over its indiscriminate acceptance of the West as over its emotional attachment to the superficial manifestations of Western thought. Nevertheless, despite his sharp criticism of propagating Western ideas merely for public consumption, Hsiung apparently never displayed any revulsion toward Western thinkers. Although his *Dialogues* included only a few comments on Kant, Bergson, and Russell, he made perceptive observations on Greek culture as well as on Marxism, science, and ontology.[40] His knowledge of Western learning was certainly limited, but his imaginative vision enabled him to appreciate the metaphysical dimensions of Western culture, which were largely ignored by the westernizers at the time.

In the language of *t'i-yung*, what Hsiung realized was the necessity of reconstructing the Chinese *t'i* as an authentic way of understanding the *t'i* of the West. Similarly, he maintained that an appreciation of the Western *t'i* would in turn deepen the level of Chinese self-awareness. Only then would creative adaptation be possible. Chang Chih-tung's formulation was a fallacy not because the dichotomy itself was inappropriate, but because in his wishful thinking he completely failed to appreciate the complexity of the relationships involved. The weakness of the westernizers was their one-dimensional approach to Western learning. Their determined effort to learn from the West brought no substantial change in the Chinese mind because they abstracted Western *yung* from its *t'i*. When the ideas were detached from their ontological structure, they became fragmentary opinions, useful only for propagandist purposes. Total adaptation was not a shortcut to westernization, but a blind alley. Hsiung was convinced that sporadic romanticization of Western ideas could never lead to a sophisticated appreciation of the underlying structure of Western thought. If the *t'i* problems in both China and the West were not even touched, any attempt to make use of borrowed ideas was bound to be futile.

One wonders what sorts of issues Hsiung envisioned as *t'i* problems. Rendered by the brilliant sinologist Peter Boodberg as "form"

237

or "body," *t'i* certainly conveys the meaning of the basic structure.[41] However, as Wing-tsit Chan has pointed out, ever since Wang Pi's (226–249) commentary on Lao Tzu, in which he interprets the *t'i* of *tao* as *wu* (nonbeing), the term has assumed a metaphysical meaning in the sense of "substance" or "essence."[42] As one of the most prominent concepts in Buddhism and Neo-Confucianism, *t'i* refers to the deepest sense of reality. Understandably, "ontology" has been translated as *pen-t'i lun* (the learning of the original *t'i*). Problems concerning *t'i* are therefore ontological issues.

To Hsiung, the main task of philosophy is to engage in ontological inquiries, and ontology, he claimed, is not a form of speculative thought or a search for external truths; the ontological quest, he insisted, is to make manifest the ultimate source of creative transformation in human culture as well as in the cosmos. Underlying his assertion is the assumption that ontology, often thought of as the intellectual game of a small group of professional philosophers, ought rather to be understood as closely linked with the welfare of the people. As a reflection on the ultimate source of creative transformation, ontology deals not only with the continuous cosmogonic process, but also with the nature of human beings.

In Hsiung's philosophy, ontology is not a variable dependent on a given sociopolitical system. Rather, by its perception of what constitutes reality, it actually shapes the general direction of social change. Of course Hsiung can be labeled as an idealist, but to characterize his approach as idealistic is no more informative than to call Wang Fu-chih a materialist. Hsiung held that consciousness can determine the mode of existence; he further argued that human will molds as well as perceives the realities of the world. Ontology, in this connection, not only reflects but also creates the intellectual ethos, which in turn charts the general direction of social change. Thus, in a tortuous but substantial way, ontology affects the life of the people.

It is beyond the scope of the present essay to give even a synoptic view of Hsiung's ontological insights. Suffice it to say that Hsiung assumed that ontology can restructure existing reality in a fundamental way, and he undertook such a task with a profound sense of relevance. His undertaking should not be thought of as simply an action-oriented enterprise, for his main concern was not social thought or political ideology. However, he believed that the kind of ontological mission he was attempting was important for China's survival and that the continuation of Chinese culture as a dynamic, living tradition depended on it. Despite the hubris inherent in such a belief, it reflected a sincere and painful realization of what he himself had to do to participate in the national effort to save China. His ontological quest was thus colored by a strong nationalist sentiment, but the way he envisioned his task and the manner in which he carried it out defies a reduction to simple sociopsychological interpretation.

Hsiung's conscious response to the intellectual crisis of the post-May Fourth period can undoubtedly be explained in terms of his perception of the current historical situation. Of course Hsiung could not avoid the kind of psychological pressures that were felt by every thinking Chinese at the time. Indeed his works would be better appreciated if the effects of such pressures were noted and analyzed. His very style of writing and the format in which his books were printed vibrantly echo the sound and fury of his generation. Still it would be wrong to argue that his ontology is reducible to a sociopsychological need to search for roots. It would be equally wrong to interpret his quest as "seeking to avoid a conflict between historical affection and acknowledgment of value," for he clearly was not an example of what Levenson conceptualized as the "traditionalist" who "drained the contemporary value from what . . . [he] perpetuated."[43] Therefore, it is misleading to characterize him either as a stale syncretist or as a token integrationist.

Furthermore, given his ontological perspective, Hsiung not only rejected iconoclasm outright; he also regarded the common slogan of selecting the best from East and West as no more than wishful thinking. Serious selection, he maintained, depended on experiential knowledge and critical examination. Hsiung's inclination was to probe the ontological dimension of Chinese culture as a way to arrive at a critical examination of the philosophical foundation of the West. He believed that only then could Chinese intellectuals really absorb wisdom from the West. What Hsiung tried to promulgate was more than an approach to Western learning. His intention was to formulate an ontological awareness that would serve as the ground for a mutual appreciation of cultural values between China and the West. One may very well ask whether Hsiung's "supposed commitment to value alone, to the generally acceptable, masks a concern with its special, historical origins."[44] Was Hsiung in the last analysis still caught in the Levensonian predicament: "the only motive which a Chinese could have in celebrating the beauty of blended values would be a desire—entirely foreign to the world of value—to see China and the West as equal partners"?[45]

If we accept the view that, in a cognitive sense, the only way for post-May Fourth intellectuals in China to relate themselves to their own cultural heritage was to measure it against the rules imported from the West, Hsiung's ontological vision must of course be subsumed under the category of psychological adjustment. According to this line of argument, the coming of the "brave new culture" compelled Hsiung to face a world that was basically non-Confucian. As a philosopher deeply rooted in Chinese traditions, he could not help being alienated by the westernizing process. His emotional attachment to China's past, a form of particularism, lingered on in his own mind and in the minds of his followers, and his universal intent in constructing a new ontology was no more than a philosophical strategy designed to make his nationalist sentiment intellectually respectable.

Such a line of reasoning is actually based on a reductionist dogma; namely, that westernization is an irreversible, one-dimensional, linear progress. Once such an interpretive position is called into question, it is no longer plausible to assume that just because Hsiung's ontological insight was Confucian in character it was necessarily an attachment to history rather than a commitment to value. Nor does it seem proper to regard Hsiung's mode of thought as a form of particularism simply because he made a conscious attempt to philosophize from a specific point of view. Similarly, to characterize his universal intent as no more than an expression of nationalist sentiment is to rule out the possibility that in a confused and chaotic setting an original mind could still perceive fundamental humanistic values as such.

The Original Mind and Ultimate Reality

Although few attempts have been made to study the genesis of

Hsiung's mode of thinking, it is generally accepted that "metaphysical idealism in the Vijñāptimātra (Yogācāra) tradition of Indian Buddhism" played a very important role in his philosophical training. He openly acknowledged his intellectual debt to Ou-yang Ching-wu, whose Nanking Institute of Buddhism (also known as the Academy of Inner Learning) was instrumental in the revival of systematic studies on the Vijñāptimātra school in modern China. This school, better known as the Wei-shih doctrine, is also referred to as the Fa-hsiang (Characteristics of the dharmas) tradition.[46]

A salient feature of the school is the subtlety of its understanding of the mind (consciousness). The prominence of the mind in the whole tradition has yielded volumes of minute analysis on the subject. To begin with, the mind is divided into eight consciousnesses. The first five are sensory perceptions: sight, hearing, smell, taste, and touch. The sixth is the sense center (manovijñāna), the conscious mind or the general perceiving agency. The seventh is the thought center (manas), the self-conscious mind or the cognitive basis of thinking, willing, and reasoning. The eighth is the storehouse-consciousness (ālayavijñāna). Each of the eight consciousnesses is supposed to be a separable reality, demanding a type of analysis suitable to its nature. While the first six sensory perceptions can be readily understood in terms of ordinary psychology, the last two require a much more complicated model of analysis.[47] Especially noteworthy is the idea of ālaya. Instead of being a mechanistic interpretation of the unconscious, the Wei-shih teaching on ālaya contains many insights reminiscent of psychoanalysis. The following quotation is a case in point:

A seed produces a manifestation,
A manifestation perfumes a seed.
The three elements (seed, manifestation, and perfume)
turn on and on,
The cause and effect occur at one and the same time.[48]

An impression, a seed of act or thought by the human subject, necessarily produces a manifestation in the external world. Thus one's mental state is not an isolated private affair, but an active agent inevitably affecting the world in flux. The manifestation is an

241

integral part of what we perceive as the universe. Simultaneously the manifestation in turn exerts influence on the quality of the seed through a perfuming (or polluting) process. However, the relation between them is not a simple causality. Rather, in accord with the principle of dependent origination, they occur "at one and the same time." The kind of analytical method required for this doctrine is, therefore, twofold: to differentiate entities as discrete for heuristic purposes, and to integrate various levels of observation for a comprehensive understanding.

Intent on "penetrating behind the veil of impermanence to attain to the absolute knowledge that transcends all conditionality and relativity," the school focuses its attention on the purification of *ālaya*. This task involves, among other things, raising the level of consciousness. This partly explains why the school has been considered the most intellectually oriented tradition in Chinese Buddhism. As Kenneth Ch'en has pointed out, while the Mādhyamika School of Nāgārjuna conceives of two levels of truth, the Wei-shih doctrine advocates three levels of knowledge that refer to three approaches to truth. The *parikalpita* view, based on "sole imagination," grasps truth in a distorted and fragmented manner. The *paratantra* view, based on the principle of dependence, recognizes only the temporary and impermanent aspect of truth. The *pariniṣpanna* view, based on the vision of ultimate reality, comprises the "rounded comprehension" of truth. Accordingly, the main purpose of the school is to teach the road to enlightenment through analytical inquiries.

What Hsiung learned in the Nanking Institute was not only the basic philosophy of Buddhism and the tenets of the Wei-shih doctrine. As the closest protégé of the Institute's master, who was one of the most brilliant Buddhist thinkers in modern China, Hsiung received a very special instruction, combining experiential knowledge with a rigorous method of detached analysis. Indeed, before his "conversion" to Confucianism, he had already established himself as a leading light in Chinese Buddhism. His *Buddhist Concepts Explained (Fo-chia ming-hsiang t'ung-shih)* and *Commentary on the Great Treatise on Buddhist Logic (Yin-ming ta-su shan-chu)* are important contributions to Buddhist literature. This perhaps explains why Father Brière, in his *Les courants philosophiques en Chine depuis 50 ans (1898–1950)*, characterizes Hsiung as an original Buddhist thinker who synthetically reconstructed the philosophical school of "mere-ideation."[49] In fact, at the time when Hsiung, under the guidance of Ou-yang in the late 1920s, was engaged in a systematic inquiry into K'uei-chi's monumental work, *Notes on the Completion of the Consciousness-Only doctrine* (*Ch'eng wei-shih lun shu-chi*),[50] he was already recognized as a potential successor to the master.

According to Hsiung's own recollection, only after a long process of spiritual quest did he decide to change his philosophical stance:

> Some people have stated that my philosophy is an attempt to adduce Confucianism as an evidence to support Buddhism. This statement might appear to be true, for my personal experience in this matter is absolutely incomprehensible to an outsider. There was a period when I was inclined toward Indian Buddhist thought. My pursuit of Buddhist studies was certainly not motivated by a mere desire to broaden my knowledge and to display my erudition. It was really driven by a great wish to search for truth as a ground for "peace of mind and a meaningful existence" (*an-hsin li-ming*). I studied the teachings of Asanga and Vasubandhu with Master Ou-yang and was thoroughly converted. Later on, I gradually rejected the theories of various schools. Totally putting aside Buddhism and other systems (including even Confucianism), I searched within myself with singleness of purpose. I thought that truth is not remote from us. We can never lay hold of truth by turning around under the spell of verbal and written words of others. Thereupon I completely trusted my own devotion and open-mindedness. I constantly maintained vigilance lest my selfish desires and prejudices deceive my (true) self. I was entirely engaged in what Ch'en Po-sha[51] termed "placing the mind in nonbeing" (*ts'o hsin yü wu*). It means to make a clean sweep of all kinds of "cognitive perception" (*chih-chien*) derived from bigoted opinions and implanted superstitions. The purpose is to make the mind large and dynamic without any trace of stagnation. Only then can we "experientially recognize" (*t'i-jen*) the truth in all places. After a long time, I suddenly awoke to the realization that what I inwardly witnessed agreed entirely with the idea of "great change" (*ta-i*)[52] in the Confucian transmission. Thereupon I completely destroyed the draft of the Wei-shih doctrine which I had written based on Asanga and Vasubandhu, and avowed to compose a new Wei-shih doctrine of my own in order to save

243

myself from the defect of the old. Hence my understanding of Confucianism was not derived from book learning. Only after my inner experience had already embodied it did I feel that my understanding of it was in complete harmony with what was recorded in the books. This kind of experience is extremely difficult to explain to the general public.[53]

Based on autobiographical accounts like this, Wing-tsit Chan suggests that Hsiung's new exposition of Wei-shih was a critique of Buddhism from the perspective of the *Book of Change*. Chan's interpretive position agrees very much with Hsiung's own justification: "I present my synthesis in the tradition of the *Book of Change* by a critical examination of the main tenets in both the Buddhist schools of Being and Nonbeing."[54] We may, on historical grounds, object to Hsiung's assertion that "both Confucianism and Taoism are based on the *Book of Change*."[55] But it seems undeniable that, as one of the oldest and most characteristic expressions of the Chinese mode of thinking, the book offers a "striking cosmology and a philosophy of human potential for creative action and freedom in the cosmic process."[56] In Jungian terminology, it is of uncommon significance as a way of probing the "inner person" and "personal wholeness" from a Chinese perspective.[57]

Among the profound insights in the book, what most directly inspired Hsiung was the ontological notion of great transformation (*ta-hua*). Contrary to the Wei-shih theory that phenomena are temporary, tentative, transitory, and thus false, the *Book of Change* asserts the reality of the great transformation. To be sure, Hsiung maintained that the external world, insofar as it is conceived as absolutely independent of consciousness, is nonexistent. Nevertheless by accepting the great transformation as the necessary manifestation of the original mind, he completely rejected the Wei-shih claim that *ālaya* is instrumental in producing phenomena. He believed that the ultimate reality, or the original mind, far from being a static substance, is a constant flux. The phenomenal world, which is inseparable from the great transformation, should thus be recognized as an integral part of reality.

As Wing-tsit Chan has noted, in Hsiung's new perception reality in the ultimate sense is understood as a "running current." Ultimate reality so conceived is not only a state of being but also a process of becoming: "It is changing because it manifests itself in countless phenomena, and yet it is unchanging because its self-nature remains unaltered in the process of change."[58] Indeed, the notion of *i* (change) in the *Book of Change* connotes the meaning of both a constant structure of rudiments and a dynamic process of transformation. Understandably, ultimate reality is also conceptualized by Hsiung as constant transformation. Fundamentally different from the Buddhist idea that the phenomenal flux of change is impermanent, without self-nature, and thus illusory, Hsiung insists that it is a concrete manifestation of the ultimate reality. Therefore, the multiplicity of the phenomenal world, far from being the figment of the mind, is intrinsically meaningful. For it shows, in a tangible form, the creativeness of the ultimate reality. In terms of Hsiung's favorite analogy, the relationship is like that between the ocean and its waves. The ocean is perceived in terms of the waves, which are its inevitable manifestations. The waves are inseparable from the ocean, which is their necessary ground of existence. It is in this sense that Hsiung advocates original substance (*pen-t'i*) and manifested functions (*tso-yung*).

Undoubtedly Hsiung's ontological vision resembles the teachings of the Neo-Confucian masters, notably Chang Tsai (Heng-ch'ü, 1020–1077).[59] Indeed, Hsiung's cosmological duality, contraction (*hsi*) and expansion (*p'i*), is reminiscent of Chang's fusion and intermingling of material force (*ch'i*) wherein lies "the subtle, incipient activation of reality and unreality, of motion and rest, and the beginning of *yin* and *yang*, as well as the elements of strength and weakness."[60] Hsiung himself has acknowledged his intellectual debt to Chang, although his appreciation of Chang's cosmology was first mediated through the philosophy of Wang Fu-chih.[61] Contraction, to Hsiung, is "the congealing operation that produces apparently concrete objects of matter."[62] This tendency toward concretization is the ontological basis of the manifold world and the multiplicity of existence. However, contraction is ever under the discriminating and directing activity of expansion. As a defining characteristic of the mind, expansion compels, as it were, "this universal flux of seemingly contradictory tensions" to become "an orderly, constant transformation rather than a static equilibrium of interacting forces." This leads to the view that ultimate reality is

245

"function or process, never completely passive but ever producing and reproducing a harmonious synthesis of heaven, earth, and human being."[63]

It is not difficult to pinpoint the influence of Wang Yang-ming in this formulation. Hsiung repeatedly acknowledged that Wang was the true transmitter of the Confucian way, and was thus a precursor of Hsiung's own philosophy.[64] It is interesting to note that Hsiung's exaltation of Wang Yang-ming's concept of mind, which was severely attacked by Wang's contemporary critics as Ch'an Buddhist, is indicative of the direction of his own thought, which was also characterized by his detractors as basically in the intuitive tradition of Buddhism. Hsiung's rejection of the Wei-shih theory of causation can probably be interpreted as a conflict within the Buddhist realm of intellectual discourse.[65] However, by stressing the unity and inseparability of the ultimate reality and its manifested functions, Hsiung significantly departs from the Buddhist claim of the insubstantiality of the world. Furthermore, in Hsiung's philosophy, human activities and relationships are integral parts of the highest expression of truth, a position difficult to support by any Buddhist teaching.

True to the spirit of Wang Yang-ming's dynamic idealism, Hsiung maintained that the mind is not only a cognitive knowing but also an affective acting. The unity of knowledge and action is so much a part of Hsiung's mode of thinking that pure intellectuality devoid of any existential implication is dismissed by him as nonsense or, at most, a playful game. According to Hsiung's contention, there should never be a bifurcation of the mind. Its indivisible unity manifests itself in a creative process wherein the separation of the external and the internal is completely transcended. Therefore, the mind acts and generates as well as comprehends. Actually it is in the sensitivity of the mind—its ability to feel and to care—that the creative potential of human beings truly lies. In a strict sense, the word "mind," used here as a translation of the Chinese character *hsin*, really stands for "mind-heart." It entails much more than what is usually envisioned in the philosophy of mind. Indeed, Hsiung argued that the human mind-heart, as the quintessence of human nature, interprets and directs the great transformation in the same way as the ultimate reality manifests itself. As an interpretive agent it gives

246

meaning to the universe; and as a directing agent, it shapes its very reality. To intend, in this connection, is not merely to will, but to will in the sense of molding and creating. The mind-heart's power of direction, Hsiung observed, is "life-force," ever developing and changing, yet without losing its inner identity.[66]

Hsiung's highly sophisticated understanding of the mind is predicated on a strong belief in the malleability of the human condition through internal self-transformation. The mind, by its experiential comprehension, not only understands but also directs and masters. Implicit in this ontological insight is the conviction that the intellectual, by raising the level of consciousness of the people, necessarily shapes the direction of social change and influences the fate of the nation. However, this form of elitism is based on self-knowledge, indeed self-direction and self-mastery. It thus points to an open system of moral community, rather than a prescribed hierarchy of control. In the light of this line of argument, Mencius' notion of "those who labor with their minds" (lao-hsin che) actually refers to the moral leaders who are responsible for the integrity of the meaning-structure of the society.[67] It is their duty to see to it that the cosmic process as well as the legal and ritual order is in a harmonious state. Of course their central concern is not to preserve the status quo. In Hsiung's philosophy, stasis means degeneration. If ultimate reality is perceived as a dynamic process of great transformation, the courage to change and to create is a prerequisite for survival. Hence, the harmonious state can never be attained merely by balancing conflicting forces. It can only be realized by undergoing a continuous process of creative integration, despite internal contradictions. The intellectual who refuses to endorse the simple-minded model of one-dimensional progress thus contributes significantly to the actual sequence of change. After all, human community is a dialectical interplay between what is and what its members insist ought to be. An ontological inquiry into the mind, far from being the pastime of metaphysicians, becomes an inalienable right and an unavoidable duty of the people. If the intellectuals fail in their task as guardians of the meaning-structure, in the terminology of Mencius, they will no longer be "fed" by "those who labor with their strength" (lao-li che).[68]

It is important to note that Hsiung's emphasis on the internality

247

of the mind presupposes a sense of community as the basis of self-realization. To be sure, the value of the individual as an integral part of social welfare is recognized. However, since a person is perceived never as an atomized entity but always as a center of relations, human dignity is demonstrated as much by the elimination of selfish desires as by the struggle for civil rights.

Jen in Hsiung's Ontology

Consistent with the Wang Yang-ming tradition of Neo-Confucianism, Hsiung observers: "Humanity (*jen*) is the original mind. It is the original substance common to people, heaven, earth, and all things. . . From Confucius and Mencius to teachers of the Sung and Ming periods, all directly pointed to humanity, which is the original mind. The substance of humanity is the source of all transformations and the foundation of all things."[69] As one would expect, *jen* occupies a pivotal position in Hsiung's ontology. This enables C. B. Day to conclude that "throughout all his philosophizing, Hsiung Shih-li placed *jen* at the center and thoroughly believed in the capacity of all men to possess a share of it, thereby proving himself truly Confucian in spirit."[70]

Hsiung's emphasis on *jen* as a life-force might have given Father Brière the impression that what he had accomplished was no more than an eclecticism, "fusing the classical doctrines of the [Wei-shih] school with the essential principles of the Neo-Confucianism of Wang Yang-ming, and drawing inspiration from Bergsonian idealism."[71] The reference to Bergson demands some explanation. Virtually all of the available sources on Hsiung Shih-li in Western languages that I have examined have made at least a passing reference to the fact that Hsiung was somehow influenced by Bergson's philosophy. Clarence H. Hamilton, in his contribution to the *Encyclopedia Britannica*, simply says that "from Western thought he gained appreciation of analytical method and the idea of evolutionary change (Bergson)."[72] In what sense was Hsiung a Bergsonian?

Actually, the question was raised by Hsieh Yu-wei in a long letter to Hsiung. Hsieh suggested that Hsiung's method of apprehending *pen-t'i* seems quite compatible with Bergson's intuitive approach to reality. Hsiung, however, rejected the comparison outright on the ground that his ontological awareness was fundamentally different from Bergson's philosophical assumptions, which, he believed, were based on a biological model. Hsiung's knowledge about Bergson was definitely secondhand. It seems that by the time he received Hsieh's letter he had only read a translated version of *Creative Evolution* by his friend Chang Tung-sun, the famous professor of Western philosophy. Hsiung emphatically denied that his ontological awareness had anything to do with Bergson's "intuition." He further argued that Bergson's notion of instinct really functions at the level of the perfumed (or polluted) mind (*hsi-hsin*) rather than at that of the original mind (*pen-hsin*).[73]

We must hasten to add that Hsiung's unwillingness to endorse Bergson's philosophy by no means suggests that other attempts to analyze his ontology in terms of Western philosophy were also dismissed. To him, comparative study of this kind, far from being objectionable, was of great significance. In his response to Hsieh Yu-wei's letter mentioned above, he accepted the interpretation that F. H. Bradley's *Appearance and Reality* contained insights quite similar to his own insistence on the unity of "original substance" and "manifested functions." However, he warned that his ontological method of "experiential comprehension," which he regarded as "the outstanding spirit of Chinese philosophy," probably differed from Bradley's intellectual argumentation in a fundamental way. Similarly, though cautioning that such an analogy might be misleading, Hsiung appreciated Chang Tung-sun's comparative observation that his *New Exposition of Consciousness-Only (Hsin Wei-shih lun)* was congenial with Whitehead's philosophical intent in *Process and Reality*.[74]

It is possible that in underlining the importance of the cardinal Confucian virtue *jen*, Hsiung's primary concern was to construct an ontology of his own, rather than to give respectability to a Confucian concept in the light of new ideas from the West. Unlike K'ang Yu-wei, who tried to universalize *jen* to suit the demands of his times, Hsiung was not very much concerned about how new or how cosmopolitan his philosophy would appear in the eyes of those who were familiar with the most recent trends in Western thought.[75] His single-minded attention was focused on the seemingly impossible mission of finding "truth" and "value" through a long and strenuous process of experiential learning. Though he did not envision his work as the lonely struggle of an isolated thinker, he strongly believed that his philosophical quest had to begin with a probe of the specificity of his own culture and the particularity of his own existence. To use a Mencian analogy, the search for the spring of wisdom commences with digging the ground of one's true self. Yet the intention is to assert neither the strength of one's ethnicity nor the power of one's cultural heritage, but the universal relevance of "authentic existence." *Jen* so conceived is an ontological idea of humanity without its sociopolitical trappings. Hsiung's philosophy is, in this connection, a conscious attempt to demonstrate that such a task is not only experientially possible but morally imperative.

If, like Levenson, we speak of intellectual history as "the history not of thought, but of men thinking," Hsiung's ontological awareness definitely does not point to a system of ideas forever meaning what it means in itself, as a logical construction. Rather, as "thinking," a psychological act as well as a philosophical pursuit, it "implies context (changing), not disembodiment, [for] men mean different things when they think thoughts in different total environments."[76] One may very well argue that the social context in which Hsiung philosophized as a Confucian thinker makes it clear that "a set of Confucian attitudes, even if one could deem them uncorroded, does not sum up the *gestalt*."[77] The theoretical attempt to celebrate history as the persistence of an "essential past" by obliterating history-as-process is certainly untenable, but to raise the fundamental issue of meaning as a way of understanding the seemingly inexorable process of history is the birthright of a thinking person. What is the meaning of "men thinking" if the types of thought involved are reducible to a mere reflection on an irreversible trend of social change? " 'Out there,' in the history men make, the web is never rent, and intellectual, social, political, economic, cultural threads are interwoven."[78] But an interconnected mode of explanation need not imply a fixity of relationships. The possibility of reorganization is always there, and the thinking individuals are never "situated" in the status quo.

250

Unlike Bradley, who maintained that philosophy, as a form of intellectual reflection, should not tamper with social affairs, Hsiung believed that ontological awareness would inevitably reorganize the constellation of given realities. True to the Confucian "oneness of knowledge and action,"[79] he believed that to think is not merely to reflect but to orient, to shape, and to create. Underlying Hsiung's study of *jen* is a basic conviction that awareness is not only an expression of reality or an evocation of truth, but also a reorganization of the basic structure of affairs. A profound awareness of the human condition is necessary both for the production of a compelling understanding of historical specificity and for the creation of a new order of social community. A systematic questioning of the deepest insights in a given culture is therefore the authentic way of formulating an ontology as a prior condition for fundamental change and adaptation. Hsiung might have argued that if China was to survive as an integrated nation, it would be in part because it had the courage to dig into its roots and drill into the very foundation of its *raison d'être*. Indeed, Hsiung assigned himself the task of such "digging and drilling." It is in this sense that his ontological awareness, far from being a happy excursion into a detached realm of ideas, was an agonizing struggle through the grounds of his own cultural heritage. And this was done with profound intellectual passion.

NOTES

[1]Joseph R. Levenson, *Confucian China and Its Modern Fate: A Trilogy* (Berkeley: University of California Press, 1968), pp. ix-x. It should be noted that the passage originally appeared in Levenson's *Liang Ch'i-ch'ao and the Mind of Modern China* (Cambridge, Mass.: Harvard University Press, 1953).

[2]*Ibid.*, p. xi.

[3]*Ibid.*, p. xvi.

[4]*Ibid.*

[5]*Ibid.*, p. ix.

[6]Wing-tsit Chan, *A Source Book in Chinese Philosophy* (Princeton: Princeton University Press, 1963), p. 743.

[7]Levenson, *Confucian China*, p. xvi.

[8]For example, see Sha Ming, *K'ung-chia tien chi ch'i yu-ling*(Confucius and sons and their ghosts; Hong Kong: Wen-chiao Press, 1970), pp. 53–68.

[9]For an excellent study on this, see Herbert Fingarette, *Confucius—The Secular as Sacred* (New York: Harper Torchbooks, 1972), pp. 1–17.

[10]It should be added that the struggle continued in a most vigorous way in the People's Republic. Levenson's notion of "'museumified" Confucius can hardly account for intellectual attack against the so-called Confucian elements during the Cultural Revolution. See Levenson, *Confucian China*, 3: 76–82. Cf. Sha Ming, pp. 54–55.

[11]Benjamin I. Schwartz, "Notes on Conservatism in General and in China in Particular," in Charlotte Furth, ed., *The Limits of Change: Essays on Conservative Alternatives in Republican China* (Cambridge, Mass.: Harvard University Press, 1976), p. 16.

[12]*Ibid.*

[13]*Ibid.* This refers to a point particularly emphasized by Levenson.

[14]Levenson, *Confucian China*, p. x.

[15]An indication of this uncommonly significant response was Hsiung's memorial service held by the Department of Philosophy at New Asia College and the Oriental Society of Humanism in Hong Kong on July 14, 1968. See a brief report on the occasion in *Young-sun*, no. 388 (Aug. 1968): 2–3.

[16]This information was given to me by some of Hsiung's closest associates, such as Professor T'ang Chün-i of New Asia College in Hong Kong. For an example of the kind of intellectual discourse T'ang had with Hsiung, see Hsiung Shih-li, *Shih-li yü-yao* (Essential sayings [Dialogues] of Shih-li; Taipei: Kuang-wen Book Company, 1962; reprint), 2:11b–20. Hereafter referred to as *Yü-yao*.

[17]One could argue that this was probably due to Hsiung's lack of sociopolitical influence. There is also reason to believe that his preferential treatment was actually sanctioned by the highest authority in Peking because of his reputation abroad.

[18]Shen Yu-ting, Ho Ch'ang-ch'ün, and Jen Chi-yü were greeted either as his junior friends or as his students. For reference, see *Yü-yao*, 3:12b–13, 3:17a–b (Shen); 2:65–69b (Ho); and 2:70b–71b (Jen). Chang Tung-sun was one of his closest friends; for example, see *Yü-yao*, 1:47b–55 and 2:2–6. Ma I-fu later invited him to join Ma's Fu-hsing Academy as a professor, but their friendship failed shortly afterwards.

[19]For a monographic account of Hu Shih, see Jerome B. Grieder, *Hu Shih and the Chinese Renaissance: Liberalism in the Chinese Revolution, 1917–1937* (Cambridge, Mass.: Harvard University Press, 1970).

[20]I have in mind particularly Professors Mou Tsung-san and T'ang Chün-i at New Asia College, Professor Liu Shu-hsien at the University of Southern Illinois, and Professor Fu Wei-hsün at Temple University.

[21]For an account of this kind of personal animosity, see Mou Tsung-san, "Wo yü Hsiung Shih-li hsien-sheng" (Master Hsiung Shih-li and I), in his *Sheng-ming te hsüeh-wen* (The learning of life; Taipei: San-min Book Company, 1970), pp. 143–144. It should be noted that the account given is based on Professor Mou's personal reminiscences.

[22]Hsiung fully acknowledged the strength of Ch'ing scholarship. What he really criticized was the mentality of scholasticism. See Hsiung Shih-li, *Tu-ching shih-yao*

(Essential ways of reading the Classics; Taipei: Kuang-wen Book Company,1960; reprint), 1:8–11. Hereafter referred to as *Tu-ching*.

[23] *Yü-yao*, 1:46–47b.

[24] *Ibid.*, 1:46b.

[21] *Ibid.*, 1:47.

[26] It should be noted that although the entire book was published more than two decades after the May Fourth movement, letters and discussions in the book actually represent his intellectual position since the 1920s. The term *Dialogue* here refers to his *Yü-yao*, for the sayings included are mainly in the format of questions and answers.

[27] *Yü-yao*, 3:63.

[28] *Ibid.*, 3:63b.

[29] In fact, since the Sung Neo-Confucian revival, Confucian learning has frequently been referred to as *shen-hsin chih hsüeh* (the learning of the body and mind) and *sheng-jen chih hsüeh* (the learning of the sages). The designation *hsin-hsing chih hsüeh* (the learning of mind and human nature) has also been widely used.

[30] *Yü-yao*, 3:64.

[31] In this connection, I have to take issue with Donald J. Munro. See his "Humanism in Modern China: Fung Yu-lan and Hsiung Shih-li," in *Nothing Concealed: Essays in Honor of Liu Yü-yün*, ed. Frederic Wakeman, Jr. (Taipei: Chinese Materials and Research Aids Service Center, 1970), pp. 197–192.

[32] *Yü-yao*, 3:64.

[33] For a discussion on this issue, see Tu Wei-ming, "Subjectivity and Ontological Reality—An Interpretation of Wang Yang-ming's Mode of Thinking," in *Philosophy East and West* 23, no. 1–2 (Jan.–April 1973):187–205. Above, ch. 10.

[34] See *Chung-yung* (*Doctrine of the Mean*) chap. 20, in Wing-tsit Chan, *A Source Book in Chinese Philosophy*, pp. 107–108. The quotation is a condensed version of the original statement.

[35] This refers particularly to Mencius' distinction between those who labor with their minds and those who labor with their strength. The idea was originally intended to advocate a form of division of labor. See *Mencius*, 3A.4. For an English version of this passage, see *Mencius*, trans. D.C. Lau (Penguin Classics, 1970), pp. 100–104.

[36] Hsiung maintained that "the greatest cultural issue today is to make analytical distinctions between China and the West." The ultimate purpose is to arrive at a mutual appreciation of cultural values. Hsiung seems to argue that without sophisticated understanding of the difference, the possibility for a new synthesis at a higher level is quite slim. See *Yü-yao*, 3:73.

[37] See Hsü Fu-kuan's introduction in Hsiung Shih-li, *Fo-chia ming-hsiang t'ung-shih* (Buddhist concepts explained; Taipei: Kuang-wen Book Company, 1961), Preface, p. 4.

[38] The late Professor Yin Hai-kuang of Taiwan University told me that although he was basically in conflict with Hsiung on philosophical grounds, he was overpowered by Hsiung's personality and style of writing. Yin, as a disciple of Chin Yüeh-lin, the famed scholar of British empiricism, was noted for his discipline in

253

logic and clarity of expresson.

[39]See *Tu-ching*, 2:31–32.

[40]For example, see *Yü-yao*, 2:102 and 3:72–73.

[41]Peter Boodberg, "The Semasiology of Some Primary Confucian Concepts," *Philosophy East and West* 2(1953):327–330.

[42]See Wing-tsit Chan, *A Source Book in Chinese Philosophy*, p. 791. For an ontological account on this issue, see Mou Tsung-san, *Ts'ai-hsing yü hsüan-li* (Native endowments and metaphysical principles; Hong Kong: Young-sun Press, 1963), pp. 128–139.

[43]Levenson, *Confucian China* 1: 132–133.

[44]*Ibid.*, p. 110.

[45]*Ibid.*

[46]For a brief account of the Fa-hsiang (or Wei-shih) school, see Kenneth K. S. Ch'en, *Buddhism in China* (Princeton: Princeton University Press, 1964), pp. 320–325. Also see Wing-tsit Chan, *Religious Trends in Modern China* (New York: Columbia University Press, 1953), pp. 105–106. A succinct account of Hsiung's association with the tradition is found in *Religious Trends,* pp. 126–135.

[47]See Kenneth Ch'en, pp. 321–322.

[48]See Wing-tsit Chan, *Religious Trends*, p. 107. It is also cited in Kenneth Ch'en, p. 323.

[49]O. Brière, *Fifty Years of Chinese Philosophy*, trans. Laurence G. Thompson (New York: Frederick A. Praeger, Inc., 1965), p. 42.

[50]The text had been lost in China for centuries; it was presented to Yang Wen-hui by the renowned Japanese Buddhist scholar Nanjio Bunyū in 1880. Its subsequent publication in China marked the beginning of Buddhist revival in modern China. See Wing-tsit Chan, *Religious Trends*, pp. 109–110.

[51]Ch'en Po-sha (Hsien-chang, 1428–1500), a leading Neo-Confucian thinker in the Ming, has been widely acclaimed as the precursor of Wang Yang-ming's dynamic idealism.

[52]*Ta-i* in this connection refers to the idea of "great transformation" in the *Book of Change.*

[53]Hsiung Shih-li, *Hsin wei-shih lun* (New exposition on the Consciousness-only doctrine; Taipei: Kuang-wen Book Company, 1962; reprint), 1: 82b–83. Cf. Wing-tsit Chan, *Religious Trends*, pp. 126–127.

[54]Hsiung Shih-li, *Hsin-lun*, Preface, p. 1.

[55]*Ibid.*

[56]Frederick W. Mote, *Intellectual Foundations of China* (New York: Alfred A. Knopf, 1971), p. 15. For a general interpretation of the *Book of Change*, see Richard Wilhelm, trans., *The I Ching*, rendered into English by Cary F. Baynes (Princeton: Princeton University Press, 1967), pp. xlvii–lxii.

[57]See Jung's foreword to *The I Ching*, in Wilhelm, pp. xxi–xxxix. Also see C. G. Jung, *Psychology and Religion: West and East* (*Collected Works,* vol. 11), trans. R. F. C. Hull (New York: Pantheon Books, Bollingen Series, 1958), pp. 82 and 96.

[58]See *Hsin-lun*, 1: 28b–29b. Quotation from Wing-tsit Chan, *Religious Trends*, p. 34.

[59]For a brief account of Chang Tsai's philosophy, see T'ang Chün-i, "Chang Tsai's Theory of Mind and Its Metaphysical Basis," *Philosophy East and West* 7, no. 2 (July 1956): 113–136. See also Wing-tsit Chan, *A Source Book in Chinese Philosophy*, pp. 495–517.

[60]Wing-tsit Chan, *Source Book*, p. 503.

[61]Wang Fu-chih's influence on Hsiung is omitted in the present study. But in a more comprehensive analysis of the intellectual formation of Hsiung's thought, it is imperative that Wang's philosophical reflections on reality be noted as a background. For a controversial study on Wang's approach to *t'i-yung*, see Chu Po-k'un, "Wang Fu-chih lun pen-t'i ho hsien-hsiang" (Wang Fu-chih on original substance and phenomenal appearance) in *Chung-kuo che-hsüeh-shih lun-wen chi* (Collected essays on the history of Chinese philosophy; Peking: Chung-hua Book Company, 1965), pp. 66–99.

[62]See *Hsin-lun*, 1: 57b–66. For the quotation, see Clarence Burton Day, *The Philosophers of China* (New York: Citadel Press, 1962), p. 328.

[63]Day, *Philosophers of China*, p. 328.

[64]See *Yü-yao*, 2:85.

[65]For a serious critique of Hsiung's new approach from a Buddhist point of view, see Yin-shun, *P'ing Hsiung Shih-li ti Hsin Wei-shih lun* (A review of Hsiung Shih-li's New exposition of the Consciousness-only doctrine; Hong Kong: Cheng-wen Press, 1950).

[66]It should be noted that Hsiung defines the original mind as an absolutely non-dependent wholeness. First, it is called *heart*, because it is the real substance of myriad things but is not itself a thing. Second, it is called (genuine) *intention*, for it develops according to the unceasing creativity of its own nature. Third, it is called (pure) *consciousness* for it comprehends as it creates. And it is in the unity of heart, intention, and consciousness where the true meaning of the original mind lies. See *Hsin-lun*, 3A: 100b–101b.

[67]*Mencius*, 3A.4.

[68]*Ibid.*

[69]*Hsin-lun*, 3A: 79b–80.

[70]Day, *Philosophers of China*, pp. 329–330.

[71]O. Briere, *Fifty Years of Chinese Philosophy*, p. 42.

[72]Professor Hamilton's piece is otherwise a pertinent summary of Hsiung's philosophical orientation.

[73]*Hsin-lun*, 3B: 66a–b. See Liu Shu-hsien, "Hsiung Shih-li's Theory of Causation," *Philosophy East and West* 19, no. 4 (Oct. 1969): 407, n. 18.

[74]*Hsin-lun*, 3B: 65–66. Reference is also made to John Dewey and Betrand Russell. Similarly, his critique of Social Darwinism is made from an ontological perspective; see *Hsin-lun*, 2B: 10.

[75]It should be noted here that although Hsiung had high respect for T'an Ssu-t'ung, he repeatedly criticized K'ang Yu-wei for his uncritical adaptation of Western ideas as a way of making Confucianism relevant to the modern times.

[76]Joseph R. Levenson, "The Genesis of *Confucian China and Its Modern Fate*," in Perry L. Curtis, Jr., ed., *The Historian's Workshop* (New York: Basic Books,

1972), p. 285.

[77]*Ibid.*

[78]*Ibid.*

[79]Cited by Levenson, *ibid.*

15. Confucianism: Symbol and Substance in Recent Times

In this essay, I shall discuss the symbol and substance of Confucianism in the light of the Cultural Revolution and the ensuing events. Although I am fully aware that issues of power and policy on the economic, political, and social levels may have exerted a greater transforming influence on the brute facts of life in present-day China, I will in this study address myself mainly to the ideological question.

As an apparent digression, which actually it is not, I shall begin by an examination of Levenson's renowned thesis on *redness versus expertise*, or *value priority*, in his works on the fate of Confucianism, and suggest that this "Levensonian" interpretation needs to be broadened and modified if it is to account for the ideological struggle in the Cultural Revolution. The Confucian element will be introduced in a discussion of the Maoist approach to vital problems in China in order to show that Confucian ideas have dominated much of the intellectual discussions in contemporary China notwithstanding the making of a new "state cult" of Maoism. The essay concludes with a series of reflections on the relevance of Confucian symbolism in identifying substantive issues in China's quest for a new value system.

1. The Levensonian Thesis

In an article entitled, "Marxism and the Middle Kingdom," published in the September 1966 issue of *Diplomat*, Joseph R. Levenson makes the following observation:

> . . . Ch'ien-lung, proclaiming that the imperial virtue was acknowledged everywhere, could write complacently to George III, "We are in need of nothing. . . ." Mao, however, knows

how desperate the needs are—the intervening century and a hal
had ruined any complacency and the Confucian pretension to
virtue that explained it—and his prescription to banish the needs
is *science* (very far from Confucian values), most especially including a 'science of society.' The *red* of *red vs. expert* is not an eternally
Chinese demand, whether Confucian or Communist, that officials
profess to a world view transcending technical skill and specialization. It implies something else, that the modern world is
incompatible with the Confucian, not congruent with it—so incompatible that science and technology are in the ascendant
everywhere, and Marxism has to own them or lose its own ascendancy.[1]

Although this observation seems incongruent with the "spirit" of the
Great Proletarian Cultural Revolution, it does point to a central
Problematik of contemporary China: how to adapt herself to the
modernizing world without losing her own cultural identity.

Reviewed from this perspective, the *red vs. expert* controversy
has been interpreted as a conflict between an emotional need to be
attached to that which defines what the uniqueness of China is, and
an intellectual choice to develop a highly sophisticated technology.
Of course the conflict between identity and adaptation is not new.
Indeed it smacks of the conciliatory attempt of Chang Chih-tung
(1837–1909) in his "substance-function" (*t'i-yung*) formula. And
Levenson's pioneering work itself suggests that the conflict was apparent in the mind of Liang Ch'i-ch'ao (1873–1929).[2] Without
stretching the point, the antitraditionalism of the *New Century* (*Hsin
shih-chi*) and the advocacy of democracy and science in the *New Youth*
(*Hsin ch'ing-nien*) can also be understood as a by-product of an inevitable confrontation between the so-called *redness vs. expertise*. The
triumph of scientism in modern China may thus be described as a
clear indication that the amateur ideal of the red will eventually be
supplanted by the "technical skill and specialization" of the expert.
The true test for Marxism as well as for Confucianism is its ability
or inability to *own* science and technology.

Actually it has been widely argued that the Cultural Revolution
represents no more than a desperate attempt to rescue the dying
fervor of the red. According to this view, the young Maoist radicals
fear that the revolutionary spirit has been seriously eroded by party

functionaries, factory managers, and academic teachers, and that the takeover generation as a whole has become bourgeois in mentality and revisionist in attitude. Therefore they contend that unless a major transformation in the political culture takes place, China will face the danger of following the capitalist road at the expense of socialism. The tasks of the Cultural Revolution, as adopted by the Central Committee of the Chinese Party, were:

> First, to struggle against and overthrow those persons in authority who were taking the capitalist road; second, to criticize and repudiate the reactionary bourgeois "academic authorities" and the ideology of the bourgeoisie and all other exploiting classes; and third, to transform education, literature, and art and all other parts of the superstructure that did not harmonize well with the socialist economic base.[3]

This program may very well be seen as hoisting a red flag against bureaucratization in the Party, systematization in the economy, and professionalization in the university. It can be seen as a declaration of war against the emergent tendencies of what Max Weber calls "rationalization" in political, economic, and educational institutions. If Levenson is right in holding that the *red* is not an eternally Chinese demand that officials profess a world view transcending technical skill and specialization, and that the ascendancy of science and technology is irresistible, then the Cultural Revolution, too, will be doomed to failure, and the *redness* will also in the end become "a shade, living only in the minds of many, treasured in the mind for its own sake after the society which has produced it and which needs it has begun to dissolve away."[4]

Levenson's thesis can be further developed against the background of modern Chinese history, which he describes in "The Province, the Nation, and the World: the Problem of Chinese Identity" as

> a history of movement from the politics of Confucian faction (deriving at times from provincial fellow-feeling, but in a world commanded, overall, by a common Confucian fellowship) to the politics of a new world, an international politics conceived in terms of class.[5]

Implicit in this description is his strong belief that science and technology as manifested in the universalizing process of industrialization will give rise to "the diversity of many vocational types that come with specialization." This is neither a Confucian nor a Maoist value. And since "specialization makes new elites, of professionals, not amateurs on the Confucian model," he concludes, the fields of expertise will eventually provide "particular identities."[6] Redness, we may add, will be seen as Confucian amateurism and neutralized, gradually being relegated to a secondary role.

If we take this line of argument seriously, how can we account for the "fantastic drenching in ideology that China began to take" during the Cultural Revolution, directed not only against the experts but against the past as well? Levenson explains the obvious dilemma in terms of a sense of danger, "the danger of a war that could not be left to experts, because they would not choose it and could not win it with their expertise alone." With a touch of irony, Levenson continues:

> And it was this danger that gave the Cultural Revolution its dual targets, the two cultures, western and traditional. The concurrent attack on the latter confirms danger as the source of attack on the former, on the cosmopolitan spirit which the experts represented. For the tendency to "museumify" the past, instead of rooting it out, belonged to the age of self-assurance. It had not been there in the early days of struggle, when the communists had the passion of engagement: and it vanished now in an embattled age of possible destruction. The god of history was a hidden god again. Relativistic historicism, coolly accounting for one-time foes by giving them their niches, went out of fashion. The dead were no longer monuments, but ghosts and monsters to be slain again.[7]

II. *Beyond* Redness Versus Expertise

However, provocative as it is, the Levensonian interpretation is flawed in both conceptual sophistication and historical accuracy. Only five years after the untimely death of the brilliant scholar, we have witnessed too many fundamental problems in postindustrial societies to feel comfortable in giving unqualified support to the assertion that "science and technology are in the ascendant everywhere." The awareness that the life-supporting resources are finite, that the available energy for mass consumption is exhaustible, that the world's ecosystems are disintegrating, and that the human environment is rapidly deteriorating, at least suggests that modernization, in the sense of industrialization, is no longer to be conceived as a process of quantitative growth. The newly emergent global consciousness recognizes basic limits not only in economic growth but in scientific and technological developments themselves. The United Nations Stockholm Conference on the Human Environment in 1972 and the politicization of natural resources engineered recently by the Organization of Petroleum Exporting Countries further testify to the vulnerability of highly industrialized countries. One wonders whether with this hindsight Levenson would still have insisted that "expertise" rather than "redness" was the wave of the future?

Historically the case against the Levensonian interpretation is even more compelling. The available literature on the Cultural Revolution seems to indicate that the *red vs. expert* controversy has not been a central concern. No serious attempt has been made to demean expertise at all. Only a few professionals in science and engineering have experienced public humiliation. Mao Tse-tung is alleged to have given special instructions to protect science and engineering professors from Red Guard assaults. Indeed, technical expertise is fully accepted as a positive value. The slogan "first red, then expert" is not intended to discourage specialized knowledge; it simply demands that such knowledge be applied in the total ideological, political, and economic context. After all, *scientific* materialism is taken seriously as a guiding principle for action. And the ability to solve concrete problems with particular skills acquired through actual experience is highly prized. If an expert is under attack, as in the case of Ch'ien Wei-ch'ang, usually it is not his expertise but his vision limited in its application that matters.

The plight of the high-level cadres and the professors in the humanities is an entirely different story. They are the real "rootless cosmopolitans,"[8] in Levenson's characterization. For the experts are neither rootless nor cosmopolitan. To be sure, they are not as ideologically secure as the peasants or the workers, but they have

261

found a permanent niche in the total scheme of "building socialism." Although they cannot yet claim the universality of science and, as Levenson observes, "see their association with professional colleagues on the other side of national and ideological walls," they are rooted and localized in China's established institutes of science and technology. The cadres and the professors, especially those in literature, history, and philosophy, are the modern counterparts of traditional China's "bureaucrat-literati" or "scholar-officials." They are the targets of attack because, from the scientistic point of view, they are the expendables (rootless) and yet, with the power of the pen, they have exercised enormous influence throughout China (cosmopolitan).

The case of Wu Han is well-known. His political power as deputy mayor of Peking, combined with his historical knowledge and literary expressiveness, gave tremendous weight to the *Dismissal of Hai Jui* (January 1961). The play was not only a satire but also an act of defiance against Mao's handling of the *rightists*, especially P'eng Te-huai, Mao's first defense minister, in 1959. Ostensibly Wu seemed to be pleading for the rehabilitation of P'eng Te-huai, but underlying the theatrical plot was a serious attempt to advocate a new cultural mode. Of course Wu Han was not alone. He was joined by Liao Mo-sha, head of the United Front Department of the Peking Municipal Party Committee, and Teng T'o, former chief editor of the *People's Daily*. The three of them, beginning in October 1961, under the joint pseudonym of Wu Nan-hsing, collaborated in writing a series of morality tales for the Municipal Party Committee's journal *Front Line (Ch'ien-hsien)*. Under the heading "Personal Notes from a Three-Family Village" (*San-chia ts'un cha-chi*), these tales comment on education, the arts, morals, and current events. As a whole, they represent a masterful use of historical allegories.[9] Again, the political message was subtle but clear: a fundamental transformation of the revolutionary way of life was in order.

What was this new cultural mode or way of life that Wu Han, Liao Mo-sha, Teng T'o, and others advocated? At first glance, it appears to be absolutely innocuous. One wonders why some of their seemingly modest protests have been labeled as extremely poisonous. A brief analysis of Teng T'o's short essays, published under the general heading of *Evening Chats at Yenshan (Yen-shan yeh-hua)* in the

Peking Evening News from March 1961 onwards, may provide part of the answer. The "chats" were originally designed to serve the workers, peasants, and soldiers, Teng explains in his preface to the first anthology of his essays; however, since the majority of the readership consists of cadres, teachers, students, scientists, technicians, and practitioners in the arts, the "chats" at the present juncture cannot fulfill the needs of the masses. After all, Teng continues, the demands of the cadres and other above-mentioned comrades are different from those of the masses. He acknowledges the duty of high-level cadres in the party, the government, and the army to represent the interests of the people, but given the present situation, he intends to satisfy those who have already achieved a considerable level of cultural sophistication.

Teng T'o's "chats," which number more than one hundred fifty articles, are all written in elegantly composed vernacular or *pai-hua*. Stylistically they are reminiscent of the "short, superfine-quality essays" (*hsiao-p'in wen*) of late Ming (1368–1644). And the essays are so rich in historical allusions that they can be fully appreciated only by those who are highly cultivated in their literary tastes. Teng does talk about mundane things, such as the earliest recorded political march of the workers in Peking and the alleged pessimism in Taipei. But the bulk of his literary effort is devoted to subjects that are historically informative and aesthetically appealing. He talks about the art of calligraphy, paintings, the difficulty of understanding the classics, the necessity of correct identification of archaeological sites, and a host of other subjects. A salient feature of his comments on a wide range of topics from natural phenomena to current events is his consistent inclusion of primary sources from historical texts, especially those of the Ming dynasty.

Indeed, Teng's "chats" are laden with direct quotations from the Four Books, the Five Classics, the writings of the pre-Ch'in philosophers, the dynastic histories, the works of the Sung thinkers, and a variety of "miscellaneous notes" (*pi-chi*) by Ming scholars. His essays on Confucius' most beloved disciple Yen Hui (521–490 B.C.),[10] the Han general Wu Han (d. 44),[11] the hero and the statesman of the *Romance of the Three Kingdoms*, Chang Fei (d. 221) and Chu-ko Liang (d. 234),[12] the T'ang poet Chia Tao (779–843),[13] the Tung-lin scholar Ku Hsien-ch'eng (1550–1612),[14] the Ming states-

263

man-scientist Hsü Kuang-ch'i (1562–1633),[15] and a relatively unknown Ming official Li San-ts'ai,[16] further indicate his preoccupation with traditional personalities.

Actually if we delete the perfunctory references to Marx, Lenin, and Mao, which are often inconspicuous and dispensable trappings, Teng's "chats" are fitting companions to Peking opera, top-grade Lung-ching tea, and other exhibits of the *haute culture* in old Peking. Teng's delightful comments on poinsettia,[17] snowflakes,[18] eagles,[19] bees,[20] dogs,[21] and a long-lost game called *"t'anch'i"*[22] may even create the illusion that the "cultural essence" of Peking has remained intact after twelve years of revolutionary education. More important perhaps is the complex of fundamental values permeating Teng's published works: it includes a respect for things past, a concern for exquisite taste, and a caution against any form of extremism. One easily detects in it a kind of self-indulgence, verging on the snobbishness of a traditional "literatus" *(wen-jen)*.

Apparently the genteel world of Yenshan (even the name itself evokes memories of old Peking) was extremely contagious. It would not be far-fetched to suggest that in the pre-Cultural Revolution days, the ethos of "intellectuals" in the capital of the People's Republic was very much a reflection of the cultural values advocated in Teng T'o's *Evening Chats at Yenshan*. From the outside, it seems that these cultural values are not necessarily incompatible with "building socialism." But if they in fact became the central concerns of the power elite, supplanting revolutionary ideas, notably the idea of "struggle," it was a real cause for alarm, especially for those who could not bear witnessing the demise of the "spirit of Yenan." The indignation of Mao and his radical comrades at this "unwholesome" development is quite understandable.

On the ideological front, the "revolutionary situation" must have been equally distressing to the Maoists. Among the forty-two issues of *Philosophical Research (Che-hsüeh yen-chiu)*, published between 1959 and 1965, only one takes note of the philosophical expressions of the masses. And it was the winter and the very last issue of the 1965 series. Before then, it probably did not even occur to the editors of the prestigious journal that philosophical inquiries could have been conducted by people other than the professional philosophers. Understandably the scholars who had gained their reputations long before the founding of the People's Republic continued to dominate the intellectual scene. To mention just a few obvious examples, an article on the principle of objective verification by the logician, Chin Yüeh-lin, attracted considerable attention;[23] the aesthetician, Chu Kuang-ch'ien, aroused great interest by publishing a couple of technical comments on the art of aesthetic appreciation;[24] and the Buddhologist, T'ang Yung-t'ung, made a rare appearance by contributing a highly refined piece on textual criticism, while his student, Jen Chi-yü, was very active in other scholarly debates.[25] The only visible new presence was the defender of genuine Marxism and Leninism, Kuan Feng. But even Kuan devoted much of his time to historical analyses of Lao Tzu and Chuang Tzu.

Several controversies surfaced in the six-year period. Fung Yu-lan made quite a few lengthy self-criticisms, repeatedly denounced his early thoughts on Neo-Confucianism, and declared that he had been seriously wrong in advocating "abstract inheritance" as a guide for appropriating brilliant ideas in the past. But in the summer 1965 issue, he again raised the problem of transmitting the Chinese philosophical heritage. He proposed that (1) the linguistic expressions of the ancients be properly used (as in Mao's modern poems written in the style of Sung *tz'u*), (2) a conscious attempt be made to link up with philosophical issues in the past (as in Mao's *Practice* and *Contradiction*), (3) stories in ancient philosophical texts be adopted for allegorical purposes (as in Mao's ingenious handling of the parable of "The Foolish Old Man Who Moved Mountains" from the *Lieh Tzu*), and (4) experiences of the past be made to serve as lessons for the present (as in Mao's creative application of ancient military tactics).[26]

The prominence of "tradition" is evident in almost every issue. With notable exceptions, such as a study on the nineteenth-century Indian philosopher, Swami Vivekananda, in the winter 1962 issue,[27] the majority of the articles dealt with philosophical interpretations of Chinese history. Although methodologically Kuan Feng, Lin Yü-shih, and others insisted that "the arena of the history of philosophy is the battlefield of the struggle between materialism and idealism,"[28] more contributors seemed to question the wisdom of imposing Western categories on the study of Chinese philosophy.

265

Some strongly urged that research emphases be placed on China's unique contributions to world philosophy, especially in areas of education, ethics, and spiritual life. Liu Chieh even declared that the Confucian idea of "humanity" (*jen*) is the primary symbol in philosophy and advocated a new appreciation of the Confucian ideal of the "unity of man and Heaven."[29]

The national Conference on Confucius (November 6–12, 1962), held in the capital of Shantung, near the birthplace of the sage, was therefore not an isolated phenomenon. Attended by 160 philosophers and historians representing sixteen provinces and cities, the conference of "scholarly discussion" (*hsüeh-shu t'ao-lun hui*) examined several position papers and heard comments made by distinguished scholars among whom were Fung Yu-lan, Yang Jung-kuo, Chao Chi-pin, Lü Chen-yü, and Kuan Feng.[30] According to a report in *Philosophical Research*, Kao Tsan-fei's essay on "The Core of Confucian Thought: Humanity (*jen*)" attracted much attention. Kao maintained that the "total thought content" of the Confucian idea of humanity must be differentiated from its concrete "forms of expression." Thus, the validity of the inner logic in the Confucian formulation of the concept of humanity cannot be negated solely on the ground of its historical manifestations. Yang Jung-kuo, on the other hand, maintained that since "class analysis" is essential to any metaphysical construct, Confucius' thought must be examined against the background of the actual economic and social conditions of his times as well as his own class origin and attitude. Kuan Feng and Lin Yü-shih further contended that Kao had significantly departed from the guiding principle of Marxism. However, Lü Chen-yü argued that the best way to study a great personality is to see him in the light of critical scholarship. Imposing alien categories on him will not advance the spirit of science in Marxism.[31]

Contrary to Levenson's interpretation, the rehabilitation of the Confucian point of view did not reflect any intention of the Party to "museumify" the Confucian heritage as an archaeological relic. Rather, it was symptomatic of a massive effort at reshaping the official ideology or, as it were, redefining the whole notion of "redness."

Whether or not Liu Shao-ch'i was instrumental in making these scholarly exchanges possible, the ethos as manifested in them has been labeled as Liu's "rightist" tendency. The implication is not that since Liu and his cohorts have adopted the "capitalist road" at the expense of "building socialism" they have put much more emphasis on "expertise" than on "redness." It seems that the real issue lies in the "superstructure" itself: at this particular juncture of the People's Republic, what should be the correct ideological line? Should bureaucratization in the Party be encouraged? Should academic elitism be justified? Should the normalization of higher education be continued? Should centralized economic decisions be maintained? Underlying these considerations is of course a host of questions concerning "value priority." What kind of cadres are to be trained? What does it mean to be an "intellectual" in a socialist country? What is education for? And what strategy of economic development is to be implemented? The "rightists" would certainly opt for a gradual, normal, institutional, and elitist approach to these problems. The operating principles would be harmony rather than struggle, calculation rather than spontaneity, and leadership rather than mass participation. This would presuppose that a high level of integration in society, even if it be achieved by conciliatory and compromising measures, is tolerable and even desirable.

If we follow this line of thinking, "contradiction," a central kernel in Mao Tse-tung's thought, would have to be relegated to the background. Whether or not he was actually instigated by Liu, the philosopher Yang Hsien-chen did urge just that. In 1964, Yang published his theory of "combine two into one" (*ho-erh wei-i*) as an obvious critique of Mao's *On Contradiction*.[32] While Mao asserts that "everything divides into two" and "the law of contradiction in things, that is, the law of the unity of opposites, is the basic law of materialist dialectics,"[33] Yang claims that Lenin's thesis on the identity of contradiction means one should seek for "common points," "common things," and "common needs."[34] He further advocates the idea of the inseparability of opposite aspects and suggests that learning dialectics means "learning how to link the two opposing ideologies." To him, "synthesis" represents a more advanced development than mere "analysis." Thus, he calls for "conciliation of contradictions" and even "class collaboration."[35]

Yang's philosophical assault on Maoism found a sympathetic echo in Fung Yu-lan's articles published in the same period. On the surface, Fung's assumption that "universal forms" transcend class distinctions has little in common with Yang's notion of "combine two into one." However, like Yang, Fung's intention is to establish a common ground on which people of different class origins can begin to share certain "basic" values. Inherent in Fung's monographic studies then is a critique of Mao's theory of "class nature," and by extension his strategy of "class struggle."[36] This demand for reconciliation is in perfect accord with Wu Han's message in the *Dismissal of Hai Jui*, and, we may add, it is also quite compatible in spirit with Teng T'o's *Chats at Yenshan*.

III. Maoism in Perspective

From Mao's perspective, the whole situation must have appeared to be extremely provocative. The record of his informal talks in this period of time clearly shows that he was deeply distressed by what was happening. He remarked ruefully that class struggle had been discontinued for a whole decade[37] and that education on socialism had become a shambles.[38] He complained that the so-called intellectuals were in fact stupid and ignorant.[39] He felt that the *People's Daily* was not worth reading,[40] and he probably refused to take seriously the intellectual debates in *Philosophical Research* for years. His distaste for scholasticism had become more intensified and his distrust of professional philosophers had become more pronounced. He contended against the facts that among the great Chinese philosophers and literati, such as Wang Ch'ung (27–91), Fan Chen(ca. 450–ca. 515), Fu Hsüan (217–278), Liu Tsung-yüan (773–819), Wang Ch'uan-shan(Fu-chih, 1619–1692), Li Chih(1527–1602), Tai Tung-yüan(Chen, 1723–1777), and Wei Yüan(1798–1856), none "specialized" in philosophy. This was also the case in the Marxian tradition. Even Hegel and Kant, he continued, were not merely specialists.[41] With a touch of sarcasm, he said that conducting counterrevolutionary activities under the guise of writing fictions was a great invention.[42] Perhaps only half seriously, he even suggested that Peking opera singers, poets, literary writers, and dramatists be chased out of the city.[43] Using the example of Russian revisionism, Mao warned that the high-salary bracket appeared first among the writers and artists in the Soviet Union.[44]

In the May 1963 address delivered at the Hang-chou Meeting, Mao instructed that five "essential points" (*yao-tien*) be implemented by the Party to ensure a higher level of efficiency among the cadres in carrying out their socialist responsibilities: (1) practicing class struggle, (2) strengthening education on socialism, (3) depending on poor peasants for actual experiences, (4) continuing the movement of "four purifications" (*ssu-ch'ing*) in economics, politics, organization, and thought, and (5) participating in collective productive labors. On June 16, 1964, Mao revealed his concerns in cultivating the "successor generation" (*chieh-pan jen*). Again, he instructed that five factors be taken into consideration: (1) adequate education in Marxism and Leninism, (2) identification with the masses, (3) ability to unite the majority, (4) democratic attitude, (5) self-criticism.[45] Undoubtedly Mao was deeply concerned about the fate of his most cherished principles, notably "social practice," "class struggle," "mass line," and "continuous revolution." Therefore, what he actually proposed was no less than a restructuring of the existing "value priority." It did not take him long to realize that the completion of the task required more than issuing directives.[46]

Historically the Cultural Revolution began with the publication of Yao Wen-yuan's devastating criticism of Wu Han's *Dismissal of Hai Jui* in the Shanghai paper *Wen-hui pao* on November 10, 1965. Recently available information confirms the suspicion that Mao was personally responsible for the publication of the article.[47] Thus, in a sense, Mao was instrumental in creating the climate of opinion in which the Cultural Revolution became possible. Whether or not Mao actually supervised the formation of the Red Guards, his sanction and encouragement of the students' demonstrations clearly show that he was very much in favor of the movement. The stabilizing effect of the Army during the period also indicates that Mao, through the apparent, if not real, cooperation of Lin Piao and other military leaders, was really in command. And the fact that the supreme rule of Mao Tse-tung's thought has become fully established only since the downfall of Liu Shao-ch'i in 1966 further points to the interpretation that Mao not only initiated the "revolution" but actually led it to its logical conclusion. However, Mao's active role in the Cultural Revolution does not at all suggest that he personally "manufactured"

269

the whole thing. Nor does it imply that he was in perfect control at each stage as the Cultural Revolution unfolded.

In an address delivered at the enlarged meeting of the Standing Committee of the Politburo on March 17, 1966, Mao remarked that the antisocialist influence of Wu Han, Liao Mo-sha, and Teng T'o was so pervasive that "cultural revolutions" were urgently needed in literature, history, philosophy, law, and economics.[48] Similarly, on April 28, 1966, Mao, in his criticism of P'eng Chen, who was listed as one of the six most influential members of the Party in September 1966, described the situation in Peking as so tightly controlled by the "rightists" that "even a needle could not stick into it, nor could a drop of water leak into it."[49] Mao's feeling of powerlessness in exerting an immediate impact on Peking is evidenced by his painful decision to initiate the Cultural Revolution from Shanghai. A recorded conversation of Mao on February 3, 1967, reveals that he originally intended to have a critique of Wu Han published in Peking, but no one there could be entrusted with the task. Therefore, he had to go to Shanghai and discuss the matter with Yao Wen-yüan. And Mao mentioned in passing that the Shanghai base had been established by Chiang Ch'ing. After Yao had completed the article, as a precautionary measure, Chiang insisted that it not be shown either to Chou En-lai or to K'ang Sheng for fear that Liu Shao-ch'i, Teng Hsiao-p'ing, or Lu Ting-i might gain access to it and intervene in its publication. Mao complained that even after it had been printed and widely circulated throughout the country, Peking still refused to cooperate.[50] However, it should be noted that a remarkable change of emphasis in *Philosophical Research* did take place in winter 1965 when a special issue on the philosophical essays of the workers, peasants, and soldiers was published on December 21, 1965. Mao happily stated that he had read three of them with great interest and encouraged others to do the same.[51]

The three 1966 issues of *Philosophical Research*, which were among the last to have been published before the journal was abruptly discontinued, contain exclusively articles denouncing Wu Han and intellectual elitism in the first and the third, and one hundred concrete examples of the principle of "identity of contradictions" in the second. On May 25, 1966, seven members of the Department of Philosophy at Peita launched an attack against the university's chancellor, Lu P'ing. Their poster of criticism, displayed on the walls of the university and commonly known as the *tatzupao* (large-character news), was the first sign of "student" rebellion against an established educational authority during the Cultural Revolution. Mao's personal decision to have the content of the *tatzupao* broadcast over the national radio system on June 1 gave a great impetus to impending student demonstrations at Peita, Tsinghua, Nanking, and other famous universities. The "initiators" of the Cultural Revolution, as the seven signers of the *tatzupao* were to be called by the press, opened the floodgate of protest with, as it were, a few strokes of the brush.[52] The story of the subsequent events is now widely known, although interpretations on Mao's "countercurrent" activities continue to proliferate. Admittedly, the intellectual confrontation thus outlined might have been a surface manifestation of what many China experts believe to be a much more substantive issue, namely an intense power struggle in the highest echelon of the Chinese communist leadership. However, the "power struggle" thesis is inadequate, not because it is "wrong" but because, as advanced in current literature, it is too restrictive even to account for the actual exercise of power in the Cultural Revolution.

Needless to say, power has been a central concern. The downfall of Liu Shao-ch'i, later the death of Lin Piao, and the displacement of an overwhelming majority of leaders in virtually all segments of the "establishment" can very well be interpreted as a change in the mode of exercising power unprecedented in the history of the PRC. The Cultural Revolution, in this particular connection, has been a "snatching power" (*tuo-ch'üan*) movement. And it does seem plausible that Mao, with the support of the Shanghai "radicals," reemerged from the Second Line to the First Line and in the process managed to destroy the power bases of his rivals: Liu's party, Lin's army, and, with a stretch of the imagination, probably also Chou's government. This interpretation is, however, oversimplified. Given the complexity of events of the last decade in the People's Republic, it is deceptively naive to subsume the whole "political" process under the rubric of power struggle, assuming the existence of a conscious design to restructure the leadership so that those who were "power holders" (*tang-ch'üan*) would be drastically replaced by those who were originally powerless. Of course the slogan that *tsao-fan yu-li* (there is

271

reason to rebel or rebellion is justified) during the heyday of the Cultural Revolution could be easily understood as a militant attempt to transfer power from one group to the other. But are we to accept the speculation that Mao was able to mobilize the Red Guards and, with the support of the People's Liberation Army, successfully destroy the Party; that through an ingenious manipulation of the government he then managed to paralyze the leadership of the army; and that now his radical supporters are busily trying to discredit the government as well? Even if phenomenologically one can perceive such a pattern, as an explanation it gives no more than an impressionistic account. For it fails to take into consideration the underlying issue of value priority, without which the Cultural Revolution could not have happened in the first place.

It is generally recognized that Mao's real strength in mobilizing a nationwide revolution did not come from the power centers of day-to-day political control but from the authority of ideology. Paradoxically Mao's ability to exert a profound influence in shaping the direction of national sentiments in the last ten years is, in a significant way, attributable to his choice of remaining relatively detached from directly exercising power through party apparatus. Had Mao been closely associated with the educational policies of the party, for example, he would not have had the leverage to deal effectively with the student revolts in the summer of 1968.[53] Indeed, without any irony at all, Mao could very well subscribe to Lord Acton's observation that power tends to corrupt and absolute power corrupts absolutely. The struggle of the Cultural Revolution, in this connection, can even be characterized as an attempt to search for an uncorruptible power base—"dictatorship of the proletariat." Whether or not this is labeled revolutionary romanticism, the Maoist strategy was to define power in so broad and comprehensive a context that it could never be legitimately "localized" to become the weapon of a special interest group. And a monolithic order, achieved through a routinized handling of public problems, was thought to have been a direct threat to social revolution precisely because it seemed that inherent in its power relationships was a tendency toward particularism. It was not power alone but power based on ideology that gave Mao the authority to challenge the everyday management of national affairs.

272

The ideology behind the Cultural Revolution, commonly known as Maoism, stresses among other things (1) social practice (*she-hui shih-chien*), (2) class struggle (*chieh-chi tou-cheng*), (3) mass line (*ch'ün-chung lu-hsien*), and (4) continuous revolution (*chi-hsü ko-ming*). Without describing in detail each of the principles, it may be helpful to discuss briefly some of their ideological implications.

Social practice superficially resembles the notion of *engagement* in modern existentialism, but since its philosophical basis is not individualism but collectivism, it points to an entirely different area of concern. The individual choice to confront the unknown as an authenticating act for one's real existence is diametrically opposed to the idea of "eradicating self-centeredness" (*ch'ü-ssu*) as a precondition for genuine practice. In Maoism, a person is perceived as an integral part of a collectivity; his real worth, as it were, can be fully manifested only by a process of objectification through which selfishness is overcome and unity with the "great self" (*ta-wo*) achieved. The idea that one's inner truth can be discovered by probing the ground of spiritual subjectivity is completely alien to this mode of thinking. Practice in Maoism must be empirically verifiable and socially recognizable. It is intended to subordinate the needs of the part to the needs of the whole. It aims at a total solution, rather than an individual response to a partial situation.

As a form of social practice, *class struggle* aims to ensure that egalitarian measures be universally implemented. The purpose of "struggle, criticize, and reform," to use a current expression, is to achieve a higher level of justice in society by destroying apparent orderliness. This is premised on the judgment that latent contradictions among people, brought about by an unequal distribution of economic commodities, social privilege, and political power, can be resolved only through struggle. Conciliatory arrangements are frequently pretexts for perpetuating injustice. The leveling of inequalities by heightening conflicts between "classes" is thus an indicator of the societal commitment to revolutionary change. Since contradictions, in a practical sense, cannot cease to exist, the struggle has to be renewed continually.

The *mass line* is to see to it that cadres, intellectuals, and other leaders do not forsake the revolutionary spirit of struggle. And the idea of "unity with the masses" is intended to foster an exemplary

273

morality of self-sacrifice. The task of socialist education therefore involves the establishment of centers for training revolutionaries with a profound sense of mission. The prominence of totalism is particularly pronounced in the principle of *continuous revolution*. Much emphasis is placed on the power of the people by their own will to bring about an egalitarian society. To be sure, revolution depends on "a capacity for building large-scale and highly disciplined forms of human organization,"[54] but the boundless creative power of the masses is believed to be more reliable as the basis for socialist transformation. Mao is absolutely serious in asserting that "the people, and the people alone, are the motive force in the making of world history."[55]

However, contrary to widely held belief, *social practice* as a form of praxis is not necessarily anti-intellectual. Mao fully recognized the significance of intellectual activities in building socialism;[56] he also acknowledged that the intellectuals themselves have a key role to play in social revolution. To him, it was vitally important that the cadres be thoroughly trained in the "theory" of Marxism-Leninism. For unless they are adequately equipped with the proper ideological tool, they cannot fully realize the creative potential of the masses.[57] Mao once stated that "truths, all truths, in the beginning, are always held in the hands of a few, and are always suppressed by the majority." And to illustrate his point he cited the examples of Copernicus, Galileo, and others.[58] His "countercurrent" thesis is therefore predicated on the assertion that the real vision of how to apply Marxist and Leninist ideas to a concrete situation is sometimes the property of a small minority in society. But only through an experiential involvement in studying and working with peasants, workers, and soldiers can the insight of this creative minority become socially practicable.

Similarly, *class struggle* and *mass line* are not necessarily antirational. It is true that faith in the people as a source of inexhaustible energy and a belief in the intrinsic value of identifying with the lower classes are unquestioned "background assumptions" of Maoism. But the actual process of achieving social goals, far from being an emotional solution to China's "authority crisis," is often pragmatic and programmatic. The emphasis on study and research further suggests a commitment to empiricism, not as a philosophical doctrine but as a practical necessity. *Continuous revolution,* accordingly, is not so much against structure itself as against any form of essentialism. Mao believed that the dynamic process, rather than the achieved equilibrium, is a more effective way to release creative energy from below. It is better, Mao seems to contend, for the present to be chaotic than for the future to become stagnant.[59]

Obviously the Maoist line is in basic conflict with, for lack of a better term, the Confucian line advocated by Wu Han, Teng T'o, and other intellectuals in Peking. As far as the Cultural Revolution is a struggle on the ideological plane, the confrontation of the two lines can very well characterize what the major points of contention have been in the cultural arena over the last ten years. With the upsurge of anti-Confucian campaigns after the Lin Piao incident in 1971, it seems that the attack on the Confucian tradition may have been a logical extension of the Cultural Revolution. If we leave genetic reasons aside, critiques of Confucianism may appear to be inevitable consequences of shaping up the cult of Maoism. This interpretation of course presupposes that Maoism is absolutely incompatible with Confucianism and that Mao himself had a very strong aversion to Confucian culture.

Despite the apparent total negation of Confucianism, however, in the light of the available information, Mao himself was ambivalent toward the Confucian heritage. It is true that Mao had repeatedly attacked intellectual elitism, academic scholasticism, and bookish knowledge devoid of an experiential basis. Yet this does not mean that he was consistently critical of Confucianism itself. He may have thought more highly of revolutionaries, inventors, poets, and folk heroes than of Confucian scholars, but there is no evidence of any systematic effort at eradicating the Confucian influence in his thought.

Suggestively, Mao time and again acknowledged that six years of Confucian education in his youth had a profound influence in shaping his world view. He was familiar with the Four Books and the Five Classics. For example, he could recite long passages from the *Book of Poetry.*[60] And he expressed the wish to go through all of the twenty-four dynastic histories.[61] He also noted that his knowledge about warfare did not come from the *Sun Tzu,* as many people suspected, but from books much closer to the Confucian tradition,

275

such as *Tso-chuan* (*The Tso Commentary to the Spring and Autumn Annals*), *Tzu-chih t'ung-chien* (*General Mirror for the Aid of Government*), and *San-kuo yen-i* (*Romance of the Three Kingdoms*).[62] Even in his philosophical writings, despite their apparent Marxist-Leninist stance, perennial issues in Confucianism are often taken into serious consideration. On the Chinese New Year of 1964 (February 13), Mao, in an informal conversation with Chang Shih-chao, Huang Yen-p'ei, and others, made a few references to the Confucian "six arts" (ceremonies, music, archery, carriage-driving, writing, and mathematics). He expressed regret that the "main stream" (*chu-liu*) of Confucianism had been lost and urged his followers not to throw away the Confucian heritage.[63]

A further evidence of this seemingly open-minded attitude toward the Confucian tradition is found in the January 1972 issue of *K'ao-ku* (*Archaeology*), the first scholarly journal to resume publication after the Cultural Revolution. The editorial reiterates the necessity of continuing the struggle of the two ideological lines. It also stresses the importance of applying Mao's policy of "making the past serve the present" to archaeological studies.[64] But the first article by Kuo Mo-jo, president of the Academy of Science and for decades a close personal friend of Mao, is on a hand-written scroll of the Confucian *Analects* dated 710 with poems and miscellaneous notes added toward the end.[65] The scroll was discovered in 1969 at T'ulufan in Hsinkiang province. The copier, P'u T'ien-shou, was identified as a twelve-year-old student of a frontier community school. Kuo claims that P'u's calligraphic skill and ability in poetic expression amply testify that his familiarity with the basic literary education in T'ang China was very high. Kuo proudly concludes that if a twelve-year-old schoolboy at an ordinary community school in the remote region of Hsinkiang was able to demonstrate such a level of competence in Confucian education more than a thousand years ago, the claim of the Russian sinologists that Chinese culture has never spread beyond Szechwan and Kansu is obviously false.[66] It should be noted in passing that this "Confucian" scroll was included in "The Exhibition of Archaeological Finds of the People's Republic of China" in Paris, London, and Toronto. It was replaced by a "land contract" only after the anti-Confucian campaign had been launched.

276

IV. Confucian Symbolism in Historical Context

It may not be far-fetched to suggest that the actual organization of massive campaigns against Confucius launched after Lin Piao's death was a surprising development even to some members of Mao's inner circle. The politics of anti-Confucianism, which is inseparable from the eradication of Lin's ideological influence in the Party, is beyond the scope of the present study. Suffice it to say that although the "power" issue is directly involved, many journalistic accounts of an implicit attack on Chou En-lai are not yet substantiated. Some guesswork, such as the attempt to prove that the target was indeed Premier Chou by suggesting the phonological approximation of Chung-ni (Confucius' style name) and *tsung-li* (the modern term for premier), is highly speculative. However, it should be noted that the recent upsurge of anti-Confucian sentiment, despite its uncertain political consequences, is not at all a new phenomenon in modern Chinese intellectual history.

In fact, underlying these uncertainties and occasional absurdities is a consistent theme not only in the political thought of the People's Republic but also in the whole intellectual development since the fall of the imperial system in the early twentieth century: cultural iconoclasm. In other words, a strong commitment to see China reconstitute herself as an integrated political system independent of Western influence has been closely linked with an equally strong commitment to see her cultural values supplanted by new ideas imported from the West. The belief that the quest for political self-determination necessarily involves a willingness to cast away traditions that account for much of China's cultural heritage has been widely shared by modern Chinese intellectuals of different political persuasions. As a result, Confucianism, the most influential value system in China since its revival in the eleventh century, has become the principal object of iconoclastic assaults.

Actually, ever since the May Fourth Movement in 1919, Confucian symbolism has been attacked from without and corrupted from within. Indeed, systematic campaigns against "Confucius and Sons" (*K'ung-chia tien*) in the twentieth century are traceable to the publication of the *New Century* in 1907 and surely to the commencement of the New Culture Movement in 1916. As a matter of fact, the effectiveness of the *New Youth* as a weapon against Confucianism significantly outweighed its ability to promulgate *Te hsien-sheng* (Mr. Democracy) and *Sai hsien-sheng* (Mr. Science). A brief survey of the well-known anti-Confucian heroes should substantiate the claim that the only consensus of virtually all articulate Chinese intellectuals at the turn of the century was that the roots of the Confucian tradition must be eradicated before China can be "modernized." The socialist Ch'en Tu-hsiu (1879–1942), the writer Lu Hsün (1881–1936), the Kuomintang leader Wu Chih-hui (1864–1953), the classicist Chang Ping-lin (1868–1936), and the anarchist Liu Shih-p'ei (1884–1919) had little in common except their anti-Confucian sentiments.

Undoubtedly these influential minds made the odds overwhelming against the possibility that Confucian ideas would reemerge as meaningful and creative symbols in Chinese intellectual circles. But ironically it was the ostensibly staunch supporters of Confucianism who really committed the devastating blow. The elaborate scheme of Yüan Shih-k'ai to make Confucianism a "national religion" as a way of legitimizing his imperial ambitions probably did more to discredit Confucian symbols than all the anti-Confucian articles of the *New Youth* put together. The haphazard efforts of the warlords, notably Sun Ch'uan-fang and Chang Ts'ung-ch'ang, to "promote" Confucian studies as a way of enhancing their prestige discouraged sensitive youth from having any association with Confucian symbols. The politicization of Confucianism in the republican era further strengthened the belief that, as a political ideology, Confucian values had always supported the despotic system in imperial China.

Damaged by external attacks and internal corruptions, Confucian symbolism seemed to have become ossified long before the founding of the People's Republic. This enabled Levenson to describe the modern fate of Confucian China as follows:

The sageliness of Confucius may still be felt in China (or felt again), like Socrates' Europe. But Confucian civilization would be as "historical" as Greek, and modern Chinese culture as cosmopolitan as any, like the western culture that reaches now, in paperback catholicity, to "The Wisdom of Confucius." In a true world history, when all past achievements are in the museum without walls, everyone's past would be everyone else's; which implies that quite un-Confucian thing, the loss of the sense of tradition.[67]

Yet recent events in the West as well as in China impel us to take issue with this observation.

For one thing, it is inconceivable that an anti-Socratic campaign, if one could ever be launched in modern Europe, could have an impact beyond the academic ivory tower. Cultural iconoclasm—and the recent anti-Confucian campaign is in a sense a variation on the same theme—may itself be a subtle manifestation of the latent power of the Confucian tradition in contemporary China. Admittedly this is most intriguing. One possible interpretation is that the Confucian civilization has been so deeply rooted and widespread in Chinese society that its influence is still pervasive, despite more than half a century of concerted efforts to extirpate it. To be sure, many Confucian symbols have been so thoroughly ridiculed and discredited that they probably can never be reestablished as meaningful guides for social action, but the "substance" of Confucian power, so to speak, as manifested in "new" values that are structurally identifiable as of Confucian origin, is an entirely different matter. Of course this claim can only be substantiated by a sophisticated analysis of what may be called the modern transformation of Confucian symbolism. Suffice it now to say that there are definite signs showing why this line of inquiry may be fruitful.

One example readily comes to mind. Systematic efforts to eradicate Confucian influence, in the case of many modern Chinese intellectuals, were frequently accompanied by "unconscious" identifications with Confucian values. Hu Shih's militant refutation of Confucian passivity, for instance, did not at all prevent himself from becoming a "mild, kind, courteous, restrained, and magnanimous"[68] gentleman. Liu Shih-p'ei's fascination with Wang Yang-ming (1472–1529) forced him to conclude that the greatest Confucian thinker of the Ming dynasty was in essence "anti-Confucian." Wu Yü's ruthless denunciation of Confucian institutions did not divert his attention from the importance of moral rejuvenation in China. Chang Ping-lin's involvement in revolutionary activities went parallel with his commitment to "ancient text" (ku-wen) scholarship. And it is probably more than an irony that the champion of anti-Confu-

279

cianism, Ch'en Tu-hsiu himself, is now labeled a "Confucianist" at heart. On the other hand, those who tried to use Confucian symbols for political gains did not fare very well either. Lu Hsün's devastating caricatures of the so-called "reactionaries" have made them laughingstocks. It is common knowledge that most attempts at the formulation of a more Confucian political ideology have met with failure.

Thus, the Confucian symbols could not be destroyed simply by intellectual critiques; nor could they be easily manipulated for political expediency. The phenomena seem to suggest that underlying the apparent trend of cultural iconoclasm was a strong sense of confidence: no matter how much destruction there might be, Chinese identity will remain powerful. This partly explains why decades of iconoclastic attacks on traditional authorities have not yet brought about a fundamental transformation of Confucian symbolism. It is quite plausible that beneath the sound and fury of current campaigns against Confucius lurks an urgent need to demonstrate the uniqueness of the Chinese ideological line.

It is certainly false to identify Confucianism with the uniqueness of Chinese culture. This not only commits the fallacy of boundary confusion but also lacks any intellectual sophistication. But since Confucianism has significantly contributed to the formation of basic Chinese cultural traits, it would be ill-advised to advance an interpretation of the salient features of modern Chinese political culture, for instance, without an adequate knowledge of some of the basic Confucian values. Unfortunately the problem is much more complicated than that. To begin with, since the Confucian tradition does not constitute one massive whole, exhibiting solid uniformity, it cannot very well be reduced to a few core ideas such as ancestral worship, filial piety, the "three bonds" (*san-kang*), and the "five constancies" (*wu-ch'ang*). Moreover, as one of the oldest and the longest humanistic traditions in the world, Confucianism involves a highly complex process of integration, enveloping many divergent currents in religion, philosophy, arts, economics, politics, and education over a very long period of time. The spiritual orientation of pre-Ch'in Confucianism was significantly different from the institutionalized Confucian value system of the Han; the appropriation of Confucian ideas in the T'ang central bureaucracy did not at all resemble the Confucian concerns as reflected in the ethos of Sung scholar-officialdom, and the struggle of Confucian "intellectuals" against the despotic rule of the Ming court must not be confused with the plight of Confucian officials under the literary inquisition of the Ch'ing.

The diversity and richness of the Confucian heritage makes it possible to accommodate many seemingly contradictory claims. This "ecumenical" nature of Confucianism helps it to coexist with all kinds of alien forces on the one hand, and in the process assimilate much of their strength on the other. Ch'ü T'ung-tsu's analysis of the Confucianization of law[69] and Kenneth Ch'en's study of the Chinese transformation of Buddhism[70] are outstanding cases in this respect. On the other hand, having adapted itself to a variety of changing social and political conditions, Confucianism has come very close to a form of eclecticism, occasionally verging on a total disintegration of its inner identity. Thus the Jesuit scholar, Matteo Ricci (1552–1610), could vehemently criticize Neo-Confucianism and find substantive compatibility between classical Confucianism and Catholicism at the same time.[71] Equally illustrative but in a different context, T'an Ssu-t'ung (1865–1898) could claim in his *Jen-hsüeh* (Philosophy of humanity) that the notion of "humanity" (*jen*) in Confucian thought is identical to the Buddhist precept of compassion and also to the Christian doctrine of universal love.[72] Numerous other examples can be cited to show that the range of possibilities in Confucian symbolism is truly great. It should be stressed that its adaptability could also account for much of its influence on imperial institutions. The pervasiveness of Confucian symbols in Chinese culture is certainly the main reason why the unprecedented change in China since the Western impact of the mid-nineteenth century has brought about many waves of anti-Confucian campaigns.

Still, one can rightly complain that generic concepts such as "Confucian China" are extremely misleading. We must not forget about other prominent traditions like Taoism and Buddhism. We should also take into account the development of Christianity since the mid-nineteenth century and the visible presence of Islam in the southwestern parts of China. If we start to probe the resources of the folk culture and the syncretic tendencies of belief systems in

281

the lower echelons of the society, the case against the domination of Confucianism in Chinese culture seems more compelling. It is interesting to know that this was precisely how the anti-Confucian forces of the May Fourth generation shaped their tactics: to relativize Confucianism as one of the several major traditions in China and to neutralize its influence by characterizing it as merely the ideology of the educated elite. In a sense, this continues to be the strategy of current anti-Confucian campaigns. It is probably too early to predict whether it will actually work, but, in the light of historical experiences, it is not difficult to detect some serious problems.

A prelude to the current anti-Confucian campaign was Kuo Mo-jo's article on the periodization of ancient Chinese history, published in the summer of 1972, more than a year before the campaign was formally launched. Kuo's article announces the official position that the end of slave society and the beginning of feudalism in China, after many years of debate, are now to be identified as the transition from the Spring and Autumn (722–481 b.c.) to the Warring States (403–222 b.c.).[73] Confucius (551–479 b.c.), as a product of the slave society, was therefore advocating an outmoded ideology at the time when inevitable social changes had already occurred. Consequently, it is only fitting that Confucius is characterized as extremely "reactionary." The historicist argument attempts not only to relativize and neutralize Confucian influence in traditional China but also to "localize" Confucian thought in a definite historical context. However, it leaves a crucial question unanswered: How did the ideology of the slave society continue to play a dominant role in the feudal period for two thousand years?

Yang Jung-kuo, whose emphasis on class analysis was noted in the 1962 Conference on Confucius, has emerged as a leading theoretician for the anti-Confucian movement. In his recent book, *Confucius: "Sage" of the Reactionary Classes*, he again focuses his attention on Confucius' class origins and class attitudes. He flatly denies that Confucian ideas of "humanity," "loyalty," "filiality," "reciprocity," "goodness," and "rectification of names" can be abstracted from their historical specificities and claim a kind of transtemporal validity.[74] He does concede that Confucian symbols were effectively used by feudal institutions. He explains that this is because (1) the land-

282

owning class changed its historical character and held on to its political power, and (2) the feudal government, in its search for an ideology of control, abandoned the more progressive Legalism and adopted Confucianism for its selfish interests.[75] He then briefly outlines how Tung Chung-shu (c. 179-c. 104 B.C.), a leading philosopher of the Han dynasty, synthesized salient elements in Confucian teaching and formulated his "idealist transcendentalism," which eventually became the reactionary ideology of feudalistic rule in China.[76]

Having characterized Confucianism as the reactionary ideology of the ruling elite in the feudal period, Yang further argues that the mainstream of Chinese intellectual history can even be seen as a continuous appropriation and manipulation of Confucian symbols for the service of despotic governments. This naturally leads to the interpretative position that those who rebelled against the Confucian tradition were the real revolutionary spirits in Chinese history. So far, only a few have been identified. Aside from the historically controversial figures, Chih of Liu-hsia and Mao of Shao-cheng, the list includes Han Fei (d. 233 B.C.), Li Ssu (d. 208 B.C.), Shang Hung-yang (150–80 B.C.), Wang Ch'ung (27–7?), Liu Tsung-yuan (773–819), Wang An-shih (1021–1086), and Li Chih (1527–1602).[77] Among the modern writers, Lu Hsün alone is considered absolutely uncompromising in his anti-Confucian stance. Great "materialists," such as Chang Tsai (1020–1077) and Wang Fu-chih (1619–1692), are no longer mentioned. The long-ignored Legalism has suddenly surfaced as a progressive ideology. The first emperor of the Ch'in dynasty, whose coercive measures at centralization have been universally denounced throughout Chinese history, has now been rediscovered as an anti-Confucian hero.[78]

Surely, far from being an intellectual exercise or a philosophical debate, the main purpose of the anti-Confucian campaign is to generate a nationwide mass movement in order to "fix up the superstructure." By that is meant, among other things, a total weeding out of the poisonous thought of elitism in order to achieve a true "dictatorship of the proletariat." Putting theoretical niceties aside, can this be achieved simply by exposing Confucianism as the most insidious reactionary ideology in Chinese history? Perhaps the anti-Confucian campaign was only designed to liquidate Lin Piaoism. If so, the implications for the formulation of new policies on arts, literature, philosophy, history, and even archaeology would be too far-reaching to be restricted to one concrete political event. The Chinese leadership today may genuinely believe that once the Confucian "shackle" is removed, the real creativity of the masses will be naturally released, and that this will at last silence what the current literature describes as the "dark spirits" (*yu-ling*) of Confucianism.[79] Perhaps Levenson was right after all in suggesting that "the dead were no longer monuments, but ghosts and monsters to be slain again."

However, we must not forget that the "fate" of Confucianism is widely thought to have been sealed before the founding of the People's Republic. Moreover, since the majority of Chinese intellectual historians outside of China still feel that the Confucian tradition definitely ended before the republican era, the attempts to salvage it in the thirties and forties are generally labeled neotraditional, if not outright reactionary. Some scholars, depending on their vantage points, further argue that the debate on science and metaphysics in 1923, or the May Fourth Movement in 1919, or the abolition of the Examinations in 1905 was really the single most devastating blow to Confucian symbolism. This inevitably leads to the puzzling question why, long after the death of Confucianism, the Confucian "ghosts and monsters" have to be slain again and again. If we take Yang Jung-kuo's interpretation seriously, this seemingly extraordinary phenomenon actually has been characteristic of Chinese thought for centuries: Confucian symbolism should have perished together with the slave society in the third century B.C., but its "dark spirits" have been haunting the Chinese for two thousand years. Without being unduly sarcastic, I contend that the modern Chinese "obsession" with the dark side of Confucian symbolism is itself a reflection of the relevance of the Confucian tradition in defining substantive issues in China's emergent superstructure.

V. Substantive Issues of Value Priority

In conclusion, I would simply note how these issues are delicately entangled with what may be called "perennial problems in Con-

284

fucianism." However, to stress the relevance of Confucian symbols in defining some major problem areas in contemporary China is not at all to suggest that Maoism is in a sense still Confucian in character. Actually the Maoist value orientation is so alien to the ethico-religious intention of Confucianism that there is absolutely no way that the "inner sensibilities" of the Confucian tradition can be holistically grasped simply by an analysis of the articulated ideology of Maoist China. On the other hand, it is inconceivable that one can have a sophisticated appreciation and critique of the "value priority" in China without being aware of the Confucian dimension both as an intractable reality of the past and as a viable alternative for the future.

(1) As an all-embracing humanist tradition, Confucianism seeks to find *integrated* and *holistic* solutions to sociopolitical problems. Any exposure to the *Great Learning (Ta-hsüeh)* or the *Evolution of Rites (Li-yün)*[80] should convey the impression that the Confucian approach is comprehensive in character. Unlike Taoism, Buddhism, or other historical religions, Confucianism is oriented toward the peaceful but fundamental transformation of this world. Although the Confucian choice is to harmonize with rather than to master the existing conditions, a confirmed Confucian often stands in tension and conflict with the status quo. As a result, one of the central concerns in the Confucian tradition is how to be an integral part of the social collectivity without losing one's sense as an individual moral person. A Confucian is a social being but never merely an atomized entity in the crowd. The notion of continuous revolution is also intended to bring about total solutions. To be sure, it aims at a radical, not merely a gradual, transformation of the existing society. But by focusing on the human factor it has so far avoided the danger of causing irreparable damage to the human environment. It is vitally important to know how this emphasis on continuous mass mobilization, equipped with a highly advanced control mechanism, can continue to adopt an "ecologically" sound policy of social development without ever trying to harmonize with the existing conditions. Is it possible to envision the cadre as an integral part of the totality and yet at the same time as a responsible critic of it? If not, the "countercurrent" phenomenon is inconceivable.

(2) One of the core ideas in Confucianism is self-cultivation.

A key passage on this matter in the Confucian *Analects* is: "To conquer yourself and return to propriety (*li*) is humanity."[81] Due to Lin Piao's alleged preoccupation with this statement, two anthologies including more than twenty essays critical of this six-character line were published in the spring of 1974.[82] Whether or not "return to propriety" means to accept unconditionally the ideology of the slave society in the Chou dynasty, "conquer yourself" as a way of learning to be human certainly resembles the whole idea of "eradicating self-centeredness" (*ch'ü-ssu*). It is true that Confucian self-cultivation, unlike self-criticism, is intended to help one to become a *chün-tzu* (a superior or profound person) rather than to become a *kan-pu* (cadre member), but the primacy of moral self-discipline is assumed in both cases. Of course the total ideological context in which the cadre is developed has nothing to do with Confucian emphasis on the "transformation of one's material nature" (*pien-hua ch'i-chih*).[83] Nevertheless, it is quite possible that once moral qualities are stressed, the way of identifying leaders becomes not only compatible with but also reminiscent of the pattern of social mobility in a Confucian value system. Moreover, even if prescriptive conditions, like class origins, are established as major criteria of selection, *kan-pu* will still be evaluated in terms of personality traits and acquired attitudes. After all, the language of "redness" as an ethical as well as political category is often indistinguishable from the language of Confucian moral philosophy. It is certain that the Confucian symbols, at least in the near future, will not be appropriated the way Liu Shao-ch'i did in his "Black Book," *On How To Be a Good Communist*.[84] But substantive issues are likely to be discussed in a similar context.

(3) The Confucian idea of human nature is thought to be in basic conflict with the doctrine of class nature. If there were absolutely no universalizable human nature, either Mencius' belief in the moral propensity of man or Hsün Tzu's belief in man's intrinsic cognitive power to know good would be considered false. For underlying the apparent contradictions between the Mencian theory of *hsing-shan* (goodness of human nature) and Hsün Tzu's theory of *hsing-o* (the evil tendencies of human nature) is a strong commitment to man's malleability, transformability, and perfectibility through self-effort.[85] This is predicated on the assumption that despite the

diversity of human conditions, which certainly include various kinds of natural environments, primordial ties, and methods of socialization, there is a common potential shared by all persons called "humanity." Without this assumption, the Confucian insistence on universal education would be groundless. The doctrine of class nature, I suppose, is intended to bring about a more egalitarian society through class struggle. Accordingly the "dictatorship of the proletariat" does not necessarily aim to destroy other undesirable classes by sheer force; a better choice is perhaps to exercise the transforming power of education so that political goals can be reached through the art of persuasion as well. Class struggle therefore entails ideological self-criticism and psychological conversion. One wonders how this can be achieved without an awareness that class nature as well as class attitude are changeable by educational processes and that these processes are not merely superimposed from outside. If such an awareness does exist, the quest for genuine mass participation will probably lead to the question whether human nature is really definable in terms of class origins alone.

(4) As of now, formal education in China is still dominated by pragmatic and scientific methods. To be sure, in Mao's later educational directives, the old university entrance examination was virtually abolished, the curriculum at all levels of schooling shortened, practical application of knowledge emphasized, and close cooperation between productivity and academic research established. On the surface, this "politicization" of education may seem likely to have an adverse effect on theoretical sciences. In the language of "redness versus expertise," this seems a clear indication of leaning toward redness at the expense of expertise. But, to reiterate an earlier point, the real issue is not the fact of technological expertise, which I believe will continue to be highly regarded no matter how "red" the country becomes. The very fact that the universities in China are in essence institutes of science and technology should make the point clear. Certainly the question of developments in basic research in the theoretical sciences is more intriguing. But there is no reason to believe that critical studies in mathematics, physics, health-related sciences, and the like will be curtailed in China because of the educational reform. The phenomenon in the humanities and social sciences is an entirely different matter. This is, in a broad sense,

287

inseparable from the complex problem of defining or redefining "redness." It seems that the "priority of values" will continue to be a crucial concern in China for years to come. Some traditional Confucian value orientations, like bias against profit-making activities and predilection for government service, will probably remain powerful. Others, such as preferring generalists to specialists, will likely be more seriously challenged.

(5) The policy that literature and art must serve the people at the present time may not be in conflict with the notion of historical continuity. Nor must the creative energy of the masses take the form of antitraditionalism. In fact folk culture in China can exhibit a wide range of possibilities beyond the comprehension of established forms of artistic or literary expressions in the "great tradition." However, the "two-culture" concept is not fully adequate as an analytical scheme for understanding Chinese history. In fact one can learn as much about substantive Confucian issues from the *Romance of the Three Kingdoms* or the *Dream of the Red Chamber* as from the Thirteen Classics. The inability of the "culture workers" to rediscover enough popular theatrical performances that have not yet been tainted by Confucian "feudal" thought of "emperors, kings, generals, and prime ministers" is also a case in point. The whole repertoire of the Peking opera tradition as well as many other local operatic literatures are now slated for extermination. But if Lin Piao, who is alleged to have been so "anti-intellectual" that he refused to read even newspapers and books, was in fact familiar with the basic Confucian ideas, the presence of similar ideas among educated Chinese must be considerable. After all, Mao himself in his informal conversation with Wang Hai-jung revealed that he had read the *Dream of the Red Chamber* five times and found its fourth chapter a good lesson for understanding the class situation of imperial China.[86] The subtle question then is to differentiate anti-Confucianism from anti-traditionalism. Such a differentiation may also lead to a distinction between the appropriation of traditional symbols as weapons for political control and the original meanings of those symbols. It is difficult to believe that just because Wu Han has "misused" Ming history, historical allegories will no longer play an important role in political education.

(6) One of the most serious charges against Confucianism is its elitist tendency. A frequently quoted documentary evidence of this

has been Mencius' distinction between those who labor with their mental strength and those who labor with their physical strength. Since the distinction is thought to have implied the supremacy of the mental laborers, it is concluded that there has been a strong bias against working people in the Mencian tradition of Confucianism. However, historically Mencius made the remark in his debate with a physiocrat. What he intended to do there was simply to point out that it is neither possible nor desirable to have every person involved in agricultural production. He stressed the functional necessity of division of labor and argued that the scholars (or, if you wish, the intellectuals) could justify their existence and usefulness without making a direct reference to productivity. For the scholars, as the articulate members of society, must perform other equally significant duties such as government service and education.[87] Since Mencius also affirmed that the people are more important than the king and that the people have the right to rebel against tyrannical rulers,[88] he was certainly not an enemy of the people by conscious choice. The current policy to send intellectuals downward and to recruit members of the least advantaged groups to become university students might have been an utter surprise to Mencius, but the Mencian concern for the role of the intellectual in society is still a very relevant issue.

(7) The Confucian emphasis on cultural diversity is being attacked as a form of "restorationism." The idea of "restoring perished states, continuing broken lines of large families, and recruiting hermitic people for government service,"[89] which is alleged to have been another of Lin Piao's favorite quotations, is a Confucian approach to displaced people and their cherished traditions. It is diametrically opposed to the Legalist demand for conformity. The issue is partly centralization versus decentralization, but in a broader sense it is a conflict between two different ways of achieving political integration. At present, the Legalist line of uniformity seems in command. But in areas like minority relations and international cooperation, the spirit of peaceful coexistence is clearly visible. The policy toward the Five Black Groups (the landed, the rich, the reactionary, the rotten, and the revisionist) is likely to be uncompromising for some time. But it seems inevitable that eventually a conciliatory arrangement will be made. After all, continuous revolu-

tion presupposes the continuous presence not only of diversity but also of contradictions in society.

(8) Confucianism, as an ethicoreligious philosophy, has put much emphasis on society as a "fiduciary community." The primacy of harmonizing human relations in Confucian political education is one of the many manifestations of the particular focus. Even the idea of ordering society in a hierarchical structure, based on merits rather than birth, is reflective of this concern for social stability. It is often thought that this Confucian model of society has been supplanted by the need to build socialism through total mass mobilization. And the harmonizing intention of Confucian social thought is believed to have been a path to stagnation, inequality, and in current parlance, revisionism. However, this is not necessarily a flat rejection of the Confucian model of "fiduciary community." It is difficult to imagine that a critique of Confucianism in this connection might lead to the reorganization of society according to an adversary system of law. Given the existing "legal" practices in China, it seems unlikely that China will soon become "legalistic" in the sense that the American society is. On the contrary, the cohesiveness of the social structure will continue to depend on the basic trust of the people. And since the appearance of control is fundamentally different from the substance of collective participation, the real challenge to the mass line is not merely the promotion of orderliness but the disciplined expression of creative dynamism. This can only be achieved when a sense of community is shared by the overwhelming majority. Psychological terms such as "pride," "confidence," and "dedication" are different ways of describing the same phenomenon. The angry response to Antonioni's movie on China[90] and the strong attack on Western music[91] may also be understood in this context as attempts to form a new group self-definition. As China enters the pluralistic world of nations, her self-image will probably undergo many metamorphoses, but it seems that the notion of "fiduciary community" will remain strong.

Undeniably, despite the fact that Confucian ideas are still relevant in identifying substantive issues in contemporary China, Confucian symbolism as a whole has been discredited and corrupted almost to a point of no return. Ironically, just as during the Cultural

Revolution every faction of the Red Guards evoked the name of Mao to justify its activities, so all conceivable "enemies of the people" are now labeled as Confucian. In his "Directive to the Great Cultural Revolution in Shanghai" on February 12, 1967, Mao remarked that even if China was completely communized, there should still be a party, a center. It matters very little whether the party is called, in his words, "the Communist Party, the Social Democratic Party, the Social Democratic Labor Party, the Nationalist Party (*Kuomintang*), or the One-Thread Way (*I-kuan tao*)."[92] Perhaps, after the Confucian "ghosts and monsters" are absolutely subdued, a new and comprehensive ideological sturcture will emerge. Call it Socialism, Humanism, Marxism, or Maoism; for the symbol is not as important as the substance of a total and integrated value system.

NOTES

[1]Reprinted in *Modern China: An Interpretive Anthology*, edited by Joseph R. Levenson (New York: The Macmillan Company, 1971), pp. 231–32.

[2]Levenson, *Liang Ch'i-ch'ao and the Mind of Modern China* (Cambridge, Mass. Harvard University Press, 1953). See a summary of his argument in his *Confucian China and its Modern Fate: A Trilogy* (Berkeley: University of California Press, 1968), general preface, ix-x.

[3]See *Decision of the Central Committee of the Chinese Communist Party concerning the Great Proletarian Cultural Revolution*, adopted on August 8, 1966 (Peking: Foreign Languages Press, 1966), p.1. This statement is taken from Chester C. Tan, *Chinese Political Thought in the Twentieth Century* (New York: Doubleday & Company, 1971), p. 370.

[4]Levenson, *Confucian China and its Modern Fate*, general preface, x.

[5]Originally published in Albert Feuerwerker, Rhoads Murphey, and Mary C. Wright, ed. *Approaches to Modern Chinese History* pp, 268–88. Reprinted in *Modern China: An Interpretive Anthology*, p. 68.

[6]*Ibid.*

[7]Levenson, "The Past and Future of Nationalism in China," *Survey*, no. 67 (April 1968), pp. 28–40. Reprinted in *Modern China: An Interpretive Anthology*, p. 15.

[8]A term used by Levenson in "The Past and Future of Nationalism in China," *Modern China: An Interpretive Anthology*, p. 14.

[9]For a succinct account of this development in English, see Jean Esmein, *The Chinese Cultural Revolution*, trans. from French by W. J. F. Jenner (New York: Anchor Press, 1973), pp. 43–54.

[10]Teng T'o (pseudonym, Ma Nan-ts'un), *Yenshan yeh-hua* (Peking: Peking Press,

1965), pp. 182–85. It should be noted that in *The Chinese Cultural Revolution,* Teng's pseudonym is misidentified as "Mao Nan-tun."

[11] *Yenshan yeh-hua,* pp. 110–12.

[12] *Ibid.,* pp. 469–72 (Chang), pp. 315–18 (Chu-ko).

[13] *Ibid.,* pp. 18–20.

[14] *Ibid.,* pp. 156–58. The essay is entitled "Shih-shih kuan-hsin," taken from part of a line in Ku Hsien-ch'eng's famous couplet in front of the Tunglin Academy.

[15] *Ibid.,* pp. 339–42.

[16] *Ibid.,* pp. 530–32.

[17] *Ibid.,* pp. 277–79.

[18] *Ibid.,* pp. 280–82.

[19] *Ibid.,* pp. 473–76.

[20] *Ibid.,* pp. 359–62.

[21] *Ibid.,* pp. 477–80.

[22] *Ibid.,* pp. 113–16.

[23] For Chin's article on the verification of objective facts and the first three basic laws of thought in formal logic, see *Che-hsüeh yen-chiu* (abbreviated as *CHYC*) 3 (1962): 1–11. Also see Chin's article on class nature and the idea of necessity in logical inference, *CHYC* 5 (1962): 69–83.

[24] For Chu's essay on Kant's aesthetics, see *CHYC* 3 (1962): 72–93; for his essay on Goethe's aesthetics, see *CHYC* 2 (1963): 62–74.

[25] For T'ang's article, see "Lun Chung-kuo Fo-chiao wu 'Shih-tsung,' " *CHYC* 3 (1963): 47–54. Jen Chi-yü has apparently emerged as a leading scholar in contemporary China. See his *Han-T'ang Fo-chiao ssu-hsaing lun-chi* (Peking: San-lien Press, 1973). It should be noted that Mao has spoken highly of Jen's works, which are basically critical analyses of Buddhist thought in China from the perspective of dialectical materialism.

[26] Fung Yu-lan, "Chung-kuo che-hsüeh i-ch'an te chi-ch'eng wen-t'i," *CHYC* 1 (1965): 63–67.

[27] The article was written by Huang Hsin-ch'uan, see *CHYC* 6 (1962): 81–91.

[28] This is, of course, merely restating A. A. Zhadanov's assertion in his *Speech in the Discussion of G. F. Alexandrov's History of Western European Philosophy*. See Kuan Feng and Lin Yü-shih's article on "Several Problems Concerning the Class Analysis in the Study of a History of Philosophy," *CHYC* 6 (1963): 29.

[29] Liu's articles originally appeared in *Hsüeh-shu yen-chiu*. For a critique of his position as well as a summary of his argument, see Liu Yüan-yen, "P'ing Liu Chieh hsien-sheng te 'Wei-jen lun' ho 'T'ien-jen ho-i' shuo," *CHYC* 1 (1964): 32–39.

[30] For a brief report on the Conference, see *CHYC* 1 (1963): 54–57.

[31] *Ibid.,* p. 57.

[32] For two rather different interpretations of the Yang Hsien-chen controversy, see Ch'en Feng, "I-fen-wei-erh te lun-chan yü Yang Hsien-chen te shih-fei chen-hsiang," *Tsu-kuo yüeh-k'an* (Feb.–March, 1965) and "The Theory of 'Combine Two into One' Is a Reactionary Philosophy for Restoring Capitalism," in *Three Major Struggles on China's Philosophical Front (1949–64)* (Peking: Foreign

Languages Press, 1973), pp. 48–66.

[33]Mao Tse-tung, "On Contradiction," quoted in *Three Major Struggles,* p. 48.

[34]*Three Major Struggles,* p. 54.

[35]*Ibid.*

[36]The case of Fung Yu-lan is too complicated to be adequately summarized here. For our limited purpose, his pre-Cultural Revolution intellectual struggles can be characterized as attempts to formulate a positive interpretation of Confucian values in the light of the ideological trend at the time. See *CHYC* 6 (1963): 45–53. However, Fung's most recent self-criticism, after having criticized his own interpretive positions on Confucius several times since 1949, took the form of a radical denunciation of the Confucian tradition. See his "Tui-yü K'ung Tzu te p'i-p'an ho tui-yü wo kuo-ch'ü te tsun-K'ung ssu-hsiang te tzu-wo p'i-p'an" and "Fu-ku yü fan-fu-ku shih lien-t'iao lu-hsien te tou-cheng." The two articles originally appeared in *Pei-ching ta-hsüeh hsüeh-pao* 4 (1973). They were reprinted in *Kuang-ming jih-pao,* December 3–4, 1973.

[37]The recently available material includes Mao's recorded conversations, directives, articles, and other sources. Most of them have never been published before. The anthology seems to have been compiled by dedicated Maoists during the Cultural Revolution. The preface is dated August 1968. My copy is based on the Hoover Institute version. Since the material is not yet widely circulated, it will be referred to as *Mao's Unpublished Statements* (abbreviated as *Statements*). The remark was made on March 28, 1965, see *Statements,* p. 480.

[38]The remark was made on April 15, 1964. See *Statements,* p. 487.

[39]See *Statements* (March 1964), pp. 476–77. It should be noted that Mao, in this connection, did not intend to be anti-intellectual; what he tried to convey was simply the necessity of social practice as the real basis for acquiring useful knowledge. In an informal conversation with his niece, Wang Hai-jung, on June 24, 1964, Mao asked Wang, a student of English at the Foreign Languages Institute, the English word for *chih-shih fen-tzu* (intellectual). When Wang failed to provide the answer, Mao himself tried to look it up in a Chinese-English dictionary. To his regret, only the English equivalent of *chih-shih* (knowledge) was found. See *Statements,* p. 503. Mao's preoccupation with the problem of the intellectual is reflected in his other conversations as well. In particular, see *Statements,* p. 469.

[40]The remark was made in his conversation with Mao Yüan-ch'ing in March 1964. Although Mao dismissed the *People's Daily* as boring, he spoke highly of the *Liberation Army News* and *Chinese Youth News.* See *Statements,* p. 471 and pp. 579–80.

[41]The remark was made at the Hang-chou Conference in March 1963. See *Statements,* p. 442. For his criticisms of Yang Hsien-chen, see *Statements,* pp. 557–627.

[42]The remark was made in an address to the Tenth Plenum of the Central Committee on September 24, 1962. See *Statements,* p. 435.

[43]The remark was made on February 13, 1964. What Mao really had in mind was to transfer them downward to the rural areas. See *Statements,* p. 462.

[44]The remark was made in his talk on the Third Five-Year Plan on June 6, 1964. See *Statements,* p. 499.

[45]*Statements,* pp. 443–45. For a monographic study on this, see R. Baum and

F. C. Teiwes, *Ssu-ch'ing, The Socialist Education Movement of 1962–1966*, China Research Monographs 2 (Berkeley: Center for Chinese Studies, 1968).

[46]*Statements*, pp. 501–3.

[47]A most comprehensive statement on this matter was made on February 3, 1967. See *Statements*, pp. 664–65. Also, see his remark on March 1, 1967 in *Statements*, pp. 673–75. However, it seems that Mao was not particularly impressed by Yao's article. He merely stated that it managed to identify the issue, but failed to tackle it. See *Statements*, p. 626.

[48]See *Statements*, p. 640.

[49]See *Statements*, p. 641.

[50]See *Statements*, p. 664. The same expression noted on p. 641 is repeated here: "Neither a drop of water nor a thin needle could enter into the Peking Municipal Party Committee."

[51]See *Statements*, p. 640.

[52]Jean Esmein, *The Chinese Cultural Revolution*, p. 99. Since the "seven signers" were actually instructors on the faculty, in a strict sense they did not themselves represent the beginning of the student rebellion.

[53]The fascinating confrontation between Mao and the student leaders took place on July 28, 1968. See *Statements*, pp. 687–716.

[54]An expression from Lucian W. Pye, *The Spirit of Chinese Politics* (Cambridge, Mass.: MIT Press, 1968), p. 235. It should become clear that the problem of what Pye calls the gap between the phenomenon of control and the substance of development is not a central concern in my study. See *The Spirit of Chinese Politics*, pp. 235–40.

[55]Mao Tse-tung, *Selected Works*, 4 vols. (Peking: Hsin-hua Press, 1961), 3:257.

[56]*Statements*, p. 496.

[57]See his conversation with the Educational Delegation of Nepal on August 29, 1964, in *Statements*, p. 574.

[58]*Statements*, p. 472.

[59]For a sophisticated analysis of some of the basic intellectual issues in Maoism, see Frederic Wakeman, Jr., *History and Will: Philosophical Perspectives of Mao Tse-tung's Thought* (Berkeley: University of California Press, 1973), pp. 302–33.

[60]*Statements*, p. 550.

[61]He further remarked that the *Chiu T'ang-shu* is better than the *Hsin T'ang-shu*, and the *Nan-shih* and *Pei-shih* are both better than the *Chiu T'ang-shu*. He was most dissatisfied with the *Ming-shih*. See *Statements*, p. 479.

[62]It should be noted that Mao's real message was the futility of bookish knowledge. Even though he learned more about warfare from these three books than from the *Sun Tzu*, they did not help him a bit in his military campaigns. The only way to learn about warfare, he claimed, was to be involved in it. See *Statements*, p. 627.

[63]*Statements*, p. 461 and p. 463.

[64]*K'ao-ku* 1 (1972): 2.

[65]Kuo Mo-jo, "P'u T'ien-shou *Lun-yü* ch'ao-pen huo te shih-tz'u tsa-lu," *K'ao-ku* 1 (1971): 5–7. And as the editor noted, the text itself, together with annotations, was published in the following issue.

[66]*Ibid.*, p. 7.

[67]Levenson, *Confucian China and Its Modern Fate*, 3:123.

[68] A statement in the *Analects* describing the virtues of Confucius. It is quoted in Mao's "Report of an Investigation into the Peasant Movement in Hunan." It should be noted that Mao's description of the brute reality of revolution here is diametrically opposed to Hu Shih's liberal approach to social change. Mao argues: "A revolution is not the same as inviting people to dinner or writing an essay or painting a picture or embroidering a flower; it cannot be anything so refined, so calm and gentle, or so 'mild, kind, courteous, restrained, and magnanimous.' " See Stuart R. Schram, *The Political Thought of Mao Tse-tung* (New York: Praeger, 1969): 252–53.

[69]See his *Law and Society in Traditional China* (Paris and the Hague: Mouton, 1961), pp. 267–79. The book was originally published in 1917 under the title *Chung-kuo fa-lü yü Chung-kuo she-hui.*

[70]See his *The Chinese Transformation of Buddhism* (Princeton: Princeton University Press, 1973), pp. 3–13.

[71]See Matteo Ricci, *T'ien-chu shih-i* (preface, 1607, Wan-li edition), 1:37b–57b, especially 46b–47b. Ricci criticized both Neo-Confucianism and Buddhism by evoking the authority of classical Confucian ideas.

[72]See Wing-tsit Chan, "The Philosophy of Humanity (*Jen*) in T'an Ssu-t'ung," *A Source Book in Chinese Philosophy* (Princeton: Princeton University Press, 1973), p. 738.

[73]Kuo Mo-jo, "Chung-kuo ku-tai-shih te fen-ch'i wen-t'i," in *Hung-ch'i tsa-chih* 7 (1972): 56–62. The article was reprinted in *K'ao-ku* 5 (1972): 2–4.

[74]Yang Jung-kuo, *Fan-tung chieh-chi te "sheng-jen" K'ung Tzu* (Peking: Jen-min Press, 1973), pp. 26–65. It is interesting to note that 560,000 copies of the book were printed for the first edition. For an English translation see Yang Jung-kuo, *Confucius: "Sage" of the Reactionary Classes* (Peking: Foreign Languages Press, 1974). References are to the Chinese edition.

[75]*Ibid.*, pp. 71–2.

[76]*Ibid.*, pp. 73–5.

[77]For this see, *Chung-kuo li-tai fan-K'ung ho tsun-K'ung te tou-cheng* (Hong Kong: San-lien Press, 1974), Ching-ch'ih, et al., ed., *Lun tsun-Ju fan-Fa* (Hong Kong: San-lien Press, 1973), and Chao Chi-pin, *Kuan-yü K'ung Tzu chu Shao-chen Mao wen-t'i* (Peking: Jen-min Press, 1973). It is not at all far-fetched to suggest that the list almost exhausts the "genuine" anti-Confucian heroes in Chinese history, even though the case of Wang An-shih is still ambiguous.

[78]See Hung Shih-ti, *Ch'in Shih-huang* (Shanghai: Hsin-hua Press, 1973), pp. 55–72. It should be noted that since its first publication in May 1972, the book has been reprinted four times, and in total 1,350,000 copies have been printed.

[79]See Sha-ming, *K'ung-chia-tien chi-ch'i yu-ling* (Peking: Wen-chiao Press, 1970), pp. 53–68.

[80]See Wing-tsit Chan, *A Source Book in Chinese Philosophy*, pp. 84–94. Also, see Wm. T. de Bary, Wing-tsit Chan, and Burton Watson, comp., *Sources of Chinese Tradition*, 2 vols. (New York: Columbia University Press, 1960), 1:175–76.

[81]*Analects*, 12.1.

[82]See *P'i* "k'o-chi fu-li" *wen-chang hsüan-chi* (Hong Kong: San-lien Press, 1974) and *Tsai p'i* "k'o-chi fu-li" (Hong Kong: San-lien Press, 1974).

[83]A very common idea in Neo-Confucian literature. It is closely associated with the Ch'eng-Chu school of Neo-Confucianism.

[84]Originally entitled *Lun Kung-ch'an-tang-yüan te hsiu-yang* (On the self-cultivation of Communists), it is a short essay on the importance of self-cultivation in the Confucian tradition to the formation of a Communist personality. Mao is alleged to have characterized the book as absolutely un-Marxian in character.

[85]For an analytical discussion on this issue, see Donald J. Munro, *The Concept of Man in Early China* (Stanford: Stanford University Press, 1969), pp. 49–83. For a discussion of the contemporary implication of this issue, see Munro, "Man, State, and School," in "China's Developmental Experience," ed. Michel Oksenberg, *Proceedings of the Academy of Political Science* 31 (March 1973): 121–43.

[86]For Mao's reference to the *Dream of the Red Chamber*, see *Statements*, pp. 444, 529, 556, and 567.

[87]*Mencius*, 3A.4. See Wing-tsit Chan, *A Source Book of Chinese Philosophy*, pp. 69–70.

[88]*Mencius*, 1B.7, 8 and 4B.32.

[89]See *Lin Piao shih ti-ti tao-tao te K'ung lao-erh te hsin t'u* (Peking: Jen-min Press, 1974), pp. 86–9.

[90]See *P'i-p'an An-tung-ni-ao-ni p'ai-she te fan-Hua ying-p'ien "Chung-kuo"* (Hong Kong: San-lien Press, 1974). The anthology includes more than twenty angry denunciatory articles on Antonioni's approach and motivation.

[91]See *Kuan-yü piao-t'i yin-yüeh wu-piao-t'i yin-yüeh wen-t'i te t'ao-lun* (Hong Kong: San-lien Press, 1974).

[92]*Statements*, p. 671.

GLOSSARY

an-hsin li-ming　　安心立命

ch'a　　察
ch'a-teng hsing　　差等性
Chan Jo-shui (Kan-ch'üan)　　湛若水(甘泉)
Chan Kan-ch'üan (see Chan Jo-shui)
Chan Wing-tsit　　陳榮捷
Ch'an　　禪
Chang Chih-tung　　張之洞
Chang Chü-cheng　　張居正
Chang Chung-yüan　　張鍾元
Chang Fei　　張飛
Chang Hao　　張灝
Chang Lü-hsiang　　張履祥
Chang-nan　　漳南
Chang Piao　　張彪
Chang Shih (Nan-hsien)　　張栻(南軒)
Chang Ping-lin　　章炳麟
Chang Shih-chao　　章士釗
Chang Shih-ch'ing　　張石卿
Chang-shih ts'ung-shu　　章氏叢書
Chang Tsai (Heng-ch'ü)　　張載(橫渠)
Chang Tsung-ch'ang　　張宗昌
Chang Tung-sun　　張東蓀
Chang Tzu ch'üan-shu　　張子全書
Chao Chi-pin　　趙紀彬
Chao Heng　　趙衡
Chao Kung　　昭公
chao-ming　　昭明
Che-hsüeh yen-chiu　　哲學研究
"Chen-che hsüeh-an"　　震澤學案
chen-ch'ieh　　眞切
Ch'en Ch'i-yün　　陳啓雲
Ch'en Feng　　陳風
Ch'en Hsien-chang (Po-sha)　　陳獻章(白沙)

Ch'en Liang　陳亮
Ch'en Po-sha (see Ch'en Hsien-chang)
Ch'en Teng-yüan　陳登源
Ch'en Tu-hsiu　陳獨秀
cheng (correct)　正
cheng (confirmation)　證
Cheng-chung　正中
cheng-hsin　正心
Cheng-i t'ang　正誼堂
Cheng-meng　正蒙
Cheng-wen　正聞
"Cheng Yen"　正顔
ch'eng (becoming)　成
ch'eng (sincerity)　誠
Ch'eng-Chu　程朱
Ch'eng Hao (Ming-tao)　程顥(明道)
Ch'eng I (I-ch'uan)　程頤(伊川)
ch'eng-i　誠意
ch'eng-jen　成人
ch'eng-ssu　誠思
Ch'eng wei-shih lun shu-chu　成唯識論述記
chi (incipience)　機
chi (continue)　繼
Chi-fu ts'ung-shu　畿輔叢書
chi-hsü ko-ming　繼續革命
chi-wu　己物
Chi Yün　紀昀
ch'i (vital force)　氣
ch'i (instrument)　器
ch'i-chia　齊家
ch'i-chih　氣質
ch'i-chih chih hsing　氣質之性
ch'i-hsi　氣習
Ch'i-yang　祁陽
Chia-li　家禮

298

Chia-shen hsün-nan lu　　甲申殉難錄
Chia Tao　　賈島
Chiang Ch'ing　　江青
chiang-hsüeh　　講學
chiang-i　　講義
chiao-hsüeh hsiang-chang　　教學相長
chiao-k'an　　校勘
ch'iao　　巧
chieh-pan jen　　接班人
chieh-chi tuo-cheng　　階級鬭爭
chien-ai　　兼愛
chien-hsing　　踐形
chien-i　　簡易
chien-jen　　踐仁
Chien-lun　　檢論
ch'ien　　乾
Ch'ien-chou　　虔州
Ch'ien-hsien　　前綫
Ch'ien-k'un yen　　乾坤衍
Ch'ien-lung　　乾隆
Ch'ien Mu　　錢穆
Ch'ien Te-hung (Hsü-shan)　　錢德洪(緒山)
Ch'ien Wei-ch'ang　　錢偉長
Chih　　跖
chih (know)　　知
chih (wisdom)　　智
chih (to extend)　　致
chih (final particle)　　之
chih-chieh　　知解
chih-chien　　知見
chih-chih　　致知
chih-hsing　　知行
chih-hsing ho-i　　知行合一
chih-kuo　　治國
Chih-li　　直隷

chih liang-chih　致良知

chih-shan　至善

chih-shih　知識

chih-shih fen-tzu　知識分子

Chih te chih-chüeh yü Chung-kuo che-hsüeh　智的直覺與中國哲學

Chih-yen　知言

ch'ih-jen　吃人

Chin Hsü-ju　金絮如

Chin-ssu lu　近思錄

Chin Yüeh-lin　金岳霖

Ch'in-Han　秦漢

Ch'in Hui-t'ien　秦蕙田

Ch'in Shih-huang　秦始皇

ching (essence)　精

ching (reverence)　敬

ching (quietude)　靜

ching-ch'a　精察

Ching-ch'ih　景池

Ch'ing　清

ch'ing　情

chiu-kuo　救國

Chiu T'ang-shu　舊唐書

Chou　周

Chou En-lai　周恩來

Chou-li　周禮

Chou Tso-jen　周作人

Chou Tun-i (Lien-hsi)　周敦頤（濂溪）

Chou Tzu ch'üan-shu　周子全書

Chu　朱

Chu Hsi (Yüan-hui)　朱熹（元晦）

Chu-ko Liang　諸葛亮

Chu Kuang-ch'ien　朱光潛

chu-liu　主流

Chu-Lu *i-t'ung*　朱陸異同

Chu Po-k'un　朱伯昆

300

Chu Tzu chi-ch'i che-hsüeh　　朱子及其哲學

Chu Tzu chia-li　　朱子家禮

Chu Tzu ch'üan-shu　　朱子全書

Chu Tzu hsin hsüeh-an　　朱子新學案

"Chu Tzu k'u-ts'an chung-ho te ching-kuo"　　朱子苦參中和的經過

Chu Tzu nien-p'u　　朱子年譜

Chu Tzu nien-p'u k'ao-i　　朱子年譜考異

Chu Tzu ta-ch'üan　　朱子大全

Chu Tzu wan-nien ting-lun　　朱子晚年定論

Chu Tzu wen-chi　　朱子文集

Chu Tzu yü-lei　　朱子語類

Chu Tzu yü-lei p'ing　　朱子語類評

Chü-yeh lu　　居業錄

ch'ü　　去

ch'ü jen-yü　　去人欲

ch'ü-ssu　　去私

Ch'ü T'ung-tsu　　瞿同祖

Ch'ü Wan-li　　屈萬里

chuan-shih　　轉世

chüan (chapter)　　卷

chüan (aloof)　　狷

Ch'uan-hsi lu　　傳習錄

ch'üan-fa　　權法

"Ch'üan-hsüeh"　　勸學

chuang　　壯

Chuang Tzu　　莊子

chüeh　　覺

chüeh-hsing　　覺醒

Ch'uen Ts'ew (see *Ch'un-ch'iu*)

chün-tzu　　君子

Ch'un-ch'iu　　春秋

ch'ün-chung lu-hsien　　群眾路線

chung (centrality)　　中

chung (loyalty)　　忠

chung-ho　　中和

301

Chung-hua　　中華
Chung-hua Wen-hua　　中華文化
"Chung-kuo che-hsüeh i-ch'an te chi-ch'eng wen-t'i"　　中國哲學遺產的繼承問題
Chung-kuo che-hsüeh shih　　中國哲學史
Chung-kuo che-hsüeh-shih lun-wen chi　　中國哲學史論文集
Chung-kuo che-hsüeh te t'e-chih　　中國哲學的特質
Chung-kuo che-hsüeh yüan-lun　　中國哲學原論
Chung-kuo chin san-pei nien hsüeh-shu shih　　中國近三百年學術史
Chung-kuo fa-lü yü Chung-kuo she-hui　　中國法律與中國社會
Chung-kuo hsüeh-jen　　中國學人
Chung-kuo jen-hsing-lun shih　　中國人性論史
"Chung-kuo ku-tai-shih te fen-ch'i wen-t'i"　　中國古代史的分期問題
Chung-kuo li-tai fan-K'ung ho tsun-K'ung te tou-cheng　　中國歷代反孔和尊孔的鬥爭
Chung-kuo tsao-ch'i ch'i-meng ssu-hsiang shih　　中國早期啓蒙思想史
Chung-kuo wen-hua yen-chiu so　　中國文化研究所
Ch'ung-chen　　崇禎
Chung-yung　　中庸
chung-shu　　忠恕
Chung-ni　　仲尼
Chung Ling　　鍾錂
Chung-yang wen-wu kung-ying she　　中央文物供應社

Erh-Ch'eng i-shu　　二程遺書

Fa-hsiang　　法相
Fan Chen　　范縝
Fan Chung-yen　　范仲淹
fan-shen k'e-chi chih kung　　反身克己之功
Fan Shou-k'ang　　范壽康
Fan-tung chieh-chi te "sheng-jen" K'ung Tzu　　反動階級的聖人孔子
fen　　分
fen-shu　　分殊
fen-ting　　分定
Feng-t'ien fu　　奉天府

Fo-chia ming-hsiang t'ung-shih　　佛家名相通釋
Fu-hsi　　伏羲
Fu-hsing　　復性
Fu Hsüan　　傅玄
Fu-k'ao　　赴考
"Fu-ku yü fan-fu-ku shih liang-t'iao lu-hsien te tou-cheng"　　復古與反復古是兩條路線的鬥爭
fu-li　　復禮
Fung Yu-lan　　馮友蘭

Hai Jui　　海瑞
Han　　漢
Han Fei　　韓非
Han-T'ang Fo-chiao ssu-hsiang lun-chi　　漢唐佛教思想論集
Han T'o-chou　　韓侂冑
han-yang　　涵養
Hang-chou　　杭州
ho　　和
Ho Ch'ang-ch'ün　　賀昌群
ho-erh wei-i　　合二爲一
Ho Hsin-yin　　何心隱
ho-i　　合一
Ho Shen-mu　　何樫木
hou-t'ien chih-hsüeh　　後天之學
Hou Wai-lu　　侯外盧
hsi　　翕
Hsi-chai　　習齋
Hsi-chai chi-yü　　習齋記餘
hsi-hsin　　習心
hsi-li　　習禮
"Hsi-ming"　　西銘
Hsia　　夏
Hsiang　　襄
Hsiang-shan ch'üan-chi　　象山全集
hsiang-shu　　象數
"Hsiang-tang"　　鄉黨

303

hsiang-yüan　鄉愿

hsiao　孝

Hsiao I-yü　蕭亦玉

hsiao-p'in wen　小品文

hsiao-t'i　小體

Hsieh Liang-tso　謝良佐

Hsieh Yu-wei　謝幼偉

hsien　現

Hsien-Ch'in chu-tzu hsi-nien　先秦諸子繫年

hsien-t'ien chih hsüeh　先天之學

hsin (mind)　心

hsin (new)　新

hsin-chih-t'i　心之體

Hsin ch'ing-nien　新青年

hsin-hsing　心性

hsin-hsing chih hsüeh　心性之學

Hsin-hsüeh (see *hsin-hsüeh*)

hsin-hsüeh　心學

Hsin-hua　新華

hsin-li　心理

Hsin shih-chi　新世紀

Hsin T'ang-shu　新唐書

Hsin-t'i yü hsing-t'i　心體與性體

Hsin-ya hsüeh-pao　新亞學報

Hsin-ya shu-yüan hsüeh-shu nien-k'an　新亞書院學術年刊

Hsin Wei-shih lun　新唯識論

hsing (nature)　性

hsing (action)　行

hsing-ch'a　省察

hsing-ch'i chih ssu　形氣之私

hsing-ch'ing　性情

Hsing-li ta-ch'üan　性理大全

hsing-o　性惡

hsing-shan　性善

hsing-t'　性體

hsiu-shen　修身
Hsiung Shih-li　熊十力
hsü　恤
Hsü Fu-kuan　徐復觀
Hsü Heng　許衡
Hsü Kuang-ch'i　徐光啓
Hsü Shen　許慎
Hsü Shih-ch'ang　徐世昌
Hsü Yüeh　徐樾
hsüeh　學
hsüeh-an　學案
Hsüeh Hsüan (Wen-ch'ing)　薛瑄(文清)
hsüeh-shu　學術
hsüeh-shu t'ao-lun hui　學術討論會
Hsüeh-shu yen-chiu　學術研究
Hsüeh-tou　雪竇
Hsün Tzu　荀子
Hu An-kuo (Wen-ting)　胡安國(文定)
Hu Chü-jen　胡居仁
Hu Hung (Wu-feng)　胡宏(五峯)
Hu Shih　胡適
Hu Yüan　胡瑗
huan　幻
Huan mi-t'u　喚迷途
Huang Hsin-ch'uan　黃心川
Huang Tsung-hsi　黃宗羲
Huang Tsung-hsien　黃宗賢
Huang Yen-p'ei　黃炎培
hui　會
Hun-t'un　混沌
Hung-ch'i tsa-chih　紅旗雜誌
Hung Ming-shui　洪銘水
Hung Shih-ti　洪世滌

I　易

i (intentionality)　意
i (righteousness)　義
i-li chih-hsing　義理之性
i-li　義理
I-li　儀禮
I-kuan tao　一貫道
"I-fen-wei-erh te lun-chan yü Yang Hsien-chen te shih-fei chen-hsiang"　一分爲二的論戰與楊獻珍的是非眞相
i-fa　已發
I-ching　易經
i-chien　易簡
I-shu　遺書
I-wen　藝文

Jan Ch'iu　冉求
jen (humanity)　仁
jen (comprehension)　認
jen (forbearance)　任
Jen che jen yeh　仁者人也
Jen Chi-yü　任繼愈
jen-hsin　人心
Jen-hsüeh　仁學
jen-jen　仁人
jen-min　人民
jen-shu　仁熟
"Jen-shuo"　仁說
jen-tao　人道
jen-yü　人欲
Jih-lu　日錄
Ju-chung　汝中
Juan Yüan　阮元

K'ai-ming　開明
kan-pu　幹部
kang　剛
K'ang-chai hsien-sheng chi　康齋先生集

306

K'ang-hsi tzu-tien 康熙字典

K'ang Sheng 康生

K'ang Yu-wei 康有爲

Kao Tsan-fei 高贊非

Kao Tsung 高宗

Kao Tzu 告子

k'ao-chü 考據

K'ao-ku 考古

k'e 克

k'e-chi 克己

ko-wu 格物

k'o-hsüeh wan-neng 科學萬能

Ku-chi tao-tu 古籍導讀

Ku Hsien-ch'eng 顧憲成

ku-kuai 古怪

ku-wen 古文

Ku Yen-wu 顧炎武

K'u-ch'a sui-pi 苦茶隨筆

Kuan Chung 管仲

Kuan Feng 關鋒

kuan-li 冠禮

Kuan-yü K'ung Tzu chu Shao-cheng Mao wen-t'i 關于孔子誅少正卯問題

Kuan-yü piao-t'i yin-yüeh wu-piao-t'i yin-yüeh wen-t'i te t'ao-lun 關于標題音樂無標題音樂問題的討論

Kuang-ming jih-pao 光明日報

Kuang-wen 廣文

K'uang 匡

k'uang 狂

kuei-shen 鬼神

K'uei-chi 窺基

kung-fu 工夫

Kung-sun Lung 公孫龍

Kung-tu Tzu 公都子

K'ung-chia tien 孔家店

K'ung-chia-tien chi-ch'i yu-ling 孔家店及其幽靈

Kuo Ai-ch'un　　郭靄春
Kuo Mo-jo　　郭沫若
Kuo-shih ta-kang　　國史大綱

lao　　老
lao-hsin che　　勞心者
lao-li che　　勞力者
Lao Tzu　　老子
Li (see *li*, ritual)
li (ritual)　　禮
li (principle)　　理
li-ch'eng　　立誠
Li-chi　　禮記
li-ch'i　　理氣
li-chiao　　禮教
Li Chih　　李贄
li-chih　　立志
Li-hsüeh　　理學
li-i (righteous principle)　　理義
li-i (oneness of principle)　　理一
li jen-chi　　立人極
"Li-yün"　　禮運
Li Yen-p'ing (see Li T'ung)
Li-wen shou-ch'ao　　禮文手鈔
Li T'ung (Yen-p'ing)　　李侗(延平)
Li Ssu　　李斯
Li Kung (Shu-ku)　　李塨(恕谷)
Li Kou　　李覯
Liang Ch'i-ch'ao　　梁啓超
liang-chih　　良知
Liang Shu-ming (see Liang Sou-ming)
Liang Sou-ming　　梁漱溟
Liao Mo-sha　　廖沫沙
Lieh Tzu　　列子
Lin Piao　　林彪

308

Lin Piao shih ti-ti tao-tao te K'ung lao-erh te hsin-t'u　林彪是地地道道的孔老二的信徒

Lin Yü-sheng　林毓生

Lin Yü-shih　林聿時

ling-chüeh　靈覺

Liu Chieh　劉節

Liu-hsia　柳下

Liu Hsiang　劉向

Liu Hsiang Hsin fu-tzu nien-p'u　劉向歆父子年譜

liu hsien-sheng　六先生

Liu Hsin　劉歆

liu-hsing　六行

liu-i　六藝

Liu Shao-ch'i　劉少奇

Liu Shih-p'ei　劉師培

Liu Shu-hsien　劉述先

Liu Tsung-chou (Chi-shan, Nien-t'ai)　劉宗周(蕺山，念臺)

Liu Tsung-yüan　柳宗元

Liu Tzu-ch'ien　劉子健

Liu Yü-yün　劉毓鋆

Liu Yüan-yen　劉元彥

Lo Cheng-an　羅整菴

Lu　魯

Lu Hsiang-shan (Chiu-yüan)　陸象山(九淵)

Lu Hsün　魯迅

Lu Lung-ch'i　陸隴其

Lu P'ing　陸平

Lu Ting-i　陸定一

Lu-Wang　陸王

Lü Chen-yü　呂振玉

Lü-shih ch'un-ch'iu　呂氏春秋

Lü Tsu-ch'ien　呂祖謙

"Lun Chung-kuo Fo-chiao wu 'Shih-tsung' "　論中國佛教無十宗

Lun Kung-ch'an-tang-yüan te hsiu-yang　論共產黨員的修養

Lun tsun-Ju fan-Fa　論尊儒反法

Lun-yü　　論語
Lun-yü chi-chu　　論語集註
"Lun-yü lun-jen lun"　　論語論仁論
Lung-ching　　龍井
Lung Tzu　　龍子

Ma I-fu　　馬一浮
Ma Nan-ts'un　　馬南邨
Ma Tzu-hsin　　馬子莘
Mao (Confucius' contemporary)　　卯
Mao Tse-tung　　毛澤東
Mao Yüan-ch'ing　　毛遠清
Mei Kuang　　梅廣
Meng Kung-ch'o　　孟公綽
Ming (see *ming*, bright)
ming (bright)　　明
ming (dynasty)　　命
Ming-Ch'ing　　明清
ming-chüeh　　明覺
Ming-ju hsüeh-an　　明儒學案
ming-liu hsüeh-che　　名流學者
Mo Ti　　墨翟
Mo Tzu　　墨子
Mou Tsung-san　　牟宗三
mu　　睦

Nan-shih　　南史
Nanjio Bunyū　　南條文雄
"Nei-tse"　　內則
nei-hsing　　內省
nei-tsai te ni-chüeh t'i-cheng　　內在的逆覺體證
nei-wai　　內外
neng　　能
Nien-p'u　　年譜
Niu　　牛

Ou-yang Ching-wu　　歐陽竟无
Ou-yang Hsiu　　歐陽修

pa-pen sai-yüan　　拔本塞源
pai-hua　　白話
Pei-ching ta-hsüeh hsüeh-pao　　北京大學學報
Pei-hsüeh　　北學
Pei-shih　　北史
pen　　本
pen-hsin　　本心
pen-i　　本意
pen-t'i　　本體
pen-t'i lun　　本體論
P'eng Chen　　彭眞
P'eng Te-huai　　彭德懷
pi-chi　　筆記
Pi-yen chi　　碧嚴集
Pi-yen lu　　碧巖錄
pi-yu-shih yen　　必有事焉
p'i　　闢
P'i "k'o-chi fu-li" *wen-chang hsüan-chi*　　批克己復禮文章選輯
P'i-p'an An-tung-ni-ao-ni p'ai-she te fan-Hua ying-p'ien "Chung-kuo"
批判安東尼奧尼拍攝反華影片中國
pien-hua ch'i-chih　　變化氣質
pien-wei　　辨僞
P'ing Hsiung Shih-li ti Hsin Wei-shih lun　　評熊十力的新唯識論
"P'ing Liu Chieh hsien-sheng te 'Wei-jen lun' ho 'T'ien-jen ho-i
shuo'"　　評劉節先生的唯仁論和天人合一說
p'ing t'ien-hsia　　平天下
Po-yeh　　博野
p'u　　樸
pu-jen　　不仁
P'u T'ien-shou　　卜天壽
"P'u T'ien-shou *Lun-yü* ch'ao-pen huo te shih-tz'u tsa-lu"　　卜天壽論語抄本后的詩詞雜錄

311

Sai hsien-sheng　賽先生
San-chia ts'un cha-chi　三家村扎記
san-kang　三綱
San-kuo yen-i　三國演義
san-li　三禮
San-lien　三聯
San-min　三民
Sha Ming　沙明
shan-o　善惡
Shang Hung-yang　桑弘羊
Shang-wu　商務
shao　少
Shao-cheng　少正
Shao Yung　邵雍
she　射
she-hui shih-chien　社會實踐
She-king (see *Shih-ching*)
shen (body)　身
shen (spiritual)　神
shen-chiao　身教
shen-hsin chih chiao　身心之教
shen-hsin chih hsüeh　身心之學
shen-hui　神會
Shen Tsung　神宗
Shen Yu-ting　沈有鼎
sheng　生
sheng-hsien　聖賢
sheng-jen chih hsüeh　聖人之學
Sheng-ming te hsüeh-wen　生命的學問
Shih　詩
shih (timeliness)　時
shih (solid)　實
shih (knight of the Way)　士
Shih-chieh　世界
shih-chien shih-yung chu-i　實踐實用主義

312

Shih-ching　詩經
shih-chuan　世轉
shih-hsüeh　實學
"Shih-jen"　識仁
"Shih-jen p'ien"　識仁篇
Shih-li yü-yao　十力語要
Shih-li yü-yao ch'u-hsü　十力語要初續
"Shih-shih kuan-hsin"　事事關心
Shou-wen chieh-tzu　說文解字
shu (writing)　書
shu (mathematics)　數
shu (reciprocity)　恕
Shu　書
Shun　舜
ssu　思
ssu-ch'ing　四清
Ssu-en　思恩
ssu-hsiang　思想
ssu-i　私意
Ssu-ku chai　思古齋
Ssu-ku jen　思古人
Ssu-ma Ch'ien　司馬遷
Ssu-ma Kuang　司馬光
Ssu-pu pei-yao　四部備要
Ssu-shu　四書
Ssu-shu cheng-wu　四書正誤
Ssu-shu chi-chu　四書集註
Ssu-ts'un　四存
Ssu-ts'un Hsüeh-hui　四存學會
ssu-wu　四無
ssu-yu　四有
ssu-yü　私欲
su　素
Sui　隋
sui　歲

Sun Ch'uan-fang　　孫傳芳
Sun Fu　　孫復
Sun Tzu　　孫子
Sung　　宋
Sung-Ming　　宋明
"Sung-Ming ju-hsüeh chung chih-shih chu-i ti ch'uan-t'ung"　　宋明儒學中智識主義的傳統
Sung-Ming li-hsüeh kai-shu　　宋明理學概述
Sung-Yüan hsüeh-an　　宋元學案

"Ta Chang Heng-ch'ü ting-hsing shu"　　答張橫渠定性書
ta-che　　大者
Ta-hsüeh　　大學
Ta-hsüeh ching-yen chiang-i　　大學經筵講義
"Ta-hsüeh wen"　　大學問
ta-hua　　大化
ta-i　　大易
ta-jen　　大人
Ta-kung pao　　大公報
ta-t'i　　大體
ta-t'ung　　大同
ta-tzu-pao　　大字報
ta-wo　　大我
"Ta yu-jen wen"　　答友人問
Tai Chen (Tung-yüan)　　戴震(東原)
Tai Tung-yüan (see Tai Chen)
Tai Wang　　戴望
t'ai-chi　　太極
"T'ai-chi-t'u shuo"　　太極圖說
T'ai-chou　　泰州
t'an-ch'i　　彈棋
T'an Ssu-t'ung　　譚嗣同
tang-ch'üan　　當權
T'ang (king)　　湯
T'ang (dynasty)　　唐

T'ang Chün-i　　唐君毅

T'ang Yung-t'ung　　湯用形

Tao　　道

tao-ch'i　　道器

tao-hsin　　道心

tao-t'ung　　道統

Te-an　　德安

te chih ts'e　　德之賊

Te hsien-sheng　　德先生

te jun-shen　　德潤身

Teng Hsiao-p'ing　　鄧小平

Teng T'o　　鄧拓

t'i　　體

t'i-ch'a　　體察

t'i-cheng　　體證

t'i-chih　　體之

t'i ch'ün-ch'en　　體群臣

t'i-hui　　體會

t'i-jen (to embody humanity)　　體仁

t'i-jen (experiential comprehension)　　體認

t'i-tao　　體道

t'i-wei　　體味

t'i-yen　　體驗

t'i-yung　　體用

Tiao Meng-chi　　刁蒙吉

T'ien　　天

T'ien-chou　　田州

T'ien-chu shih-i　　天主實義

t'ien-li　　天理

T'ien Ming (see *T'ien-ming*)

T'ien-ming　　天命

t'ou-nao　　頭腦

Tsai-hsing yü hsüan-li　　才性與玄理

Tsai-p'i "k'o-chi fu-li"　　再批克己復禮

ts'ai　　才

Tsang Wu-chung　臧武仲

tsao-fan yu-li　造反有理

tsao-hua chih ching-ling　造化之精靈

Ts'ao Tuan　曹端

Tseng Kuo-fan　曾國藩

Tseng Tzu　曾子

Tso-chuan　左傳

Tso Chuen (see *Tso-chuan*)

tso-yu ming　座右銘

tso-yung　作用

ts'o hsin yü wu　措心於無

Tsou Ch'ien-chih　鄒謙之

Tsu-kuo yüeh-k'an　祖國月刊

ts'un　存

Ts'un-chih pien　存治編

Ts'un-hsing pien　存性編

Ts'un-hsüeh pien　存學編

Ts'un-jen pien　存人編

ts'un t'ien-li　存天理

ts'un t'ien-li ch'ü jen-yü　存天理去人欲

tsung-chih　宗旨

tsung-li　總理

Tsung-lun　總論

Ts'ung-shu chi-ch'eng　叢書集成

"Ts'ung Sung-Ming ju-hsüeh ti fa-chan lun Ch'ing-tai ssu-hsiang shih"　從宋明儒學的發展論清代思想史

Tsze-kung (see Tzu Kung)

Tu-ching shih-yao　續經示要

tu-shih　篤實

Tu-shu lu　讀書錄

Tu Wei-ming　杜維明

Tuan　段

tuan　端

tuan-ch'ang　斷常

tuan-hsü　端緒

316

"Tui-yü K'ung Tzu te p'i-p'an ho tui-yü wo kuo-ch'ü te tsun-Kung ssu-hsiang te tzu-wo p'i-p'an"　　對於孔子的批判和對於我過去的尊孔思想的自我批判

Tung Chung-shu　　董仲舒

Tung-fang Jen-wen Yu-hui　　東方人文友會

Tung-lin　　東林

Tung-sheng　　東昇

T'ung-chien kang-mu　　通鑑綱目

T'ung-shu　　通書

tuo-ch'üan　　奪權

Twan (see Tuan)

Tzu-chih t'ung-chien　　資治通鑑

Tzu-hsia　　子夏

tzu-jan liu-hsing　　自然流行

Tzu-kung　　子貢

Tzu-lu　　子路

Tzu-ssu　　子思

tzu-ssu　　自私

tz'u　　詞

Wai-shu　　外書

Wan-li　　萬曆

wan-wu　　萬物

Wang An-shih　　王安石

Wang Chi (Lung-hsi)　　王畿（龍溪）

Wang Ch'uan-shan (see Wang Fu-chih)

Wang Ch'ung　　王充

Wang Fa-ch'ien　　王法乾

Wang Fu-chih (Ch'uan-shan)　　王夫之（船山）

"Wang Fu-chih lun pen-t'i ho hsien-hsiang"　　王夫之論本體和現象

Wang Hai-jung　　王海蓉

Wang Hsing-hsien　　王星賢

"Wang-hsüeh ti fen-hua yü fa-chan"　　王學的分化與發展

Wang Ken　　王艮

Wang K'un-shen　　王崑繩

317

"Wang Lung-hsi hsien-sheng chuan"　王龍溪先生傳

Wang Lung-hsi yü-lu　王龍溪語錄

Wang Mou-hung　王懋竑

Wang Pi　王弼

Wang P'in (Hsin-po)　王蘋（信伯）

Wang-tao lun　王道論

Wang Wen-ch'eng Kung ch'üan-shu　王文成公全書

Wang Yang-ming (Shou-jen)　王陽明（守仁）

Wang Yang-ming ch'üan-shu　王陽明全書

Wang Yang-ming chih-liang-chih chiao　王陽明致良知教

Wang Yü-chung　王于中

Wang Yüan　王源

wei　味

wei-chi　爲己

wei-fa　未發

wei-jen　爲人

Wei-shih　唯識

Wei Yüan　魏源

wen　文

Wen-chiao　文教

wen-chien chih chih　聞見之知

Wen-hsing　文星

Wen-hui pao　文匯報

wen-jen　文人

Weng Fang-kang　翁方綱

"Wo yü Hsiung Shih-li hsien-sheng"　我與熊十力先生

wu (nonbeing)　無

wu (thing)　物

wu-hua　物化

wu-hsin chih hsin　無心之心

Wu Han (writer)　吳哈

Wu Han (general)　吳漢

Wu Chih-hui　吳稚暉

Wu Ch'eng　吳澄

wu-ch'ang　五常

Wu-ch'ang　武昌

318

Wu-li t'ung-k'ao　五禮通考
wu-lun　五倫
Wu Nan-hsing　吳南星
wu-so-pu-pao　無所不包
wu-wei　無爲
Wu Yü　吳虞
wu-yü　物欲
Wu Yü-pi　吳與弼

yang　陽
Yang Hsien-chen　楊獻珍
Yang Jung-kuo　楊榮國
Yang Lien-sheng　楊聯陞
Yang-ming ch'üan-shu　陽明全書
"Yang-ming hsien-sheng mu-chih-ming"　陽明先生墓誌銘
Yang-ming-hsüeh shu-yao　陽明學述要
Yang P'ei-chih　楊培之
Yang Shih　楊時
Yang Wen-hui　楊文會
Yao　堯
yao-chih　要旨
Yao Wen-yüan　姚文元
Yen　鄂
yen　驗
yen-chiao　言敎
Yen-ching-shih chi　揅經室集
Yen Chün　顏鈞
Yen Hsi-chai (see Yen Yüan)
Yen Hsi-chai che-hsüeh ssu-hsiang shu　顏習齋哲學思想述
Yen Hsi-chai hsien-sheng nien-p'u　顏習齋先生年譜
Yen Hsi-chai hsien-sheng p'i-i lu　顏習齋先生闢異錄
Yen Hsi-chai hsien-sheng yen-hsing lu　顏習齋先生言行錄
Yen Hsi-chai hsüeh-p'u　顏習齋學譜
Yen Hsi-chai yü Li Shu-ku　顏習齋與李恕谷
Yen Hui　顏回
Yen-Li　顏李

"Yen-Li hsüeh-p'ai yü hsien-tai chiao-yü ssu-hsiang" 顏李學派與現代教育思想

Yen-Li ts'ung-shu 顏李叢書

Yen-shan yeh-hua 燕山夜話

Yen-shih hsüeh-chi 顏氏學記

Yen Yüan (Hsi-chai) 顏元(習齋)

Yen Yüan yü Li Kung 顏元與李塨

Yin 殷

yin (female principle) 陰

yin (compatibility) 婣

Yin Hai-kuang 殷海光

Yin-ming ta-su shan-chu 因明大疏刪注

Yin-shun 印順

yin-yang 陰陽

yu (concerned) 憂

yu (friendship) 友

yu-ling 幽靈

yu-tao 有道

Yu Tso 游酢

yü 御

yü-lu 語錄

Yü Ying-shih 余英時

Yüan 元

Yüan-hsüeh yüan-chiang 原學原講

Yüan Jang 原壤

Yüan-ju 原儒

Yüan Shih-k'ai 袁世凱

yüan-t'ung 元同

Yüan-wu 圓悟

yüeh 樂

yung (courage) 勇

yung (function) 用

SELECTED BIBLIOGRAPHY

Abe Yoshio 阿部吉雄. *Nihon Shushigaku to Chōsen* 日本朱子學と朝鮮 (Japan's Chu Hsi learning and Korea). Tokyo: Tokyo daigaku shuppankai 東京大學出版會, 1965.

—— *Ri Tai-kei* 李退溪. Kōbe: Bunkyō shoin 文教書院, 1944.

Adorno, Theodor W. *The Jargon of Authenticity*, trans. Knut Tarnowski and Frederic Will. Evanston: Northwestern University Press, 1973.

Araki Kengo 荒木見悟. *Bukkyo to Jukyo: Chūgoku shisō o keisei suru mono* 佛敎と儒教—中國思想を形成するもの (Buddhism and Confucianism: The formation of Chinese thought). Kyoto: Heirakuji shoten 平樂寺書店, 1963.

Balazs, Étienne. *Chinese Civilization and Bureaucracy: Variations on a Theme*, trans. H. M. Wright. New Haven: Yale University Press, 1964.

Baum, R., and F. C. Teiwes. *Ssu-ch'ing: The Socialist Education Movement of 1962–1966.* Berkeley: Center for Chinese Studies, 1968.

Bellah, Robert N. *Tokugawa Religion: The Values of Pre-Industrial Japan.* Glencoe, Ill.: Free Press, 1957.

—— ed. *Religion and Progress in Modern Asia.* New York: Free Press, 1965.

—— *Beyond Belief: Essays on Religion in a Post-Traditional World.* New York: Harper & Row, 1970.

Boodberg, Peter. "The Semasiology of Some Primary Confucian Concepts." *Philosophy East and West* 2.4:317–32 (January 1953).

Booth, Wayne C. *Modern Dogma and the Rhetoric of Assent.* Chicago: University of Chicago Press, 1974.

Brière, O. *Fifty Years of Chinese Philosophy*, trans. Laurence G. Thompson. London: Allen & Unwin, 1956.

Bruce, J. Percy, trans. *The Philosophy of Human Nature by Chu Hsi.* London: Probsthain, 1922.

—— *Chu Hsi and His Masters.* London: Probsthain, 1923.

Burke, Kenneth. *The Rhetoric of Religion.* Boston: Beacon Press, 1961.

Chan, Wing-tsit. *Religious Trends in Modern China.* New York: Columbia University Press, 1953.

—— "The Evolution of the Confucian Concept *Jen.*" *Philosophy East and West* 4.4:295–315 (January 1955).

—— trans. *Instructions for Practical Living and other Neo-Confucian*

Writings by Wang Yang-ming. New York: Columbia University Press, 1963.

———— "The Evolution of the Neo-Confucian Concept of *Li* as Principle." *Tsing-hua Journal of Chinese Studies,* n.s. 4.2:113–48 (February 1964).

———— *Neo-Confucianism, etc.: Essays by Wing-tsit Chan.* Hanover, N.H.: Oriental Society, 1969.

Chang, Carsun. *The Development of Neo-Confucian Thought.* 2 vols. New York: Bookman, 1957.

Chang Chi-yŏn 張志淵. *Chosŏn Yugyo yŏnwŏn* 朝鮮儒敎淵源 (The origins of Korean Confucianism). Reprint, Seoul: Asea munhwasa 亞細亞文化社, 1973.

Chang Chün-mai (Carsun) 張君勱. *Pi-chiao Chung-Jih Yang-ming-hsüeh* 比較中日陽明學 (A comparative study of the Wang Yang-ming school in China and Japan). Taipei: Chung-hua wen-hua ch'u-pan-she 中華文化出版社, 1955.

Chang Hao. *Liang Ch'i-ch'ao and Intellectual Transition in China, 1890–1907.* Cambridge, Mass.: Harvard University Press, 1971.

Chang Tsai 張載. *Chang Tzu ch'üan-shu* 張子全書 (Complete works of Master Chang). SPPY ed.

Chang Tung-sun 張東蓀. *Hsin che-hsüeh lun-ts'ung* 新哲學論叢 (A new collection of essays on philosophy). Shanghai: Commercial Press, 1934.

———— *Tao-te che-hsüeh* 道德哲學 (Moral philosophy). Reprint, Taipei: Lu-shan ch'u-pan-she 廬山出版社, 1972.

Chao Chi-pin 趙紀彬. *Ku-tai Ju-chia che-hsüeh p'i-p'an* 古代儒家哲學批判 (Critique of ancient Confucianism). Shanghai: Chung-hua shu-chü 中華書局, 1950.

———— *Kuan yü K'ung Ch'iu sha Shao-cheng Mao* 關于孔丘殺少正卯 (On the question of Confucius' execution of Shao-cheng Mao). Peking: Jen-min ch'u-pan-she 人民出版社, 1974.

———— *Lun-yü hsin-t'an* 論語新探 (Fresh probes into the *Analects*). Peking: Jen-min 人民, 1976.

Ch'en Ch'i-yün. *Hsün Yüeh: The Life and Reflections of an Early Medieval Confucian.* Cambridge: Cambridge University Press, 1975.

Ch'en, Jerome. *Mao and the Chinese Revolution.* London: Oxford University Press, 1965.

Ch'en, Kenneth K. S. *Buddhism in China.* Princeton: Princeton University Press, 1964.

———— *The Chinese Transformation of Buddhism*. Princeton: Princeton University Press, 1973.

Ch'en Teng-yüan 陳登源. *Yen Hsi-chai che-hsüeh ssu-hsiang shu* 顏習齋哲學思想述 (A survey of Yen Hsi-chai's philosophical thought). Nanking: Chung-kuo wen-hua yen-chiu-so 中國文化研究所, 1934.

Cheng Chung-ying 成中英. *Chung-kuo che-hsüeh yü Chung-kuo wen-hua* 中國哲學與中國文化 (Chinese philosophy and Chinese culture). Taipei: San-min 三民, 1934.

———— *Tai Chen's Inquiry into Goodness*. Honolulu: East-West Press, 1971.

Ch'eng Hao 程顥 and Ch'eng I 程頤. *Erh-Ch'eng i-shu* 二程遺書 (Surviving works of the two Ch'engs), in *Erh-Ch'eng ch'üan-shu* 二程全書 (Complete works of the two Ch'engs). SPPY ed.

Chiang Wei-ch'iao 蔣維喬. *Chung-kuo chin san-pai-nien che-hsüeh-shih* 中國近三百年哲學史 (History of Chinese philosophy in the last three hundred years). Reprint, Taipei: Chung-hua 中華, 1972.

Ch'ien Mu 錢穆. *Kuo-hsüeh kai-lun* 國學概論 (Introduction to national learning). Chungking: Commercial Press, 1931.

———— *Chung-kuo chin san-pai-nien hsüeh-shu-shih* 中國近三百年學術史 (History of Chinese scholarship in the last three hundred years). Shanghai: Commercial Press, 1940.

———— *Chung-kuo ch'uan-t'ung cheng-chih* 中國傳統政治 (Politics in traditional China). Hong Kong: Chung-kuo wen-t'i yen-chiu-so 中國問題研究所, 1950.

———— *Chung-kuo wen-hua-shih tao-lun* 中國文化史道論 (An introduction to Chinese cultural history). Taipei: Cheng-chung shu-chu 正中書局, 1951.

———— *Sung Ming li-hsüeh kai-shu* 宋明理學概述 (A general discussion on Sung-Ming Neo-Confucianism). 2 vols. Taipei: Chung-hua wen-hua ch'u-pan shih-yeh wei-yüan-hui 中華文化出版事業委員會, 1953.

———— *Yang-ming hsüeh shu-yao* 陽明學述要 (A summary of Yang-ming's learning). Reprint, Taipei: Cheng-chung 正中, 1954.

———— *Hsien Ch'in chu-tzu hsi-nien* 先秦諸子繫年 (Chronological studies of pre-Ch'in philosophers). Reprint, Hong Kong: Hong Kong University Press, 1956.

———— *Lun-yü hsin-chieh* 論語新解 (A new explanation of the *Analects*).

Hong Kong: New Asia Institute Press, 1963.

———— *Chu Tzu hsin hsüeh-an* 朱子新學案. (A new scholarly record of Chu Hsi's philosophy). 5 vols. Taipei: San-min 三民, 1971.

———— *Chung-kuo wen-hua ching-shen* 中國文化精神 (The spirit of Chinese culture). Taipei: San-min 三民, 1971.

Chin Hsü-ju 金絮如. *Yen Yüan yü Li Kung* 顏元與李塨 (Yen Yüan and Li Kung). Shanghai: Commercial Press, 1935.

Ching-ch'ih 景池, et al. *Lun tsun-Ju fan Fa* 論尊儒反法 (Essays on supporting Confucianism against Legalism). Hong Kong: San-Lien 三聯, 1973.

Ching, Julia. *To Acquire Wisdom: The Way of Wang Yang-ming.* New York: Columbia University Press, 1976.

Chou Tun-i 周敦頤. *Chou Tzu ch'üan-shu* 周子全書 (Complete works of Master Chou). Wan-yu wen-k'u 萬有文庫 ed.

Chow Tse-tsung. *The May Fourth Movement: Intellectual Revolution in Modern China.* Cambridge, Mass.: Harvard University Press, 1960.

Chu Hsi 朱熹. *Chu Tzu ta-ch'üan* 朱子大全, also known as *Chu Tzu wen-chi* 朱子文集 (Collected literary works of Master Chu). SPPYed.

———— *Ssu-shu chi-chu* 四書集註 (Collected commentaries on the Four Books). Reprint, Taipei: Shih-chieh 世界, 1952.

Chu Po-k'un 朱伯昆. *Chung-kuo che-hsüeh-shih lun-wen-chi* 中國哲學史論文集 (Collected essays on the history of Chinese philosophy). Peking: Chung-hua 中華, 1965.

Ch'ü T'ung-tsu. *Law and Society in Traditional China.* Paris and The Hague: Mouton, 1961.

Ch'ü Wan-li 屈萬里. *Ku-chi tao-tu* 古籍導讀 (Guide to ancient texts). Taipei: K'ai-ming 開明, 1964.

Chung-kuo che-hsüeh-shih wen-t'i t'ao-lun chuan-chi 中國哲學史問題討論專集 (Proceedings of discussion on problems in history of Chinese philosophy), ed. Che-hsüeh yen-chiu pien-chi-pu 哲學研究編輯部. 2 vols. Peking: K'o-hsüeh ch'u-pan-she 科學出版社, 1957.

Cox, Harvey. *The Secular City.* New York: Macmillan, 1965.

Creel, Herrlee G. *Confucius, the Man and the Myth.* New York: John Day, 1949. Paperback ed. retitled *Confucius and the Chinese Way.* New York: Harper and Row, 1960.

Cua, A. S. *Dimensions of Moral Creativity: Paradigms, Principles, and Ideals.* University Park: Pennsylvania State University Press, 1978.

Danto, Arthur C. *Mysticism and Morality: Oriental Thought and*

Moral Philosophy. New York: Basic Books, 1972.

Dardess, John W. *Conquerors and Confucians: Aspects of Political Change in Late Yüan China.* New York: Columbia University Press, 1973.

Day, Clarence Burton. *The Philosophers of China.* New York: Citadel Press, 1962.

de Bary, Wm. Theodore, et al., comps. *Sources of Chinese Tradition.* New York: Columbia University Press, 1960.

———— ed. *Self and Society in Ming Thought.* New York: Columbia University Press, 1970.

———— ed. *The Unfolding of Neo-Confucianism.* New York: Columbia University Press, 1975.

Deutsch, Eliot. *Humanity and Divinity: An Essay in Comparative Metaphysics.* Honolulu: The University Press of Hawaii, 1970.

Dimberg, Ronald G. *The Sage and Society: The Life and Thought of Ho Hsin-yin.* Honolulu: The University Press of Hawaii, 1974.

Dubs, Homer H. *Hsuntze, the Moulder of Ancient Confucianism.* London: Probsthain, 1927.

———— trans. *The Works of Hsuntze.* London: Probsthain, 1928.

———— "The Development of Altruism in Confucianism." *Philosophy East and West* 1.1:48–55 (April 1951).

Dumoulin, Heinrich. *A History of Zen Buddhism.* Boston: Beacon Press, 1969.

Durkheim, Émile. *On Morality and Society; Selected Writings,* ed. Robert N. Bellah. Chicago: The University of Chicago Press, 1973.

Eisenstadt, S. N. *The Political Systems of Empires.* New York: Free Press, 1963.

———— ed. *Protestant Ethic and Modernization.* New York: Basic Books, 1968.

Erikson, Erik H. *Gandhi's Truth: On the Origins of Militant Nonviolence.* New York: Norton, 1969.

———— *Toys and Reasons: Stages in the Ritualization of Experience.* New York: Norton, 1977.

———— ed. *Adulthood.* New York: Norton 1978.

Fairbank, John K., ed. *Chinese Thought and Institutions.* Chicago: University of Chicago Press, 1957.

———— ed. *The Chinese World Order.* Cambridge, Mass.: Harvard University Press, 1968.

————*The United States and China*. 3rd ed. Cambridge, Mass.: Harvard University Press, 1972.

Fan Shou-k'ang 范壽康. *Chu Tzu chi ch'i che-hsüeh* 朱子及其哲學 (Chu Hsi and his philosophy). Taipei: K'ai-ming 開明, 1964.

Fang Tung-mei 方東美. *Chung-kuo jen-sheng che-hsüeh kai-yao* 中國人生哲學概要 (An outline of philosophy of life in China). Taipei: Hsin-chih ch'u-pan-she 新知出版社, 1974.

Fingarette, Herbert. *The Self in Transformation: Psychoanalysis, Philosophy and the Life of the Spirit*. New York: Basic Books, 1963.

———— "Human Community as Holy Rite: An Interpretation of the Confucian *Analects*." *Harvard Theological Review* 59.1:53–67 (1966).

———— *Confucius—The Secular as Sacred*. New York: Harper & Row, 1972.

Freeman, Manfield. "Yen Hsi-chai, a 17th Century Philosopher." *Journal of the North China Branch of the Royal Asiatic Society* 57:70–91 (1926).

———— trans. *Yen Yüan's Preservation of Learning with an Introduction on His Life and Thought*. Monumenta Serica Monograph 16 (1973).

Fung Yu-lan 馮友蘭. *Chung-kuo che-hsüeh shih* 中國哲學史 (A history of Chinese philosophy). Shanghai: Commercial Press, 1931.

———— *Hsin li-hsüeh* 新理學 (A new discourse on the learning of the Principle). Ch'ang-sha: Commercial Press, 1939.

———— *Hsin shih-hsün* 新世訓 (A new discourse on instructions for the world). Shanghai: K'ai-ming 開明, 1941.

———— *Hsin yüan-jen* 新原人 (A new discourse on humanity). Chungking: Commercial Press, 1943.

———— *Hsin yüan-tao* 新原道 (A new discourse on the Way). Shanghai: Commercial Press, 1946.

———— *Hsin chih-yen* 新知言 (A new discourse on understanding words). Shanghai: Commercial Press, 1946.

———— *Hsin shih-lun* 新事論 (A new discourse on human affairs). Shanghai: Commercial Press, 1947.

———— *A Short History of Chinese Philosophy*, ed. Derk Bodde. New York: Macmillan, 1948.

———— *A History of Chinese Philosophy*, trans. Derk Bodde. Princeton: Princeton University Press, 1952–53.

———— *Chung-kuo che-hsüeh-shih lun-wen-chi* 中國哲學史論文集 (Collection of essays on history of Chinese philosophy). Shanghai: Jen-min 人民, 1958.

—— *Ssu-shih-nien ti hui-ku* 四十年的回顧 (Reminiscences of the last forty years). Peking: K'o-hsüeh 科學, 1959.

—— *Chung-kuo che-hsüeh-shih hsin-pien* 中國哲學史新編 (A new compilation of History of Chinese philosophy). Peking: Jen-min 人民, 1962.

—— "Chung-kuo che-hsüeh i-ch'an te chi-ch'eng wen-t'i" 中國哲學遺產的繼承問題 (Problems concerning the succession of Chinese philosophical inheritance). *Che-hsüeh yen-chiu* 哲學研究 (Philosophical Research) 1:63–67 (1965).

—— *Lun K'ung Ch'iu* 論孔丘 (On Confucius). Peking: Jen-min 人民, 1975.

Fumoto Yasutaka 麓保孝. *Hokusō ni okeru Jugaku no tenkai* 北宋に於ける儒學の展開 (The unfolding of Confucianism in the Northern Sung). Tokyo: Shōseki bunbutsu ryūtsū-kai 書籍文物流通會, 1967.

Furth, Charlotte, ed. *The Limits of Change: Essays on Conservative Alternatives in Republican China*. Cambridge, Mass.: Harvard University Press, 1976.

Geertz, Clifford. *The Interpretation of Cultures*. New York: Basic Books, 1973.

Graham, A. C. *Two Chinese Philosophers*. London: Lund Humphries, 1958.

Granet, Marcel. *Chinese Civilization*, trans. Kathleen E. Innes and Mabel R. Brailsford. New York: Knopf, 1930.

Grieder, Jerome B. *Hu Shih and the Chinese Renaissance: Liberalism in the Chinese Revolution, 1917–1937*. Cambridge, Mass.: Harvard University Press, 1970.

Hampshire, Stuart. *Thought and Action*. New York: Viking Press, 1967.

—— *Freedom of Mind and Other Essays*. Princeton: Princeton University Press, 1971.

Ho Lin 賀麟. *Wen-hua yü jen-sheng* 文化與人生 (Culture and human life). Shanghai: Commercial Press, 1947.

—— *Tang-tai Chung-kuo che-hsüeh* 當代中國哲學 (Contemporary Chinese philosophy). Nanking: Sheng-li ch'u-pan-she 勝利出版社, 1947.

———— *Ju-chia ssu-hsiang hsin-lun* 儒家思想新論 (A new treatise on Confucian thought). Peking: Cheng-chung 正中, 1948.

Hou Wai-lu 侯外廬. *Chung-kuo ku-tai she-hui-shih* 中國古代社會史 (Social history in ancient China). Shanghai : Hsin-chih shu-tien 新知書店, 1948.

———— *Chung-kuo tsao-ch'i ch'i-meng ssu-hsiang shih* 中國早期啓蒙思想史 (A history of early enlightenment thought in China). Shanghai: Commercial Press, 1956.

———— et al. *Chung-kuo ssu-hsiang t'ung-shih* 中國思想通史 (A comprehensive history of Chinese thought). 5 vols. Peking: Jen-min 人民, 1957–1963.

———— et al. *Chung-kuo chin-tai che-hsüeh-shih* 中國近代哲學史 (A history of modern Chinese philosophy). Peking: Jen-min 人民 1978.

Hsiao Kung-ch'üan 蕭公權. *Chung-kuo cheng-chih ssu-hsiang-shih* 中國政治思想史 (History of Chinese political thought). 2 vols. Chungking: Commercial Press, 1945–46.

———— *A Modern China and a New World: K'ang Yu-wei, Reformer and Utopian, 1858–1927*. Seattle: University of Washington Press, 1975.

Hsiung Shih-li 熊十力. *Hsin Wei-shih lun* 新唯識論 (New exposition of the Consciousness-only doctrine). 3 vols. Peking: Peking University Press, 1933.

———— *Shih-li yü-yao* 十力語要 (Essential sayings of Hsiung Shih-li). Peking: Pei-ching ch'u-pan-she 北京出版社, 1935 .

———— *Shih-li yü-yao ch'u-hsü* 十力語要初續 (An initial supplement to Hsiung Shih-li's essential sayings). Hong Kong: Tung-sheng yin-wu-chü 東昇印務局, 1949.

———— *Yuan Ju* 原儒 (On the origins of Confucianism). Shanghai: Lung-men shu-chu 龍門書局, 1956.

———— *Tu-ching shih-yao* 讀經示要 (Essential ways of reading the classics). Reprint, Taipei: Kuang-wen 廣文, 1960.

———— *Fo-chia ming-hsiang t'ung-shih* 佛家名相通釋 (Buddhist concepts explained). Reprint, Taipei: Kuang-wen 廣文, 1961.

———— *Ch'ien-k'un yen* 乾坤衍 (An elaboration on the hexagrams of Ch'ien and K'un). Reprint, Taipei: Hsüeh-sheng shu-chü 學生書局, 1976.

———— *Ming-hsin p'ien* 明心篇 (An essay on enlightening the mind)

328

Reprint, Taipei: Hsüeh-sheng 學生, 1976.

—— *T'i-yung lun* 體用論 (On substance and function). Reprint, Taipei: Hsüeh-sheng 學生, 1976.

sü Cho-yün. *Ancient China in Transition.* Stanford: Stanford University Press, 1965.

sü Fu-kuan 徐復觀. *Hsiang-shan hsüeh-shu* 象山學術 (On Lu Hsiang-shan's scholarship). Hong Kong: Min-chu p'ing-lun she 民主評論社, 1955.

—— *Hsüeh-shu yü cheng-chih chih-chien* 學術與政治之間 (Between scholarship and politics). Taichung: Chung-yang shu-chü 中央書局, 1957.

—— *Chung-kuo ssu-hsiang-shih lun-chi* 中國思想史論集 (Collection of essays on history of Chinese thought). Taichung: Tunghai University Press, 1959.

—— *Chung-kuo jen-hsing-lun shih hsien-Ch'in p'ien* 中國人性論史先秦篇 (A history of Chinese views on human nature in the pre-Ch'in period). Taichung: Tunghai University Press, 1963.

—— *Chung-kuo i-shu ching-shen* 中國藝術精神 (The spirit of arts in China). Taichung: Tunghai University Press, 1966.

—— *Hsü Fu-kuan wen-lu* 徐復觀文錄 (Collection of essays by Hsü Fu-kuan). 4 vols. Taipei: Huan-yü ch'u-pan-she 環宇出版社, 1971.

—— *Chou Ch'in Han cheng-chih she-hui chieh-kuo chih yen-chiu* 周秦漢政治社會結構之研究 (Study of the political and social structures in the Chou, Ch'in and Han dynasties). Hong Kong: New Asia Institute Press, 1972.

—— *Liang Han ssu-hsiang-shih* 兩漢思想史 (Intellectual history of the Western and Eastern Han dynasties). Hong Kong: Hong Kong Chinese University Press, 1975.

Isü Shen 許慎. *Shuo-wen chieh-tzu* 說文解字 (Ancient words discussed, modern characters analyzed). Reprint, Taipei: I-wen 藝文, 1958.

Iu Shih. *The Development of the Logical Method in Ancient China.* Shanghai: Oriental Book Co., 1928.

—— 胡適. *Chung-kuo che-hsüeh shih ta-kang* 中國哲學史大綱 (An outline of history of Chinese philosophy). Shanghai: Commercial Press, 1928.

—— *Tai Tung-yüan ti che-hsüeh* 戴東原的哲學 (The philosophy of

Tai Chen). Taipei: Commercial Press, 1967.

Huang Siu-chi. *Lu Hsiang-shan, a Twelfth-Century Chinese Idea Philosopher*. New Haven: American Oriental Society, 1944.

Huang Tsung-hsi 黃宗羲. *Ming-ju hsüeh-an* 明儒學案 (Schola record of Ming Confucians). SPPY ed.

———— *Sung-Yüan hsüeh-an* 宋元學案 (Scholarly record of the Su and Yüan). SPPY ed.

Hucker, Charles O. *China: A Critical Bibliography*. Tucson: Unive sity of Arizona Press, 1962.

Hughes, E. R. *Chinese Philosophy in Classical Times*. London: Der 1954.

Hung Shih-ti 洪世滌. *Ch'in Shih Huang* 秦始皇 (The First Emper of Ch'in). Shanghai: Hsin-hua 新華, 1973.

Hyŏn Sang-yun 玄相允. *Chosŏn Yuhak sa* 朝鮮儒學史 (A history Korean Confucianism). Seoul: Minjung Sŏwan 民衆書舘, 194

Jen Chi-yü 任繼愈. *Han-T'ang Fo-chiao ssu-hsiang lun-chi* 漢唐佛 思想論集 (Collected essays on Han-T'ang Buddhist though Hong Kong: San-lien 三聯, 1973.

———— et al. *Chung-kuo che-hsüeh-shih chien-pien* 中國哲學史簡編 (concise account of the history of Chinese philosophy). Pekin Jen-min 人民, 1974.

Jung, C. G. *Psychology and Religion: West and East*, trans. R. F. Hull. New York: Pantheon Books, 1958.

Jung Chao-tsu 容肇祖. *Ming-tai ssu-hsiang-shih* 明代思想史 (Intelle tual history of the Ming period). Shanghai: K'ai-ming 開明 1941.

Kant, Immanuel. *Foundations of the Metaphysics of Morals*, tran Lewis W. Beck. New York: Bobbs-Merrill Co., 1969.

Kojima Yūma 小島祐馬. *Chūgoku shisō shi* 中國思想史 (A history Chinese thought). Tokyo: Sōbunsha 創文社, 1968.

Ku Chieh-kang 顧頡剛. *Hsien-Ch'in ti fang-shih yü ju-sheng* 先秦的 方士與儒生 (Taoist practitioners and Confucian scholars in th pre-Ch'in period). Shanghai: Jen-min 人民, 1957.

Kuan Feng 關鋒 and Lin Yü-shih 林聿時. *Ch'un-ch'iu che-hsüeh-shi lun-chi* 春秋哲學史論集 (A collection of essays on history of philo ophy in the Spring and Autumn period). Peking: Jen-min 人民 1963.

K'ung-tzu che-hsüeh t'ao-lun-chi 孔子哲學討論集 (Collected essays o the discussions of Confucius' philosophy), ed. Che-hsüeh yen-chiu pien-chi-pu 哲學研究編輯部. Peking: Chung-hua 中華, 1963.

Kuo Chan-po 郭湛波, *Chin wu-shih-nien Chung-kuo ssu-hsiang-shih* 近五十年中國思想史 (History of Chinese thought in the last fifty years). Peking: Jen-wen shu-tien 人文書店, 1936.

———— *Chung-kuo chung-ku ssu-hsiang-shih* 中國中古思想史 (History of Chinese thought in the medieval period). Hong Kong: Lung-men 龍門, 1967.

Kuo Mo-jo 郭沫若. *Shih p'i-p'an shu* 十批判書 (Ten critiques). Chungking: Ch'un-i ch'u-pan-she 群益出版社, 1945.

Kwok, D. W. Y. *Scientism in Chinese Thought, 1900–1950.* New Haven: Yale University Press, 1965.

Lao Ssu-kuang 勞思光. *Chung-kuo che-hsüeh-shih* 中國哲學史 (A history of Chinese philosophy). 2 vols. Hong Kong: Hong Kong Chinese University Press, 1968–1971.

———— *Wen-hua wen-t'i lun-chi* 文化問題論集 (Collection of essays on cultural problems). Kowloon: Tzu-yu ch'u-pan-she 自由出版社, 1971.

———— *Chung-kuo wen-hua yao-i* 中國文化要義 (Essential features of Chinese culture). Hong Kong: Chinese University of Hong Kong, 1972.

Lau, D. C. "Theories of Human Nature in *Mencius* and *Shyuntzy*." *Bulletin of the School of Oriental and African Studies* 15: 541–565 (1953).

———— trans. *Mencius*. London: Penguin Books, 1970.

Legge, James. *The Chinese Classics.* 5 vols. Oxford: Clarendon Press, 1893–1895.

Levenson, Joseph R. *Liang Ch'i-ch'ao and the Mind of Modern China.* Cambridge, Mass.: Harvard University Press, 1953.

———— *Confucian China and Its Modern Fate: A Trilogy.* Berkeley: University of California Press, 1968.

———— *Modern China: An Interpretive Anthology.* New York: Macmillan, 1971.

———— "The Genesis of *Confucian China and Its Modern Fate*," in *The Historian's Workshop*, ed. Perry L. Curtis, Jr. New York: Basic Books, 1972.

Lévi-Strauss, Claude. *Totemism*, trans. Rodney Needham. Boston: Beacon Press, 1963.

——— *Structural Anthropology*, trans. Claire Jacobson and Brooke G. Schoepf. New York: Basic Books, 1963.

——— *The Raw and the Cooked*, trans. John and Doreen Weightman. New York: Harper & Row, 1969.

Li Tu 李杜. *Chung-hsi che-hsüeh ssu-hsiang chung te T'ien-tao yü Shang-ti* 中西哲學思想中的天道與上帝 (The Way of Heaven and God in Chinese and Western philosophical thought). Taipei: Lien-ching ch'u-pan shih-yeh kung-ssu 聯經出版事業公司, 1978.

Liang Ch'i-ch'ao 梁啓超. *Hsien-Ch'in cheng-chih ssu-hsiang shih* 先秦政治思想史 (History of political thought in the pre-Ch'in period). Shanghai: Commercial Press, 1925.

——— *Ch'ing-tai hsüeh-shu kai-lun* 清代學術概論 (Introduction to Ch'ing scholarship). Shanghai: Commercial Press, 1927.

——— *Chung-kuo chin san-pai-nien hsüeh-shu-shih* 中國近三百年學術史 (History of Chinese scholarship in the last three hundred years). Shanghai: Commercial Press, 1935.

——— *Intellectual Trends in the Ch'ing Period*, trans. Immanuel Hsü. Cambridge, Mass.: Harvard University Press, 1959.

Liang Shu-ming 梁漱溟. *Tung-hsi wen-hua chi ch'i che-hsüeh* 東西文化及其哲學 (Eastern and Western cultures and their philosophies). Peking: Ts'ai-cheng-pu yin-shua-chü 財政部印刷局, 1921.

——— *Chung-kuo min-tsu tzu-chiu yün-tung chih tsui-hou chüeh-wu* 中國民族自救運動之最後覺悟 (Final awakening of the national self-salvation movement of the Chinese people). Shanghai: Commerical Press, 1932.

——— *Chung-kuo wen-hua yao-i* 中國文化要義 (Essential meanings of Chinese culture). Shanghai: Commercial Press, 1949.

Lin Mou-sheng. *Men and Ideas, An Informal History of Chinese Political Thought*. New York: John Day, 1942.

Lin Yü-sheng. "The Evolution of the Pre-Confucian Meaning of *Jen* and the Confucian Concept of Moral Autonomy." *Monumenta Serica* 31:172–204 (1974–75).

Liu, Alan P. L. *Communication and National Integration in Communist China*. Berkeley: University of California Press, 1971.

Liu, James T. C. *Reform in Sung China: Wang An-shih (1021–1086) and His New Policies*. Cambridge, Mass.: Harvard University Press, 1959.

——— *Ou-yang Hsiu: An Eleventh-Century Neo-Confucian*. Stanford:

University Press, 1967.

———— "How Did a Neo-Confucian School Become the State Orthodoxy?" *Philosophy East and West* 23.4:483–505 (October 1973).

Liu Shu-hsien 劉述先. *Hsin shih-tai che-hsüeh ti hsin-nien yü fang-fa* 新時代哲學的信念與方法 (Belief and method of philosophy in the new era). Taipei: Commercial Press, 1966.

———— *Wen-hua che-hsüeh ti shih-t'an* 文化哲學的試探 (A preliminary inquiry into cultural philosophy). Taipei: Chih-wen ch'u-pan-she 志文出版社, 1970.

Liu Wu-chi. *A Short History of Confucian Philosophy*. London: Penguin Books, 1955.

Liu Yüan-yen 劉元彥. "P'ing Liu Chieh hsien-sheng te 'Wei-jen lun' ho 'T'ien-jen ho-i' shuo" 評劉節先生的唯仁論和天人合一說 (Critique of Mr. Liu Chieh's discourse on the "primacy of humanity" and the "unity of Heaven and man"). *Che-hsüeh yen-chiu* 哲學研究 (Philosophical Research) 1: 32–39 (1964).

Lo, Winston Wan. *The Life and Thought of Yeh Shih*. Hong Kong: Chinese University of Hong Kong, 1974.

Lovejoy, Arthur O. *Essays in the History of Ideas*. Baltimore: Johns Hopkins Press, 1948.

Lu Hsiang-shan 陸象山. *Hsiang-shan ch'üan-chi* 象山全集 (Complete works of Hsiang-shan). SPPY ed.

Lukes, Steven. *Individualism*. Oxford: Basil Blackwell, 1973.

Mak Chung-kwei 麥仲貴. *Wang-men chu-tzu chih-liang-chih hsüeh chih fa-chan* 王門諸子致良知學之發展 (The study of conscience by the scholars of the Wang Yang-ming school in the Ming dynasty). Hong Kong: Chinese University Press, 1973.

Mao Tse-tung. *Selected Works*. 4 vols. Peking: Hsin-hua, 1961.

Marcel, Gabriel. *Creative Fidelity*, trans. Robert Rosthal. New York: Farrar, Strauss & Co., 1964.

———— *Searchings*. New York: Newman Press, 1967.

Metzger, Thomas A. *Escape from Predicament: Neo-Confucianism and China's Evolving Political Culture*. New York: Columbia University Press, 1977.

Mishima Fuku 三島復. Ō *Yōmei no tetsugaku* 王陽明の哲學 (The philosophy of Wang Yang-ming). Tokyo: Ookayama 大岡山, 1934.

Moltmann, Jürgen. *Man: Christian Anthropology in the Conflicts of the Present*, trans. John Sturdy. Philadelphia: Fortress Press, 1974.

Mote, F. W. *The Poet Kao Ch'i, 1336–1374.* Princeton: Princeton University Press, 1962.

———— *Intellectual Foundations of China.* New York: Alfred A. Knopf, 1971.

Mou Tsung-san 牟宗三. *Li hsing ti li-hsiang chu-i* 理性的理想主義 (Rational idealism). Hong Kong: Jen-wen ch'u-pan-she 人文出版社, 1950.

———— *P'i Mao Tse-tung ti "Mao-tun lun"* 闢毛澤東的矛盾論 (Critique of Mao Tse-tung's "On Contradiction"). Hong Kong: Jen-wen 人文, 1952.

———— *Wang Yang-ming chih-liang-chih chiao* 王陽明致良知教 (Wang Yang-ming's teaching of extending innate knowledge). Taipei: Chung-yang wen-wu kung-ying-she 中央文物供應社, 1954.

———— *Li-shih che-hsüeh* 歷史哲學 (Philosophy of history). Taipei: Ch'iang-sheng ch'u-pan-she 强生出版社, 1955.

———— *Jen-shih-hsin chih p'i-p'an* 認識心之批判 (Critique of the cognitive mind). Hong Kong: Yu-lien ch'u-pan-she 友聯出版社, 1956–1957.

———— *Tao-te ti li-hsiang chu-i* 道德的理想主義 (Moral idealism). Taichung: Tunghai University Press, 1959.

———— *Cheng-tao yü chih-tao* 政道與治道 (The way of politics and the way of government). Taipei: Kuang-wen 廣文, 1961.

———— *Ts'ai-hsing yü hsüan-li* 才性與玄理 (Native endowment and metaphysical principles). Hong Kong: Jen-sheng ch'u-pan-she 人生出版社, 1962.

———— *Chung-kuo che-hsüeh ti t'e-chih* 中國哲學的特質 (Characteristics of Chinese philosophy). Hong Kong: Jen-sheng 人生, 1963.

———— *Hsin-t'i yü hsing-t'i* 心體與性體 (The substance of the mind and the substance of nature). 3vols. Taipei: Cheng-chung 正中, 1969.

———— *Sheng-ming ti hsüeh-wen* 生命的學問 (The learning of life). Taipei: San-min 三民, 1970.

———— *Chih ti chih-chüeh yü Chung-kuo che-hsüeh* 智的直覺與中國哲學 (Intellectual intuition and Chinese philosophy). Taipei: Commercial Press, 1971.

———— *Hsien-hsiang yü wu-tzu-shen* 現象與物自身 (Phenomenon and the thing-in-itself). Taipei: Commercial Press, 1975.

———— *Fo-hsing yü po-jo* 佛性與般若 (Buddha nature and *prajñā*

wisdom). 2 vols. Taipei: Hsueh-sheng 學生, 1977.

Mungello, David E. *Leibniz and Confucianism: The Search for Accord.* Honolulu: The University Press of Hawaii, 1977.

Munro, Donald J. *The Concept of Man in Early China.* Stanford: Stanford University Press, 1969.

——— *The Concept of Man in Contemporary China.* Ann Arbor: University of Michigan Press, 1977.

Naess, Arne and Alastair Hannay, eds. *Invitation to Chinese Philosophy.* Oslo: Universitetsforlaget, 1972.

Nagel, Thomas. *The Possibility of Altruism.* Princeton: Princeton University Press, 1970.

Needham, Joseph. *Science and Civilization in China.* Vol. 2. Cambridge: Cambridge University Press, 1956.

Nelson, Benjamin. "Self-Images and Systems of Spiritual Direction in the History of European Civilization," in *The Quest for Self-Control*, ed. S. Z. Klausner. New York: Free Press, 1965.

——— "Scholastic *Rationales* of 'Conscience,' Early Modern Crises of Credibility, and the Scientific-Technocultural Revolutions of the 17th and 20th Centuries," *Journal for the Scientific Study of Religion* 7.2:157–177 (1968).

——— *The Idea of Usury from Tribal Brotherhood to Universal Otherhood.* Chicago: University of Chicago Press, 1969.

——— "Science and Civilization, 'East' and 'West,': Joseph Needham and Max Weber," in *Philosophical Foundations of Science*, ed. Raymond J. Seeger and Robert S. Cohen. Dordrecht, Holland: D. Reidel, 1969.

——— "Conscience and the Making of Early Modern Cultures: *The Protestant Ethic* Beyond Max Weber." *Social Research* 36.4:4–21 (1969).

——— "The Quest for Certitude and the Book of Scripture, Nature, and Conscience," in *The Nature of Scientific Discovery*. ed. Owen Gingerich. Washington, D.C.: Smithsonian Institution, 1975.

——— "Copernicus and the Quest for Certitude: 'East' and 'West,'" in *Vistas in Astronomy*, vol. 17, ed. Arthur Beer and K. A. Strand. Oxford: Pergamon Press, 1975.

Nivison, David S. *The Life and Thought of Chang Hsüeh-ch'eng.* Stanford: Stanford University Press, 1966.

——— and Arthur Wright, eds. *Confucianism in Action.* Stanford:

Stanford University Press, 1959.

Ogihara Hiroshi 荻原擴. *Shū Ren-kei no tetsugaku* 周濂溪の哲學 (The philosophy of Chou Lien-hsi). Tokyo: Fuji Shoten 藤井書店, 1935.

Okada Takehiko 岡田武彦. *Ō Yōmei to Minmatsu no Jugaku* 王陽明と明末儒學 (Wang Yang-ming and Late Ming Confucianism). Tokyo: Meitoku shuppansha 明德出版社, 1970.

Otto, Rudolf. *Mysticism East and West*, trans. Bertha L. Bracey and Richenda C. Payne. New York: Macmillan, 1960.

Pae Chong-ho 裵宗鎬. *Han'guk Yuhak sa* 韓國儒學史 (A history of Korean Confucianism). Seoul: Yŏnsei taehakkyo ch'ulp'anbu 延世大學校出版部, 1974.

Pepper, S. C. *Sources of Value*. Berkeley: University of California Press, 1958.

Pocock, J. G. A. *Politics, Language and Time: Essays on Political Thought and History*. New York: Atheneum, 1973.

Polanyi, Michael. *Personal Knowledge: Towards a Post-Critical Philosophy*. London: Routledge & Kegan Paul, 1962.

Poole, Roger. *Towards Deep Subjectivity*. London: Penguin Press, 1972.

Pye, Lucian W. *The Spirit of Chinese Politics: A Psychocultural Study of the Authority Crisis in Political Development*. Cambridge, Mass.: M.I.T. Press, 1968.

Rawls, John. *A Theory of Justice*. Cambridge, Mass.: Harvard University Press, 1971.

Ricci, Matteo. *T'ien-chu shih-i* 天主實義 (The real meaning of the Heavenly Lord). Wan-li 萬曆 ed., 1607.

Richards, I. A. *Mencius on the Mind*. London: Kegan Paul, Trench, Trubner & Co., 1932.

Ricoeur, Paul. *The Symbolism of Evil*, trans. Emerson Buchanan. Boston: Beacon Press, 1969.

―――― *The Conflict of Interpretations: Essays in Hermeneutics*, ed. Don Ihde. Evanston: Northwestern University Press, 1974.

―――― *The Rule of Metaphor: Multidisciplinary Studies of the Creation of Meaning in Language*, trans. Robert Czerny. Toronto: University of Toronto Press, 1977.

Rongen, Ole Bjorn. "A Chinese Marxist Study of the *Analects*." *Bulletin of Concerned Asian Scholars* 10.1:1–53:62 (1978).

Sakai Tadao 酒井忠夫. *Chūgoku zensho no kenkyū* 中國善書の研究 (A

study of Chinese morality books). Tokyo: Kōbundō 弘文堂, 1960.

Schram, Stuart R. *The Political Thought of Mao Tse-tung*. New York: Praeger, 1969.

Schuon, Frithjof. *The Transcendent Unity of Religions*, trans. Peter Townsend. New York: Harper & Row, 1975.

Schurmann, Franz. *Ideology and Organization in Communist China*. Berkeley: University of California Press, 1966.

Schwartz, Benjamin I. *Chinese Communism and the Rise of Mao*. Cambridge, Mass.: Harvard University Press, 1951.

——— *In Search of Wealth and Power: Yen Fu and the West*. Cambridge, Mass.: Harvard University Press, 1964.

——— *Communism and China: Ideology in Flux*. Cambridge, Mass.: Harvard University Press, 1968.

——— ed. *Reflections on the May Fourth Movement: A Symposium*. Cambridge, Mass.: East Asian Research Center, Harvard University, 1972.

Sha Ming 沙明. *K'ung-chia-tien chi ch'i yu-ling* 孔家店及其幽靈 (Confucius and sons and their ghosts). Hong Kong: Wen-chiao 文教, 1970.

Shestov, Lev. *Kierkegaard and the Existential Philosophy*, trans. Elinor Hewitt. Athens: Ohio University Press, 1969.

Shimada Kenji 島田虔次. *Chūgoku ni okeru kindai shii no zasetsu* 中國に於ける近代思惟の挫折 (The frustration of modern thought in China). Tokyo: Chikuma shobō 筑摩書房, 1949.

——— *Shushi gaku to Yōmei gaku* 朱子學と陽明學 (The Chu Hsi school and the Yang-ming school). Tokyo: Iwanami 岩波, 1967.

Smith, D. Howard. *Chinese Religions*. New York: Holt, Rinehart & Winston, 1968.

Smith, Huston. *The Religions of Man*. New York: Harper & Brothers, 1958.

——— "Transcendence in Traditional China," *Religious Studies* 2:185–96 (1967).

——— *Forgotten Truth: The Primordial Tradition*. New York: Harper & Row, 1976.

Smith, Wilfred C. *The Faith of Other Men*. New York: New American Library, 1963.

——— *The Meaning and End of Religion*. New York: The Macmillan Company, 1964.

——— *Religious Diversity: Essays by Wilfred Cantwell Smith*, ed. Willard B. Oxtoby. New York: Harper & Row, 1976.

——— *Belief and History*. Charlottesville: University Press of Virginia, 1977.

Solomon, Richard H. *Mao's Revolution and the Chinese Political Culture*. Berkeley: University of California Press, 1971.

Ssu-ma Ch'ien. *Les mémoires historiques de Se-Ma Ts'ien*, trans. Édouard Chavannes. Paris: E. Leroux, 1895–1905.

Takahashi Tōru 高橋亨. "Richō Jugakushi ni okeru Shuriha Shukiha no hattatsu" 李朝儒學史に於ける主理派主氣派の發達 (The development of the schools of principle and material force in the history of Confucianism in Yi Korea), in *Chōsen Shina bunka no kenkyū* 朝鮮支那文化の研究 (Studies in Korean and Chinese cultures), ed. Tabohashi Kiyoshi 田保橋潔. Tokyo: Tōkōshoin 刀江書院, 1929.

Takase Takejirō 高瀬武次郎. *O Yōmei shōden* 王陽明詳傳 (A detailed biography of Wang Yang-ming). Tokyo: Bunmeidō 文明堂, 1905.

Takeuchi Yoshio 武內義雄. *Chūgoku shisō shi* 中國思想史 (History of Chinese thought). Tokyo: Iwanami 岩波, 1957.

Tan, Chester C. *Chinese Political Thought in the Twentieth Century*. New York: Doubleday, 1971.

T'ang Chün-i 唐君毅. *Tao-te tzu wo chih chien-li* 道德自我之建立 (The establishment of the moral self). Shanghai: Commercial Press, 1946.

——— *Chung-hsi che-hsüeh ssu-hsiang chih pi-chiao yen-chiu chi* 中西哲學思想之比較研究集 (Collected essays on a comparative study of Chinese and Western philosophies). Shanghai: Cheng-chung 正中, 1947.

——— *K'ung Tzu yü jen-ko shih-chieh* 孔子與人格世界 (Confucius and the world of human personality). Hong Kong: Jen-wen 人文, 1950.

——— *Hsi-yang wen-hua ching-shen chih i hsing-ch'a* 西洋文化精神之一省察 (An investigation of cultural spirit in the West). Hong Kong: Jen-sheng 人生, 1951.

——— *Chung-kuo chih luan yü Chung-kuo wen-hua ching-shen chih ch'ien-li* 中國之亂與中國文化精神之潛力 (Disorder in China and the inner strength of Chinese cultural spirit). Taipei: Hua-kuo ch'u-pan-she 華國出版社, 1952.

—— *Hsin-wu yü jen-sheng* 心物與人生 (Mind, matter, and human life). Hong Kong: Ya-chou ch'u-pan-she 亞洲出版社, 1963.

—— *Chung-kuo wen-hua chih ching-shen chia-chih* 中國文化之精神價值 (The spiritual values of Chinese culture). Taipei: Cheng-chung 正中, 1954.

—— *Jen-wen ching-shen chih ch'ung-chien* 人文精神之重建 (The reconstruction of the humanist spirit). 2 vols. Hong Kong: New Asia Institute Press, 1955.

—— "Chang Tsai's Theory of Mind and Its Metaphysical Basis." *Philosophy East and West* 7.2:113–36 (July 1956).

—— *Ch'ing-nien yü hsüeh-wen* 青年與學問 (Youth and learning). Hong Kong: Liu-wang ch'u-pan-she 流亡出版社, 1957.

—— Mou Tsung-san 牟宗三, Hsu Fü-kuan 徐復觀 and Chang Chün-mai 張君勱. *Chung-kuo wen-hua yü shih-chieh* 中國文化與世界 (A declaration to the world for Chinese culture). Hong Kong: Min-chu p'ing-lun she 民主評論社, 1958.

—— *Wen-hua i-shih yü tao-te li-hsing* 文化意識與道德理性 (Cultural consciousness and moral rationality). Hong Kong: Jen-sheng 人生, 1958.

—— *Chung-kuo jen-wen ching-shen chih fa-chan* 中國人文精神之發展 (Development of Chinese cultural spirit). Hong Kong: Jen-sheng 人生, 1958.

—— *Jen-sheng chih t'i-yen* 人生之體驗 (An experiential understanding of human life). Hong Kong: Jen-sheng 人生, 1961.

—— *Che-hsüeh kai-lun* 哲學概論 (An introduction to philosophy). 2 vols. Kowloon: Meng-shih chiao-yü chi-chin-hui 孟氏教育基金會, 1961.

—— "The T'ien Ming (Heavenly Ordinance) in Pre-Ch'in China." *Philosophy East and West* 11.4:195-218 (January 1962) and 12.1:29-49 (April 1962).

—— *Chung-kuo che-hsüeh yen-chiu chih i hsin-fang-hsiang* 中國哲學研究之一新方向 (A new orientation for the study of Chinese philosophy). Hong Kong: Hong Kong Chinese University Press, 1966.

—— "The Development of Ideas of Spiritual Value in Chinese Philosophy," in *The Chinese Mind*, ed. Charles A. Moore. Honolulu: East-West Center Press, 1967.

———— *Chung-kuo che-hsüeh yüan-lun* 中國哲學原論 (An original exposition of Chinese philosophy). 2 vols. Hong Kong: Young-sun 人生, 1965–1968.

———— *Chung-kuo che-hsüeh yüan-lun* 中國哲學原論 (An original exposition of Chinese philosophy). 3 vols. Hong Kong: New Asia Institute Press, 1973–1975.

———— *Chung-hua jen-wen yü tang-chin shih-chieh* 中華人文與當今世界 (Chinese culture and the present world). 2 vols. Taipei: Hsüeh-sheng 學生, 1975.

———— *Sheng-ming ts'un-tsai yü hsin-ling ching-chieh* 生命存在與心靈境界 (The existence of human life and the realm of the spirit). 2 vols. Taipei: Hsüeh-sheng 學生, 1977.

T'ang Yung-t'ung 湯用彤. "Lun Chung-kuo Fo-chiao wu 'Shih-tsung'" 論中國佛教無十宗 (On the absence of the so-called "Ten Schools" in Chinese Buddhism). *Che-hsüeh yen-chiu* 哲學研究 (Philosophical Research) 3:47–54 (1963).

T'ao Hsi-sheng 陶希聖. *Chung-kuo cheng-chih ssu-hsiang shih* 中國政治思想史 (A history of Chinese political thought). 4 vols. Chungking: Commercial Press, 1942.

Teng Ssu-yü and John K. Fairbank, eds. *China's Response to the West.* Cambridge, Mass.: Harvard University Press, 1954.

Teng T'o 鄧拓 [Ma Nan-ts'un 馬南邨]. *Yenshan yeh-hua* 燕山夜話 (Evening chats at Yenshan). Peking: Pei-ching ch'u-pan-she 北京出版社, 1965.

Tomaeda Ryūtarō 友枝龍太郎. *Shushi no shisō keisei* 朱子の思想形成 (The formation of Chu Hsi's thought). Tokyo: Shunjūsha 春秋社, 1969.

Trilling, Lionel. *Sincerity and Authenticity.* Cambridge, Mass.: Harvard University Press, 1972.

Ts'ai Shang-ssu 蔡尚思. *Chung-kuo hsüeh-shu ta-kang* 中國學術大綱 (An outline of Chinese scholarship). Shanghai: Ch'i-chih shu-chü 啓智書局, 1931.

———— *Chung-kuo san-ta ssu-hsiang pi-chiao* 中國三大思想比較 (A comparative study of three major currents of thought in China). Shanghai: Ch'i-chih 啓智, 1934.

———— *Chung-kuo ch'uan-t'ung ssu-hsiang tsung p'i-p'an* 中國傳統思想總批判 (General critique of traditional Chinese thought). Shanghai: T'ang-ti ch'u-pan-she 棠棣出版社, 1950.

Tu Kuo-hsiang 杜國庠. *Hsien-Ch'in chu-tzu ssu-hsiang kai-yao* 先秦諸子思想概要 (An outline of pre-Ch'in philosophies). Peking: San-lien 三聯, 1949.

—— *Hsien-Ch'in chu-tzu jo-kan yen-chiu* 先秦諸子若干研究 (Several studies of pre-Ch'in philosophers). Peking: San-lien 三聯, 1955.

Tu Wei-ming 杜維明. *San-nien ti hsü-ai* 三年的蓄艾 (Three years of cultivating the moxa). Taipei: Chih-wen 志文, 1970.

—— *Jen-wen hsin-ling te chen-tang* 人文心靈的震盪 (The resonance of the humanist mind). Taipei: Shih-pao 時報, 1976.

—— *Centrality and Commonality: An Essay on Chung-yung.* Honolulu: The University Press of Hawaii, 1976.

—— *Neo-Confucian Thought in Action: Wang Yang-ming's Youth (1472–1509).* Berkeley: University of California Press, 1976.

Twitchett, Denis and A. Wright, eds. *Confucian Personalities.* Stanford: Stanford University Press, 1962.

Voegelin, Eric. *Order and History.* 4 vols. Baton Rouge: Louisiana State University Press, 1956–1975.

Wakeman, Frederic, Jr., ed. *Nothing Concealed: Essays in Honor of Liu Yü-yün.* Taipei: Chinese Materials and Research Aids Service Center, 1970.

—— *History and Will: Philosophical Perceptions of Mao Tse-tung's Thought.* Berkeley: University of California Press, 1973.

Waley, Arthur. *Three Ways of Thought in Ancient China.* London: George Allen & Unwin, 1953.

—— *The Analects of Confucius.* London: George Allen & Unwin, 1938.

Wang Chi 王畿. *Wang Lung-hsi yü-lu* 王龍溪語錄 (Recorded conversations of Wang Lung-hsi). Reprint, Taipei: Kuang-wen 廣文, 1960.

Wang Hsien-chien 王先謙, ed. *Hsün Tzu chi-chieh* 荀子集解 (Collected annotations on the *Hsün Tzu*). Reprint, Taipei: Shih-chieh shu-chü 世界書局, 1958.

Wang Mou-hung 王懋竑. *Chu Tzu nien-p'u* 朱子年譜 (Chu Hsi's chronological biography). Ts'ung-shu chi-ch'eng 叢書集成 ed., 1937.

Wang Tch'ang-tche. *La philosophie morale de Wang Yang-ming.* Shanghai: T'ou-Sè-Wè Press, 1936.

Wang Yang-ming 王陽明. *Wang Wen-ch'eng Kung ch'üan-shu* 王文成公

全書 (Complete works of Wang Yang-ming). Ssu-pu ts'ung-k'an 四部叢刊 ed.

——— *The Philosophy of Wang Yang-ming*, trans. Frederick G. Henke. Chicago: Open Court, 1916.

——— *Wang Yang-ming ch'üan-shu* 王陽明全書 (Complete works of Wang Yang-ming). Taipei: Cheng-chung 正中, 1955.

——— *Instructions for Practical Living and Other Neo-Confucian Writings by Wang Yang-ming*, trans. Wing-tsit Chan. New York: Columbia University Press, 1963.

Weber, Max. *The Religion of China: Confucianism and Taoism*, trans. Hans H. Gerth. Glencoe, Ill.: Free Press, 1951.

Welch, Holmes. *The Buddhist Revival in China*. Cambridge, Mass.: Harvard University Press, 1968.

Wilhelm, Hellmut. *Heaven, Earth, and Man in the Book of Changes*. Seattle: University of Washington Press, 1977.

Wilhelm, Richard, trans. *The I Ching*. Rendered into English by Cary F. Baynes. Princeton: Princeton University Press, 1967.

Williams, Bernard. *Morality: An Introduction to Ethics*. New York: Harper & Row, 1972.

Wittgenstein, L. *Philosophical Investigations*. New York: Macmillan, 1965.

Wright, Arthur F., ed. *Studies in Chinese Thought*. Chicago: University of Chicago Press, 1953.

——— ed. *The Confucian Persuasion*. Stanford: Stanford University Press, 1960.

——— and Denis Twitchett, eds. *Confucian Personalities*. Stanford: Stanford University Press, 1962.

Yamashita Ryūji 山下龍二. *Yōmeigaku no kenkyū* 陽明學の研究. 2 vols. Tokyo: Gendai Jōhō sha 現代情報社, 1971.

Yang Jung-kuo 楊榮國. *K'ung-mo ti ssu-hsiang* 孔墨的思想 (Confucian and Moist thought). Shanghai: Sheng-huo shu-tien 生活書店, 1947.

——— *Chung-kuo ku-tai ssu-hsiang-shih* 中國古代思想史 (History of ancient Chinese thought). Peking: San-lien 三聯, 1955.

——— *Chien-ming Chung-kuo ssu-hsiang-shih* 簡明中國思想史 (A concise history of Chinese thought). Peking: Chung-kuo ch'ing-nien ch'u-pan-she 中國青年出版社, 1962.

——— *Chung-kuo li-tai fan-K'ung ho tsun-K'ung te tou-cheng* 中國歷代反

孔和尊孔的鬥爭 (The Struggles between Confucian supporters and critics throughout Chinese history). Hong Kong: San-lien 三聯, 1974.

―――― *Confucius—"Sage" of the Reactionary Classes.* Peking: Foreign Languages Press, 1974.

Yen Yüan 顏元 and Li Kung 李塨. *Yen-li ts'ung-shu* 顏李叢書 (Collected works of Yen Yüan and Li Kung). Peking: Ssu-ts'un hsüeh-hui 四存學會, 1923.

Yi Pyŏng-do 李丙燾. *Charyo Han'guk Yuhaksa ch'ogo* 資料韓國儒學史草稿 (A draft history of Confucianism in Korea). 3 vols. Seoul: Sŏul taehakkyo 서울大學校, 1959.

Yi Sang-un 李相殷. *Han'guk ŭi Yuhak sasang* 韓國의 儒學思想 (Korean Confucian thought). Seoul: Samsong ch'ulp'ansa 三省出版社, 1976.

―――― *Yuhak kwa Tongyang munhwa* 儒學과 東洋文化 (Confucian learning and Oriental culture). Seoul: Pomhak tosŏ 汎學圖書, 1976.

Yin Hai-kuang 殷海光. *Chung-kuo wen-hua te chan-wang* 中國文化的展望 (An appraisal of the prospects of Chinese culture). 2 vols. Taipei: Wen-hsing shu-tien 文星書店, 1966.

Yin-shun 印順. *P'ing Hsiung Shih-li ti Hsin Wei-shih lun* 評熊十力的新唯識論 (A critique of Hsiung Shih-li's *New Exposition of the Consciousness-Only Doctrine*). Hong Kong: Cheng-wen 正聞, 1950.

Yü Ying-shih 余英時. "Ts'ung Sung-Ming Ju-hsüeh ti fa-chan lun Ch'ing-tai ssu-hsiang shih" 從宋明儒學的發展論清代思想史 (Ch'ing thought as seen through the development of Sung-Ming Confucianism). *Chung-kuo hsüeh-jen* 中國學人 (Chinese Scholar) 2:19–41 (September 1970).

―――― *Lun Tai Chen yü Chang Hsüeh-ch'eng* 論戴震與章學誠 (On Tai Chen and Chang Hsüeh-ch'eng). Hong Kong: Lung-men 龍門, 1976.

―――― *Li-shih yü ssu-hsiang* 歷史與思想 (History and thought). Taipei: Lien-ching 聯經, 1976.

Zen, Sophia H. Chen, ed. *Symposium on Chinese Culture.* Shanghai: China Institute of Pacific Relations, 1931.

INDEX

a posteriori learning (*hou-t'ien chih hsüeh*), 173–174

a priori learning (*hsien-t'ien chih hsüeh*), 173–174

Academy of Science, 276

activism, 12, 195, 200, 202; *see also* relationship; self and society; sociality

Acton, Lord, 272

adolescence, 40

ālaya vijñāna (storehouse-consciousness), 241, 244

amateur ideal, 258, 260

Analects (*Lun-yü*): on *jen*, 6; on *hsiang-yüan* and *chün-tzu*, 22; and Confucian tradition, 111; on *hsi* (practice), 195; in *K'ao-ku*, 276; quoted by Mao Tse-tung, 295 n. 68; passages from, 6–9, 11, 13, 14, 21–23, 27, 29, 30, 31 n.11, 34 n.42, 36–53, 55 n.49, 89, 94, 107, 205, 279, 286

anthropocosmic experience, 156, 159

anti-Confucianism, 252 n.10, 275, 277–284

Antonioni, Michelangelo, 290, 296 n.90

Appearance and Reality, 249

Asaṅga, 243

attachment, 168, 171

Augustine, St., 83

Balazs, Etienne, 31 n.15, 71

being and becoming, 142–144

Bellah, Robert, xxii

Bergson, Henri, 229, 237, 248–249

Blondel, Maurice, 84

Boodberg, Peter, 18, 237

Book of Change (*I-ching*): quoted by Chou Tun-i, 72; and Confucian tradition, 88, 111, 115; Chu Hsi's conception of, 115, 132; in Ch'ien

Mu, 121; and Hsiung Shih-li, 232, 244–245

Book of History (*Shu-ching*), 121, 132, 165, 199

Book of Odes (*Shih-ching*): quoted, 39, 45, 100 n.26; in Ch'ien Mu, 121, 132; Chu Hsi's study of, 132; in Yen Yüan, 199; and Mao Tse-tung, 275

Book of Poetry, see *Book of Odes*

Book of Rites (*Li-chi*), 29, 33 n.40, 35, 121, 133–134

book-reading, 194–195, 198–199, 210, 275, 294 n. 62

Bradley, F.H., 249, 251

Brière, O., 242, 248

Bruce, J.P., 119

Buber, Martin, 83, 109 n.2, 223

Buddhism: Pure Land, 10; challenge of, 122; reality and illusion in, 172–175; and Wang Lung-hsi, 174–175; and Liang Ch'i-ch'ao, 186; and Yen Yüan, 208–209; and Confucianism, 122, 223, 243, 281, 285; and Hu Shih, 227–228; in modern China, 254 n.50; *see also* Ch'an Buddhism

Buddhist Concepts Explained (*Fo-chia ming-hsiang t'ung-shih*), 242

bureaucracy, 219

Canton, 232

capping ceremony, 35

celibacy, immorality of, 207–208

Chan Jo-shui, 148, 159

Chan Kan-ch'üan, 189

Chan, Wing-tsit: on *jen*, 9, 10, 21; on *t'i* (to embody), 109 n.3; and categorization of Neo-Confucians, 113; on Chu Hsi, 114, 119, 134–135; on "spirit of creation," 177; on *t'i* (essence), 238; on Hsiung

345

Shih-li, 244

Ch'an Buddhism: and Neo-Confucianism, 10, 85; and human relatedness, 19; and Chu Hsi, 126; and Wang Yang-ming, 149, 162, 246; and Yen Yüan, 201–202

Chang Chih-tung, 237, 258

Chang Chü-cheng, 181, 184

Chang Fei, 263

Chang Lü-hsiang, 190

Chang-nan Academy, 196

Chang Piao, 232

Chang Ping-lin, 188, 213 n.13, 278, 279

Chang Shih (Nan-hsien), 116–117, 129

Chang Shih-chao, 276

Chang Shih-ch'ing, 198

Chang Tsai (Heng-ch'ü): on Heaven and Earth, 73–74; and Buddhism, 85; on humanity, 95; on physical nature, 110 n.18, 127; and Confucian tradition, 85, 112–114, 117, 123, 192; and Chu Hsi, 128, 204–205; and Yen Chün, 186; and Yen Yüan, 192; and Hsiung Shih-li, 245; on ch'i, 245; as materialist, 283

Chang Ts'ung-ch'ang, 278

Chang Tung-sun, 222, 226, 249, 252 n.18

change (i), 245, 254 n.52

Chao Chi-pin, 266

Chekiang School, 129, 130, 187

Ch'en Hsien-chang, 80

Ch'en, Kenneth, 242, 281

Ch'en Liang, 214 n.54

Ch'en Po-sha, 187, 189, 243, 254 n.51

Ch'en Teng-yüan, 189

Ch'en Tu-hsiu, 278, 280

Cheng-meng (*Correcting youthful ignorance*), 117

ch'eng (sincerity): in *T'ung-shu*, 73; in *Chung-yung*, 73, 94–98; in *Mencius*, 94; etymology of, 95; and

Way of Heaven, 96; transforming power of, 96–97; transcendence of, 98, 112; as creativity, 97–98; and humanity, 98; as God-term, 112

Ch'eng-Chu School: and Wang Yang-ming, 105; and Lu-Wang School, 113, 126, 129; ritualism of, 133; and Yen Yüan, 192, 195, 199, 201, 203, 210; and material nature, 296 n. 83

Ch'eng Hao (Ming-tao): on *jen*, 74–75, 154, 159; on *t'ien-li*, 152; on mind, 154; quietism of, 85; and Wang P'in, 110 n.16; and Confucian tradition, 85, 112–114, 117, 123, 192; and Chu Hsi, 128; and Yen Yüan, 192

Ch'eng I (I-ch'uan): on self-cultivation, 75–76; and Confucian tradition, 86, 106, 112–115, 117, 123, 192; and Chu Hsi, 114–115, 122, 128; and Yen Yüan, 192, 194–195

ch'eng-jen (adulthood), 40, 55 n.57

ch'eng-ssu (sincerity and cogitation), 125

chi (incipient activation), 125, 164

Chi Yün, 213 n.13

ch'i (material force): and sensitivity, 74; and *li*, 76–77, 127; as stuff of mind, 78, 115, 127–128, 130; in Chu Hsi, 115, 127–128, 130, 204; and *liang-chih*, 156; in Yen Yüan, 207; in Hsiung Shih-li, 245; see also *ch'i-chih chih hsing;* corporality

ch'i-chih chih hsing (physical nature): in Chang Tsai, 110 n.18; 127, 204; in Mencius, 205; in Chu Hsi, 110 n.18, 127, 204, 206–208; in Yen Yüan, 207–208; as creative agent, 208; transformation of, 286, 296 n.83; see also *ch'i;* corporality

Ch'i-yang, 198

Chia-li (Family rituals), 133, 194, 214 n.33

Chia-shen hsün-nan lu (A record of the Loyalist deaths of 1644), 203

355

and good and evil, 162, 167, 168–170; rectification of, 163, 169, 173; without thingness, 164, 168–169; and *liang-chih*, 167–172; and principle, 168; and attachment, 168; and intention, 169; see also *ko-wu*
Thirteen Classics, 288
Three Character Classic, 231
Three Teachings, 85, 227
t'i (structure; to embody): -*jen* (to embody *jen*), 10, 18; in various compounds, 103–104, 109 n.3; as "substance, essence," 238; see also *pen-t'i*; *t'i-yung*
t'i-yung (substance and function): of *jen*, 8–9, 15 n.10; in Ch'ien Mu, 125; in Levenson, 221–222; and Hsiung Shih-li, 237, 245; and cultural identity, 258
Tiao Meng-chi, 198
t'ien, *see* Heaven
T'ien-chou, 162, 172, 175
T'ien-ch'üan Bridge, 176
t'ien-li, *see* Heavenly principle
Tientsin, 190
Tillich, Paul, 109 n.2, 223
timeliness (*shih*), 30, 90
transformation (*hua*), 244–247, 254 n.52; *see also* transforming power
transforming power: of sage, 68; of Heaven and Earth, 73, 96–97, 99, 106; of *ch'eng*, 96
ts'ai (ability, power), 205, 207
Ts'ao Tuan, 106, 109 n.7
Tseng Kuo-fan, 12
Tseng Tzu; on *li*, 11; on inward examination, 27; on Knight of the Way, 35–36; on fear and trembling, 39, 94, 100 n.26, 201; and adulthood, 53; in *tao-t'ung*, 192; and Yen Yüan, 192
Tsinghua University, 271
Tso-chuan (*Tso's Commentary on the Spring and Autumn Annals*), 14 n.1;3, 276
Ts'un-chih pien (On the preservation

of statecraft), 192
Ts'un-hsing pien (On the preservation of human nature), 194
Ts'un-hsüeh pien (On the preservation of learning), 194, 198
Ts'un-jen pien (On the preservation of humanity), 195
ts'un t'ien-li ch'ü jen-yü (to preserve Heavenly principle and extirpate human desires), 138, 149, 152–156
T'ulufan, 276
T'ung-chien kang-mu (Outline and digest of the *General Mirror*), 134
Tung Chung-shu, 283
Tunglin Academy, 263, 292 n.14
T'ung-shu (Penetrating the *Book of Change*), 73, 117
Two Chinese Philosophers, 113
Tzu-chih t'ung-chien (Comprehensive mirror for the aid of government), 191, 276
Tzu-hsia, 46
Tzu-kung, 50
Tzu-lu, 49
Tzu-ssu, 192

ultimacy of man, 84, 111, 204
Ultimate Reality, *see* Great Ultimate
Understanding Words (Chih-yen), 116–117, 129
United Nations Stockholm Conference on the Human Environment, 261
University of Southern Illinois, 252 n.20
utilitarianism, 188, 189

value priority, 257, 272, 284–291; *see also* "redness vs. expertise"
value system, 228, 279–280, 284–291
Vasubandhu, 243
Vietnam, 135
Vijñāptimātra (Yogācāra), see *Wei-shih*
Vivekananda, Swami, 265

Index prepared
by Joseph A. Adler